# The Time of Our Lives
## Women Write on Sex after 40

edited by
### Dena Taylor &
### Amber Coverdale Sumrall

Introduction by Marge Piercy

Foreword by Sadja Greenwood, M.D.

The Crossing Press • Freedom, CA 95019

## Other Books by
## Amber Coverdale Sumrall and Dena Taylor

Amber Coverdale Sumrall and Dena Taylor are the editors of *Sexual Harassment: Women Speak Out* (The Crossing Press, 1992), *Women of the 14th Moon: Writings on Menopause* (The Crossing Press, 1991). Sumrall is also co-editor of *Catholic Girls* (Penguin/Plume, 1992) and *Touching Fire: Erotic Writings By Women* (Carroll & Graf, 1989). She is the editor of *Lovers* and *Write to the Heart* (both from The Crossing Press, 1992). Taylor is the author of *Red Flower: Rethinking Menstruation* (The Crossing Press, 1988).

### Cataloging-in-Publication Data

The Time of our lives : women write on sex after forty / edited by Dena Taylor & Amber Coverdale Sumrall.
      p. cm.
    ISBN 0-89594-613-0. -- ISBN 0-89594-612-2 (pbk.)
    1. Women--United States--Literary collections. 2. Middle aged women--Sexual behaviors--Literary collections. 3. Sex (Psychology)--Literary collections. 4. American Literature--Women authors. 5. Erotic literature, American. I. Taylor, Dena. II. Sumrall, Amber Coverdale.
PS509.W6T56 1993
810.8'09287--dc20
              92-40774
              CIP

# Acknowledgments

Some of the work in this book has previously appeared in the following publications to which authors and publisher gratefully acknowledge permission to reprint:

"The Middle-Aged Blues Boogie" by Gaye Todd Adegbalola (Hot Toddy Music ASCAP) is from Sapphire's album *The Uppity Blues Women*, copyright 1990, Alligator Records. It won the W.C. Handy Award for "Blues Song of the Year" in 1990.

"What Can You Do About Love" by Naomi Feigelson Chase was originally published in a longer version in *A Wilder Giving* (Chicory Blue Press, 1988).

"Sleeping with Soldiers" excerpt by Rosemary Daniell is reprinted from *Sleeping with Soldiers* (Holt, Rinehart and Winston, copyright 1984) by permission of the author.

"It Is a Very Good Year" by Ayofemi Folayan is reprinted from *Lesbians at Midlife: The Creative Transition* (Spinsters, 1991) by permission of the author.

"Based on Experience" by Candida Lawrence was published originally by *Berkeley Poets Cooperative*.

"She Said We'd Never Fall in Love Again" by Deena Metzger is reprinted from *A Sabbath Among the Ruins* (Parallax Press, 1992) by permission of the author.

"The Loneliness of the Middle-Aged Women" by Susan Moon first appeared in *This World*.

"White Eggplant" by Elizabeth Searle first appeared in *Ploughshares*, Fall 1991.

"No Words for It" by Tilly Washburn Shaw originally appeared as a Broadside (Moving Parts Press).

"The Bookkeeper at H.G. Smithy's" by Enid Shomer originally appeared in *New Letters*.

"Sestina for Indian Summer" by Enid Shomer won the Celica B. Wagner Award of the Poetry Society of America and first appeared in the *PSA Newsletter*.

"Giving the Cat Your Tongue" by Deborah Shouse first appeared under a different title in *Potpourri*.

"Kingdoms Are Clay" by Madelon Sprengnether is reprinted from *Rivers, Stories, Houses, Dreams* (New Rivers Press) by permission of the author.

"Grave Dance" by Christina Sunley first appeared in *Backbone*.

"A Tooth for Every Child" by Abigail Thomas was originally published in *The Missouri Review*, 1991, and won their William Peden Prize for fiction.

"Penelope's Silver Wedding Anniversary" by Rima de Vallbona is reprinted from *Short Stories by Latin American Women: The Magic and the Real* (Arte Publico Press, 1990) by permission of the publisher.

"HE 2-104: A Planetary Nebula" by Gloria Vando won the 1991 Billee Murray Denny Poetry Prize.

"A Season for Sex" by Gail Weber was first published in *Healthsharing*, Fall/Winter 1990.

"Reconstruction" by Hannah Wilson is an abridged version of the story that is forthcoming in *Other Voices*.

# Contents

For Elaine Goldman Gill, who said,
when asked about older women's sexuality,
*"You're hotter than hell. There's no cessation."*

———————————————

*One thing is certain, and I have always known it—*
*the joys of my life have nothing to do with age.*
                                                    —May Sarton

# Preface

This book grew naturally out of our work on *Women of the 14th Moon: Writings on Menopause*. We met so many spirited, sensuous women through their writings and on tour with the book that we were inspired to explore further the sexuality of midlife and older women.

We present here sixty-six stories, personal accounts and poems by women from their forties to eighties. They are heterosexual and lesbian, sexual and celibate, outrageous and conventional, serious and humorous—voices from Tucson to Toronto, Savannah to Vancouver, and Portland, Maine, to Portland, Oregon.

These are honest stories. They reflect the chaos, freedom and new definitions of sexuality that emerge during this time of our lives. Some women say sex after midlife is the best it's ever been. They know what they want. Inhibitions are gone and, after a certain point, so is the fear of pregnancy. For some it is a time of being alone, although not necessarily lonely. We heard from many women who shattered the myth, or the lie, that at their age they should or would not be interested in sex. And many said sex was no longer the driving force in their life, and thus they were free to follow other paths. Several women told of a kind of letting-go after menopause, a lightness. We found a sense of adventure and humor woven through much of the work.

Sexuality can be expressed in many ways. We may experience increased desire, a change in sexual preference, a need for celibacy, alternatives to traditional relationships, non-sexual sensuality, an awakening of new feelings. There are many choices, and the choices are ours.

We live in a time when youth is venerated, but middle and old age, at least women's, are denied and degraded. We are bombarded with media messages telling us that wrinkles, weight gain, the inevitable pull of gravity and *aging* are to be avoided at all costs. And thus many of us spend inordinate amounts of money and time on cosmetics and cosmetic surgery, diets, pharmaceuticals, exercise programs and equipment, trying to look like something we no longer are, and in a non-misogynist society, would not long to be. The male-defined standards of beauty leave us feeling something is wrong with our older bodies. Seeing no positive images, our sexuality is all too often curtailed or rejected. How we would love to see midlife and older women reveling in their bodies, their sexuality, their good feelings about themselves the way they are, not as a parody of younger women.

We had fun thinking of titles for this collection, tossing around "It's Not Over Till the Fat Lady Sings," "Wicked Old Witches," and "Go Down Moses." Mostly it was known rather awkwardly as "our book on women's sexuality in midlife and beyond." The *beyond* part was very important to us, because certainly many of the stories are by and about women well past midlife. We finally decided on "The Time of Our Lives," realizing it may be confused with a soap opera or a Frank Capra film, but hoping to convey the message that herein are the stories of vibrant, feisty and sexy women.

This is not a collection of erotica, but rather a book about women's relationships to sex—and the sensuality, wisdom and humor that are found there. We hope it flies in the face of all the stereotypes about older women's sexuality.

Dena Taylor
Amber Coverdale Sumrall
Santa Cruz, CA, November, 1992

2

# Foreword

I tucked the galleys of this book under my bed every morning so I could chuckle or cry over it that night as I savored one story, poem or essay after another. Recognition, remembrances, revelations. Varnished and unvarnished truths. I called one author, Madelon Sprengnether, in the middle of the night to rave about her story, "Kingdoms are Clay." Fortunately (because of the lateness of the hour) I got her answering machine.

The essays define the terrain. In "A Season for Sex," Gail Weber describes sexuality as a moving stream flowing through our lives. "As young girls it is narrow, and as we reach maturity it widens, is full and spilling over. As we age, it may narrow again but it never stops flowing." Chris Karras ("To My Middle-Aged Sisters") writes, "It seems to be an affront, if not a severe shock, to the mainstream culture that we define ourselves, celebrate our sexuality and sensuality at any age in spite of physical and metaphorical castration (how many unnecessary hysterectomies are performed on menopausal women?). That we find our sexuality reflected in our affections, our friendships, our humor, our voices, and our shining eyes. That we dare write about it."

And they have written about it! The writing is poignant, erotic, anti-erotic, complex. Words flowing from the imagination define and intensify longing, fulfillment, dreams and disappointments. Cultural constraints which limit the actions and self-esteem of older women are shown in these stories, and then broken or transcended as the heroines find new ways to think and to live.

You will find a reflection of your polymorphous self in these tales. Some are heterosexual, others about lesbian love, and some bisexual. Some are breath-taking in their erotic power, some angry and political, and others painful in their depiction of rejections, embarrassments and self-doubt. The protagonists range from their early forties to mid eighties. All are heroines of self-disclosure.

In my medical practice I often hear women in their forties say that everything in their cycles is intensified: the sensations of ovulation, premenstrual symptoms, cravings, cramps, blood flow—and also the intensity of their sexual desire, their ability to understand it, affirm it, delight in it, or mourn the lack of a partner. From Chris Karras again: "My sexuality is no more separable from me than is my breath. Nor does it need validation through reflection in others' eyes. Past the age of sexual assessment and evaluation, based on my sexiness or desirability, I am no longer object, but subject. To become aware of this shift is liberating."

Read this book to be liberated, to laugh, to cry, to be turned on, to appreciate the varieties of sexual experience, to find new voices in literature.

—Sadja Greenwood, M.D.

# Introduction

## Tales from the Dark Side of the Moon

Here are stories, essays, memoirs and poems from a bright and bushy bouquet of older women. In reading them, I was struck by a correlation between women represented as having cleaved to the traditional roles for women—wife, mother, housewife, helpmate—and trouble in later life. The conventional wisdom that avoiding risks, following the customary guidelines, being a good woman produces the most satisfaction would not seem to be borne out in these stories. Women who have taken the wildest chances seem the most pleased with their lives.

By the midpoint of a woman's anticipated life, she has often learned what she can ask from sex. Whether she loves men or women, she has often found as she bumps along that love cannot in itself give shape to a life. Young girls often expect the loving regard of an exciting man to provide them with a transcendent experience, to change them like lightning striking or like a starlet being discovered by a producer. The lover is seen as a transformer, a magician, giving entrance to another world. Perhaps that is the world of the ideal marriage, the perfect safe place, the sunlit home. Perhaps it is ecstasy, the god descending into flesh.

There are romantic older women in these stories who are still looking for the potless wonder at the rainbow's end, but many have learned to seek pleasure and relish that for itself. They do not expect their sexuality to provide them with much besides company, perhaps occasional, and physical satisfaction. Some value companionship before pleasure, but they do not usually anticipate that sex is going to lay any golden eggs. It is what it is, marvelous in itself, renewing like the sun, but evanescent and finite. Often they remark that they know how to please themselves. They seem less apt to confuse pleasure and pain, to cower in a masochistic crouch awaiting what will befall them.

A number remark that they understand their bodies. What works may not be heterosexual. It may not be the Big Bang of mutual orgasm they were raised to expect. They may enjoy sex in less traditional ways. They may be more open to experimentation and alternatives.

Younger women often experience themselves as the pursued. Sex is something they submit to or they acquiesce in. Older women generally are aware that they must pursue and capture sex. Rarely does it chase them. The more open-minded the woman may be as to what kind of sexual partner she will try, the more likely, if we can judge by these writings, she is to achieve satisfaction. It seemed sometimes that the more a male is described in traditionally handsome or suitable terms, the less likely he is to prove a solution for the needs of an older woman.

We have wit on the pot luck table and we have bleak reportage, but all are the authentic voices of older women trying to understand and improve the hands they have been dealt. Some are professional writers; some are less polished. All have much to pour into your ear. This is not a titillating anthology; rather think of an honest conversation among women late at night when there is no one to overhear. In this living room of the mind, women from forty to seventy and a couple older, come together to drop their masks and talk about their adventures and their disappointments in bed. There are boastful pieces and erotic pieces, but mostly you will hear the voices of women talking about the most personal of all matters in a conversation you may want to join.

— Marge Piercy

# It's About the Day to Day
## Mary Allison

I tell my lover of many years that I'm writing an essay on women's sexuality in midlife. She tosses me a look and laughs out loud. "Well, that'll certainly be brief," she claims.

"No," I say. "I'm serious. What do you think about sex at forty-five, about how it differs from sex when you were, oh, say twenty-five or thirty?"

She laughs again. "When you're young, all you think about is sex. But it's different now. In fact, someone in class just the other night told that bit about the three phases of sex.

"The initial phase is the 'all over phase.' That means you do it everywhere. In the car, in the woods, in the kitchen, at the beach.

"In time you progress to the 'bedroom phase.' Discretion develops, sensibility returns. There are often small children around," she continues.

"Then finally the third phase, the 'hallway phase.' You're fortyish, there are probably teenagers still living in the home. You pass one another in the hall and mutter 'fuck you.'" She laughs again.

"Frequency is certainly a factor indicating change," I say, "but how else does it differ?" The topic initially brought nothing but foolishness from her.

"Want to go to bed and do some research?" she quips.

I turn away from her. Tonight I don't feel like being made light of. During the night our bodies settle into their usual fashion: my belly to her back or turning, asleep, one always follows the other, the slowest of dance, somnambulate, together.

In the morning she cuts off the alarm, snaps on the coffee pot then comes back to the warmth of the bed. We are heading into winter; ours is an energy-efficient relationship.

Five minutes or so pass before the coffee maker starts its sputtering and gurgling ritual, my signal to greet the day, at least briefly. I fetch a cup of coffee for her, stir the ashes from the coals, add kindling, carefully place logs, set damper and vents before returning to the warmth under the quilts.

One sixty-watt bulb burns. Her hands are wrapped around the coffee cup; she sits propped with bed pillows. Her face is soft, her new haircut brings attention to her right ear, now framed, and punctuated by a streak of silver hair emerging at the temple. Her blue eyes scan me, regard the morning.

"It's twelve degrees," I say.

"If I could have a lover who would give me orgasms all day long, or I could have one who knows how to tend fires and keep this house warm, which one do you think I'd choose?" she asks.

"What, on a morning like this?" I say, as we both break into a laugh. I climb back under the covers.

# Multiple Orgasm
## Karen Alkalay-Gut

a rush of birds
flushed
from their hiding place

# After Making Love

## Karen Alkalay-Gut

"Finish eating," my grandmother
would urge her children
hoping to clear the table
for the next meal. But they
would laugh, "Finish?"
and nibble their bread.
"When you've finished eating,
you're dead."

# Old, But Not Dead
## Brenda Bankhead

I am old that does not mean I am dead. Some people would rather think of me as dead. They think old people are dead anyway but that's beside the point. I don't care what they think. I am 70 years old and alive and breathing, thank you. And everything that breathes has some kind of sex life. I read that in one of those women's magazines. My niece says so, too. I like my niece a lot. She's just like me when I was a young woman. Don't take nonsense off nobody and not interested in all the unnecessary frills. She is interested in the real things. You couldn't get her to wear make-up or paint her fingernails for nothing. Now, I used to own a beauty parlor but I understand what she's saying. That stuff can take a lot of energy you'd rather be spending on something else. And shaving her legs! Lord. One time her Mama started fussing at her bout that and Lydia, that's her name, puffed right up back at her.

"All adult human beings have hair on their legs, Mama," she said. "Why is it considered normal on men and abnormal on women? Do men want to have sex with children?"

Well, that shut her mother right up. My sister has always been more concerned with what people think than what really is. But on the subject of children. Some people would call Raymond a child but my God! The man is 50 years old. That's never been a child no kind of way unless there is something seriously wrong with a person. And there is nothing wrong with Raymond. I met him at the convalescent center. I was visiting a friend and so was he. We met in the hallway and started right up talking like we had been friends for a long time. You know how it is with some people. He asked me out to dinner right then and there. I sort of looked at him funny cause I knew how old I was but I couldn't quite tell with him. I knew he was way under 70 though. So I asked. Fifty, he said. How old are you? Real clear. Raymond is like that. I hesitated. Well, I said to myself, there goes a little fun and adventure. I used to lie about my age. It was one of my true vices. I guess I felt that so much of life had passed me by and I had nothing to show for it. But I'm past that now. I told Raymond straight out how old I was. That I'd be 71 come next November. Oh, he said. Is dinner on or not? Then he smiled at me. I smiled back at him and looked him deep in the eyes. I liked what I saw. We been seeing each other ever since. Been almost a year now. Tessie had a fit. That's my sister, Lydia's mama. I already told you bout her. She went on and on. Bout how he was just looking to see what kind of money I had. That he was making a fool out of me. And the shame! People would say that I was robbing the cradle. They'd always thought I was crazy before but now! Oh they'd really start to talk. I told her, I said I don't have any money to speak of and if I'm a fool then I'm a fool. I got to take risks. You know me well enough by now to know I never run my life by what people are gonna think bout me. So why don't you just go in the mirror and fuss at yourself? Cause it sure ain't doing me any good. That made her mad. She called me a dried up old woman who didn't know she was dried up. I may be dried up, I said, but there's always vagina lubricating gel. There's some in my medicine chest, you want it? I thought her head was gonna bust the way her face got all red. She didn't speak to me for a while after that.

The first time me and Raymond had relations. Well. It was so nice. I never had a man who knew much bout pleasing a woman. Always had to make sure I got my own if you know what I mean. But Raymond. Well, this is how it started. Me in the bathtub getting ready to go out with him to Sizzler's. We were celebrating our sixth month together. Isn't that just like a couple of kids? Feels good too. Anyway, Ray showed up early. So he was waiting in the living room while I took my bath. The best thing bout my place is the bathtub. It's big and long enough for me to stretch out. It has those claw feet. You know the kind. Well, I'm in there splashing warm water up on my chest and I start to think what it would be like to kiss Raymond hard on his mouth. I get thoughts like that sometimes in that tub. It's magical, it is. Before I have the sense to stop myself I calls out to Raymond. Could you hand me a towel, I say. I hear his footsteps approaching my bedroom and my heart starts pounding to beat the band. Where, he asks. Right in here, sugar, I say. I hear him hesitate. He just sort of stops in his tracks. For a minute I'm afraid he don't want me, that I'm just an old woman. Then I see his face peeking round the door. Where is that towel again, Bea? he says. He's smiling that smile again. I point to the towel rack on the side of my head. Raymond comes in and sits on the edge of that clawfooted tub, reaches over to get the towel, then brings his lips to my throat and starts kissing me there. That was so sweet I got tears in my eyes. But then the passion built up in me and I gave him that hard kiss I had been thinking bout. We never made it to Sizzler's that night.

I was a looker in my day. I lost most of it now but sex ain't all bout good looks. I can attest to that. Some of the prettiest men I had in my bed couldn't please a woman to save their lives. Sex ain't bout good looks. A lot of it is cooperation and adventure. You look at what you got and see how far you can take it. You want to take your partner over that hill. Leave 'em panting and pawing for more. Sometimes that ain't pretty but, child, it sure is worth it. Beats pretty any day. As you get older sex can't be all huff and puff like when you was young. You really got to know the person you with. You got to be good friends. I like that. The main thing bout Raymond is that he is considerate. He cares bout my needs. Makes sure I'm satisfied. You don't find that in men too often. Sometimes I think they ought to go to school and learn bout it. Lord knows there's classes for everything else. Maybe I can teach one someday. But let me quit, and tell you bout Ruby.

Ruby and me been knowing each other since we was girls together in Louisiana. We call each other every week. Every other Saturday I call her in Los Angeles. Then we switch and she calls me in Chicago. We been doing this for years. She's the best friend I got. Me and my sister never got along but me and Ruby, we been close. And I guess that's why I was so afraid to tell her bout Raymond. I kept it a secret a long time. Months. It was a delicious secret but it bothered me. If you can't be open with your best friend who can you be open with? But I was afraid with Ruby. Cause I didn't want her to spoil it. Much as I love her she can sure spoil the fun and magic of things sometimes. That's just the way she is. Sensible. Durable. Ruby lasts. She gets on no matter what. She's like a rock. Lord knows I clung to that rock many times when I was feeling down here in cold, windy Chicago. When I was young and not so young. I suppose Ruby's greatest fault is also her greatest strength. Guess we all like that. Faults and strengths, God knows what He's doing, let me tell you. But what Ruby thought was important to me. I wanted her to accept me and Raymond, especially since he was moving into my place and I'll tell you bout that in a minute. I wanted her blessing is what I wanted. She means that much to me.

How'd it come bout that Raymond's moving in with me? Surprised me too especially since I haven't lived with a man since my first and only husband died a lifetime ago. I married for all the wrong reasons when I was young. Both me and my husband tried to be something out of a fairy tale, not real. We ended up not liking each other very much. So when my husband died, I figured nope, marriage ain't for me. I liked my freedom and I could take care of myself. And I did. Opened my own beauty parlor with the insurance money and did all right till a few years ago when I got sick off and on and it sort of fell apart. I had to sell my place. I got some money but not enough to live on a long time. The rents are so expensive. And food. Well, I don't have to tell you bout it. Social Security say I made too much money when I sold my parlor, they think I got money stashed away is what they think. Holding everything up with their red tape. Me not being able to pay my rent. When I finally told Raymond, he offered what he could but he's a working man and he has no savings left after having to pay all those medical bills for his wife. She died six years ago after a long illness. It worried Raymond though, my worrying. He told me I could move into his place. I said no. I don't like the neighborhood. It's all right for a man but for a woman? No. I like my street. I know the places to avoid. I don't see as good as I used to, it'd be hard to learn new tricks. I told him he could move in with me if he wanted. My place is nice. When I first moved here the whole neighborhood was white. It's got all mixed up now and I likes it like that. Must be one of the two mixed neighborhoods in all Chicago. Raymond and me living together seems natural. And he's neat. I been to his place enough to know. I even dropped in unexpected a few times just to see the up and up.

So after all my troubles, all I'd gone through, I wanted Ruby to understand bout us but she didn't. She started sounding just like Tessie. Asking bout Ray's money and questioning how he could want me.

"Oh Bea," she said, real quiet-like.

And I knew what she was thinking. What man would want an old woman like you? Child, it hurt me so bad I almost doubled over.

"He makes me feel like a woman," I tried to explain, feeling foolish. "He made me realize I still got needs." I wanted to cry.

"At your age?" Ruby said. "You'd better watch that high blood pressure."

I got mad then. "Ruby, I am old. I ain't dead." I slammed down the phone. And then I did cry. I called Raymond and he came over and held me.

Funny how people can see an old man falling for a girl half his age and understand that. Not condone it but at least understand. Cause what is there not to love? Beauty and youth is something everybody's attracted to. But when a younger man falls for an old woman? Well. Something's wrong with him, he's simple-minded. Or he's up to no good. Cause nobody can't see a person falling for wisdom and experience or just an aged personality. Somebody who's really there, you know? Most people my age been on this earth too long to worry bout what people think anymore. If we grouchy, we grouchy and stay out our way. If we in a good mood, come round. If we got a passion, watch out! A realness. Old people is real. The more the body goes the more the personality shines through, you hope. There's some that don't advance that way but those the ones been hiding from themselves all their lives. I never hid from nobody. Never learned to hide my heart either. It just shines right through my eyes. I been hurt lots of times that way but I never got the trick of hiding it. And I guess that's what people just can't understand. And I guess that's why I'm telling you this. Cause I couldn't tell my dearest and closest friend how an old, fat, yella woman, who's getting arthritis so bad she can't barely walk, found that warm space inside herself again and fell in love. It amazes even me. My soul feels leathery sometimes it's been through so much. One tender spot was left and Raymond found it. And we'll get on. I'll work on Ruby. She's stiff but she will bend. She'll come round. Me and Raymond, well, we'll just have to keep on stepping.

# Grave Dance
## Christina Sunley

I can believe I'm dead.
What I can't believe   is the blue eyeshadow
the mortician is stroking onto my lids.   *But in life—*
I protest   through stiffened lips   *I NEVER wore make-up!*

*Exactly*   she replies   dusting my cheeks with rouge
*Let's make your mother happy!*   and then   as she braids
my hair   she whispers into my naked ear   *I'll wash it off*
*—after your funeral...*
I must not be completely dead yet:   the nerves
in the back of my neck   are tingling   from her hot breath.
She stands behind my head   so that I cannot see her face
and cannot help but see her breasts   as she bends over
greeting me   from her low-cut satin dress.   *Odd*   I think
*a mortician wearing such a slinky thing*   then just as she's
on the verge of smearing pink lipstick   a shade my mother
would approve of   onto my lips

she kisses them.
Now for the first time I can see her face
—not for the first time:   *Oh it's you*   I gasp   between
kisses   *I should've known!*

*That's the way it's always been*   she declares   nibbling
my neck   *You dig me—*

*—and I dig you!*   She flings the first shovelful
of dirt over her left shoulder like salt   for luck
and soon my grave is so deep   she has to jump into it
so her shovel can reach.   *Don't worry*   she assures me

sunk chest high   *This is just for decoration. Soon as
the big black cars drive off   we're out of here!*

    Spadefuls of dirt   fly up from the dark hole
like exclamation points   and from my graveside seat
a cream-cushioned coffin   I can study the many lovely creases
in her aged face   like furrows   some so deep   you could
plant in them   and I run my hand   through the sweet
damp earth   dropping
seeds   one by one   in a row.   She is in my wake   covering
them over with dirt.   When I hear her say the name of Luna
I know we have arrived in the ancient world again   when women
were lunatics   planters   dancing   under the full moon
the full belly   *Of the goddess?*   I ask.
    *Oh yes the goddess*   she answers.
    and we join the dancers   until the moon herself   drops
from exhaustion   and a sun hotter than I've ever known
rises.   *Lay me to rest*   I plead collapsing into the soft
cream cushions

    of a canopied bed.
    I hear a worn-out knock on the door   and in she comes
wearing a crisp white uniform   bearing a tray which she places
almost in reach:   tea & white toast & Blue Bonnet margarine.
    *Just the way you like it missus*   she announces   smirking.
    *But...the goddess?*   I ask her.
    *I don't know nothing 'bout no goddess missus.   Must be
some dream you having.   I'll be ironing now.*   And she shuts
the door behind her.   I stare   at the wallpaper   red & green
paisley   until my eyes ache   I search   for my face
in the vanity mirror   but the small round bulbs that frame it
shed only feeble light.   This plastic altar   with its sacred
instruments:   lipsticks   compacts   eyebrow pencils   tweezers
and an assortment   of eyelashes and eyeshadows   including
a shade called Heavenly Blue.   My lids are caked with it
and my lips are drawn out   pink   perfect—

    I take a soft ball of cotton   and start scouring
my made-up face   until I am again

    *all clean.   That is some putrid shade of blue*
she remarks   before tossing the blue-streaked cotton puff

into my grave   pushing dirt over it   with her foot.
I hear a car door slam   and watch the last of the black limos
depart.   She starts filling up the hole   and it makes me think
of the body in a grave   like a seed planted   and of old ways
long buried:   the moon-struck   moon-touched   moon-calves
planting   dancing   planting   and of how I once gazed
through Luna's deep reflection   and then into the shallows
of a vanity mirror:   the ways we have buried our selves
and each other:   she and I   all of us.   *We go way back*
is what I say.

    She smirks her paisley smirk.   *You sure picked out some*
*ugly wallpaper, huh?   That was a pasty life you lived*
*back in your Blue Bonnet days   back when I was your Black maid.*
She leans on her long-handled spade   and sweat streams
down her face   like tears.

    *It was better the next time around*   I say   *When we both*
*came back Black.*

    She nods.   Then she stabs her spade   into the earth
the handle left   like a life unfinished

quivering

from my quick touch   in her wise old cunt   she moans
*It just never stops   feeling so good.*   Flesh that is old
really knows its way around.   I still pinch her butt
in the supermarket.   Having covered a lot of ground
in the past eighty years   we take our steps slowly now.
We do not always know   what day it is   or care.
Set deeper   with age   our eyes lose one kind of vision
and gain another.   I had not foreseen that along with
a wandering mind   comes a certain freedom: the terms
past, present, future   obsolete.   Having suffered
in this life   the inflexibility of time   we delight
in our new mobility   slipping into and out of
our many lives together   some nice, some not so nice:
fish in a tank   secretaries   in a steno pool   lovers
and unrequited lovers   high priestesses   cheerleaders
wild dogs in heat   we were once called sinful spinsters
we were even around   back when *Old Woman*   was a title
of respect.

    *Nowadays* she observes   *only the men get distinguished*
*with age.   Us women   we just get old.*   She is examining

a jar of skin cream in the drugstore  "Younger You"
which promises to erase the wrinkles—of women.  Erase
the evidence of a lifetime  our hard-won wrinkles
the tendencies of our faces  memorialized  like the many rings
of an ancient trunk:  indicators of a vast span  of experience.
   She drops the jar and it shatters—
—as if we  would have our faces  made blank!

   Pain  has come to her lately.
Her once straight spine bent by arthritis.  She feels most
her fingers' lost dexterity.
   *No good anymore* she complains  *for gardening.*
*Or sex.*
   One day she loses patience with aging  leaves life
—the last day of spring planting.  I told her I would wait
for the harvest.  Many days have passed now  without anyone
to braid my hair in the morning  the tomatoes are quite ripe
she would run her fingers through my hair  like a comb
I didn't weed much this year  won't bother with canning.
And finally a day comes  when I am so lonely for her I could
die.  So I do.
   She drops the last shovelful of earth onto my grave
and we stamp it down
      bare-footed.

# Wicked Old Witches
## Erica Lann Clark

*The aging woman well knows that if she ceases to be an erotic object, it is not only because her flesh no longer has fresh bounties for men; it is also because her past, her experience, make her willy-nilly, a person; she has struggled, loved, willed, suffered, enjoyed, on her own account. This independence is intimidating...*
—From Simone de Beauvoir's classic, *The Second Sex*, A. Knopf, 1935.

Armed with the above, and not quite sure how to finish the unfinished sentence, how to get beyond intimidating independence, I pestered friends and relatives. "So, what do you think about sex after midlife?" I asked.

"Not much," they answered.

"Do you mean sex or sexuality?" they asked.

"When is midlife?" they wanted to know.

Disheartened by the apparent fruitlessness of my quest, I took to the streets. When a subject is threatening, often folks more readily speak to strangers. Into the health food store I went. Isn't that where those who honestly care about a vibrant, radiant lifestyle congregate? Who better to lecture me on the best possible model of aging sex?

I bought the obligatory bottle of supplements. Feigning a casual stance, as I lingered over the writing of the check I asked in an off-hand way, "So, what do you think about sex after midlife?"

"Excuse me?" The two middle-aged women behind the counter weren't sure they'd heard right. They exchanged looks as I repeated the question, then burst out laughing.

"Are you kidding? What sex?" asked the older one.

"I'm not there yet, am I? I'm only 36!" said the younger woman. She was gasping for breath, laughing hysterically. Nervous laughter, I wondered, but dared not ask. Instead I raced to reassure her and so did the older clerk. "No, no, no," we cried, "you're not there yet. If you figure on living to 90, you've got another nine years to go before you hit midlife."

Now we were all laughing, but she most of all, till the tears streamed down her face. Us older women, the older clerk and I, we let our hair down now, rambling on about how the hormones ebb and steal away the heat of our desire. Then we touched on the side-effects of long-term partnerships, and the old adage of how familiarity breeds contempt rose to our lips.

"Also," added the young one, in a confiding whisper, "I've had customers tell me how, after their menopause, women's vaginas will get dry and sore because the skin gets too thin on the—you know—the wall." Her face showed what she thought that might feel like. Ah, yes, the dryness! Us aging ones, we nodded like veterans and exchanged looks.

Just when things were getting juicy between us, in came the UPS man with a delivery. "Damn!" I thought. On the other hand, I could use the interruption to my advantage. Taking the bull by the horns, I leaned toward the UPS man and asked softly, "Say, what do you think about sex after midlife?" Startled, he looked up from his clipboard. We three waited with gleeful anticipation. He looked at each of us in turn. The silence grew.

"Well," he said, breaking the awkward silence, "when's midlife anyway?"

"About 45," we chimed.

"I guess that does it for me. That's right where I am. I just turned 45 last week."

"So, what do you think?" I pressed my point.

"It's all downhill from here," he said and flashed us a wry smile. We three women pursed our mouths in the conciliatory expression of sympathy that women often wear when they speak of a man who cannot get it up or keep it up or who is much too small to satisfy.

With a synchronicity that smacked of divine intervention, the UPS man was saved from further embarrassment, for at that precise moment, the Mother-Daughter team entered the health food store. Mother was tiny, shriveled, at least 80 years old. Daughter was well into her 50s, edging up on 60, and had the weight of middle-age on her well-built frame. While they shopped, our talk dwindled and the UPS man escaped.

Faithful to the purpose of my quest, I malingered, idly browsing shelves of wellness formulae, until at last mother and daughter came to the counter to pay for their purchases. Quickly, I joined them and fired off my question. "Say, ladies, the three of us have just been talking about sex after midlife and we were wondering what you think about it."

Old mother reacted first, shot me a piercing look of pity and contempt. "Sex! Haven't got a man. I'm single!" she snapped. The words hit the air flat and final. Her hand made a sweeping gesture, waving away all hope, or questions, or commentary. Is that it? I thought. What happened to the sexy old women who keep on enjoying the fruits of passion well into their 90s—the ones we hear about in the media? Not in this health food store!

As we sank in the silence of her finality, I caught a glimmer of malicious delight in the old woman's eyes. My cousin Myra floated into memory. Cousin Myra, who had smiled when she heard my question and said in a voice tinged with malice, "Honey, I don't have sex anymore and what's more, I don't miss it. I never even think of it and that's all I've got to say." I winced, even now, as I thought about the course my future was likely to take.

But wait! Daughter wasn't about to let mother have the final word. Edging her mother aside and stepping closer to the three of us, she eyed us suspiciously, then said with a toss of her head, "Now *I* don't find any change at all! *My* sex life is as good as it ever was." Well, look at that. Old mother was gazing up at her daughter with pride and admiration, and perhaps even a touch of envy. I guess the rest of us must have had our mouths agape, because as she surveyed us all, a sly smile turned up the corners of her mouth and she added, "Maybe the sex is *even better!*"

Suddenly the suspicious, overweight middle-aged woman changed and I could see the peachy down on her cheeks, that downy skin that D.H. Lawrence had found so sexy in his novels. I could see the fullness of her lipsticked lips. In a flash, she'd transformed herself from one of us aging women into a living Helen Trent. In the radio days of my childhood, Helen Trent dared, in her soap opera, to be divorced and in midlife and in love with one lover after another. Some disaster always happened to prevent the marital outcome. Either Helen would get hit over the head by a burglar and develop amnesia, completely forgetting her former life and lover, or her lover would mysteriously disappear in a plane crash in the Brazilian jungle. So, one way or another, Helen could remain a vibrant, passionate, sexy island in a sea of middle-aged and married peers. Here she stood before me in the health food store, radiant and ageless! Wow!

My vision was short-lived. As abruptly as she'd spoken, she shut down now. "Well, I don't have anything else to add. Come on mother, let's go." I wanted to say, Wait, give me a chance to think of the next question, but she had already turned away. Helen Trent had disappeared. Out came the scent-less, sexless, church-going slouch. As she led her mother out of the store, there was nary a hormone, much less a pheromone, visible in her demeanor. She looked like anybody's good wife, a fit companion for a decent man, a perfect product of generations of puritan tradition.

I wanted to follow her out, wanted to shout after her, What did we do wrong? Should we have laughed? Weren't you serious? How do you shut it down like that, as if it weren't there—you know, your sexiness? Why do you hide it? And I might have, but just then Eleanor showed up. The saleswomen behind the counter saw her before I did. Joyfully, they cried out, "Here comes Eleanor, oh, you've got to ask her, she's the boss, she'll have plenty to say. She's divorced, she's got a boyfriend. Eleanor, come here and listen to this."

A successful entrepreneur, Eleanor owns her health food store, her home, her car. She can afford to pay employees and take vacations. I explained my mission.

"You're not kidding?"

"No, really, what about sex after midlife—from your point of view?"

"Well, I'm torn. In a way, I enjoy sex as much as I ever did, maybe even more, because now I know what I like. I'm just plain better at it. When I was young, I wasn't so sure of myself. I didn't really know yet. On the other hand, nowadays sex is just not as important to me as it used to be. Ten years ago, when I first got divorced, I was sure I'd be remarried inside of two years. I was not going to become an aging, single woman. But, after a couple of years of living independently, having my freedom, I was not at all eager to get married, even though I had a man who was interested. That was quite a surprise to me. Now here it is ten years later and I'm a happy, single woman. I have my lover and my life. But, you know, I'm really a lucky woman because I have the economic independence to do what I want. So, does this answer your question?"

She was ingenuous and sincere, so willing to address the issue. She was free and sure of herself. She reminded me of Aunt Anne, whose husband, Uncle Fred, had died when she was in her early 50s. The family pestered the heck out of Aunt Anne to re-marry, but—to our astonishment—she had no real interest in remarrying. She was a successful entrepreneur, with a thriving glove factory under her belt. For years, Aunt Anne had a man, Albert, a fellow with a handlebar moustache and a cane. But he was just a friend.

I must have looked blank, because Eleanor pulled me back to the moment. "Maybe you should carry a tape recorder to do these interviews," she admonished.

I mumbled something lame. I could see I had lost her. Off she went, wishing me luck. As she disappeared into her office, her employees had to look sharp. I lingered for a moment indecisively, and left.

I was heading home when I remembered an errand I needed to do at a friend's house, which just happened to be on my way—a ten minute delay, at most. And probably it would have been just ten minutes, but my friend had a handsome young visitor and one word led to another, till at last, there I was, blabbing about sex after midlife again.

"You're kidding!"

"No, I'm seriously asking. What do you think about sex after midlife?"

"What do I think, or how do I feel?" Stan, the handsome, young visitor smiled at me playfully.

"Either one." I smiled back. My God, he was very attractive.

"Are you sure you want to know?" he challenged.

"Why not?" I flirted.

We were all sitting in overstuffed armchairs. Stan jumped up out of his chair and leaped over to mine. He slid onto his knees like a baseball player sliding into home plate. His penetrating eyes looked directly into mine. He put his warm hand on my arm. His eyes were alight with a look I can hardly remember most days. But, in that moment I remembered.

"Come on, let's go. I'll show you my answer. I mean it." His voice was like music. His eyes were wonderful. From down behind my belly, a pleasing warmth spread along my groin, up my skin, through my heart, into my cheeks. I reddened—and if I had been 20 or 30 years young, I surely would have surrendered to pleasure on the spot! Instead, I heard myself chuckle like a nice lady, an aunt, and patted his arm as you would a child. I fought for and found my own pheromone-free slouch and slouched down into the safety of the overstuffed armchair.

My friend gave me a look that mixed pity with contempt. "If I had an offer like that, my dear, I would ask to borrow a bedroom. Please feel free to use mine now."

He grinned. Stan's delight showed in his eyes. He grinned, too. It was an invitation. Suddenly, the UPS man zoomed to mind. He had shining eyes, and he grinned, too. Could this be how men look when they're watching a woman trying to decide whether or not she'll take off her dress, her pants, her bra? Whether or not she'll lie on her back, whether or not she'll lean into the kiss, whether or not she'll assume the position?

My turn to laugh hysterically. My turn to say, "Well, whatever, I've got to go." My turn to run like hell. What was I running from? Embarrassment about my wrinkled, flabby and overweight body compared to young, lean Stan? Or was it rage toward the men in my past who wanted my body, but not me? Or fear that Stan would draw me into past behavior and I'd end up hurt as hell, wanting more and rejected?

My thoughts tumbled over each other as I drove home in turmoil. But when I arrived, my heart only felt grateful. Stan had reminded me that my desire is still alive, that my heart is still soft and all it would take to kindle my flame is an appropriate someone.

As I rolled that first sheet of blank paper into the typewriter, I found myself drifting back to Woodmere High School, to Mademoiselle Megritte's French class. It was the 50s. French was still the language of love, and I took four years of it. Mlle. Megritte was a stern, tight, sour woman, but an excellent teacher. She was a task-master, a bully, a slave-driver. She was like the ballet-master who went along our ranks as we lined up at the bar in first position. With his baton, he would tap our chests and rap our inelegantly elevated rear ends, shouting, "Pull up on that sternum and tuck your bottom. Tuck it! Tuck it! Tuck it! We don't dance from the bottom. We dance from the heart."

Like him, Mlle. Megritte demanded excellence and terrorized us into learning. But in the summer of our junior year, something happened to Mlle. Megritte. When we came back to school in September, she had become Madame Holtzkamp. Her sour manner was gone. Her mouth didn't have that tight look. Her cheeks were pink and her skin looked more alive. And she began each class with a monologue that always started with the same words, "Mon mari..."

I loved the sound of her voice as she purred those two words. That year, the new Madame Holtzkamp let us get away with murder. We all knew why she did and, God, we loved her for daring, at her age, to discover love.

So the question is, what do you think? What about sex after midlife?

# Even When She Sings
## Maude Meehan

'They' tell us it's not over
till the fat lady sings,
and we want to tell 'them'
there are a lot of
fat ladies, skinny ladies,
middle aged and old and
*very, very* old ladies,
who are singing duets,
and even a cappella,
and the lyric from
those fat ladies, skinny ladies
middle aged and old ladies is,
it just *never* seems to *be* over
So, we're wondering,
where does whomever said
it wasn't over till, etc.
get their information,
or - don't they - get theirs,
and, could that be the problem?

# Back of Her Neck
## Janice Levy

I know she was married once, to a fat man, who slept like a turtle on his back and whose skin smelled of red wine and onions. She pointed him out to me in a pub. He was talking in the direction of a group of women. His words were floating above their heads, like the empty bubbles of a comic strip. His hand was on his crotch.

He needs something to hold onto, she says.

We all do, I say.

Still, it is easier for you, she says. You are used to being alone. When I talk to myself, nobody answers.

He made rocking chairs, she says. And oxcarts for the farmers to carry their coffee beans. He told me the wheels he carved made music as they turned. He fanned me with his hat. His English was good enough.

We went to Puerto Limon by train to meet his mother. He said the mountains looked like the shoulders of strong men, the palm trees like feather dusters. He bought me *papas calientes* from a lady with a dirty apron and yucca and hot fish from a boy who ran up and down the aisles. When nobody was looking, he chewed on my thighs. He called them *chuletas*, pork chops, and smacked his lips.

We lived here once, she says, taking a photograph from her wallet. I see a small house, the color of tarnished silver, the stone roof looking like a row of crooked teeth. A man sits in a rocking chair on a porch next to tin cans filled with red flowers, a rooster on his lap. A woman kneels at his feet, her arms wrapped around his legs. I cannot make out her face.

She tells me she was married for three falls and three winters. When the weather turned warm, he paced like a dog in heat and followed the scents of strangers.

Postcards, she says and shows me the wall of her apartment she has made into a collage. Most of the pictures are of churches.

I watch her fingers glide over the cards like reading Braille.

She feels my question through her back.

He said my breasts were getting droopy and my thighs took up too much room in bed. That I was getting lines above my lips and snored like one of his aunts. He said I made him old.

Bottles of wine lie together as if necking, sweet liquid dripping, leaving left over wet kisses on her bedroom floor.

My husband made love like a fish, she says. He never used his hands.

Her laugh sounds like a cello. She sits naked with her knees up, pinching the bottom of her thighs with her fingers.

Pin cushions, I say and her laugh goes down a few notes.

He was better when I was younger, she says. Then I could remember anything, whether it happened or not.

We make love on the floor and she sits on my shoulders with her knees. I hear my bones crack.

I think you just broke me in two, I say.

Then I better make a wish, she says and closes her eyes for a long time, the years slipping from her face, as she sucks her bottom lip.

I sit alone and it comes again to me like the puzzle piece of a split eyebrow or the chip of a tooth—the one that fits somewhere in the middle, if you wait long enough.

The fingertips of someone who wanders first in night darkness. Coolness oozes up my spine. Sharp toes scratch my calves. I taste his breath through my nose.

My father comes when shadows nibble at the corners of the sun. He leaves wiping crumbs from his mouth. I am eleven, maybe twelve.

My mother moves in slow motion, chews her lips and tastes her words in silence. She disappears except for the little noises she makes—the moaning of a leftover puppy, lying broken on the road.

My mother's back is brittle now like the shell of a walnut. Her head has grown tiny and her tongue whisks in and out. She breaks things when she visits.

I pull back my skin and imagine it tied tightly behind my ears. I am looking for my face. The hair near my earlobes is the color of granite.

Then the phone rings. It is the new woman I have met.

She wants to see the baby condors at the zoo.

I rub my eyes and see her face in my palms. I press my hands to my cheeks to hold in her heat.

I have decided not to grow old. It has no future.

This new woman likes my mother. She tells stories that make my mother's eyes spin.

In the bathroom, my mother whispers to her, "I haven't dropped my pants in front of someone in twenty-five years."

My mother's laugh sounds like static.

I am vaguely jealous.

Yesterday, I saw Parker. I watched him watch me as I stared at my reflection in the store window. Then I made it easy for him. I put on my sunglasses and crossed the street.

As he leaned against the telephone pole, his arms folded across his chest, his legs wrapped in blue denim, he still looked as solid as a stone house. Once we ran from a church, under a sky charged with lightning; his hands an umbrella for my head.

A butcher's son, he hacked up wild beasts and came back with a six-pack and dried blood under his nails. He sucked on my fingers, his head thrown back, like a blind baby bird. We drank 'til our eyes turned gray and cloudy, then curled up like old mutts and slept, my hair a web over his face.

Sometimes I'd awaken and tease my teeth up his leg.

It was easy to be fed.

But I was always hungry.

Some nights I hold onto my pillow and call out a name from a long time ago. My voice stumbles around and around the room like a bat bumping into the walls of a cave.

I dream of happy Iris, laughing, giggling Iris, dancing naked like a go-go girl from "Laugh-In." Yodeling on an escalator at Bergdorfs, pinching my ass in the shower. Funny, silly Iris, charging into a crowded elevator, demanding who had eaten pizza with pepperoni for lunch.

Then, too, I think of Iris wrapped in a sheet, roaming the apartment like an unmade bed. Circling me, bumping into furniture, her voice falling on me like an avalanche. That last night, I found her body spilling off the sofa, a white bathrobe twisted under her stomach, her hair stuck to her sweaty face. She looked like a ripped bag of flour. The cleft in her chin held a little red pill I had never seen before.

I watched her relatives place small rocks on her headstone. I sat in my car and chewed on the ties of my plastic raincoat. Iris loved me so softly, so gently, that she made me weep. I held her at night and lay in her breath. If any of them had asked me, I could have told them things. About Iris, my Greek Goddess of the Rainbow. That I made her laugh. But maybe not enough.

This new woman I have met? The back of her neck is long and sleek like a horse's thigh. I know she can't hurt me. I have nothing left to feel.

I don't listen to my friends. Besides, I know they are jealous. This new woman is big, tall, almost six feet and wears clothes that let you know her weight has gone up and down. Her hands are the size of ping pong paddles. Her fingers are painted red. I think about how her feet hang down over the edge of my bed. She calls her ex-husband the Sperminator.

She moves with the force of one who is used to working a room, of doing presentations, of showing things off. She tells a story, first to you alone, bathing you in sunshine. Then when she's grabbed you, she raises her voice and looks around a bit, catches the eye of another person, and tells her story again, raising the heat a few degrees. Soon, everyone is simmering and ready to go home with her. Her voice is husky.

She tells me she has started to think of me when she wakes up in the morning.

I tell her, that's good.

She says it isn't, that maybe we are moving too fast.

You have been with a woman before, she says. I have yet to be with myself. You don't tell me things, but I know.

It's a new feeling, although I don't tell her. It's like probing with my tongue after the root canal clamps are unscrewed. Or maybe like yanking off a Band-Aid from a hairy spot. How my skin tingles when it first hits the air. I can smell her. Maybe it's my imagination, but I can smell hot chocolate and candy corn, none of which I keep in my house, except when she stays for breakfast. I can feel her, too. She's barely touching me, as lightly as a cloud floating by, but I can feel her breath as if she were standing near my shoulder.

It's a new feeling, this thinking of her in the morning, one I don't know what to do with. And when the phone rings and I jump across the room and pounce on it like a mountain cat, all prickly and hot throated...I'm not sure about anything at all.

Iris smelled of satisfaction.

Humping soap, she had said.

Brown, in the shape of a camel, we steamed its legs down to stubs.

Spicy, feisty Iris.

Her last name was Mustard.

In the bedroom with a rope.

In the kitchen with a knife.
I did not see all the clues.

This new woman likes icy showers. Alone and quick.
She rests her breasts on my head like a shelf.
She is sticky, then tingly in my arms.
I dry her with my body.
It's the back of her neck I want to touch again.
But still she jumps, her eyes frozen bits of chocolate. As if I have shone a flashlight under her chin. She stares right through my forehead.
She does not like her doughy thighs.

She tells me her younger sister is pregnant. That she's going to name the baby Rosa. Sometimes she dreams of pushing her sister down a flight of stairs. All of her children are named after flowers.
My ex-husband has lots of children too, she says, some with names he can't pronounce.
If I had a baby, she smiles, I'd name her Esmerelda. I'd tie her arms around my neck and wear her like a sparkling necklace. She would smell sweet like me and have her father's green eyes.

You promised that you'd fill me up, she says.
I can feel her shivering under her green coat. The goosebumps on the back of her neck feel like pinpricks against my tongue.
You promised, she insists. Up to the very top.
I put my arms around her waist and she trembles. She pulls her hat down over her ears and puts one hand on her hip. She looks like a coffee mug. Her words steam the air.
Then why do I feel so empty? She yells at the space above my head and stomps the ground with her boots.
Maybe you're just leaking, I say.
After she has gone, I see the line she has drawn in the snow with the heel of her boot.

You talk too much about yourself, she says and cracks her knuckles as she looks about the room.
You don't ask enough questions, she says and pulls her chin into her face like a pigeon.

It is the back of her neck I want to touch again. Under her hair, it is the back of her neck. I think her bones will feel warm.

And then she meets me late one day, chewing on a nail, cuffing and uncuffing the sleeves of her raincoat.

I'm moving, she says. I'll be busy for awhile. I'll call you. Have you over.

To his place or yours? I ask.

A look passes quickly over her face, as fleeting as the shadow of a dragonfly. Her eyelashes touch my cheek. Like a hummingbird's kiss, I hear her sigh.

The back of your neck, I think. But I don't tell her.

Then the look is there again in her eyes.

And I know she knows that I know.

Maybe she was no more real than a shadow of a shadow.

# Rituals

## Carol Potter

The set of knives in the stand,
a slot for each blade
on the counter. A woman is sharpening
the blade. I watch her, thinking of
rituals, of my father at the head
of the table and the rasp of knife
on metal, then the blade against the
meat. Delicate, an easy pull
against the grain. She is sharpening
the knife. Is it the same knife
she pulled across her arm?
What happens in that moment
when a woman pulls a blade
through her flesh then drives off
with the arm in a bandage?
She found herself turning against
that ridge. She pulled herself
along the point as if to test
the envelope of the body, open this
package up, give it some air.
I think of the circus performer
climbing a ladder balanced on a chair
while he juggled nine hoops. He was pulling
himself up through the air
hoping the air
would not collapse around him.
This is what we do, I wanted
to tell her as if the breath was a body

slipping in and out of our mouths
trying to haul us along behind it.
I ran my finger along that place
on her arm that she opened up
to the sky, that edge she leaned
against as if to give herself
more air, more light. Other places
I wanted to tell her, people do this
to each other, the body with its lid
open to the air, faces hanging
on trees. Is this what happens
when love fails, slide the blade
across the wrapper to lay it open
like a present? Untie the bow, cut
open the tape. She is sharpening
the blade. I watch her test it
against her thumb. Later, making
love, I go deep inside her. She sings
at the end of my tongue. I hold her
tight as I can.

# Two Conversations
## A.D. Ross

Rachel was suddenly awake and wondering why. Hawaii. Right. Moonlight streamed through an unusually large window oriented strangely to the bed. Single bed. This was the Hawaii condo. What was that noise? A kind of clinking, no, now a rustling. What was that muttering? Was that Linnis? Where was Linnis? Disturbed, Rachel reached for her robe and got out of bed. The door to the big bathroom was open and the light was on.

The condo was all view and balcony. Clearly it had been built on the cheap; the teak-trimmed rooms were cramped. But space had been lavished on the big bathroom. A round tub was sunk into a raised tile platform. A long counter with cosmetic lighting held two sinks. The toilet seat was teak; teak bordered the stall shower, and the frame of the very large tilt-back mirror was teak. In front of this mirror Linnis was standing, naked, looking at her back over her shoulder. Her eyes met Rachel's. She was holding a glass of what looked to be brandy, and as she straightened up she drank.

"Here I am," she said, "looking in the mirror at 4 a.m."

"Is this a common practice? Because you didn't tell me. And when we were roommates? I didn't know."

"I can explain everything, Rachel. I'm old. I know this because I'm looking at myself naked in a full-length mirror. I can't remember ever having done this particular thing at this particular time."

"Middle of the night, or in a Hawaiian condo?"

"You know, I never had so much as a pimple in my life until I was 40 years old. I had really good skin. Now look. God. Broken veins and mysterious red splotches and even little lumps and bumps. Everywhere. That's not counting the wrinkles. The wrinkles are dense. The only cure for wrinkles is to go under the knife and I'm not having it."

"Did I even suggest."

"Last year I had a little collagen work done. Lines around my mouth."

"I didn't notice."

"I didn't want anyone to notice. Don't even think about it. It's nothing. But I felt sexier. No one noticed. Perfect. This was all for me."

"Right," Rachel said, "self-image."

"Yeah. And dance class every day. However, you'll notice my thighs have not become less flabby, nor has all the dancing in the world fluffed up my saggy ass. My breasts droop and my upper arms are a scandal. Look," she wailed. Linnis was strangely pale in the bathroom light. Her light medium-length hair, which was usually combed straight to her shoulders, showing a flash of the crystal or beaded earrings she liked, had been pulled back into an untidy knot. She wore no earrings now, Rachel noticed, and this, together with the hair, made her look colorless and ghostlike. Well, she was naked. She was thin compared to Rachel, whose own dark hair was cut short. "The collagen's all worn off," Linnis went on. She turned away and examined her face closely in the mirror. "I can't feel myself to be physically attractive. And all the time in my head I know, I've always known, the power of wit and the charisma of intellect, the seduction of good timing. But the flesh is overpowering."

"As flesh is wont to be."

"Appearance is not my only manifestation of aging. My lower back hurts. I got a new prescription for my reading glasses but I can't see things the way I remember them to look. God. We're in the age group. One of us could croak at any minute. My cousin died of cancer only five days before Eddie and I kissed at that party."

Rachel sighed. "Right. Eddie."

"I miss the sex. I miss the supreme moments of connection, you know, the gazing and so forth."

"It's wonderful."

"It is."

"Nothing like it." Rachel knew what Linnis was talking about. She'd had her share of ecstatic moments. She'd been secretly seeing a married colleague of Kay's for three years. Only Linnis had been told of this affair.

"Well, and that's why I can't get it together with aging. That's it. That's the ball game. I just don't feel sexy and juicy and compelling and musky and irresistible."

"You have to feel all those things?"

"Two out of three."

"They say it's just as scary for men."

"Yes, but you know it's not true. We're the ones. We're the objects. We have the pheromones. We have the tits."

Rachel sat down on the toilet seat. She picked up Linnis's brandy glass and sipped from it. "Give me a cigaret," she said.

"Oh my god," said Linnis, "am I that far gone?" She handed her cigarets to Rachel.

"Dire," Rachel said. She lit a cigaret, coughed, and passed it to Linnis who began to smoke it greedily. "Well, dramatic. Momentous. The discovery of aging."

"Have you thought about this, Rachel? I mean, when you're with your boyfriend?"

"Yes. Well. A little bit." Rachel lit another cigaret and they smoked together silently. Linnis slipped her pajamas off the hook and put them on. She took the glass from Rachel and drank.

"Let's get some more," she said.

"Good idea." In the tiny kitchen area, they sat across from each other at a narrow table, their knees touching, drinking brandy.

"You know, Kay went to see Eddie." Linnis sniffled and her voice trembled.

"When?"

"Couple days ago. She was worried about him, she said. What about me, I asked her. Oh you, you'll be okay." Linnis burst into tears. "But I'm not."

"Yes you are."

"No I'm not."

"Kay trusts women more than men."

"Who doesn't? So what?"

Rachel yawned. It was about noon on the mainland. "Look, Linnis. The sky's getting light."

"God. We're going to see the genuine Hawaiian sunrise."

"Did you unpack the Peets?"

"Not yet. I will now."

"Oh good. Dawn under the volcano."

"And aged Indonesian."

While Linnis found and brewed the coffee, Rachel hunted for her purse. She knew she had some lifesavers or gum or breath mints or something. The cigarets and brandy had changed the ecosystem of her mouth, which now felt terrible. They'd only just arrived in the afternoon. They'd eaten at the hotel on the beach, two blocks away, and walked back to the condo at 10 p.m. Three a.m. real time. Then Linnis had to watch L.A. Law while Rachel began to carelessly and listlessly unpack. Jet lag had her in its zoned grip. When Linnis snapped off the TV, Rachel got into the other bed immediately. The bedroom was tiny. The huge windows didn't leave much room for amenities like shelves and closets. But both the bedroom and the living room/kitchen opened out onto a large balcony, which faced the sea. Beneath the balcony was a landscaped garden edged by a little parapet and a short stairway to the street and the beach.

"You know, when we first fell in love I was miserable." Linnis set down two cups of dark coffee. It tasted wonderful. "That should have told me

36

something. I wanted to be with Eddie all the time. Even when he droned on about the CIA conspiracy to control ethnic minorities so that they could kill them all, even when he droned on, I stared at him in rapture. On one hand I was bored beyond belief. On the other hand I was captivated. I couldn't take my hands or my eyes off him. When we made love I pitied the toiling striving population of the earth. Oh god, oh god. If only I could hold him between my legs forever. Why isn't life like that."

Rachel sipped from her cup. She knew exactly what Linnis meant. But she'd never trusted Eddie. "I've always thought Eddie's long hair looked ridiculous," she said. "I mean, it's not an attractive hairstyle even on a younger man, or a thinner man. He's probably like most men, doesn't have a good sense of his looks. Like most people, really."

"All I can think about is my age. When I think of Eddie I think of his age, which brings me back inexorably to my age."

"But do you feel it on the inside? Your age, I mean."

"Yes, I do. I feel very unlike the way I felt at 18 or 25 or 30. I feel bitter, doomed, remorseful. I have the perspective of the aged. I have a history."

"Memory?"

"Yes. I remember having a sense of myself as beautiful and sexy, a sense which was mainly realized through sex. But now, you know, tonight, looking at my body, I feel like I'm saying goodbye to sex. Aloha."

The sky was by now yellow, slowly becoming blue over the jagged rim of the volcano to the northeast.

"Beautiful."

"Yes." Linnis gulped coffee. They sat in silence for a moment. "But I don't want to say aloha. You know?"

"Men are a mystery," Rachel said.

"They bore me when it's not eroticized."

"They?"

"Men. Eddie."

"It?"

"The encounter, the being together."

"No flash of friendship, no eyes meeting, no secret smiles?"

"Well, yes. Sure. Sometimes. But no conversation. So rare, so difficult to maneuver."

"I wish I knew what to tell you."

"Answer me this. What did I do wrong, you know. Why did he get so cold so fast?"

"Changed his mind."

"So what? Does that automatically erase everything?"

"I'm not saying it's forgivable."

"Why didn't he make me feel okay?"

"It's not forgivable."

"Just to drop me with one phone call. God."

"I thought you called him back."

"I did. Twice. He just said he couldn't see me or make a date. He wouldn't say anything else, god, he sure knows me well. He knew I wouldn't lose it, he knew I'd behave well. He knew that about me."

"Right. He made you do all the work although it was his decision. Typical male oppressive pattern."

"Exactly. I feel pissed off. But at the same time kind of proud."

"Well you were smart. You avoided days, maybe weeks, of pain and bickering. You're a hero."

Linnis blew her nose. "So you don't think I'm a coward, that I should have hung in there and cossetted him and coaxed him back?"

"They say that's what it takes."

"I haven't got it."

"Me neither."

"I want everything to be as it was two months ago, when we lay in each other's arms. But I don't want him as I see him now.

"Which is?"

"I see him as essentially stupid in that bull-like enraged puzzled way that men are." It was clear Linnis was feeling less distressed. Her eyes were still swollen and red, but she had lost her defeated slump. "And I knew it from the beginning because I was bored. God, his lame clichés. I was stupefied with disinterest when he talked. It was natural to slip away from his soliloquies into a reverie of my own."

"Didn't he notice?"

"I don't think so. I think it was dense masculine thickness of skull and crudeness of synapse. I remember a phone conversation I had with Kay. She said, 'You have to make a kind of post-feminist decision. Men are self-centered and boring, and that's the price you pay if you want a man in your life. There aren't any other kind.'"

"Yes there are."

"That's exactly what I said. Exactly. And Kay said, 'Well, do you know one?' Her voice was all sharp and dry and cynical and bitter."

"What did you say then?"

"I said, 'No, not right now.' And my voice was all sad and disappointed."

"Come on. Aren't there any men you like, just as people. Friends. How about Martin. Lenny."

"Oh of course. I'm just, you know, pissed off. Polemical."

"Well it's a kind of bigotry."

"Kay always says: 'I can't help it, I was born in this country.'"

"I think you can be conscious of it. Become familiar with your own point of view. In context."

"Make friends with your prejudices, you mean?"

"Right. Better than not knowing what they are, and sort of at their mercy."

"Am I misanthropic?"

"Not as a rule. But definitely tonight."

"This morning."

Rachel put down her cup. "You know," she said, "it's like the gender war has finally resolved itself into the acquisition of all psychic wisdom by women, and the surrender of all inclination toward it by men."

"Yes. Exactly. I had a flash that I was in on the downfall of the masculine empire." The two women sighed.

"You and Eddie seemed to be in sync," Rachel offered. "I will say that."

"But what's being in synch about, Rach?" Linnis sat up straight. "The nature of the commonality. To boldly go beneath the ostensible content. God. You know another thing that bothered me? 'Everything is wonderful,' he kept saying, 'Everything is fine.' It's like that funny old hippy girl, remember her? That jingle bells hippy, who used to go around saying, 'Oh I'm so happy, I'm just so happy all the time.'"

"I remember. That was a long time ago."

"Some things are wonderful but I don't understand how everything can be wonderful. Not to discount it. But what else is there? What's in the interstices? Something important is being ignored. I mean, god, one time we were talking cautiously about maybe moving in together. After about ten minutes of really interesting highly charged conversation he said, 'Have we talked enough? Can we stop talking about this now?'"

"Gross."

"And yet he examined every tiny minute speculative aspect of the Iran-Contra scandals. Something's weird here, is it me? Have I got something wrong? Am I missing something?"

"Right," Rachel said, "you're the one who's missing the point, talking about real life."

"Well, it's frightening. Risky. I didn't want this love affair to fall apart because I questioned it. But I did and it did."

"So you made him end it?"

"He said he was open to me, I had but to ask. But it wasn't that he was open to what I said. He was only open to me saying it. He assumed the posture of endless generosity of heart. I questioned it. If it, the posture, was real, why did it feel phony. Oh god, but as I talk his good traits are pressing in on me from all sides."

"Tell me one good trait."

"Well. He taught me about keeping my knives sharp. And he's fair. He understands about fairness."

"That's it? He's fair? Was he fair when he just dried up on you?"

"Well, he's also passive."

"He's a drunk, Linnis."

"I wonder if all drunks talk in clichés. He's got that silly long hair. God. Why did I pretend he was as smart as me. I'm so glad I got out of town. The experienced escape artist went into action. The travel agent, the Hawaiian condo, you. The note. Ah god the note."

"What'd you say?"

"How I agonized. But in the end decided to spare him."

"Not a word?"

"I went for discretion."

"How civilized you are."

"A civilized hero." Linnis looked almost cheerful. She had regained her former arrogant posture. "Is it time to call Kay? Speaking of civilized."

"Sure, it's afternoon back home."

Rachel listened to Linnis speaking to Kay on the phone.

"Well, its weird here," Linnis was saying, "It's a tiny little place with a huge bathroom and a huge ocean. It's cramped but cozy. (Pause.) Not really. (Pause.) I've got Rachel smoking and drinking. Kay, we saw the sunrise. Right over the volcano. (Pause.) Of course I'm still blue. God. (Pause.)" She started to laugh, "Yeh," she said, "we're out on the beach this very minute in our $100 swim suits, looking for two gorgeous Hawaiian men who want to fuck our brains out because they're turned on by middle-aged women. (Pause.) No, what do you think? We're talking. Okay." She handed the phone to Rachel who attempted to pace with it and soon found herself in the hall.

"Well," Kay said, "How's it going?"

Rachel saw through the open door of the bathroom the large stand-alone mirror which reflected the bright room in back of her and Linnis sitting by the big window. "Fine. We've been here about 15 hours."

"Time enough for me to drive home, get a good night's sleep, and have a fight with Neal."

"Oh no."

"Oh yeah."

"What—"

"He says I've been bad vibing him all week. He says ever since I went to see Eddie I'm on a vendetta to castigate all men."

"Oh Kay. What—"

"Eddie was an asshole. What can I tell you. Quintessential denial. He's drinking heavily. I think he misses Linnis. I don't suppose there's any possibility."

"No, Kay. Snowballs in hell."

"No. Well."

"Why did you promote this affair, if I may be so bold as to ask."

"I like to look at lovers. Young love is so inspiring when it's not wasted on the young." Kay sounded far away. Well, right. She was far away. Rachel moved, tracking the big mirror, and saw herself within it. Linnis was a tiny backlighted figure behind her. Rachel turned sideways and tucked in her stomach. Oh dear. How did Linnis stay so thin. Cigarets no doubt. Kay went on. "Neal and I are just like brother and sister these days."

"Except when you're fighting."

"Except when we're fighting. I guess that's what we do for excitement between us now. A spark. I guess I'm disappointed. I want couples. You're no good."

"I'm between engagements."

"You've been between engagements for three years, Rachel." Kay's voice was sharp.

Rachel took off her pajama bottoms. Linnis was her only confidante, but she was pretty sure that Kay guessed about her affair. There was only a slim possibility that Kay, who worked in the same office as her lover, didn't know. Rachel conducted all conversations as though that possibility were conclusive. Her thighs looked even fatter naked, and her woolly socks and slippers made her legs look lumpy. "I'm not worried," she told Kay serenely.

"God we had fun with Eddie and Linnis. We even got it on a few times after they went home."

Rachel hastily pulled off her slippers. By craning her neck she could see dark varicosities patterning her heavy thighs. Or imagined them there. Yuck. "Kay," she said, "Do you feel old?"

"Obsolete."

"Because this coming and going is hard on a person."

"I wouldn't mind a vacation."

Rachel almost dropped the phone. By squinting she could see her plump neck. When had she got so very fat? Could collagen help? "You could have come with us."

"No I couldn't."

"What are you going to do?"

"About Neal? Fix coq-au-vin. Explain I've been pissed at Eddie but he's not Eddie. Let him tell me about the Lakers. The usual."

"You're all heart."

"Is it true you drank and smoked?"

"I did."

"Ah well. Call me tomorrow. Aloha, Rach."

Rachel reclothed herself and went back into the kitchenette, which looked very different now. Brighter. Sun streamed in through the windows. "Hey, it's daytime," she said.

"God. What shall we do?"

"The beach? Or a little nap?"

"Oh god. Those are our choices. We're in Hawaii."

"We could put on something floppy and concealing and go to breakfast at the hotel."

"All right. And then take a nap."

"I'm hungry. Or something. Not my usual self."

"I know. It's jet lag."

"Right. And alcohol."

"And the blues." It took them a long time to get dressed. Rachel couldn't remember where she'd put her shoes. Linnis had to have a shower. They drank more coffee. Finally they stood side by side, gazing in the mirror. Linnis, standing very straight, was elegant, slender in her rose and grey striped sundress. Rachel wore pale blue. These drop-waist dresses are great, she thought, I look pretty good.

"We look pretty good," Linnis said. She smiled at Rachel in the mirror.

"Kay says she feels obsolete." Rachel stared at herself with pleasure.

"I feel obsolete too."

"Old, you said."

"Well. Aging. Maybe not old yet." Rachel relayed Kay's sad story to Linnis. Linnis clicked her tongue. "Relationships," she said.

"Kay," said Rachel.

"We did have some awfully good times with them. Kay works so hard on that relationship. Neal is, well, you know how he is, and you couldn't describe Kay as easy. As we know."

"We know."

"They both work hard."

"Too hard for me."

"But don't you ever yearn for it, Rachel? I know you get along well with your sweetheart, but you only see him every week or so."

"Yearning for it is better than doing it. Doing it is just what was so impossible for you with Eddie. Impossible for him with you."

"Yes. Sure. Kay has the true dedicated temperament." Their eyes met in the mirror. Linnis was definitely revived by the news of Kay's struggles with Neal. A little drunk, alerted by several cups of coffee, skin stretched by multiple time zones, the two women set out for breakfast arm in arm. First Linnis, then Rachel, turned back to look at the long mirror which now reflected only the window and through it the bright Hawaiian sky.

# Fifty Is Fine
## Dena Taylor

Lenny stood in the shower with her eyes closed, feeling the almost-too-hot water rain down on her head, her back, and then run along the curves of her rather ample and very tired body. She had looked up ample in the dictionary and found *of generous proportions* and *quite enough*, and thought that was a pretty accurate reference to her fifty-year-old body.

She was tired because she hadn't slept enough. She hadn't slept enough because Paul had been over last night. She wasn't complaining. In fact just thinking of it sent little currents of pleasure radiating from a spot just below her belly button to the far corners of her body.

Lenny rubbed her soapy hands over herself, between her legs, and lifted each generous breast to wash underneath. I should do a cancer check, she thought, but didn't, because she hated doing them. By the time she finished her shower, the hot water had done a pretty good job of lifting the fog from her brain.

She'd never had a relationship before like the one she was having with Paul. Sex was the only thing they did together. She called him or he called her. And usually the other was agreeable. And the sex was wonderful. And that was that. No being in love, no wondering what the other was doing, no hurt feelings. Once a week, sometimes more, occasionally less. It seemed perfect to Lenny. If she wanted to go out dancing or partying with a man, there were others she could call. Usually, though, she preferred her women friends for company.

The phone rang in Lenny's kitchen. Damn, she thought after the fourth ring, I forgot to put the machine on. She threw a towel around herself, ran out of the bathroom, and grabbed the phone just as Jess was about to hang up.

"I'm on my way to the Farmer's Market. Want to come?"

"Hmmmm...not now...I had *such* a good time last night," she said, drying her feet.

"Well, I'm glad...if that's what you like to do."

"Oh, come on, Jess, you can't *always* be alone, can you?"

"Yes I can, and I like it that way. How about coming over for dinner tonight?"

"Sounds great. I'll bring the wine."

Lenny and Jess had been friends for years. Not long after they met, they formed "The Two-Member Mothers of Teen-agers Support Group," which later was changed to "The Two-Member Women in Failing Marriages Support Group," and now they were "The Two-Member Over Fifty Divorced Women's Support Group."

Driving to Jess's that evening, Lenny rolled down her window and smelled the fog. She loved fog, the way it erased all the hard edges of things, the way it changed an ordinary landscape into a kind of furry fairyland. The coolness of it.

Ah, the coolness of it. That was the best part. Even before she was middle aged, even before that time in her life when being hot was a more or less permanent state of being, she loved the cool of the fog.

Lenny had that feeling that something was changing in her life, stirring up. Maybe it was nothing more than The Change itself, and one of these days she'd be back to her old self, just as the menopause literature promised. But she knew that sometimes life surprises you with things you're not really prepared for. Like the time she got up to get the paper in the early morning darkness and saw someone, a large someone, sleeping on the couch. She went over to see who this could possibly be, and found it was her sixteen-year-old daughter and her daughter's boyfriend.

Momentarily stunned, she went back to bed without the paper. And pondered this new development. She was pretty sure it was new, anyway. Was she angry? No. If they wanted to sleep together, they would find somewhere to do it, and they might as well be comfortable. Lenny had always encouraged her daughter to be open with her, but she wasn't quite ready for this. Was she worried or afraid for her daughter? No. She was very levelheaded, she knew about birth control, and Lenny thought this boy was a pretty nice person for her daughter's first experience with sex. Was she jealous of her daughter's youth and the life that stretched out ahead of her? No, Lenny felt fine about her life and the freedom of being fifty. But this was definitely a milestone. They were all growing up, growing older. Lenny got up again, went out the side door to get the paper so she wouldn't wake them, and got back in bed.

When she told Jess about this incident, Lenny could see that Jess was a little shocked. It amused Lenny that they could be such good friends while having rather different lifestyles. Lenny had never seen Jess's house be anything but calm and orderly, while hers was rarely in that state. Jess had one very nice, very quiet son who was a Buddhist; Lenny had two outspoken, passionate daughters. And Jess's lovers, when she had them, were women.

But they liked spending time together, and they shared a great enthusiasm for cooking and eating exquisite meals. Lenny said eating was her second favorite indoor sport, and that Jess was the best cook in town. Jess would often call her up with a new recipe she discovered, and they'd eat and drink and talk the night away. They said this was practice for when they were old and living together in San Francisco near Chinatown where they could easily shop for good things to eat.

Lenny ate with gusto and didn't give a damn that she was "quite enough." She liked her body. It hadn't given her any problems so far. Quite a bit of pleasure, in fact. She figured that if she ate in a reasonably healthy manner, and did a certain amount of exercise, and felt good, that she must be doing something right.

Two of her men friends had recently told Lenny she was their hero.
"What?" For one thing, she would've thought *heroine*. "Why?"
"Because of what you've done. Because you live the way you want."
"Oh." It was true that she lived the way she wanted. "What have I done?"
"Books. Kids."
Books, hmmm. Kids, yes—they were great young feminists with a good sense of humor and justice. There was nothing like your children for giving you such a feeling of sing-your-heart-out love and gut-wrenching anguish. And through it all, Lenny loved being a mother.

The girls were gone now. Off to college. Lenny had tried to prepare herself for this event by talking to other women who had gone through it. Some said she'd go crazy in her empty house, be sure and call them for support. Others said she'd love the freedom of just having herself to think about. One friend said it was terrible for her—for two weeks. And Lenny talked to the girls about it, the way they talked about everything. They were all a little anxious, although excited, about the coming changes.

They decided to have a ceremony to mark this point: the ending of their life the way it was and the beginning of new directions for all of them. They asked some of their closest women friends to come and share memories, thoughts about what the future might hold, and food. Each woman brought something that symbolized her relationship to Lenny and the girls. There was much laughter and some tears.

Later, Lenny learned that some of her men friends felt hurt that they weren't invited. Some had known the girls all their lives and were indeed very dear to them. Lenny thought about this a long time, and about how different a ceremony might be where men were present. Perhaps it was time to try a different way of doing things.

The night that she came home after helping the last child get settled into her new apartment, Lenny took a bath, put on her new Emmylou CD, cleaned up some of the disaster area left from packing, and called Paul. They had a wonderful night of making love, and could be as noisy as they wanted.

Her mother called the next morning to see how she was doing. "Well, Lenore, how was your first night by yourself?"

Lenny grinned. "Fine, Ma. I think I'm going to be fine."

# Avocado Nights
## Barbara Unger

"**N**ew York men," said Dina. "Not a normal one in the lot." To Dina, the city was one huge outpatient clinic, making it statistically impossible to meet a nearly normal man over 40 in New York. After her divorce and a short interlude on the Single-Again circuit, Dina had given up. She had now undertaken to introduce me to a kaleidoscopic range of cultural pleasures on those alternate weekends when I remained inconsolable without Boris's body. Unmoved by both dismal marriages and dismal affairs, Dina became an ideal friend for those times when Boris disappeared from my life without a trace.

It was simple to ascertain Boris's current state of mind from the phone messages left on his answering machine. One never knew if one would reach a passage from Anna Livia Plurabella, some Henry Miller erotica or an Emily Dickinson quatrain. Once, in an incautious moment, Boris himself picked up the receiver and, from his non-literary riposte, I knew at once that he was playing games with his medication. When I reported this to his shrink, the good doctor Feigenbaum, he informed me that Boris was about as functional as he was ever going to be and that I should consider making an appointment to come in. Feigenbaum had helped many women in my situation. But I turned instead to Dina.

"I knew he was a certified nut job. All New York men, darling, are mental cases. You're thinking of giving him up, aren't you?"

"Giving him up? No. Murdering him? Yes."

"Then we'll just have to keep him from driving you crazy. See others," said Dina. "It's the only way."

We were lunching at our favorite haunt. I put a bite of spinach salad in my mouth and Dina waited expectantly for me to chew it so we could get on with the question of Sam, the new man.

"He's nice enough," I said.

"You mean for someone else. What's his problem?"

"Terminally boring."

"At our age," replied Dina, "what's a little boredom? After Boris, it might be a pleasant diversion. By the way, how is Mr. Manic these days?"

"Well, if you must know, he wants me to sleep over his mother's house in Forest Hills. He's depressed because his mother's in Florida. He waters her plants while she's gone."

"What's so special about Forest Hills?"

"In the living room of her apartment is this couch," I stuttered. "This *avocado* couch."

"Yes, yes." Dina's eyes were glazed, transfixed on the tremor in the corner of my mouth. "And he wants you to do it with him on his mother's avocado couch?"

"How did you know?" I was stunned by Dina's perspicacity.

Dina closed her eyes, her face lit by a maniacal smile. "Is it one of those great semi-circular damask affairs *circa* 1958 in three parts, covered in crinkly plastic?"

I wasn't sure except that it was on this very couch that a seventeen-year old Boris experienced sex for the first time, in his mother's old apartment on Morris Avenue in the Bronx. Still in pristine condition, thanks to the zippered plastic covers, the couch had moved, along with his mother, from the Bronx to Queens. There he wanted to replicate with me his moment of bliss with Taft High's Teen Queen, Susanna Schechter, his first love.

"Now you know me, Dina. I draw the line at Boris's mother's couch." Dina fell into sharp gusts of laughter.

"Women are such fools," she gasped.

"You don't understand. Susanna Schechter dumped him. Boris says it will never be the same for him again."

"His mother's sofa." Tears formed in Dina's eyes. I nearly choked on my spinach salad, despising myself for having told Dina.

"Every Don Juan's wet dream," she muttered and struck her bosom to keep herself from another paroxysm of merriment. Adrift again, I stared at the mouse-colored tablecloth, hoping to calm my caffeine nerves.

"So what did you tell him?"

"I tried to make light of it. I said I have an aversion to the color avocado."

Dina wiped her runny mascara with a tissue and blew her nose. "So what's that supposed to mean?" she asked.

"It means a no. A definite *no*."

"You'll go back to him," Dina said. "You can't help yourself."

I drained the cup of coffee. Couldn't she understand?

Never again could he recapture those avocado nights back on the primal luxury of his mother's sofa, unzipped for that one stolen moment of abandon. How could he ever again recapture that Dionysian moment when his boy-body radiated fire, when he felt such indescribable rapture that, to this day, he can only evoke the epiphany by returning, as it were, to the scene of the crime?

"Where's your *joi d'vivre*?" I inquired.

"Honestly, Lenora, I do admire your tenacity," she said.

"I'm just not as self-sufficient as you, Dina," I reminded her.

"See others. That's my advice."

The new man, Sam, was due at six. By five-thirty I was searching frantically for his self-published curriculum guide for teaching good citizenship, the one he'd personally inscribed to me the night we'd met at the Singles mixer at the temple. "To a Fellow Author. Love, Sam." I had promptly surrendered it to the top shelf of the bookcase where I kept books I never intended to read again. I had already abandoned Genet, Celine, *Coming of Age in Samoa*, *The Lonely Crowd* and the complete works of Hermann Hesse to the shelf; Sam's spine-stapled *ouevre* would moulder in distinguished company. By five of six, I still hadn't found it, a symptom of something-or-other. I forget what. Still, I had high hopes for Sam.

A small, sad-mouthed man, Sam arrived on time. In his hands were yesterday's mildewed roses from the corner Korean grocer.

"How thoughtful," I said, burying my nose in the soggy petals. Next I ran tap water into a vase, fanned out the roses to make them seem fuller, and set the display on the coffee table. In a moment of inspiration, I excused myself, ran into the bathroom, removed a bottle of aspirin from the medicine cabinet and popped four into my palm. I swallowed two for good measure. When I returned to the living room I put the other two into the vase and swished around the stems.

"A life extender," I explained to Sam.

"How marvelous!" Pink sweat exuded from his facial pores. He followed me into the kitchen where I started the veggies in the steamer.

"I love to watch women cook. May I?" he asked.

"Be my guest."

"You don't object?"

"Not at all." Once a year I performed my *balaboosta* act just to keep my hand in. Naturally, I wasn't going to tell Sam that. I handed him the wok stirrers and told him what to do. I sensed a certain restfulness with Sam after the maelstrom of Boris. Clearly, there were no avocado nights in store with Sam.

"How do you like your rice?" I inquired.

"Firm," he said. All the while, Sam stirred the veggies, none the wiser.

"Tell me, do you enjoy poetry?" I inquired.

A lock of thinning white hair fell across his forehead and lent a Byronic moodiness to his moist face. "Oh, yes."

"So do I," I said, reaching among the cookbooks for one of Boris's translations. "Let me try this one on you." I began to read a passage Boris had penned for me on the flyleaf. "With great love comes great suffering." Hadn't Boris always said that it sounded better in German? Sam's expression remained unchanged. What did he need? *Monarch Notes*?

Sam removed his handkerchief, wiped his eyes, blew his nose and the talking resumed. "I hope you'll forgive me. Generally I enjoy poetry, but my therapist recommends more cheerful pursuits. You know. Social dancing, bowling, Group, bridge."

"But you haven't said what you think," I insisted.

"Those were words of despair," he said, pointing to Boris's book.

"Despair, yes. Of course they were," I replied. Boris's words were always full of despair.

"Poetry should affirm. We need happy poetry, poems that celebrate life." He turned an offended teacherly face to me to see if I agreed or not. I considered offering Marianne Moore's proposition about poetry teeming with visions of real toads in imaginary gardens, but thought better of it. My stomach churned with hunger and the wasted audition. I stared down at the shorn snow pea pod strings on the counter.

"Maybe we should eat. The rice is done," I said. Boris liked his rice fluffy; Sam, firm. Now there would be two men disappointed in my rice.

After Sam left, I called Dina.

"So how was the new man?"

"Sam really has fine qualities," I said.

"That bad, hmm?"

As I mentioned Sam's artistic credo, Dina groaned into the earpiece. "Forget him. The man has a 4H Club mentality. A man who likes happy poems could never penetrate your spirit. He has the soul of an Eagle Scout."

"I tried, Dina. Truly I did."

"You did," she replied in a soothing tone. "You certainly did. You see, I tried to warn you. There's something wrong with all of them, darling. But at least he took your mind off that psychopath."

"If it's Boris you mean, Boris is a *sociopath*."

"You're already planning to go back to him," said Dina, barely disguising the note of triumph in her voice. "You can't help it. Women are such fools."

I hung up and chucked Sam's wilted roses into the sink.

Two barely dissolved aspirins dove into the drain. I ran tap water until they finally flushed.

To restore my sense of Entitlement, Dina invited me to go shopping in Soho for divine *drek*. In a world as capricious as this, we were entitled to shop, as per the maxim that when things get tough, the tough go shopping. We traipsed up and down the streets, she regaled me with her philosophy of the single life. I would be a fool to think there was anything but flawed goods out there. One man sicker than the next. As for marriage, an institution designed for men. Ask any married woman. Her face was full of veiled warnings and conspiratorial innuendoes. She counted herself blessed with an excellent divorce settlement, an ample older home in Teaneck and some solid investments. She wasn't like me—she couldn't just *give it away* to any Tom, Dick or Harry. I assured her that I was giving up Boris.

"You'll go back to him. This is just the alternate weekend." We stopped at the window of a vintage clothing boutique off Spring Street. Dina wanted to go in. When, if not today? For whom, if not for Numero Uno? Life was short.

A salesgirl with a spiked platinum hairdo asked me if I needed anything.

"Do you have anything in avocado?" I asked, summoning an uncommon bravura. The girl disappeared into the back room. Meanwhile Dina examined the garter belts on the rack and held a black one up to her stretch pants.

"Too bad I don't have somebody to wear this for. But then again, who knows? My plane could go down. My mammography could come out positive. You never know. What do you think, Lenora?"

"You deserve it," I replied. Just then the salesgirl returned carrying an avocado dressing gown that Jean Harlow might have worn with silver high heels in a Thirties film. It was darling. I slipped into its softness and paraded in front of the mirror. I heard laughter tinkling among teacups and almost thought I saw Boris as Priapus in the shrubbery. Women might come and go but there was always my hairy upper arm and the decollete of this Art Deco avocado negligee. "Wrap it," I announced, removing the plastic from my wallet. Two could play the Entitlement scenario.

Not to be outdone, Dina removed a black felt bowler hat from the head of a pink male mannequin and offered the salesgirl her card.

"Isn't this decadent?" she asked.

"Take it," I said. "We could cross the street and get struck down by a bicycle messenger turning a sharp corner. We could get caught in crossfire between two rival drug gangs." As I enumerated various other entitling contingencies, Dina selected a strudel-colored silk Marilyn Monroe pajama set. With our purchases tucked safely inside our pink shopping bags, we exited.

"Don't you feel good about yourself now?" said Dina. We exchanged our most crystalline looks as we practically danced towards West Broadway on our twinkletoes.

At home, I modelled the avocado dressing gown with high heels on. Immediately my heart started to pound and I gasped for breath. It's a well-known fact that certain colors, tastes, smells have the power to release a torrent of impossibly painful buried childhood memories. Forget Rita Hayworth chartreuse and Jane Fonda turquoise; for women of my interim generation, *the* color was avocado, the bile color of The Fifties, the color of my first marriage and the Chinese Wall of appliances that symbolized my domestic entrapment back in the heartland of Indiana. Neither Emerald City nor the Yellow Brick Road, it was the cast of cloud cuckoo-land. No wonder it struck me with such revulsion. Suddenly I understood why I had vacillated at the idea of sleeping on Boris's mother's couch. But I could learn. I could grow. Now I comprehended the cause of my color phobia. I was free. I needn't forever flinch from the hue of avocado. Wasn't I the image of Theda Bara in this voluptuous dressing gown? As I strutted in front of the mirror, I realized I had to speak to Boris at once and tell him *yes yes*, I could be a fit companion to him when he fell into those moods when only a tryst on his mother's old sofa could sustain him. I could satisfy his strange obsessions. We could heal our rifts, for was I any less the victim of my own psychic traumas than Boris? I now had a whole new *zeitgeist* about avocado. But when I dialed his number, steadying myself for massive compromise, I found a strange message on the machine, a voice reading a passage from Freud's patriarchal treatise, *Moses and Monotheism*. A female voice. I learned later that her name was Marlene.

"Why are we talking about Marlene?" demanded Boris. "I don't see her steady. I warned you. I don't see any woman steady. Not you. Not anyone."

"Did you give her your battered first edition of Henry Miller yet?" My voice was raised over the amplified rock video at the bar. "Yes or no."

"I'm trying to raise Marlene's aspirations. She's not as independent as you are. Marlene's having a hard time meeting men. I'm trying to give her a little help."

"I think you and I should stop seeing each other," I barked over the bellow, as cilia-like hands groped for their MTV idol.

"Have a heart, Lenora. You're my longest relationship." Where was the poet who wrote, "With great love comes great suffering?" Elsewhere. With Marlene.

"I'm giving you an ultimatum, Boris. Give her up. See only me." I hated the whine in my voice but Dina would have been proud.

"I can't."

"Why not?"

He winked mysteriously, then lifted a bewitching eyebrow.

"What is that supposed to mean?"

"Marlene understands certain needs of mine."

I steeled myself for the worst, swallowing hard and taking zen-like breaths.

"My sexual needs."

"Your mother's avocado couch?"

He nodded. Now it is perfectly clear. "I would have done it with you on your mother's avocado couch," I announced resolutely. "I promise I would have done it. I swear I will."

"Don't force yourself on my account. I asked you, remember? You said no. Someday you'll walk right past me on the street and you won't even recognize me. You'll stare at me as if I'm a stranger. Just like Susanna Schechter." Boris's face was tragic. The thought of his lost love back in the old Jewish Bronx never failed to leave him bereft of human hope.

"Dina is right," I muttered aloud. "Women are fools."

"You don't understand," said Boris. His face brightened as he began to discuss William Carlos Williams's poem on Demuth's painting. For about ten minutes I listened to him talk about multi-media. His face got bigger and bigger as he kept on talking...*something more organic...multi-something* ...alternatives. He kept talking, gesticulating, his mouth getting bigger and bigger until his teeth grew into moving vans.

Before I could stop myself, I rolled my fist into a ball and socked him in the eye. He didn't fall backward but just stood there covering his eye with both hands. I could see a thin trickle of blood underneath his hand. By now, I had passed through the looking glass, already on the other side looking in.

When I came to hug him, I could feel his body tighten and freeze as if his balls had turned to pale green ice, the kind that Sonja Henie skated on. Now I was about as far away as the Lusitania. I just stood there saying I was sorry, over and over again. "Remember, this was your idea," he called after me as I strode out of the restaurant.

Funny, but my new husband and I never mention Boris. It's as if he disappeared over some cliff into the tide of the past. We do, however, talk about Dina, whom we can't help seeing from time to time at the neighborhood laundromat or at the corner McDonald's or on the line for Lotto at the stationery store on Third Avenue.

I can't stop thinking about how things ought to have been. The place Dina once filled in my life is still vacant. It's sad because now, more than ever, we ought to be friends. But I realize that it's like the laws of zen or physics. Without sickness there is no health. Without dark there is no light. Without Boris there is no Dina. I feel a certain pathos when I consider this dialectic, knowing at what cost it has been wrested. What I had imagined as a major crossroads was merely an interesting byway.

When I meet Dina at the laundromat, we smile shyly, like strangers, exchange a few words and walk away. I always wind up with trembling fingers and spill the socks all over the floor. I suppose I'm no different from most women. I can't accept it when someone vanishes from my life like a wrinkle in the dark. I had always pictured Dina and me, friends for a lifetime, chuckling over Boris's mother's avocado couch and combing Soho for divine *drek*.

I never thought when I joined Dr. Feigenbaum's co-dependence group that

I'd meet a *mensch* that, like me, was ready for commitment. A second marriage at my age is not for the timid of heart. But I have great hopes for it, although I sense Dina lurking in the wings, hoping for something to go awry.

There are moments when I feel a sense of loss for that time when hungry men could pick up my scent a mile away. So I play Dina's old game with my new husband who suffers from fear of closed-in places. I tell him we deserve to stay in Group even if health insurance won't cover our therapy in full. I need to work on my Dina problem. He needs help with his claustrophobia. He could get stuck in an enclosed elevator during a power outage, which is a genuine statistical reality during these greenhouse summers here in Manhattan. We're entitled.

# Notions of Men
## Barbara McDonald

Time to give up
notions of men,
at least for awhile,
to regroup,
be alone with myself,
listen to
the jays squawk,
watch hummingbirds
light on the naked walnut tree,
plant crocus, primroses,
sand the bookcase.
The years click by,
a domino design
falling.
I only recognize
the passing in
faces of friends
porcelain lines,
a certain settling in
of the hips,
walkers' shoes,
professor glasses.
The men look like my father.
A few months of solitude,
maybe I'll be ready.

# Honeycomb
## Gail Donovan

Wanda squatted among the ferns, shivering, her feet spaced apart, her jeans bunched down around her ankles. The seven o'clock morning sun had not burned all the moisture from the foliage, and next to her bare skin, the earth was cool and damp. Fifteen years ago, she had taught her daughter to position her feet on a slope, so her urine did not trickle back onto her; thirty-five years ago, she and Grace had peed in the twilight, one watching out for the other, standing guard by the willow and the bird bath at the edge of the backyard, not wanting to go inside and be told to wash their hands for dinner.

As she stood, the soft fronds of a fern brushed the backsides of her thighs. She walked down toward the sandy shore.

Grace and Ray, her arm around his waist, bent their heads; when Howard leaned forward, his green t-shirt came untucked, revealing a pudgy band of pale white skin. Surely he was studying the map, pointing out the turn-offs, the mouth of the stream, the river, then the estuary and lagoon to a portage around the waterfall. Instead, he patted a small mound of sand atop a larger mound. Pebbles circled a moat, filled with lakewater. A sprig of elderberry adorned the castle's pinnacle.

The sight of this enraged Wanda. Why? It might just as well have endeared her to him. It was always like that, a trivial incident filling her with nonsensical anger. Her heart became like a vase of flowers, crystalline and cold, filled with stagnating water. Not until the jar was thrown against a wall and cracked open would she be able to make sense of the anger she felt descending upon her. She clenched her teeth. The muscles in her face tensed, her body poised for stubborn silence. "Howie," she said, stepping into the stern of an aluminum canoe. "I'll go with Grace. You can go with Ray. Obviously we should have taken separate vacations, but at least we can take separate boats." She pushed off on the sandy bottom with the paddle. Scratched and silver, the canoe floated out onto the lake.

"Don't worry," Grace called back to Howard. "She's just *joking*."

The early morning lake was free of whitecaps, and the water lay flat and steely blue. Imperceptibly, the eastern horizon dropped away from the July sun. Wanda dug her paddle into the lake; she felt her heart begin to pump. It always did so, but these pumps were distinct and aggressive. As a child, Wanda's father had diagnosed a heart problem, and ordered her to stay in bed for a year. She remembered reaching up, clasping her hands behind his neck as he lifted and carried her outside to a lawn chair on the first warm spring day. It had been late April, yellow forsythia fringed the backyard, and broad orange petals bent the long stems of languishing tulips.

"Grace," she said. "Remember how Daddy used to carry me everywhere because of my heart?"

"Sure I do. And did any other doctor ever find a thing wrong with it?"

"Well, no. But that's because Daddy made me stay in bed for a year to fix it."

Wanda had looked forward to this vacation—no mirrors, no huge plates of storefront glass to catch a reflection of her face. It seemed to her she hadn't aged for years, still youthful with her golden hair in a ponytail. But over her forty-fifth winter, wrinkles had deepened, she felt that everything about her was sagging, like the tulips had, their petals wide, just about to drop, no longer hiding the hints of yellow and black at their center, the pollen already blown from the stigmas. When Grace twisted around to face her in the stern, it only reminded Wanda of herself, the image of which she'd hoped to avoid, Grace so like herself, the same hair, golden, without the first gray strands, the same hazel eyes without the crow's feet, the same long neck without the slightly drooping chin. Wanda stopped paddling too, the beating of her heart extra loud without the noise of their paddles dipping into the lake, and their windbreaker sleeves brushing against their torsos. Her heart beat in her still body; the lake's surface, smooth when they'd set off, now rippled in the rising wind.

"And it never occurred to you that he might have been wrong? That maybe you weren't as helpless as he made you? Face it," Grace said, "you were dominated."

In a pale blue windbreaker against the deepening sky, thirty feet ahead of Wanda and Grace's canoe, Howard unfolded a map and held it aloft. Somewhere on the eastern edge of Attean Lake, a stream ran from it, into the Moose River. This was the plan: to paddle downstream until they met the river, at which time they would turn left, and continue downriver. They had skirted the shore but found no outlet. The women stopped paddling, coasting toward Howard and Ray.

"Wanda!" Howard called out across the water. "Let's turn around and go back."

At her name, a crane startled, lifted and spread its wings and, seemingly into the marsh grass, disappeared. Its thin legs dangled beneath its blue-gray body. Wanda did not believe in omens. However, this seemed obvious: the crane had shown them where the mouth of the stream flowed from the lake, and beating its tremendous wings, it flew over the clear but hidden path cut by the water. "Thank you, Mr. Crane," she said.

Wanda had a theory. She thought the natural world, from her vantage point out here on the water, was divided into three colors: the sky-water color, usually blue, sometimes gray, always the same; the foliage color, the moose maple and quaking aspen and evergreens, at this time of year, all hues of green; and the neutrals from the white clouds to gray rocks to almost-black tree trunks. Wanda's theory was that the division of the world into three colors produced feelings of peace in her body, due to the lack of visual stimulus she was forced to take in and interpret most days. Sometimes, when she pulled into the garage after a shopping trip, she sat in the car a while, eyelids closed, an inertia strapping her to the seat, while the engine, cooling, pinged. She simply grew fatigued of visual stimulus. Too many things were put in front of her eyes—newspapers to decipher, traffic signals to attend, faces that needed appropriate responses from her face (joyful smiles, empathetic scowls, when he said he loved her, when he complained about the government), dishes to be washed, their aging bodies to ignore, her mother's broken teapot and flaws in the social system (inept sewage systems ruining the New England coastline, and the lack of an equal rights amendment) that cried out to be glued, mended, and the look of perplexity on Howie's face, the wrinkled skin between his blue eyes, and the pursed lips, when she cried afterward, or this morning, when she'd slighted him.

The stream and sky, today, were blue, the cumulus clouds white, and the marsh grass they glided through green. Wanda decided she needed to simplify her life.

"I disagree," Grace said. "There's nothing more romantic than waking up together for two decades."

"What's romantic is the way the air practically vibrates when you and Ray stand next to each other. It's just not like that for us anymore. Why does he infuriate me so?"

"It's just because we're new. It won't last." Grace stopped paddling to light a cigarette. "Now Howard, he's a rock. He's there for you—that's romance. The trouble with you is, you mistake his boyish charm for immaturity. Just because we're all growing older doesn't mean you have to get all stodgy."

"Smoking dehydrates you, Gracie. You'll get wrinkled like me. Ugly, old and stodgy."

"So what if I smoke a little, drink a little? Remember when you'd call me up and tell me you were going crazy? I'd come over with a bottle of liquor. Since you were breastfeeding you couldn't really put a shot of anything in the baby's bottle, so we'd warm up some milk, mix in some kahlua, and drink it for ourselves. Very soothing. Maybe you should have another one, for me. It doesn't look as if I ever will."

Dipping her fingers into the stream, flinging the cool water against her heated face, and throat, Wanda said, "Grace! Don't flick your ashes in the water. That's polluting. You'll spoil it for everyone."

"Yeah, look at all this natural beauty. Kind of makes you sick, doesn't it? All that beauty."

"I know," said Wanda. "There's just nothing to say."

A beaver had dammed up the stream.

"It's their job," said Howard. "Everybody's got a job to do." He ran his hand up from his brow, over the crown of his head, as one would do to pull the hair from the face of a vomiting child, or to stroke a feverish forehead. His sandy hair thinned in ever-widening concentric circles, and she admired his plain haircuts, no brushing the hair to all ends of his scalp. Other times, Wanda would have wanted to kiss his halo of balding skin.

Positioning themselves on the interlacing branches, Howard and Ray gently heaved their canoe, hand over hand, out of and back into the stream. The bottom of the boat scraped across the sticks. Howard was wearing his windbreaker, jeans, and the shiny sunglasses you couldn't see into. As he stood on the sturdy dam, Wanda thought of how all people, when they marry, think they're mating for life, like beavers or eagles. That's part of the package deal. You think it's forever, though you know your chances are possibly fifty percent, now, in the latter half of the twentieth century. You're gambling on the chance that for you, the package might be fulfilled. These things were no tragedy, they were simply a gamble. Beavers never lost; people did.

Grace hopped out from the bow, and paddling on the left, Wanda pulled over the stern. Ray reached to help her out; she grasped his hand, smoother than Howie's, the fingers soft, the palms uncalloused. Finally, he shook her hand, saying, "Pleased to renew our acquaintance," and she, startled, released his. Howard busied himself with the other canoe, his back to her. Blushing, secretly sweating, she walked along the weave of branches. The noon sun beat down, but a midday sun in Maine is never overbearing, even in the heat of July. The four of them stood on the beaver dam—Wanda, her husband Howie, her sister Grace, and Grace's new lover, Ray. On either side of the dam a canoe floated, laden with tents, sleeping bags, packbaskets, and a cooler. Wanda held a line to the upstream canoe, Howie held one to the boat downstream of the dam. Innumerable sounds blended together in the air: the minute trickle of water through the tangle of gnawed sticks, the calls of invisible birds, the breeze in the marsh grass, and their own rustling and breathing. For a few moments, no one moved. The two couples stood stockstill on the dam in the midday sun, in the huge expanse of blue sky and green grass.

"Well," said Ray. Thin, wearing shorts and a sweater, he pulled a Yankees baseball cap over his black wavy hair. "What say we switch the seating arrangement for the afternoon? Howie and I have had enough male bonding."

"You keep going for a few squiggles," Wanda said. "When the river forks, you bear left. That's an estuary or something. Then you take your immediate right, into a sort of creek that eventually runs back into the river. But before it does, you take your second left, into a lagoon—it says that's a dead-end body of water—and you find the portage trail there, to the base of the falls." Wanda sat in the bow. She rolled up the map, sealed in Contac paper, with a light blue marker traced over their route. It was impossible to tell, from the small sandy beaches on the riverbank's curves, little oases among the weedy alder bushes, which squiggle the map represented. The river here was wide, slow and meandering.

"Talk to me, baby," said Howard. "We never talk anymore. Let's talk."

"Just have your lawyer talk to my lawyer."

Downriver, a family of ducks startled but didn't take flight. They scooted over the water's surface, feet paddling and wings flapping. Every time the canoe rounded another bend, the mother urged on the baby ducks. Half flying and half swimming, they led Howard and Wanda, in short springs, down the river.

"Tell me the truth. You're having your period, right? That's why you took so long in the bushes. Ever since they announced this PMS stuff, you think it's a license to be brutal."

"I am *not*. You think my emotions are just hormones. And then when I *am* menstruating, it's like I'm defiled or something."

"Maybe," snapped Howard, "I just don't like being fingerpainted with your blood. Maybe I just don't think that's fun."

"That was seven *years* ago. Can't you forget it?"

"Forget the year you convinced our daughter to have an abortion?" Sitting, digging the blade into the river, compensating his stronger stroke and larger paddle by flipping it out sideways, he kept them headed straight downriver, behind the frantic birds.

"You want she should marry, maybe? Given my experience in this department, I couldn't advise that."

"Foul," he cried. "That is just not fair."

"Ever heard of teenage mothers? It's not a pretty sight. You certainly weren't prepared. Admit it: you can't wait till I'm barren, I bet, so you can screw all you want without coping. You could never deal with any of my bodily functions."

"Never? Never? I was there at the birth, I didn't faint."

"You grimaced," she insisted. "I saw you grimace." The ducks began their frenzied scuttling again, veering off to the right. "Take a left," Wanda said. "Steer us left, there's the turn-off. Goodbye, ducks."

"That's the stupidest thing I ever heard," said Wanda. "We could get killed."

"No," Howard said. "I walked ahead and scouted it out. This creek leads back to the river, but there's plenty of time to get out. It's July—look how slow the water's going—we're not going to rush over any gorges. Besides, I don't want to go down that dead-end thing, that lagoon, and then spend an hour carrying all our gear on some trail, when we can float it all down this way."

"Let's wait for those two."

"No," said Howard. "They're probably back on one of those little beaches, fooling around. What's the matter—you think he knows more about river travel than I do? We're doing it now."

Wanda succumbed. Trees had fallen across the creek's path, so rather than paddling and ducking, they left the gear in the canoe and began walking down the banks, lining the boat down the narrow body of water. Their own route, climbing over tree trunks, passing the ropes underneath, was halted and slow, but the long boat glided through, unheeded, even graceful. In the distance, the river flowed past boulders, a constant rush of water.

Wanda stopped, turned around, faced Howie a few yards back. "I have to go to the bathroom."

"You always have to go. Can't you wait till we finish?"

"No," Wanda said. "I cannot. You're such a riot I'm about to wet my pants." Earlier in the afternoon, she'd held onto a canoe on one side of the dam, and he held one on the other. Now they held the same canoe, guiding it down the narrow stream, as if they were walking a mutual but difficult pet, a bobbing, tippy, silver boat. The foliage fluttered in the shiny lenses of Howard's sun-glasses—the trees grew thick here, but the sun shone through the empty path of sky cut by the creek.

"Go ahead," he said. "I'll hold the boat." He tightened his grip on the stern line, coiling it up.

Wanda had not let go of the bow line. When Howard shortened his line, he pulled the canoe back, tugging on her rope, and throwing Wanda off balance. She slid down the steep bank and into the water, over her head. It was warmer than she had expected.

Howard ranted as he tied the stern line to a tree. "Are you okay? What did you do that for? Watch out for snakes."

"Howard!" she shrieked.

"I heard this story about a guy who fell down waterskiing in North Carolina. When they circled back to get him he was dead—fell in a nest of snakes." He held onto a tree branch, reaching out his other arm to her.

"Don't you talk to me about snakes. You pulled me in. And on purpose, you brute."

"Not me. You must have the wrong guy. At least you seem to think you do."

Wanda reached for his hand. "I can't reach," she said. "Come closer."

"Come closer," he moaned. "Come closer. So now you want me." Leaning further, weighing down the maple branch so the leaves dipped wildly, his fingers grazed hers.

Wanda lunged, her wet hand clutching and crushing Howie's with the fierceness of her exasperated mother, who, finally ordering Wanda and Grace inside for dinner, had scrubbed them clean under the faucet. Swimming backwards, she didn't let go.

"Bitch," yelled Howie, slithering into the creek. Surfacing, he splashed her.

"Admit it, you brute," she giggled.

"Maybe accidentally on purpose, but not on purpose on purpose. You deserved it. You have absolutely no reason to be mad at me." He grinned, dousing her again. "And if you did, we're even now."

Once, she remembered, she'd been so mad at Grace she had pissed, for spite, in their bathwater. What had Grace said? That she was faking it, that she wasn't sick at all, that her heart was fine. What would Grace say now? That Wanda had let herself be dominated again, that she had been angry at Howie's boyishness, building sandcastles, and had wanted him to be the one in charge, reading maps, telling people what to do, taking care of her. Wanda urinated now in the stream. It felt lovely, her salt water into the fresh. What her sister wouldn't say, what she didn't know, was how Wanda longed for Howard to want her more, and she him, longed for the violence of new love, not stability, and how she thrilled at the petulant fear and resistance in his voice, how the anger he gave back to her in turn reminded her of their essential desperation for each other.

In all of their fights (except that one battle over the fate of their daughter's pregnancy, which still rankled and could still be summoned from the past to illustrate one another's faults), in all of their arguments, the causes had been forgotten. They mused: Remember the time you slammed the window so hard you shattered the panes? or, Remember that awful day you said, Do you want to get out and walk, and I got out at the next red light and ran into traffic? How, they asked, did all that begin? The causes, in all of their fights, eluded; only what ensued remained. Wanda knew this time would be no different.

Treading water, she stared at Howie, already clambering up the bank. The small space between them was filled with the cool air above the dark and shiny creek, the sound of the distant river over the rocks, the twenty years of time before she even met him, the nights in the following twenty-five years when they had turned away from each other while awake and woken curled together, and now the calls of her sister, as she'd called out years ago from the willow, "Ready or not, here I come."

"They're here," said Howard, dripping. "Come on, Mrs. Get-your-own-way. I'm sorry. Get out of the water."

Howard climbed onto the rock and handed Wanda a slice of bread with honeycomb. She lay on one of the huge boulders that skirted the river, drying out. Shining with an oblivious light, a gentle heat, the four o'clock July sun showed no signs that the western horizon was creeping up on it. Wanda accepted the snack. The wax walls of the comb disintegrated in her mouth, the tiny crystals of honey crunching between her teeth.

The waterfall was anticlimactic. Rocks and boulders filled a stretch of river where the land dropped; in the spring it must have run fast and dangerous, but now the water flowed calmly, widening into a swimming hole at the base. Clean, dry, warm, the taste of honey in her mouth, Wanda lay on the boulder. Howard lay down beside her.

Now her delicious warmth increased, until she felt flushed and burning. There were no sweaters to be thrown off, no windows to be flung open. "Hot," she said. "Howie." She pulled off her t-shirt, lay half naked and sweating on the boulder, waiting for the hot flash to pass.

Leaning on one elbow, Howard caressed her belly with his other hand. In the reflection of his sunglasses, her hair curled on the boulder, and the river flashed past. "Shall we make up?" he asked. The water glinted off his lenses, how cool it must be. The stream had been warm compared to the ocean, cold compared to bathwater.

"Okay," she said. It would pass in a minute. Let him think she sweats for him; how could even she tell with certainty, in the moments between one and the other, what was the sign of menopause and what the heat of desire? Her catechism teacher had told her once, trying to assuage her doubts, "Act as if you have faith, and faith will come to you." The flash still engulfed and permeated her, but the river breeze cooled her torso and breasts. Above her, Howard smiled. From here, she couldn't see his balding halo at all, could only see his face, and the bright sky, rimmed with green at the edges. Now, in the intimations of infertility, wanting to tempt life, Wanda acted on that long-ago advice. Knowing the evasive nature of the emotions that inspired their struggles, how only the after-effects remained, she would simply begin the motions of love, and hope desire would follow. She wanted to want him. In the waning flushes of heat, Wanda wrapped her arms around Howard's waist. The last gritty crystals of honey dissolved between her teeth.

# After the Second Time Around
## Claudia Kenyon

"Any particular reason you keep your spices in five different locations? Or have six different kinds of seasoning salt?" He's gone through my cupboards and now wants to file his new and intimate knowledge of me. He's what I call a techie, and he wants to know my system—there *must* be a system—so he can find things when it's his turn to cook. He's only going to be here for three weeks, so even if I did have a system, which I don't, *he* doesn't have to learn it.

"Just tell me what you want and I'll tell you where it is," I said. "And right now your dog is barking."

"It's the dog that will break you up," an all-knowing friend had said. She knows I've lived alone for seven years. No dependents. My children are grown and away somewhere not paying their phone bills. Even my plants can go over a week without water. When I go out, I'm outgoing, with my friends, family, students, and strangers, but when I'm home, I need the solitude of my idiosyncratic sanctuary. Now some man is possibly thinking about organizing my cupboards.

Replacing the kitchen sink spray nozzle (I didn't know it *could* work) was fine, and figuring out how to make the washing machine let in cold water, and programming channels into the TV I never got before—that was great.

"Men are good for sex and fixing things, aren't they?" he asked, putting insulation in the door jamb.

"Yes," I agreed enthusiastically, carelessly stowing the groceries. He continued to look at me. "Oh, did I leave something out?"

I know the hand of fate when I see it, I just don't know whether to eat out of it or bite it. This man in my kitchen I met on a train station in Mexicali. We slid through the impoverished countryside in an open-air gondola car, mostly talking, mostly he was talking. I have to remember the trip by looking at the photographs he took, because my camera broke. ("You have to clean these things from time to time.") "It's nice to talk to someone who understands," he said, as I listened to the interminable story of the machinations of Graham's Department Chair who was trying to get rid of him because he wouldn't be "one of his whores."

We worked at the same university, and since Graham was going to give me duplicates of his photos, we agreed to have dinner when we got back, then he'd get fired, and that, I thought, would be the end of that. Instead, he touched my elbow in passing on the train. I think he was saying one of the two phrases I heard most: "Let me finish the thought" or "Sarcasm doesn't become you." I've been training in the martial arts for three years, and I know how to interpret all kinds of touches. His had both gentleness and plenty of energy. When I got off the train to go home—I hate to say goodbye so I didn't—I had his number, he had mine, and my ears didn't know what to do with the sudden silence.

I think he did mention that he had a dog, but that didn't register until our first date when he said, "Let's take your car, there's a dog in mine." A dog that could spare 2,000 hairs at regular intervals as I learned later by examining the artifacts on my black coat, my rug, and my books. Though I had quit dating three years ago, my life was full. I had to make constant changes to let him in, and he pursued me relentlessly. He called me to tell me every single turn of the screw that turned him out of the university after only two semesters. "You managed to get axed by the President?" I asked, incredulous. His main worry was that his university-paid dental insurance would terminate before he got his eleven permanent crowns. He'd located a young Chinese dentist who needed the work and was so thrilled to have such a large project that he'd lowered the price; of course the man took forever, but he was so meticulous, and so cheap, that one had to be patient. Graham's life was full too: he was fighting with a university back east that was refusing to give him either a Ph.D. or an accurate transcript for time served, and fighting with some company that hadn't sent a replacement for his non-functioning car radio, and moving every three months to avoid fighting with intransigent landladies. We had to leave plays and restaurants because he was having a gout attack ("Stress, you know"), and his arthritis was acting up, especially in the little finger his last wife had twisted, but also in the next finger which he had bent the wrong way when his dog got loose and tripped him during the ensuing chase. "Got loose? Chase? Can't you just call him?"

"He flunked obedience school. He doesn't obey the 'come' command, but other than that he's no trouble." He didn't consider it trouble that Bobby had chewed up his $200 favorite briefcase and an entire apartment full of furniture when he was a puppy ("I shouldn't have left him alone, you see").

I got stomach flu. He waited till I felt a little better to tell me the next installment of his dismal saga. As soon as I was on my feet he wanted me on my back. God, how he wanted me. The first time he kissed me was the first time I saw him smile. The next time I saw him smile he was missing a front tooth. I had been invited to his latest apartment for what I knew was to be my seduction dinner, and I came prepared for everything but that. "Oh well, what's the hurry," I thought, discovering instantly that I was a tooth snob. The hurry was that he had just enough time before sauteing the onions. "You gotta love this man," I thought, "or leave him alone because he already has so many problems." I was a little elated that after ten years alone he had chosen me, because I am not a beginner woman. "Let me look into your eyes a little," he said, and suddenly sarcasm didn't become me.

After a month he began to mention Seattle. Some people at the University there had mentioned a Visiting Professorship, a chance to complete his Ph.D. Someone wanted him. "Yes, I know the feeling. Did I mention that I don't do long-distance relationships well?"

There must have come a day when he had no job and no place to stay, but before that day I said he could come stay with me as my guest for three weeks before he went back east to do battle with the Ph.D.-deniers and to fetch his trailer so he would never be without a roof again.

I made room in my closet, I cleared out two drawers—apparently that's all you need if you fold clothes as neatly as he does. I even let the dog in the house until he peed on my couch. "Takes the edge off a nice morning," he said as he shampooed the cover. "He never does this. It's jealousy. Love me, love my dog," he added with a staccato laugh.

"Oh now, don't make that requirement. I'd hate to lose both of you."

I need that dog more than he does. Because of Bobby I don't have to consider permanently living with Graham. I can show the mean and petty side of my nature ("Why would anybody want a dog? It's like having a child that always loves you but never grows up and leaves"). I can focus on Bobby's barking instead of Graham's too-incessant chatter. I can make him choose between us to test my power ("I'm not going to meet you in Chicago to trailer back with you if you take the dog"), or I can be merciful ("But maybe Denver"). But I don't have to love him if I don't love his dog.

"I woke up this morning picturing your face above me registering the movement of my hands on your body," I wrote to him back east.

"I'm having trouble getting the back end off the trailer, but a friend loaned me some tools and I picked up some others at a garage sale," he replied in a weekly phone call. Maybe he's too shy to say much in a public phone booth, I thought. He's British after all, he's never had a woman worth being nice to before, and he is, we must remember, a 56-year-old *man*. "Write to me," I begged. "Make me remember you."

I eventually received a Garfield card that said, "Sometimes I wonder why I put up with you. Oh yeah, now I remember—you put up with me." In small neat writing was this personal message: "The little TV you loaned me has been really useful."

The man should be shot. No way am I meeting him in Chicago, birthday or no birthday. For one thing a pulled muscle had delayed my long-awaited brown belt test, so I couldn't leave when I'd tentatively planned. And he had taken the dog ("Go ahead, take him, you need someone to talk to"). And he had hurt my feelings with that card. After six weeks of "I don't know when I'm leaving, I don't know if I'm going to Santa Cruz or Seattle," suddenly it was "I'm only a little behind schedule, meet me in Chicago."

"You still think I'm meeting you in Chicago? You remember a little mention of my test?"

"After that?"

"I think I'll go to Hawaii."

"I don't know what you're so upset about," he said, and he didn't. He didn't have a clue.

I passed my test. I found I could get to Hawaii if I left immediately, but I couldn't get back. "Find me some place remote," I told the travel agent. She was new, she was clueless. There are many places you can't go on the spur of the moment, but Rapid City, South Dakota, isn't one of them. "I can do that," said the travel agent.

"Do you still want me to join you?" I asked Graham.

"Yes. I'll really look forward to it."

Rapid City's airport was deserted because the tourists, 60,000 bikers, were heading into the area on Harleys. Some of them were staying in the same campground Graham had picked to park his traveling home in, and they came in handy when he needed a couple to lift his new generator ("I got it on sale") out of the Suburban and into position to charge the battery when he accidentally left his ignition key in the "on" position. In the morning I heard the women discussing pit bulls and tattoos.

The trailer was immaculate. The only dog hairs around still clung to Bobby, who greeted me with his "He says I'm no trouble" look. "He really likes you," Graham beamed. The bed with red sheets was already turned down. "I usually keep it in the three-quarter position so I can work at the table," he said, "but you see this way there's plenty of room." Since he had never had it fully open, how could he have known that the plenty of room was made by felling the two upright bolsters into an area too big to keep them together. I spent ten days in a trough; I almost left after six.

He bought and tested equipment interminably. I know all the major auto chains between Rapid City and Seattle, the cheap ones. He kept records, he kept lists, he calculated expenses he could deduct, he studied maps and tour books— he even read the condom instructions. Well, he had *his* obsessions; he knew what *I* was good for, or should have, but no, he had to tell me how everything worked. "When we're on 12-volt, this switch is up, you have to turn on the stove outside, and only these lights work; on 9-volt, however...Always be sure to close cupboards so I don't bump my head (when he left a drawer open and the dog came in and bumped *his* head I actually shuddered) and always fasten the extra lock on the outside of the refrigerator, even when we're not traveling."

On the fifth day, more tired than usual, Graham suddenly decided I could help navigate. He handed me the map a few yards from an exit and asked about campsites. As I struggled to make sense of the map and the tour book and the trip guide, the exit advanced and Graham became excited. "How many, how many?" he yelled. "Fifty?" I said without conviction.

"Fifty *campgrounds*?"

"No, fifty camp*sites*. Isn't that what you were asking?"

"Oh no, now we've missed the turn." At this point, since the window was closed, he received the map, the tour book, and the trip guide ("all you have to do is follow the orange line") in his lap, and my steamy silence continued until he finally found a place, beautiful place really, but no showers. "We had to backtrack twelve miles on this road because we missed the turn." I got out of the vehicle and walked up into the hills until I got blisters on my heels.

"I'm at the mercy of a maniac," I thought, as I settled into the Valley of Death bed. "No one gets to yell at me anymore." The next day he nattered on about freight trains, the way the vehicle responds to cheap gas, the clouds in the sky, the absence of road kill—as if I cared, as if I were listening, as if it mattered. This man does not have a clue.

"Do you want to take an interest in where we stay tonight?"

"You can pick. All I want is a shower."

"We're staying in a national forest, but there's plenty of water in the tank. You can shower in the rig." That's not actually possible since the stall is so cramped that you have to step out of it to be able to elevate your elbows enough to soap and then you re-enter in the corpse position to rinse, but to conserve water during your absence there's a handy little gadget that halts the water for you if you turn it to the right...or was it the left?

"Fine." He stopped in a small town to rest and snack. I went exploring and bought local books, returning in a slightly elevated mood I was careful to not let him see. He kept himself awake talking while I nodded off, the dog breathing down my neck trying to get to the open window. ("I keep his window pretty well closed so he won't get conjunctivitis.") When it got close to the end of the time allocated for driving, he had three possible campgrounds in mind.

"There's that one." He pointed as he drove past the exit of a nice open place with trees at a respectful distance. I looked wistfully at it, knowing he would find the kind he likes, with trees all around so I can't see anything, but I wouldn't speak. Sure enough. Once he had me guide him into the space, always a traumatic experience, he asked, "Do you want me to look for a more open space?" And have to park you again? Are you kidding?

"No, this is fine. I just want a cup of tea and a shower, but first I'll go for a walk." I walked down the road looking for light. He let the dog loose and Bobby bounded after me. Another trauma. If he gets into trouble I can't call him, and people assume he's my dog the way he watches and seems to follow me. He isn't too bright about dodging cars either. Bobby had the time of his life running, jumping, and tearing around. "With my luck he'll give me poison oak again," I thought. "But, I have to admit, he's really a handsome dog when he runs around like this." I walked into a pretty little stream; he drank from it. "Do dogs get the same parasites humans do?" I wondered. I didn't want him dead, just quiet and obedient.

There was a great deal of commotion in the trailer. "Can I come in and make a cup of tea?"

"No. The refrigerator came open and there's food all over the floor. Here Bobby—treat," he called hopefully, pointing at the floor. Bobby wasn't giving up his freedom in order to be a mop. I reflected quickly. *He* had been the last one to close the refrigerator and *he'd* forgotten the secondary lock. It wasn't my fault.

"OK, I'll wait." My smugness vanished when he said he'd had to use so much water cleaning up that there wasn't enough for a shower.

The next morning Bobby, back on his leash, had managed to flush out a gopher from the tool compartment and had chased it until his head got wedged between one of the trailer wheels and whatever is next to it. Graham examined the situation from every angle, thoughtfully, meticulously, slowly. "You'll have to take the wheel off," I said. "There's some people over there with southern accents, I bet they'll have a jack." He went off to get a jack muttering, "It's not that simple." It wasn't that simple, as he explained to me later in excruciating detail, but I couldn't stand to see that yesterday-bounding animal now thrashing helplessly, and I couldn't understand why Graham wasn't more upset—this was his love. I remembered my first husband sleeping through my first labor and my second husband going off to Easter dinner at his mother's leaving me hemorrhaging and saying I'd be fine. What if that were *me* under there. Would he still be that calm?

As soon as Bobby was free, I said, "Let's get out of here, go get a hot breakfast in town."

"Why can't we eat here? I need food now." I had been debating whether or not to bail out during the last 24 hours. Now my mind was made up.

"OK, take me to the nearest airport instead."

"Yes, I was going to suggest that." I'm a quick packer, so I was ready and sitting out in the cold while he was still readying the rig.

"Just *how* were you going to suggest I leave?" I asked out of curiosity. I discovered my anger had left me. I didn't want to quit losers. And I loved him. "Do you understand the concept 'love'?"

"No, not really."

"Is it something you think you might want to learn?"

"Yeah."

"OK, you work on it, because sex is not enough. I will hold out for love."

I don't know if Coeur d'Alene has an airport. It does have an RV Campground with nice hot showers and laundry facilities. I woke up smiling...too early. Graham was already up. "What are you doing?" I asked.

"I'm doing laundry. Separate your clothes."

"Into what?—What time is it?"

"Six o'clock. If I wait any longer all the housewives will be using the machines."

"Are you crazy? Come back to bed."

"Later. Give me the sheets." *I* should shoot him.

I left him to the laundry and waited for him at the lake with a lunch I bought for our boat ride. His face did not change from its British reserve when he saw me, but his locomotion did: he was skipping. The man should not be shot.

As soon as he got on the boat he said one of the things guaranteed to annoy me, and I left him eating his favorite sandwich to go off to the rail where I started talking to some kid. He saved me a place in vain. Finally he came up to me, put his arm around me In Public, and called me his love. I guess he *can* learn. It has been obvious to me for a long time that the best way for him to get through to me is to touch me.

I never managed to leave him. He's in Seattle now in his trailer with his dog and his Ph.D. project. His address is Interstate 90. Perfect. The night before he left to pursue what had been denied him, I had to know: "Graham, do you love me?"

"I'm not sure."

I admit it, I secretly asked for a man to love. I didn't think to specify that he have a real address and a job and all his teeth and no dog and be able to listen as well as talk. But I took to this man. Even now he tears at my heart. He is no longer calling to tell me something I don't want to know ("The price of milk is much higher here, but eggs are cheaper. Surprising really, because...") instead of something I want to hear: "I miss you more than I can say" (*that* I would believe). Like Psyche, I did all my tasks. "No holding back," he said when we first began sleeping together.

"No holding back," I replied when we got out of bed.

I told him everything he needed to know to keep me. I learned him, I loved him, and he let me go. And he didn't even tell me. No; he said, "I'll be back to fix that last faucet." I can hear it dripping now.

# His Lip, His Beguiling Lip
## Clare Braux

**B**eyond a splashing, molded-plastic scarlet fountain in the shape of a hibiscus, Kay spies an individual who makes her do a double take. She quickens her step, her purse swinging from her shoulder, and approaches, her neck extended. A sickeningly handsome man, a man for all desires.

Her heart all bunched, she looks up at the sullen, finely chiselled features, at the deep sensual lower lip, and her eyes travel over the perfection of him, admiring his lofty eyebrow ridges, his smooth square jaw, his padded shoulders, his fist on his hip—lovely tanned knuckles. He stands tall on the step above her, indifferent to her, his left leg thrust forward.

O, the flawlessness of that leg—she presumes a strong thigh underneath the cloth. A suit of the best English worsted, pearly gray and elegantly cut, a vest of rose viyella. His shoes! Variegated leathers sewn together: ivory, tan, oxblood, bunny brown. She examines his handsome pale face again, his straight sandy hair falling over one eye, the other electric-blue eye bleak with the ineffable, loves his pouting underlip, softly rosy. Her own lips pucker and tremble. Nervously, she looks down the broad marble-floored aisle of the Sarasota Square Mall, hands thrust deep in the pockets of her Alice-blue jeans.

There's no one to pay any attention to her as she stands alone in front of the manikin, under a fake palm tree. Gazing at him, she mumbles, her lips hardly moving: Such is the well-favored person, so much like Daddy, as a child I wanted to be when I grew up: my opposite, my Double, the one I am to love and to cherish. Who is he? Who am I? Kay's mind clatters like a toy train going over cracks in the tin tracks, under mock bridges, past tiny unreadable signs. She reaches furtive fingers toward his leg, so straight, his body in the age-old stance of the proud, the self-assured, the arrogant male animal.

Abruptly she's struck by how familiar that stance is. Why, that's how he stood...her husband who'd left her a year ago—O my, yes, just a year ago! That's how he stood when he said: This is the day I'm leaving you. At first, bewildered and a little sad, she thought he meant a trip, an extended trip, he was always going on business trips. But no...this was IT. The END. After twenty-five years of marriage. Don't worry, he added with curling underlip, there's no one else; I want my freedom is all. Her heart or some big thing inside her vaulted. She began to scream, trembling all over. She couldn't stop screaming and shaking. He called his brother who came immediately, and, unable to control her, they had her put away for a "rest cure": the Gulf Shores Institute in Lecanto, Florida. Days, weeks of crying, delirious with grief and pent-up rage. What had gone wrong?

Inside the high walls, a secret garden, commiserating mourning doves, their murmured wheedling: concede, confess, own up. What kind of wife were you, anyway? The usual: submissive, convenient, a little too demanding of affection. Be honest now. Yes, it was true, sometimes she reprimanded him, even in public; felt one with him, whatever he did reflected on her.

She was released yesterday, the day after her birthday with the cake and the candles. Forty-nine already. Next year...half a century! Kay regards her Proud Prince again. His stance of rejection renews the discomfort of her nightmares in the home, nightmares of walking blind streets, hiding in dark alleys, her face wreaked with shame, a shame from childhood, re-animated. O, the stinging shame of being female in a world of self-serving males. But she's better now, released into the sane world, her zest restored. And where might he be now, her part-time-husband with his furtive, hostile glance? Was he still into amorous pursuits, her flourishing Florida man, President of a frenetic real-estate business? Of which she'd been, for years, the underpaid secretary. She looks at the doll's shapely knuckles again. A heavy spastic hand he has. To ward off danger? To console himself?

We all need consoling. From the age of eight, she'd often tumbled into daydreams of a boy's, a man's lips, the full, straining lips of desire, eager to zip onto hers. Life is two mouths kissing (It was pounded into her never to love women). O what a ravishing thing is the beginning of an Amour, wrote Aphra Behn, that gutsy genius.

The first years of their marriage, they'd been what's called lovers although a meeting of minds was beyond them. Third year: he'd come home late from work, tired and touchy, with a defiant mouth, his lip curled. Not tonight, dear, he'd say, ducking into the bathroom. When they did "make love," she glimpsed a baffled soul, subverted by ambition. Through her thirties and early forties, she bit her own fist, wishing away the insistent need for coupling of her young body; her tedious and wounded years, an absurd existence. A son who'd proven peevish had gone off. Even St. Augustine in his shameless unbosoming admitted: I sought what I might love, in love with loving. But the busy husband spoke of other women he knew who liked sex the way he did. This is how he described them to her: Most women are like men, he said, they're not like you, they want it no matter what. They don't need cuddling and this sweet-talk twaddle and this silly foreplay you talk about. They know what they want. He would grin then, remembering some quirky escapade in the office lounge. Where, O where, was the generosity of intimacy?

While in the "madhouse," she reviewed her short life, her missed opportunities, and masturbated in the shower, an unsatisfactory but clean and neat operation and sad to the point of weeping, kneeling in the tub and weeping. She'd lain on her bed and reviewed her botched good times—stuck in solemn troth as she'd been—saw again the long come-hither look of that man in the diningroom of their hotel on their first trip to Rome. She'd refused him, fool that she was; mindful of his wife, she'd refused—demurely, she suspected, she was always goddam demure despite her horny body. The tall, exuberant German she'd met on Mallorca, a beautiful person, refused him too—mindful of the woman he was with. The sardonic Englishwoman in that Japanese restaurant in London—her pained look as she sat on that bench, haunted Kay. The lonely Texan in Cuernavaca had shrugged, walked slowly away. What would he have been like as a lover? A lusty French-Canadian on Siesta Key beach said he felt sorry for her.

But, when she was forty-five, a Jewish boy of eighteen kissed her passionately out on the windblown terrace of the Nepenthe Restaurant on Big Sur, while her husband used the Men's Room. It was then and there on that flagstone terrace, resplendent with sun and a glorious view of the Pacific, that she metamorphosed. Walked away from there a different person. Four years ago now, she'd continued on the bus tour to the San Simeon mansion, a new woman. In those crazy baroque rooms, she felt herself coming to life, felt half-free for the first time, unmarrying herself, no longer one with him, seeing herself a transient being, like Mehitabel the cat, whose great-hearted hunger for surcease of loneliness prompted her to seek love in endless alleys. Kay had an affair then. When he found out, he left her. She gazes at Gorgeous and smirks. His eye ineffable stares into space.

Sitting by a window during long hot afternoons, indifferent to the constant wheeling and screeching of the gulls littering a pale sky, her dog-eared marriage peered at her. His occasional thoughtful gestures seemed always to awaken her original tenderness toward him. Looking up with a quizzical expression on her face she asks the Spiffy Gentleman a question, her voice conspiratorial: Even today, after all the talk, what young woman knows what the word "marriage" means, huh? She pulls a clown face and answers her own question: Has little to do with love, or sex for that matter, don't you think, you papier-mache hunk? She blows him a kiss and immediately smirks at him again. Of course men have always known this. The hundred-watt glare of his azure eye intensifies. Heedless and versatile, she continues talking to herself, a habit she acquired during her isolated housebound years: Has to do with brooms and dustpans, vacuum cleaners, gucky leftovers in the fridge, poo-full diapers, urine-sprinkled bathroom floors, smelly socks, a husband going out the door. Kay shakes a finger at her Deluxe Edition still flashing his hollow facade. A snare is what it is, Kay tells him, to a young female person's will, ambition and passion, sexual or otherwise.

The hell with it! she says, loud enough so that, several yards away, a petulant woman, wearing a full-backed, loose cotton dress like a peignoir or a vestment and fretting through racks of windbreakers—looking for promised bargains—turns to stare at her. Like a shot, Kay slumps down on her haunches and brushes some imaginary lint from the eyecatching, outthrust pantleg. Don't be so jumpy, she tells herself, take it easy. Her ears catch the benediction of sunny Muzak coming from above. She takes a deep breath, catches the scent of epoxy, lacquer and wool, feels the warmth of the arc light caressing her back. O, where else but to a shopping center can one go for comfort, for some cheer, for pollution-free, climate-controlled security? Kay closes her eyes for a second, thinks: My ceaselessly pulsing, 98-degree body with its secret chaos of lungs, stomach, intestines, genitals. In lonely abstinence, O Body, thou criest in the wilderness. O my body, I love thee, Byron once said. Kay squints sideways at the woman, notices her graying hair piled flat on top of her head, giving her the look of a caryatid. Kay strains to recapture her train of thought. Oh, yes, marriage, that canonized trap. Is it, in today's rosy capitalist era, more of an artful ploy to get a young couple to become lifetime consumers? She rises from her squat position. The woman is still glaring. Kay's impulse is to ask her what she thinks, but just at that moment, the woman turns away. Kay glimpses her shabby garment, frayed at the hem, trailing a long thread.

How had he seen it, that tight-lipped husband of hers? An inattentive man given to habitual silences. Kay tweaks the manikin's sleeve to see what he thinks. He ignores her, his eye persisting in its unmoving, vacuous gawking. According to male writers, she tells him, they don't much like wedlock either, the demands it places on them, the prison it is, confining love to one person. Can it be revitalized, this wishful institution? Kay wonders, contemplating the man's phony pose. Can it grow, branch out? Can it be compensated? She watches the caryatid ambling down the aisle, sadly bent from some hidden conflict. It's money, isn't it? This antiquated system of straining for financial stockpiling in a world gone thin with greed. This antiquated system of stifling couple connections, convenient but dishonest. During their long childhood, are women and men lovingly prepared to live together? Where is our new world order?

With the suddenness and numbing of a blow, an image rises before her, the ghost of him, her lord and master. The glimpse she had had of him from the window of a bus on Manatee Avenue, years ago, an image her psyche had deliberately forgotten. Her husband walking on Manatee with another man, slapping him on the back, his hand lingering, something epicene about the two of them, so awkward in their queerly boisterous camaraderie.

Who can say, I am not deprived? thinks Kay, looking up, admiring the winsome, beguiling lip and appreciating his listening in silence. Taking a step back, she feels her perspiring forehead with a trembling hand, expels her breath in a sudden burst, a fluid sob, a fluid laugh, who can say? Gave me back my freedom, he did. I'm free now to go from troth to throw-of-the-dice, for to live is to play, the fruit of long experience. She brushed back her mussed shining hair, dyed the right shade to go with her sallow-buff complexion and her chrysolite-green-gray eyes.

I do love you, man, she whispers, I should never have married you, is all. I craved an embrace, a natural, elemental embrace, is all. For the rest, I should be able to look after myself, huh? I should be adequately paid to look after myself, huh? She purses her lips and cocks her head to one side. In a daze, she gazes at the paragon before her. Ooo...his sensual underlip, savagely curved, lugubriously bowed, sardonic, satisfied, libidinous, lascivious. She becomes suffused with warmth, devouring him with wide-open, blinking eyes, her hands lifted as if in supplication. She swallows with difficulty and her breathing becomes shallow as she struggles not to smile stupidly. O, my Body, who can flee from thee? O Garden of my Soul.

I'm a little fleshy around the hips, she whispers to Him, and under the arms, but I try to think therapeutic thoughts. Ooo, the power of desire: seducing the two genders to embrace, creating the one who will succeed them. She climbs onto the step next to him. Do I dare and do I dare? she asks herself, recalling a high school poetry class. She stretches up to his level, peering searchingly at the fine features, placing her open palm on his breast, slipping it under the vest, rubbing the back of his thigh through the cloth. She puts her arms around his neck, kisses him full on the lips and pulls away as if stung. He almost falls over.

Lady! What are you doing? she hears someone shout. She nearly loses her footing, totters on the edge of the podium or whatever it is, clinging lightly to the summer-wool sleeve. This someone helps her down, a floorwalker probably, alerted by her ardent attention to his dummy.

She stares at the manikin with sad-eyed bewilderment. How hard he is! How frigid! How rigid his obstinate chin, his Heidelberg jaw. She frowns, forgetting her looks. A crowd has gathered, so swift is it to congregate at someone's discomfiture! For a second she's embarrassed, then decides: they'll think I'm a window-dresser, one of those arty decorators, kissing my Pygmalion, my supermanikin, unremorseful of my complicity with the man. She looks up at the doll's blank face and salutes him, so like old hubby he is.

O, the lip on that dummy! Kay looks gloomily at the floor, thinking: often, what he says is meant to obscure what he is, what we all are, what the earth is; his impulse to *maya*, cosmic illusion, is strong, an impulse, the sages have written, dependent upon *avidya*, ignorance. All those systems that pull the wool over his own eyes. Look at him. Look intently at him. Gaze. What do you see? As Colette says somewhere, his handsome male features reveal both the weaknesses and charms of his character.

Well! Kay says loudly, boldly looking at the onlookers, he's quite a piece of work, isn't he? Oh, what a piece of work is man! she says, quoting Shakespeare, unthinking, nodding forcefully. A guffaw from the back of the crowd, a sprinkling of laughter. She sees people's eyes popping, mouths open. A fierce tremor rushes through her. She takes a deep breath and goes on, louder than before: You see, it took three thousand years of enslaving women to produce such a champion, such a prime rib you might say, but there's no life in it. She turns her head, leans over and pulls his leg. He swivels, reels, topples and crashes to the floor from his high perch, unharmed except for his lovely lower lip which is sliced off. Kay's friend, the petulant caryatid, rushes forward and tries to cradle the dummy's head in her arms but her shopping bag falls open revealing three windbreakers of assorted colors. She tries to stuff them back in with nervous jabs. Fails. Struggles up and takes off, bag half-open, three different colored sleeves trailing on the floor behind her.

He's not hurt! Kay screams, picking up the lip. She sees the mob moving back, moving away from her. He's got all his armor on! The best protection, select English weave. She shakes her head. It'll take generations to strip that sterling stuff off him, but I've got his lip. She holds it up and shouts: The lip is mightier than the sword! A Dadaist slogan of the twenties falls in with her thinking: Destruction is also Creation! She shifts her gaze to the fallen god again. She puts the fractured lip in the pocket of her jeans, bends down and, panting, begins yanking at the dummy's pants. Yes, she says, yes, yes. And again, Yes, O yes. She wonders if what she feels is faith, hope or charity.

The manager, for he says he is, I'm the manager, he says, and soon-to-be director of operations, he adds, grasps Kay's arm in a viselike grip. He glares at her, his face full into hers, to make sure she knows she's being assailed. The onlookers, bug-eyed, keep staring at the interesting scene. Two or three are heard to say, O! The woman in the vestment has abandoned her, creeping away, carting her heavy load.

As she's led away, Kay glances at the officiating manager, the soon-to-be whatever, who growls at her in a low baritone, Come with me to the custodian's. He seems to her like her lost husband with his gesture of—is it gleeful?—hand-washing as he speeds ahead on important business of no consequence, taking her with him with his glittering eye and stiff upper lip.

I know something about you, man, she thinks, observing his heedless advance on life's racetrack. I know your dark secret, a secret so profound, even you, in your proud business cunning do not yet suspect, perhaps cannot soon admit to: You have become so fearful in this cruel world that you yourself have made that you can only hang onto your phallus for dear life, a narcissist sadly incapable of love. Before entering his puny glassed-in office, she stops him and holds him with her frail hand and asks him in polite and gracious tones: Was Pygmalion the one who came to life? Or was it Galatea?

# The Bookkeeper at H.G. Smithy's
## Enid Shomer

sits at the end of a long hall.
Her polished nails leave no tracks
on the tundra of paper.

Her hair is dyed young. She wears
button earrings, shoulder pads
and seamed stockings. At lunch

she crosses her legs tightly
on the stool and swivels like a lure
on its line. Her breasts stick

to her rayon slip. From one sleeve
a lace strap peeks like the deckled
edge of an invitation.

When she lights up in the No
Smoking section only one old man
objects. "They say," she tells him,

"when you're not being beautiful,
make trouble." Her gaze drifts upward,
astonished, with the smoke.

# Penelope's Silver Wedding Anniversary
## Rima de Vallbona

The preparations for the party have created an atmosphere of anxiety, you'd think we were going to be entertaining royalty. Maybe something exciting is finally going to happen in this sleepy place. Even I'm restless. I try to fit the nervous hours into my daily work, but it's no use. Everything breaks away from the habitual routines, the well-defined limits and rolls on towards the unexpected. Damn it! Will it happen? What?

A party's a party, fool. Relax those nerves. They're tightening like violin strings. Don't jump every time the china clinks as Julia, the old housekeeper, washes it.

"To think that I once held her in my arms when she was just a tiny little thing. Look at her now! I never would've believed that I could hang on for so many years. It's just incredible!" Julia goes on whistling her litany through the black gaps in between her few remaining teeth. She washes and washes, conducting a kitchen symphony of porcelain, crystal, silverware and running water. That unbearable garlic and fried-food smell pervades the air and turns my stomach. Though I really can't tell if it's the smell or what may happen tonight.

The noise, the smell of cooking mixed with the piercing aroma of jasmine, roses and gardenias all nauseate me and open chasms between me and the things I normally handle with ease, almost with disdain. It's as if I were desecrating a sacred object. When I picked up a teaspoon, I dropped it superstitiously. Damn nausea! The cigarette I was about to light seemed alive in my mouth, so I let it fall and then lacked the energy to pick it up.

In the next room Charito and Laura sing while they make their beds. Magical, impossible sailboats form in the air as they flap the fresh, clean sheets whose whiteness dazzles in the sunlight. As I lie unraveled on the couch, their young arms invite me to enter their intimate circle of laughter and song, to taste their kissing. "They're your cousins, David, orphaned cousins, and you must love and respect them always. You're bad, David! You'll pay in hell for what you've done. You have to go to confession and never sin with them again!" How soft and tender was their skin in the river waters! Never again have I experienced such complete and total paradise: the multicolored vegetation cascading into the water in a transcendental suicide of branches thickened with parasites and bulrushes. And the silence pierced by a thousand noises, bursting into a locust's soft whir, or into the plop of a ripe peach striking the earth, or into the river's rush, or the rush of the blood laden with new, healthy pleasure. "You'll be damned to hell! That's a mortal sin!" Ah, but it was paradise, Mom, the paradise which opened its door to me at fourteen. The taste of moist virginal flesh inviting me to joyously sample it like a fresh, crisp apple! Swollen with pleasure, their young bodies would sway in the river waters. I closed my eyes and let myself go...let myself go...let myself go...They allowed me to penetrate the boundaries of their sensuous arms and legs that wrapped around my body like a fleshy net. There I surrendered myself to the magic of release after long nights calming the hard, shameful pain in my groin. Surrender was paradise. Hell was each night in my bed as I suffered the sinful swelling. That was hell.

But Mom—such a good woman, poor thing—was unable to understand then as she is now, that games, bicycles, marbles, desks, books and multiplication tables aren't everything. There she sits knitting on the sofa next to the window—waiting for something? Knitting, always knitting. She's waiting for something. I know she is waiting for something. Every quick, nervous movement of her needle says that she is waiting. She's been waiting for so long! What has she knitted all that time? She must have collected a roomful of bedspreads, pillows, sweaters, booties, hats, scarves. Where does she find room for them all? Now, amid the bustle and getting ready for the party—damn it—Mom's knitting is making me strangely uneasy. Where on earth could she put all those things if she has never worn them or given them away? Is there a secret stash somewhere in the house? Where? White wool, always pure white. Ever since I was a child, I would watch her knit by the window, humming some sad old waltz, and then she would kiss me as she shook with anguish. "Why do you knit so much, Mom?" She would just keep knitting, and teardrops trickled down her cheek whenever I asked her. "Where's that white sweater you knitted last week?" Then she would silently rise from the sofa and go to check on Julia's dinner preparations. I always asked her about it but Mom's knitting never bothered me as it does today. The very first words I can remember her saying to me were "Sinful boy! You'll go to hell! You're a bad boy!" Then she would trail off muttering "Sausage, potatoes, beans, laundry, roses, knitting. I must knit, I must finish these booties." As she intones "I must," it's as if everything alive in her drains off into the grave and she goes on making soup or kneading dough.

When she hears a love song or the canary's warble, something suddenly seems to stir within her...but then she starts up again talking about the same old things as if life were routine and just a household chore. Dad just tolerates the chatter; it isn't coherent, not at all. Strings of words, apparently meaningful, but not really. The funny thing is that each word sounds as if she carried the thing named right there in her mouth.

"Leave her alone, David, she's happy there in her own world, a simple woman's world. Married twenty-five years and not a single complaint, not one. She's happy just to knit, cook, arrange flowers and move the furniture around. If the real world were like that, everything would be a bed of roses. Look, look here at this gray hair—that's what you get chained to a desk all day."

Mom doesn't have a single gray hair but her eyes suggest gravestones and the life entombed inside. In the mornings when she awakes her complexion is moist, as if the dew had watered the slight wrinkles that are starting to appear around her eyes. Not a single gray hair. Shining hair, always clean, done up in an elegant bun. As long as she doesn't open her mouth—*bring the potato salad, Julia*—you'd think she had popped out of a museum painting of some royal family. But once she starts talking about everyday things in her unpretentious way and with that peculiar accent from her home town, she seems crude and common. It makes you want to muzzle her, hide her in a corner, plug your ears and block out the awful sound that clashes with her beauty and elegance. Why can't she leave the bananas, cabbage and vegetables alone? Mom, Mom! How many times has she embarrassed me with that *Oh, these tomatoes are overripe!* and *Mmmm, what tender green beans!* They look at me and shrug their shoulders, unable to understand her simple world, and then resume their conversation...

Today's party. What for? What is it that's bothering me? Just another party. I feel like gagging. Is there any more room at all in Mom's knitting room? Is she going to stay by the window? White wool, white wool, white wool..."Oh, those nights at the Opera House, the Music Hall...to take in the splendor of the chandeliers! To dance every night until your shoes wore out, a new pair every night, just to wear them out." When did she say all that? No, she never did. I just dreamed it in one of those childhood daydreams that so easily pass for reality. "And the girls were always jealous of my dance card. All the boys wanted to dance with me." A vague remembrance of hearing it from her lips. Maybe it wasn't her. Someone else. Probably one of those vain old bags that always talk your ear off when they visit. White wool, kitchen—nausea, nausea—it's the same little world she'll never escape. Poor thing. Just like grandmother and all the others, no wings to fly away towards the endless horizon, no dreams of conquest...Oh hell, what a bunch of tripe. It's all so dumb, the knitting room, the fragile little woman, a shadow, empty inside...What silly thoughts!

Charito is warm, vibrant as she trembles against me for a moment and then slips away like a fish. She is so tender pressed against me, alive with unquenchable ardor in her beautiful, perverted virginity. "You'll suffer in hell! You're bad!" Mom said that because she just doesn't understand how Charito feels when she rubs up against me and we go for it. Mom doesn't know anything about that. I wonder if she has ever felt it with Dad—or anyone? No way. She's different, all she cares about is white wool and kitchen. Strange, when the teacher would talk about the Tinoco dictatorship I would think about Mom, vivacious and laughing, with curly hair and a low-cut dress—*Pelico Tinoco made a pass at me too, but I...*It's absurd, she's not that old and besides she's my mother, who can say...

The party finally starts, guests arrive. Little by little the pretense, lies and gossip penetrate and solidify in the interstices between them. Laughter, greetings, all bullshit. Nausea haunts me, will Mom start stuffing herself with bananas, tomatoes, stew and pies? She looks so beautiful in that black dress that sets off the reddishness in her hair, just regal. If she would just keep quiet, stay away from the commonplace. What? What are they saying? She's going to make an announcement? Everyone's eyes are on her. Dad is dumbfounded. This can't be happening! She has never spoken to a crowd before. With all those vultures waiting around for someone to slip up, how could she dare to speak up?

"Mom, for crying out loud...why did you have to have that damn drink, you know what it does to you. Come on, let's go..."

"No, I have an important announcement for my friends. Let me go, David, and tell your father I haven't had a drop to drink."

"Mom, please shut up for the love of God!"

She climbed up on a platform and majestically silenced everyone. She had the most marvelous, regal air about her. If she could just stay that way and be quiet...

"I would like to be candid with all our dear friends, you who have known us all our twenty-five years of marriage. How could I celebrate our silver wedding anniversary without sharing *my* happiness with you?" (Why did she emphasize *my*? What about Dad? She's drunk, she just can't handle champagne.)

"Can you imagine what it is like to be married to a cruel, selfish, stubborn, lecherous man for twenty-five years—*God damn it, she's gone crazy!*—the sleepless nights and exhausting days working, living by his side?—*Christ, this is unreal! Nightmare! This can't be happening, she's no good at expressing herself, she's drunk, get her out of here!*—I won't bore you with the details, all the tears I've shed during the past twenty-five years...What's that murmuring? I just want to share with you why I'm so happy. Well, here it is: David is now a man and no longer needs me. As for my husband...Today I celebrate my freedom. Have you ever seen a prisoner who has just paid his debt to society? Well, you're looking at one now.—*I can't take any more, everything is coming down around my ears*—Today I am throwing off the yoke of marriage. I am now free to dispose of my time as I please. No more crummy trips to Galveston or Freeport while he takes his mistress to Acapulco, Capri and Biarritz! I'm going around the world.—*She's crazy, crazy, crazy!*—And the best thing about today is the end of the silence that practically destroyed me. Drink up; drink, my friends, to freedom, to this joyous day for both me and my husband!—*Dad, poor Dad, how humiliating!*—Right dear, isn't that a relief? I'm the one that made the stink so you can play the suffering husband, just as always. Let's just drink to it, no bad feelings, good friends like we've always been."

The feeling of unreality that had pursued me since morning hit me with such force that I thought the martinis had finally done me in. I had the strangest sensation that the distance between other objects and myself was somehow sacred. Material objects which I once touched without noticing now disappeared from sight. They shunned contact, slipping away into nothingness, vanishing in the nightmare.

Mom was still on the platform when I noticed the black dress had a very provocative neckline. Her neck—I'd never seen it that way before—was firm, young, like Charito's, disquieting. No, for Christsake, what's happening to me? She's my mother. There she is, laughing...laughing...laughing with that good-looking gray-haired fellow. They gaze at each other raptly, lustfully, whispering things I can't even imagine. The martinis...I'm plastered. Mom, Dad, twenty-five years, the anniversary, that man: Dr. Manzione, yes, it was Dr. Manzione, the one that pulled her through that long illness. He saved her life...now he's saving her from...hell...slut...She's bad just like all the rest...They're just looking at each other...And Dad? It's the martinis, I can't even remember my name.

She can't. She can't leave the salads, tortillas, soups...Dammit! Let her keep knitting by the window! I'll buy her all the white wool she wants so she'll fix that sinful neckline and stop staring at Dr. Manzione that way. She was born to knit.

"I still have the rest of my life to enjoy, just for me. Why not now while there's still time? Slavery is illegal now, isn't it? (She's no good, she's looking at Dr. Manzione like Charito looks at me when we're together. She's gone to hell. My clean, pure mother, tireless knitter of useless things. This is pure hell, I thought that...)

Things got even stranger when she produced her knitting (white wool, white, white everywhere!) and started passing it out among the guests: they all got into it and started putting things on until they were completely covered in whiteness, white, white wool...finally fusing into a white mass of arms, legs, a shrieking, frenzied confusion of freedom and lust.

# Just Say No

## Constance Mortenson

Rita fell apart. She folded herself into a fat comforter and hid her head, twisting her right leg around her left in what Don called her "uptight" position and remained unmoving, the lights out and the curtains drawn shut. She didn't notice the day ebbing into dark or the sounds from the street rising and falling.

Her cleaning woman tip-toed in and out on Tuesday. On Wednesday her friend Audrey knocked loudly and later in the day came back and banged on the window shouting "Let me in, you dumb cluck. Let me in!"

Rita, clutching the edge of the quilt, agreed with the "dumb cluck" but couldn't make her hand open, couldn't get out of bed. After Day One, when she slept and cried, slept and cried, she just existed. She stumbled to the bathroom and stumbled back into bed.

It wasn't until the fourth day that her mind began to work. This behavior was very, very unproductive. She was acting as if a loved one had died when her husband had merely left her for another woman.

After Audrey visited for the fifth time, and again grumbled off home, Rita rolled over and came up for air. She felt stiff and older than her fifty-one years. She smelled like hell and needed a shower. She fell asleep again and it was dark when she awoke. She slid quietly out of bed and, as usual, tip-toed towards the bathroom; as she eased open the door she suddenly remembered that she was alone in the room. She deliberately closed the door with a bang and then opened it to let the light shine carelessly into the darkened bedroom.

She showered and washed her hair, lingering in the warm water, stepping out tingling, squeaky clean. She selected a sheer batiste nightgown she had never worn before, but when the long mirror in the door told her every line of her slender frame was visible, she quickly stepped into her padded navy blue robe and zipped it up to the top.

She was starving; the thought of toast and eggs brought moisture to the corners of her mouth. She crept quietly downstairs and pushed into the kitchen enjoying the cool, clean feel of the linoleum on her bare feet. She winced automatically when the fry pan she used for scrambling eggs clanged against the edge of the stove drawer, and then relaxed when she remembered that there was no one upstairs to be wakened. No one to call, "Come back here woman."

She lathered butter on toast feeling that a four-day fast earned a few extra calories and ate every bite. The clock over the stove told her it was five-thirty in the morning and the street was quiet. The only light was John Jay's at the end of the block; he worked the early shift on the ferry. A thousand mornings she had opened her eyes to see the reflection of his light on her bedroom ceiling and waited, not daring to move, until the sunrise faded it out, and the children clamored for breakfast, lunch pails, and school books; then she whisked out from under Don's restricting arm and murmured about being late and having to hurry.

Rita brewed a fresh pot of coffee and took it out to the patio to watch the morning unfurl. Ervine had mowed the lawn next door and the scent of dry hot grass filled the August air. In the goldfish pond a coral-tinted water lily lifted its head still folded shut waiting for full sunshine to open. Like me, she thought, clenched tight, shut; she untwisted her legs and planted both bare feet firmly on the tiles.

She felt a stirring of shame when she thought of the past four days. The neighbors would be gossiping enough about Don's desertion without her acting like a fool, not returning phone calls or answering the door.

She wondered what was the matter with her. Sniveling in bed was a luxury she *never* permitted herself.

The day warmed and after stripping her bed, packing the dishwasher and wiping up the bathroom floor, she wondered if it was too early to phone Audrey. A knock on the kitchen window and the accompanying shout, "It's me. Let me in, dumb-dumb," answered the thought. She slid back the bolt and her friend hugged her close, suffusing her with warmth and a depth of feeling that brought tears to her eyes.

"Are you crying over that jerk?" Audrey asked bluntly. "Whatsa matter you. You are free and rid of Simon. What the hell more can you want?"

"I'm not weeping over him."

"Well what have you been doing for the last four days? Partying it up?"

"No, silly, I've been weeping. And don't ask me why. I don't know why."

"It's bonding." Audrey said. "You get bonded to the apes like a duckling does to a mother hen even though you know you are bonding to the wrong party. He is family. Hell, you've had him for thirty-one years, remember."

Rita poured her a cup of coffee and found a can of shortbread cookies. Audrey dug in happily; she always ate like a horse and was still slim as a young birch tree.

"Now tell all," she said between bites. "The whole neighborhood knows that Don packed everything into his new convertible and moved into the Beach Gardens, and John Jay said he heard he has a new woman and is divorcing the old one."

Rita burst into tears and Audrey rushed to apologize. "Me with my big foot in your mouth! I didn't mean that to come out the way it sounded."

Rita laughed. "I know but I don't want to think about the fact that Karen is thirteen years younger than me. I hope she screws him into an early grave."

"Rita don't say things like that. Isn't it bad for that dumb Karma you are always worrying about?"

"Karma, be damned!" Rita said. "I don't wish him any good luck. So why pretend?"

"Well, no...I'm just not used to hearing you talk tough, I guess."

"That's probably been my trouble all along, too wishy-washy."

"Oh Rita! Whatever I say, you take it wrong."

"I know. I'm just feeling fragile."

"Will you be poor? They always say a woman's income goes down and a man's goes up after a split."

"Divorce. Dear. *Divorce* is what we are talking. I have my own money. Mother left me scads of it. Don will get one hell of a shock when he gets out into the real world and finds out how much housekeeping and family raising really costs."

"Family!"

"Yep. She's pregnant. That's what drove him to telling me, or I guess he'd have kept fucking us both. His idea of Pig-heaven."

"Wow! How did he get it up for her if what you always said is..."

"The *truth*?"

Audrey flushed. "I've got hoof-in-mouth disease really bad this morning," she said.

"Believe me. It's the truth. In fact I've never told it all because no one would credit it, not even Doc Patterson."

"You're kidding! You mean he did it morning and night every day?"

"And in the middle of the night. And at lunch if he was home."

"God almighty! What a stud!" There was awe in Audrey's tone.

"You can't imagine," Rita said.

"No I can't. Not with that old once-a-month-except-for-anniversaries man of mine. I can't imagine a sex-craving guy like Don, but I must admit there have been times I've sort of envied you."

"Don't! I'd rather go short than O.D. on the stuff."

"I'll take your word for it. But anyway, are you okay?"

"Yes, I think so. I don't know why I've felt so bad. I can't understand it."

"Come shopping with me this afternoon. Let's throw away all your blue dresses and buy some shocking pink and burgundy. You know how great you look in jewel tones."

Rita's mouth automatically opened and said, "Don doesn't like me in..." and they both collapsed in giggles. What Don liked no longer mattered in this house.

"I'll do it," she said. "I'll meet you downtown about four o'clock. When Don left he said he would be by today to pick up some things and talk about lawyers and stuff."

"Not wasting time, is he?"

"No. But then babies come fast and he doesn't want Karen to suffer."

"Tough beans!" Audrey said with a grin, and grabbing another cookie left through the kitchen door.

Rita felt much better. Audrey always had that effect on her. She went right to the root of a problem and there was nothing she wouldn't discuss openly and with loving concern.

Don didn't care much for her but that didn't matter; Don wasn't crazy about any of her closest friends. She kept them just the same. She felt if she gave into him constantly on what her mother called "The Basics" she could be stubborn about other things.

Don was in for a shock. What if his new young friend (Rita couldn't even think the word wife yet) hadn't been taught the BASICS?

Rationally, Rita knew that her mother had been very wrong but in her gut she couldn't convince herself. Her mother never talked about sex or men, except to tell her to watch them, they were all out for what they could get, until the day she turned twenty and was getting married within the week. Then her mother sat her down on the edge of the bed and solemnly told her never to refuse her husband "in bed." Never! It was her duty to "accommodate" him and if she didn't he would, *and rightly so*, go out and get IT elsewhere and shame her before the whole human race. Rita could never quite decide why she took that lesson as gospel except it was the only sex advice she was ever given at home. If her mother thought it important enough to discuss, when she always evaded every question Rita asked, it must be *absolutely vital*.

She had never, or at least hardly ever, refused Don sex, and the more she gave into his demands the more he seemed to require. One doctor she shyly asked about it refused to believe her. Another laughed but never forgot and when she went back fifteen years later he asked with a grin if her husband was "still as good as he used to be." She had not replied, but she had been heartsick.

She knew wives often complained about their husbands' sexual demands, but she believed they had nothing to complain about. Their men wanted it two or three times a week usually, and didn't know what a double-header was. When she explained to Audrey that Don meant a second orgasm without getting off, her friend had laughed too. Rita wondered why everyone thought it was so excruciatingly funny.

She shivered as she sat over the last dregs of her cold coffee and hugged herself, rocking gently back and forth.

Sometimes she felt as though her skin had been rubbed thin and tender from the hours of patting and stroking and squeezing it endured. She took a deep shuddering breath and a wave of relief that was distinctly physical washed through her body. Would his new woman like sex more? Don always managed to make her feel like a cold fish if she was too obviously reluctant or if she found excuses like, "the children are coming home for lunch."

She hadn't been reluctant during the first few months of their marriage, quite the opposite. She thought it was because he was so crazy about her that he came rushing home for lunch and threw his arms around her and dragged her protesting but laughing into the bedroom, but because he was so obdurate and demanding she soon doubted it was love.

She wondered if there was a word that matched nymphomania as pertaining to the male. If there was, it wasn't used much. There were times when she believed Don suffered from a kind of mania, but when she told him so he laughed and said he was just an ordinary healthy male. She was the peculiar one; most girls would have been delighted to get lots of sex. Look at them! They grumbled like hell about their husbands and crawled into bed with any available male who offered. She foolishly thought that Don was too busy at home to be one of those "offering"!

In one of the supermarket scandal sheets she read about a wife who undressed and donned her nightgown in the closet; everyone she knew who read it pronounced it ludicrous, except her. She sympathized and thought of all the times she stayed in the bathroom hoping Don might fall asleep. How careful she was not to wake him in the morning so he wouldn't have time for sex before he left for the office.

Fifty-five is old to start having a new family, but she knew he couldn't have resisted bragging around the office that Karen was pregnant, and he would want the "credit" for it. Damn his rotten soul! She walked into the living room and crammed piles of paper and kindling into the fireplace. When it was burning well she emptied case after case of Don's tape collection into the flames. The plastic curled and melted horribly. She was probably polluting half the town. Her rage turned to fear when she recognized the last box; it was his pet Dave Brubeck collection and he would be livid. She threw it in anyway and stood back watching until every last one had burned. She moved slowly back into the kitchen and slumped in a chair feeling nothing.

The kitchen door lock clicked and brought her fearfully to her feet until she remembered Don still had his key.

"It's only me. I've come for my tapes. I miss them." She stared at him uncomprehending for a moment.

"Give me the key," she said and he placed it in her outstretched hand. She stared down at it as if it were a foreign object. She didn't know what to say or do. Automatically she went to the stove to heat the coffee, twiddling unnecessarily with the knobs stalling for time. He moved up behind her and put his hand on her hair.

"I love the way your hair looks when it's all wet and curly." His other hand slid out to pull her back against him. "You know what? You've turned me on again. How about for old times sake...?"

"No," she snarled. "Never. Not ever again! Not on the floor or the back seat of the car. Not in your office. Or in the morning, or at noon or night. Or in the house or out. Never again. Not ever." He stepped back and his hand fell away.

"No," she said, "No! No! No!" and as the words tumbled out, joy and relief began to wash up her body. It started at her ankles and moved like a wave of pure ecstasy through her blood. Never again would she have to have sex with this man or any other if she didn't feel like it. She was free! Free! FREE...and she felt like she had taken a cool shower on a hot day. Wonderful from head to toe. Born again to herself, private, untouched and belonging to no one. No more faking orgasms or downing water glasses full of brandy to blur her reluctance.

She stood still waiting for the explosion but not caring. She heard the front door close with a slam and knew she was alone in her own house. Still, not quite trusting him, she locked the doors. She felt a rush of incredible energy, a suffusion of wild joy, as she ran up the stairs. Tearing off her robe she flung herself full length on the crisp white cover and made "angels in the snow" spreading her arms and legs wide and free as she hadn't done since she was a teenager.

# Glasnost
## Deborah DeNicola

I've done some terrible things for men.
Like the day I paid $12.50 for a designer lipstick
then told my young son we were too poor
to stop for pizza on the ride home.

Later I looked in the bathroom mirror.
Feeling anxious, I put a cigarette in my right hand.
Feeling guilty, I brushed my teeth with my left—
I was thinking of how you said we were only friends

wondering if I bleached my hair, would you like me better.
Not thinking of what an ass I was to both cleanse
and pollute myself in the same moment, wasting water and air.
But this is the last decade of the twentieth century

and everybody's confused! Statistics say
there are more divorces than marriages. The news
still refers to US and THEM, although I know it's just you
and me among millions of other poor souls, locating each other

on cellular phones, the light distance of hyperspace
filtered with openness—*Glasnost*
shot through a fax machine. I tried, anyway
to summarize the net result of our encounters:

on my end, a devised allowance for condoms,
a few hard-won orgasms, two or three melodramatic poems.
On your end, you could say you were practically loved
straight out for doing nothing

but looking aroused and bewildered at once.
I think of my adolescent son's
intensely insightful appraisal
of his current heartthrob:

"Mom, I don't think Jeanine likes me anymore—"
"How do you know for sure?" I countered. "Because
she's gotten really boring over the phone."
I walked away sober, wiser, almost empowered

by his inductive logic. I thought I'd apply my own to you
but the computer doesn't compute. All I get is a mixed message
in iridescent green letters. And everytime I hit Enter
a door closes somewhere behind you climbing the stairs

to your ratty apartment, unpacking the orange juice
and the decaf on the chipped formica counter.
I send you a senti*mental* telepathic laser:
*Just call her machine. Just say Hi.* Is there life

after the death of relationships? Are relationships
part of our death wish? Or is time in the afterlife
just another long stretch of the relationship
you can't seem to bring to an end?

# The Perfect Opportunity
## Carly Rivers

Good. They were all gone! Her husband and three children had just piled into the car, high on excitement and anticipation of their day at the lake. Marilyn waved goodbye to their flushed faces framed by the back window of the car. As they turned the corner, she sighed with relief. She could do anything she wanted to do, go anywhere she wanted to go, the possibilities were endless...

Inside, she shut the door behind her, immediately aware of the sudden quiet. The cat walked past, rubbing up against her ankles, asking to be petted. "Oh no you don't," she said, closing the door firmly behind him. "I'm not taking care of anyone today."

Marilyn looked out on the sunny street through the leafy green of her climbing wisteria vines. The flowers had just finished blooming and the vines were sending out new tendrils wildly, in all directions. They desperately needed trimming. She thought about getting out her garden tools, then firmly pushed that idea as far away as she could.

She felt the quiet as a presence enfolding her, soothing and healing her frazzled edges, taking all her accumulated worries, cares, responsibilities—all those things that took her away from herself and left her wanting.

She was breathing easier now, feeling almost weightless in the chair...anything she wanted...The bookstore! She could go to the bookstore.

Now why had she thought of that? It was at least six months ago, that talk show, when she had first heard about the bookstore. She'd forgotten all about it. Well, maybe not forgotten, just not remembered it till now. The perfect opportunity. But she wasn't sure she wanted to go anymore, even felt a little nervous at the prospect.

Without realizing she'd decided anything, she moved to the bedroom to change clothes. She remembered that the women on the show were nicely dressed, but casual. Pants, not a dress. With that settled, she stepped quickly into a pair of black slacks, pulled on her favorite lightly flowered blouse, slid her feet into comfortable black loafers, grabbed up her purse and jacket and was ready to go.

She called information for the phone number, then the bookstore for the address. It was in an unfamiliar part of town, so she got out her map to try to place it, but was feeling too restless. Unable to stay in the house any longer, she grabbed up her things, locked up the house and climbed into her Honda Civic.

She loved her car. She'd gotten it recently to drive to her new job. Now that all the kids were finally in school she felt free to go back to teaching. Ed argued that they didn't need the money, but she loved teaching, especially the spirited discussions with her students, young adults who were learning to question and search for their own opinions.

Driving down the freeway she opened the window and turned on the radio, loud. Approaching the city, she wondered, now which exit? Pulling over onto the shoulder she pulled out her San Francisco map, it probably wasn't far. She slid off the freeway and followed her map in the direction of the bookstore. Turning right onto Valencia Street she checked the numbers, just about four more blocks now.

Someone behind her honked, startling Marilyn out of her reverie. She'd slowed down without realizing it. Well I don't have to go there if I don't want to, I can go somewhere else instead. A trip to San Francisco on my own is quite a treat, no matter what I decide to do. The aquarium might be a good place to go today, or downtown shopping, or maybe I...Maybe I could just go to the bookstore. Having come this far I might as well find it, see what it looks like, at least. And she looked again at the numbers on the little shops lining the street. I've passed it. Marilyn made a U-turn at the next corner and started back, looking more intently at the numbers across the street. No wonder I didn't see it. The sign was small, black and white and written with funny spindly little letters.

Looking back over her shoulder at the sign above the shop, she read, Old Wives' Tales. That name had intrigued her from the first time she'd heard it. It spoke of dispelling all the old myths and lies about women. Maybe, in this shop, she would find works by women who wrote to tell the truth about their lives.

Old Wives' Tales looked like an ordinary bookstore. But, remembering the talk show that had started all this, she knew she was nervous about what she'd find inside, what kind of women might be there.

The women she'd seen on the talk show identified themselves as lesbians, lesbian mothers living together and sharing the load of raising children with partners and friends. She'd listened intently to what the women had to say, intrigued with some of their ideas. She certainly didn't agree with everything they said: the lack of role models for boys, for one thing. When she speculated more about it, she knew that having other—what was that term they used—co-mothers?—anyway, other women to share the load would have eased some of the pressure she'd felt to be the perfect mother. Boy, I sure could've used some help with my kids. Those women just might have something...but...Stopping her train of thought abruptly, Marilyn jumped to the heart of her fear. If she went in the bookstore would people think she was a lesbian?

Her rational mind immediately took exception—what people? Marilyn didn't know anyone in San Francisco, and it's just a bookstore, for crying out loud! Even men could walk in there and look around, so, what was her problem?

She stopped in front of the display, pretending to read the titles in the window, while trying to peer around them and see inside the shop. She could see vague shapes and movement, but not much was clear from outside on the street. As she tried again, from a lower angle, she saw a pale round face, with wavy brown hair pulled loosely back into a ponytail at the nape of her neck and large curious eyes, staring intently into her own. Startled, she jerked back and at the same time recognized her own reflection in the window. She was appalled at the image, her tall, substantial body all crunched over trying to sneak a peek inside. Completely irritated with herself, she took a deep breath, and walked in.

Her eyes settled on the nearest bookcase. She moved to it and ran her finger along the titles, looking surreptitiously out of the corner of her eye to assess her surroundings. It was quiet. There were a few women here and there looking at books and reading, and a couple of women going through the records and talking about the artists. She had always liked bookstores and was beginning to feel more at home.

Looking up at the top of the bookcase in front of her, Marilyn noticed the sign, "Psychology," posted above the section. Oh good, subject headings, she thought as she looked around the room, reading the other signs, "History," "Children," "Women's Health," then down at the end of her aisle, "Lesbian." As blatant as that? Then she looked again, desire to know more getting the best of her.

She moved casually down the aisle to the mystery section. I wonder if they have an Agatha Christie I haven't read? No, no Agatha Christie, but a lot of new names, women writers I've never heard of. She picked one off the shelf at random. "Murder in the Collective," by Barbara Wilson. That's what the women on the talk show called their group home—a collective. She carried the book with her as she continued moving on down the aisle.

Soft laughter interrupted her thoughts. Marilyn glanced across the room to see the two women who had been going through the records laughing and talking about one they'd just found. "Remember when we first heard Holly and Ronnie sing this song?" she heard one woman ask in a low voice. "Course I do," the other replied, "it was our first date." Reaching out, she gently caressed the other woman's cheek. Marilyn watched the two women smile into each other's eyes, touched by their gentle affection. Then, feeling like an intruder, she quickly turned away.

The bulletin board caught her attention and she wandered over to see the ads for workshops and performances. *Support Groups for Midlife Women in Transition*, that sounded like something she was right in the middle of, she thought, intrigued. *Coming out support group for midlife women exploring their lesbian sexuality.* Coming out at midlife? Didn't women know whether or not they were lesbians before that? Marilyn started to walk away, but turned back and took down the lavender colored flyer. Could a woman be a lesbian and not even know it? She went back to looking at book titles, sliding the flyer into her purse as she moved on down the aisle.

Her eyes focused on a title, *The Joy of Lesbian Sex*. Looking up she read "Lesbian." Without quite realizing it, she'd reached the very section she'd been slowly working her way toward. The show on lesbian mothers had intrigued her, made her wonder. She wanted to know what those women were like. She wasn't sure just what she'd expected, maybe women trying to look and act like men, but they hadn't. She found herself relating to their concerns more often than not. Scrupulously avoiding *The Joy of Lesbian Sex*, she chose *Suzanne and Mary on Vacation*, opened it at random, and began reading.

*Suzanne slid her hands under Mary's soft, warm buttocks, cupping them hungrily in her hands. Aroused by their full sensual roundness, Suzanne lifted Mary's hips slightly and breathed deeply the tantalizing scent of her wet, enticing cunt. Then she slid one hand farther under until her thumb was stimulating the sensitive tissue around Mary's anus. Suzanne's tongue and thumb pulsed as Mary's responding body arched in Suzanne's hands vibrating urgently...*

Marilyn groaned aloud.

Closing the book abruptly, she glanced nervously around. No one was paying any attention. Even so, the recognition of the erotic responses in her body had shocked her. She felt the hot blush rising up her neck and suffusing her cheeks with color.

Quickly returning the book to the shelf, her fingers pulling back as if burned, Marilyn turned and swiftly headed for the door. Realizing she still had the mystery by Barbara Wilson in her hand, she put it down on the nearest shelf and left the store fast, her heart pounding loudly in her ears.

Marilyn kept walking until her excitement and nervous energy began to abate. Her breathing slowed, her heart quieted, and she drove off, still excited, but relieved to be on her way home. As she rummaged in her purse for a stick of gum, she pulled out the lavender sheet and read again, *Support Groups For Midlife Women In Transition*. Her stomach started to churn.

# Stepping Out
## Verna Wilder

We're at the beach, a long stretch of sand and ocean and sea gulls. It's windy. We lie next to each other on our backs. I turn my body toward her. She turns her body toward me. We lie on our sides talking. Not touching. Then not talking. I lean toward her just enough to brush my lips across hers. The wind blows sand all around us. Her lips are soft against mine. Her brown eyes hold me. She moves her hand to touch mine. We intertwine fingers. Clouds blow past, covering and uncovering the sun. We lie facing each other, fingers laced in fingers. I have never held a woman's hand like this. Her hand is soft. I want to kiss her again. I want to never stop.

I rush to be home before the kids get home from school. I throw my pack on the bedroom floor, grab an apron from the hook in the broom closet, pull it over my head and tie it, throw a cut of sirloin into the microwave to defrost. Dana gets home first, grumbling about homework as she walks in the door. I drop four potatoes into the sink, scrub at them with a brush. I am drying potatoes with a towel when Laura walks in. She thumps her books onto the dining room table and one falls to the floor. "Come back and get your books," I call to her as she turns on the radio in her room. I wrap potatoes in foil to bake, preheat the oven. Dana walks into the kitchen, opens the refrigerator, and pulls out the milk carton. I reach into the cabinet above my head and hand her a glass. She thanks me and pours. "Do you have much homework?" I ask.

She drinks the full glass of milk before she answers. "A little. I can do it tonight after dinner. I want to go to Debbie's."

"OK," I say. "Dinner is at 6:00." I dry my hands, looking at the fingers that have so recently been part of another woman's hand.

"Mom?" Dana is talking to me.

"What?"

"What's for dinner?" Oh. Dinner.

"Sirloin, baked potato, french bread, a salad." Thank god for routine.

I kissed a woman on the beach. I just moved my lips to hers and I kissed her. What made me do that? I was a 40-year-old married woman who claimed to love her husband and her life. What in the world made me kiss a woman on the beach in the sunlight? I knew nothing about my own sexuality, nothing about loving a woman, nothing.

Everything. I knew everything I needed to know. I wanted her. My body felt good in her presence. My heart was full. I was beautiful, lovable, strong. I was smart and clever. I knew myself. I loved myself, oh how infinitely I loved myself. How did I do it? How did I go to school, love her in the corridors, on the beach, in my living room before the kids got home from school, love her in her car, my car, Main Street Fish and Poultry, how did I love her and come home and be wife to David, mother to Dana and Laura? But I did. I was the mother the other kids wished they had. I drove Laura to school, carpooling with five pre-teen girls all reeking of Tabu, Aqua Net, and strawberry lip gloss. I picked Dana up from Debbie's, chatted with the girls about dresses and make-up and boys. I was the wife I was supposed to be: I'd ask, "What do you want for dinner tonight?" and he'd answer, "I don't know. Not chicken again." I'd ask, "When will you be home?" and he'd answer, "I don't know—late." And when I made his coffee in the morning, he'd say, "Not enough sugar, and the color needs to be lighter—less like mud, more like pumpkin. You've been doing this for 15 years. You'd think you could get it right." I planned dinner parties, knew what our guests took in their coffee, every guest an entry on a 3x5 card in a recipe box: Michael takes cream and sugar; Linda drinks hers black. I cooked, cleaned, shopped, did laundry. I made all of his white shirts pink once. I never got it right.

I sit in Dr. Owen's waiting room reading a novel while I wait for my annual pap smear. I am tense in this comforting room: blue carpet, soft lighting, Muzak sifting over the other waiting women. Ferns and loose-limbed trees brush softly against the windows. The nurse behind the glass talks to someone on the phone, laughs, hangs up gently, and hums as she sifts through the papers on the desk. The woman on my left sits with her head thrown back, eyes closed, lips parted, and hands folded over the drum-tight skin of her very pregnant belly. On my right a woman with grey hair and grey stockings knits a grey sweater with six intertwined strands of yarn. She mumbles something at me and I lean slightly to catch her words. "You here for a pap smear? Me, too. My sister in Portland she just had both her ovaries removed. Full of cancer. They can't get it all. Didn't show up on the pap smear." A nurse calls my name and when I enter the examining room, the instruments wink at me from the pink counter top. I look away.

Dr. Owen comes in, says hello, how are you, you look good, lost weight? How's the hubby (blood pressure), doing fine (stethoscope on my chest, my back), I'll check these breasts now. Checking them yourself monthly? That's good. He pushes the buzzer for his nurse, slips on rubber gloves, and helps me slide to the edge of the table and place my feet in the stirrups. "Just a slight bit of pressure here," he says. The examining light feels warm. "No problem there. You are, as usual, in excellent condition. Built for having babies." He smiles and helps me sit up as the nurse leaves. "So," he says, "you get a clean bill of health for one more year." He keeps talking while he bends over the table, filling in the blanks on my folder. "Hubby still in school? Ah, good, good. Kids fine? Um-humm. And you, how are you?" He's still scribbling.

If I don't tell him now, if I don't ask his advice, he will be into the goodbye stage of the routine I know so well. "I need your advice," I say in a long sigh.

His pencil stops and he looks up. "Yes?"

I take a deep breath, not looking at him. "I don't like sex."

He nods, smiles, pats my shoulder. "It's like that for most women," he says.

I am trying not to cry. "I want to like sex."

"Is it intolerable?" he asks.

"No," I answer, "but it's causing problems with my marriage." I am crying now.

"Tell you what," he says, "I know a man who may be able to help you. He's a psychiatrist up at UCLA who specializes in women's sex problems." He pulls out a prescription pad, writes a name on the back of it, hands it to me.

I dress slowly and step out into late afternoon heat. When I pull the office door closed, the welcome bell jingles softly behind me.

The first time I go to a women's bar, I am wearing dark blue polyester pants, a white polyester shirt, and Birkenstocks with socks. I lock the car door, close it, and walk around to the driver's side of the car to meet Joanna.

"Stop," she says to me, getting out of the car.

"What?" I ask.

"The purse," she says, rolling her eyes. "You can't take a purse into a bar."

"Oh." I've always carried a purse. Now I don't know what to do with it, so I throw it into the seat. Then I lean in, open it, and take out some cash. I stuff it into my pants pocket.

"Driver's license, too," Joanna says, holding the door open.

I lean back in, pull out the driver's license, slide it into my other pants pocket. I wonder how lesbians dance without dumping money and ID onto the dance floor. I watch Joanna walk across the parking lot and I see that her pants have back pockets. At the door, she pulls a money clip out of one back pocket, her ID out of the other. The woman at the door stamps the back of her hand with a stamp that looks like pursed lips. I do as Joanna did, my hand held out for the stamp, and she pulls me into the dark, smoky bar. I follow women with my eyes, watch them dance together, laugh together, touch in a way I have never seen women touch each other—a hand to the face, fingers in the hair, arms casually draped over shoulders. Joanna laces her fingers with mine, pulls me to the bar, puts her lips to my ear to ask, "What do you want to drink?" I don't know what to ask for. I don't drink, but I want to.

"I don't know. What are you having?"

"Scotch and soda."

"OK. Me, too."

She nods at the bartender, who moves to the music as she pours the scotch over ice, lifts the nozzle to the soda, and shoots soda into both glasses, all the time dancing behind the bar. She slides the glasses to us, mouths the amount to Joanna, and slaps the change down in one smooth movement. I sip the drink, trying not to grimace at the taste. I feel the heat in my chest and I want to dance, right now. Joanna moves on the dance floor the way I imagine her moving in bed, gliding and weaving, her hands stroking her own thighs, moving in the air around her as I imagine they would move on my body.

I look in the mirror and for the first time in over two years I see *me* looking back. "Hello," I say, "where have you been all my life?" My hair is short and very curly and I feel light and free and confident in a way I have not felt since I was in high school. I am smiling as Pat picks up the curling rods and opens the windows wider to let out curling solution fumes. My long, straight hair is scattered all over Pat's kitchen floor.

"It's strange seeing you without all that hair," she says. "You don't look so much like a little girl now, so Alice-in-Wonderland. I like it." She reaches out and fluffs my hair again with her fingertips. I reach up and touch it myself. God, it feels good. When I leave her apartment, a wind is starting up and I know from the moist-earth smell that it's going to rain. I walk home, wanting to run, wanting to feel the wind in my short, short hair.

When I get home, David is already home from work. I call, "Hi! Sorry I'm late." I hear a drawer close and I remember that tonight is the dress rehearsal for Ted's wedding. David is going to be best man. "Do I have time to change before we leave?" I call to him.

"That depends on what you're wearing," he says as he comes out of the bedroom buttoning his shirt. I stand in the middle of the living room floor, very still, while he looks at me. "What happened to your hair?" Wind pushes through the living room window, lifting the curtains, gently at first and then into full flap, slamming the bedroom door shut. "Shit," he says, "you know I like your hair long. You look like a chrysanthemum." He walks to the hall closet and starts to pull on his windbreaker. I lace my fingers together, and my shoulders tighten and pull forward in the old familiar way. If I concentrate on the pattern in the carpet, maybe this time I won't cry. My back is to him now. I hear him zip the jacket, hear the keys jingle in his pocket. "Maybe if you shampoo it a couple of times tonight it won't be so frizzy." I push my ring with my thumb so the diamond doesn't bite into my little finger. "And if it doesn't rain too hard you can leave the windows open. That damned perm smell is already making me sick to my stomach."

He has the door open before I can speak. "I thought I was supposed to go with you."

"You don't want to go looking like that, do you?"

"No," I answer, turning to look at him, "I guess I don't." He clenches his jaw and I turn away. This time he isn't going to see me cry. He calls goodbye, says he won't be late, and he closes the door behind him, deliberately gentle. Cars shush past on the rain-wet street and the acacia bush outside the bedroom window shudders in the wind.

"We're going to The Blue Moon to dance. Want to come?" Do I. Yes. I hang up the phone, pull clothes out of my closet, black cotton pants with back pockets, a white cotton shirt. I get dressed, stuff some money in one back pocket, driver's license in the other back pocket. I pull on black socks and soft gray shoes. I roll the sleeves of my white cotton shirt, collar up, neck open. I strap my big, black watch on my tan arm, the weight satisfying against my wrist. I pull on a vest and a black leather tie that is knotted loose against my shirt. Dana comes in and watches me get dressed.

"Where are you going?"

"Dancing with Joanna and some other people from the writing group. I should be home about midnight."

"What if Dad calls?"

"Tell him I'll call him tomorrow." He's in Seattle on a business trip. Laura is sleeping over at Wendy's. Dana's boyfriend will be over later to watch TV. I hear Joanna's knock and I run to the front door, waving good-bye to Dana.

"You look great!" she calls to me as I go out the door. I run back and kiss her. "Have fun," she says.

At The Blue Moon, I pull out money, hold out the back of my hand for the stamp, wave at my friends as I walk to the bar, pulling out a couple of dollars for a scotch and soda. I look around the dark room as the bartender pours scotch. The music thumps and I move to the beat before I hit the dance floor. I take a sip of scotch, set the glass on a table, and I find Joanna, who's smoking in a corner with three women from the writing group. "Hey, Joanna," I say to her, looking up into her face, touching her blonde hair. I slide my hand down her arm to link fingers with hers. "Let's dance." We step to the beat, down three stairs, onto the dance floor, moving, moving. The music flashes colors, mirrors, rainbows, and I let it in, move with it, rhythm in my body, shoulders, thighs, feet, my own hands moving up and down my body the way I remember Joanna doing the first time we went dancing together.

Later I dance with Carrie and then with April. I come off of the dance floor breathless and happy. Joanna is at the bar by herself. I walk up behind her and drape my arms around her neck. She hands me a shot glass and I down it in one swallow. The peppermint schnapps glows warm in my chest. She nods to the bartender for another round and we knock them down. I pull her to her feet and we dance a slow dance, close. I feel her breasts against mine and I want her, but I know I've had too much to drink and I don't trust myself. At the end of the dance, she whispers in my ear, "Come out to the car with me." I take her hand and we go outside where a fine mist has coated the windows of her Honda. She opens the door, gets into the driver's seat, and reaches across to open the passenger door for me. I get in, pull her to me, and kiss her. Her hands are on my breasts and in my hair and on my thighs. I want her on me and in me. I want her in a large bed, in a soundproof room, in a motel in Carmel, a bed-and-breakfast in Mendocino, a hotel in San Francisco, and I know I can't have her, not here and not now, not while I'm married to a man, not in a car outside a women's bar on a night when my daughter is waiting up for me.

"No. Joanna, I can't." We stop, so reluctantly that I can still feel her lips on mine. I don't feel high anymore. I feel sad and tired and lonely. Joanna brushes my hair back away from my face.

"I love you in curls," she says, and she kisses each temple. I put my arms around her and she pulls me close while I cry. "You've got a long fuse, sweetheart," she says, and I laugh. We go back into the bar and dance ourselves sober. At midnight, I go home.

I leave the class on the metaphysical poets and meet my friends for coffee before the Milton seminar begins. I call home to talk to the kids. Dana is breathless, "Mom, you've gotta come home. Dad's in the hospital—they don't know what's wrong." I throw my backpack in the car and drive to the emergency room at the hospital. I find David in a white bed, the emergency blinkers staining the white walls red, his partners hovering in the halls, clucking in their pinstripe suits. The doctor meets me in the hall after examining David, and when Ted joins us, the doctor directs his explanation to Ted, as if at 45 years old I need to have medical language filtered through another man. Suddenly I am just tired, very tired—of being polite, of folding away my own hurt, my own needs, my own strength. So I ask the doctor to please direct his remarks to me, that Ted is there only because I allow it. The doctor's eyes grow slightly rounder and he almost smiles—the bastard—and he looks directly at me to tell me the rest of the bad news, which to him means euphemisms about possibilities. I finally ask, "Do you think he had a stroke?"

He pauses a moment before answering, "Yes, that's a strong possibility."

David is in the rehab center after the stroke and has been there long enough to come home on the week-ends. I help him into the car, load the wheelchair into the trunk, drive him home. I pull into the driveway, lift the trunk lid, and set up the wheelchair, an alien construction of metal and vinyl. David sits in the car waiting for me to get it together, push the footrest into place, open the seat. I find the brake and help him into the chair. I can smell his after-shave as he settles himself into the vinyl seat—all so familiar, all so different. He looks the same—softwashed Levis, cotton plaid shirt, blue running shoes, brown hair going gray. How odd to be helping him into a wheelchair. I feel like he could get out anytime, stand up, walk away, but of course he can't, not by himself, not yet. I push the chair up the walk, feeling like the neighbors are all watching this, peering through their curtains at the intimacy of it—David in a wheelchair, me pushing. Dana opens the front door. I turn his chair around, pull it up the steps to the porch, up another step into the house, hoping I have the strength, hoping the chair won't thump down and roll onto the front lawn before I can catch it. But it doesn't. Then I lower his chair down the step into the living room and push it to his desk where he'd always sat when he was well. The kids greet him politely, as if he were a guest in our home, and ask him how he is. I escape into the kitchen to make coffee for David—cream and two sugars, the color of pumpkin—and hot tea for me. Then the kids say good-bye. Dana goes to Debbie's and Laura goes to the movies with Wendy. I sit in a chair facing him at the desk. I fiddle with my cup, burn my tongue on the hot tea, make small talk. He smiles, trying to act like everything is normal. Sunlight pours through the living room window, making a warm spot on the carpet. He finishes his coffee and sets the cup down on the desk with his left hand, not trusting his right hand yet. "Bill tells me I can begin to do things I used to do," he says, his head cocked to one side in the way I know so well. I know what's coming.

"That's good," I say.

"He says I can have sex again anytime." I nod, not looking at him. Bill is his doctor. I had just told him two days ago that David and I had been talking about a divorce before the stroke and that I need to leave him. Bill tells me I should tell David now while he has a support system at the rehab center. Sometimes I think that's how I excuse myself for causing David so much pain: Bill told me to do it.

"Want to?" he says, still smiling. I look at him then. I had made my decision the day he had the stroke.

"I can't," I whisper.

He nods, thinking he understands. "You don't have to be careful around me. I'm well enough to have sex." He is still smiling. He's in a wheelchair recovering from a stroke and *he* is taking care of *me*.

"No," I say. "David, I can't do that anymore."

He understands me then, but he doesn't want to. "What do you mean?"

"I can't have sex with you anymore." And then I don't remember if I said, "I want a divorce" or if he asked, "Do you want a divorce?" but we said it out loud—between us the words are said out loud there in that blue living room on that sunny Sunday while neighborhood kids play on their bikes up and down the block and a breeze blows the sheer curtain into the room, a full billow of thin white. He looks at me. I look at him. His mother's Seth Thomas clock ticks on the wall over the fireplace. Everything is the same. Nothing is the same. My husband of 20 years sits in a wheelchair in the living room of the house we bought together and I am his wife, telling him I can't have sex with him anymore, telling him I want a divorce, telling him I am not who he thinks I am, and the sun doesn't stop shining, the clock doesn't stop ticking, and in the next moment we both begin to breathe again.

Afterwards, I can't talk for some time. How can I give voice to what I have done? I don't even have images, and that's how I know I am in trouble. No image, no words, no voice. "It isn't your fault," the silence whispers, but the whisper is far away, and I never do believe it. I know it is my fault, know I have to leave him, would make the same choice over and over again, knowing it would break him, knowing he could commit suicide, as he keeps threatening. I have to take the risk right now or I'll die, crinkle up inside like plastic wrap too close to the hot stove. He has finally come home from the rehab center, walked in the front door with a cane, stiff-legged, but upright, and every night he cries, and every night I go cold inside, lie in our bed not touching him, far enough away that I cannot feel his warmth, but I can feel the bed shake when he cries, berating me for ruining his life, begging me to have some compassion. Every night, like rehearsal for a play, we say our lines, he cries, I do not, and finally he sleeps. I lie in bed looking at the ceiling, listening to his even breathing beside me. I will myself to go to sleep, as if I could control this process that threatens to eat me alive, eat me from the inside where no one will notice at first, starting with the space behind my eyes, eating away at soft tissue, sucking the warm heart out of me, out and away, long drawn-out arcs of me, fading like the contrail of a jet at 30,000 feet. But the air itself holds my shape, forever remembers where I stood in the living room when I said to him, "I don't love you anymore—I can't make myself love you." He mutters in his sleep and I lie very still, a nothing in the bed beside him, so weightless I do not disturb the sheets, do not leave my warmth on the pillow, do not make the shape of my body beneath the comforter. Far away a train whistles, and I let myself breathe again, sigh into sleep that isn't sleep.

I come home from school every day, round the corner onto our street of neat lawns with flower trims and I hope—oh, please—that his car will not be in the drive, that today maybe he'll be off somewhere else, anywhere else, just so I don't have to brace myself once again for his misery. But his car is always there, shining silver-gray in the sunlight, and I park my little car next to his big car, let myself into the house, stand in the entry looking into that quiet suburban void, and I wonder if this time he will not be asleep on our bed, arm thrown across his face as if warding off my blow, and he will not be in the kitchen sipping coffee and staring out into the yard, he will not be in the bathroom, the kids' rooms, the backyard. This time I will find him in the garage—as he'd promised—twisting slowly from the end of a rope tied to a beam he pointed out to me once as the one he had chosen for this final task. Finally, finally, I had had enough, that night we ate out at the restaurant in town. He was sunk in that fog of despair that he wore so well, as if his Korean tailor had measured it to fit and delivered it with his three-piece suit. We were waiting for the waitress when he told me he didn't know how much more he could take. I played with my fork, turning it over and over as he spoke, lining it up with the edge of the napkin.

"Sometimes," he said, "I think I should just get it over with and kill myself."

I had heard this threat late at night when I started sleeping on the sofa and he would call to me from the bedroom, yell at me across the dark rooms, threaten me with his misery. I had heard it over coffee in the morning, louder than Tom Brokaw on the morning news. I had heard it in the car, on the front lawn, whispered, muttered, yelled, and reasoned. I snapped then in that restaurant where divorced daddies ate hot dogs with their kids and young couples drank sodas after a round of miniature golf. "Listen," I hissed at him. "If you're going to kill yourself, then do it, get it over with." The waitress put down my salad with a hard thump and looked at me as if I were the monster at the table. I glared at her and she left. "But quit threatening me with it. If you want to do it, do it. If not, shut up and get on with your life." I picked up my fork and started eating my salad.

I'm ironing: black pants that hang easy over my hips, white rayon shirts. I'm listening to a Jane Siberry song about playing hockey. I'm ironing and I'm crying. David has finally moved out, and I am single, wildly in love with myself, and scared. I push the iron over the black cotton. Laura and Dana come and go, not children anymore, not adults yet, their lives rich with possibility. Tonight I feel like I, too, am a teenager. I am electric with awareness, every encounter a nugget that could be gold. I go out into the world, to grocery stores, restaurants, shopping malls, moving gently in this awareness of myself that feels so strong and so good that it spills over into a deep ache. Tonight, earlier, I write with my friend Carrie. We look at each other across the table until I finally look into my water glass, move it half an inch to the right on the kitchen table. We write. Then we stand and stretch. I put my arms around her, smooth her hair away from her face, look at her. Will we kiss? Her phone rings and I walk away. When we say good-night, we hug and I slide my hand across her back. She lets me out the front door and watches me until I've walked down the street. I walk home in the dark, tall bare trees towering over me, the sky overcast. My footsteps are the only sound on the street. I think about all the women I see in the grocery stores, the shopping malls, the restaurants. I think about possibility. I think about Joanna.

My plane is coming into Phoenix. From my window seat in the back, I can see an oasis of lights in the vast darkness of the desert. I'm flying to Phoenix to make love with my old friend Joanna, a woman who makes love to me on the phone so intensely that I cry, who writes letters that let me in to her mind and her heart, a woman who is not afraid to let me love her. Well, afraid, yes, afraid like I'm afraid, but willing nevertheless. We've been corresponding since she moved to Phoenix two years ago, intensely corresponding for about six weeks— no, less—how could that be? And I know we are going to make love this weekend. We touch down, smooth landing, and roll down the tarmac to the terminal. I'm in the aisle, pulling my coat out of the overhead rack. I'm one of the last to leave the plane.

I feel Joanna out there in the terminal. I say to her on the phone, "When I get off the plane, I want you to be standing where I won't see you right away. I want to look for you and I want you to watch me walk toward you. I want you to stand in one spot and not move." She breathes in my ear on the phone and agrees. "How did you know that's how I wanted to meet you in the airport?" she asks. I don't know. We do that sort of thing, Joanna and I.

I come into the terminal and I can see Joanna across the room. A pillar partially hides her body, but I see her blonde hair and I know it's her. I move around a grandmother greeting her kids and her grandkids. I walk among a family—husband, wife, kids—I move toward Joanna, not taking my eyes off of her. She watches me walk toward her. I had practiced this walk at work, how it would feel to move with her watching me. And then at the airport while I waited for my flight, I had to practice again with the backpack on one shoulder, duffel bag on the other. I don't stumble. I walk toward her deliberately and she stands deliberately against a pillar watching me. Joanna. White shirt, black pants, black boots. My eyes travel her body. Black jacket, sleeves rolled. Bracelets, a row of bracelets on her wrist and up her arm. This registers on my eyes, resonates in my body, bracelets on her wrist. Blonde, tall, standing in the terminal waiting for me, knowing that we're going to make love. I am across the walkway from her, other travelers moving between us. She says my name, soundless, her lips on my name. She is smiling just a little. I pause to cross the flow of travelers on the walkway. "Joanna." I move among the grey pinstripe suits, navy blue dresses, airline uniforms, rolling luggage, children, grandparents, teenagers, I cross their path to stand in front of Joanna, drop my bags to the floor, drop the coat on top of them. Joanna. I slide my arms under her jacket and she hugs my body to hers, full body hug, her voice in my ear moaning.

When we pull into her driveway, I see into the living room: dim lights and a deeply cushioned sofa, a cat curled on a chair, iris on the table. I look up and

Joanna is looking at me with such pleasure that I have to look away. She picks up my suitcase, opens the front door, and bows as I enter. I turn slowly to take in lamplight, cushions, cat, rows and rows of books, Joanna the poet, my friend. She wraps her arms around me from behind and I turn in that circle, ease my hips to her hips, and we dance slowly to Nina Simone, her voice like silk sliding across bare skin. We stop in a pool of light, not breathing, not moving and finally my fierceness rises, there where I feared I would never find it, finally my hands are in her hair, in her long blonde hair, my hands slide down her back, over her ass as I hold her with my eyes, trace the hollow of her throat with one finger down to the curve of her breasts, unbutton her blouse, and she does not move. I trace her bare throat with my hungry mouth, hear her breath quicken, feel her shiver under my hands as the blouse slides down her shoulders and drops to the floor, and then she leans into me, and then my mouth is on her mouth, on her throat, on her breasts, her nipples hard under my tongue. I undress her, she undresses me, and I take her with my hands and my tongue, all of her, and I let her love me. Her hair trails over my breasts, my stomach, my legs, her hair and her tongue and her voice whispering me back to myself, at last.

# She Said We'd Never
# Fall in Love Again
## Deena Metzger

She said 'we'd never fall in love again'   I thought I'll follow
the body   the way I haven't followed it   as a river is
followed   low for lack of rain   still flowing green and
warmer   warmer   for the lack of water   through the
curving banks   or to follow the body like the ocean   the
swell of tissues   the constant reminder of desire   the
fullness from the rub of things against each other   we are
all almost water   and love increases us   whether it exists
or not   waiting for the ocean wave to spill   when the blond
and thoughtless boy plunges his body   into a hole in the
wave   bringing it crashing down   it doesn't happen that
way   the waves persist

She said 'we'll never fall in love again   not any of us'
and I had said the same words years before in Greece   I
had said 'I'll never fall in love again   let the body
take what it can'   making love in the soft Mediterranean
at full noon with a stranger   I thought I'll never fall
in love again   this twitch of the body is the best that
we can manage   the sea breaking over me   our bodies linked
shark on shark in the gentleness of it   And days later on
a ferry from Piraeus to Brindisi I thought   I'll never
fall in love again   and followed a man in unmatched pants
and coat   until he followed me   and pressed himself
against me   making love   no fucking   in a room too
small to love in,   I thought   I'll never   the
waves tossed us against   the rhythm of our own bodies
we rocked against the waves   the sea always wins   it

crests   and you can plunge into the wave breaking it
at its height   or foot   a surfer puncturing the circular
swell like a sleep whale   but the water closes up again
behind the whale and the swell continues   a tense
relentless crest   and the swell of desire in the body
maintaining itself   like the waves crossing the Pacific
sweeping relentlessly toward another coast   the toe rooted in
the underbelly of the sea   moving with the urgent cry of tide

She said 'we'll never fall in love again   not any of us'
plunging   parting the water recklessly without regard
for the wave seeking the camaraderie of molecule and flow
and in the early morning   breaking into the air without
announcement   walking without thought of that which opens
for us   forgetting to ask permission of the fire   before
we split one flare from another   moving the coals and flames
arbitrarily   and without notice   digging the earth   the
spade incising the surface without a 'by your leave'   these
rude gestures   do not serve us to enter the elements

The dreams I had this week   of being parted   sundered
exposed by some Moses issuing orders   to the Red Sea   divided
as the waters are split by a stone thrown into them   the air
torn by bodies which pierce its fabric   my own body unraveling
unseamed   shabby from the discourtesy of entrances and exits
and needing to be mended   to become the seamstress of the
waters   learning from the dolphin   not to make love
in the sea   like divers   rudely in harpoon pursuit of
anything which flashes   not charging against the waves
foam for foam   the dolphin has an agreement with the sea
to seal the nest behind it as it exits

I said 'I'll never fall in love again'   she said 'we'll
never fall in love again   not any of us'   but we followed
the body like a river   green and warm   nudging the
bank   and swimming that afternoon   after the long walk
down to the waters   hidden by the tall grasses   after we
had thought we would never get to the banks   of the green
snake   for everything was high and dry   we found the
water and   swimming cautiously   as if I were a maiden
preparing to fall in love   respectfully asking the river
god to let me enter   I knew we would fall in love again

if we could honor the currents   and enter the sea   as
the   river does   mingling atom for atom   allowing the
body to suck into itself   the new water   the waves building
up in the retreat and the new peak   desire   in the forward
motion   mingling sweet water   into salt.

# Kingdoms Are Clay
## Madelon Sprengnether

Let Rome in Tiber melt, and the wide arch
Of the rang'd empire fall! Here is my space.
Kingdoms are clay; our dungy earth alike
Feeds beast as man; the nobleness of life
Is to do thus
  —Shakespeare, *Antony and Cleopatra*

I want to touch you, to feel the angles of you, the sharp curve of your ribs from the flat plane of your belly. I draw my hand up the inside of your thigh, smooth, turning neatly toward your buttocks. Your skin is fair, but your pubic hair is medium brown and lush. I nose it, brushing your penis with my mouth. I feel pleasantly aroused. Slowly I begin to lick you, and as you come alive I take your penis in my mouth, sucking. The head gets large, and I begin to taste you, faintly acrid and saline, the taste of the sea. The base of your penis is not wide, but the head is engorged and throbbing. You arch toward me and touch my hair, my cheek. I want to tell you that it is all right to come.

One spring in the country, lying in the sun, still heavily dressed in shirt, sweater, coat, I eat sliced apples, salami, cheese with milk, fresh and cold, then, half dozing and warming on the bank of the river, I turn toward the man beside me, wanting to give him pleasure. I put my hand on his crotch and ask if there is anything I can do for him. He lets me arouse him, then tries to direct me, quickening the pace when he needs it. My mouth begins to ache, and I wonder whether I can sustain the movement. My mind drifts and then relocates. We are both unsure of ourselves. Orgasm is a form of concentration, I tell myself, as I begin to kiss him more slowly, as though there were only this moment, this soft skin, this mouth.

Last summer, my first night with a man who is large, fair, with heavy shoulders and a small waist, we turn toward each other from every angle, awkward, urgent, longing. He enters and re-enters me, sucking hard on my nipples when he begins to get soft. He wants me on top and, holding me by my hips, moves me until he comes, his head thrown back, his expression open, abstracted. In the morning he wakes me with an erection and pushes into me from behind. As I climb out of bed, he reaches for me again, and I finish on the floor, on my hands and knees, bracing myself with one arm outstretched against the wall. He tells me he is stunned, that he feels he could become addicted to me. For weeks, we seem to lock into each other at every opportunity, with my back against the refrigerator door, on the dining room floor, with my legs wrapped around him on the stairway. In his dream, one night, he comes into his kitchen to find the freezer blown open and a pack of dogs tearing at the meat and snarling.

One fall, a man I have just met moves into my house for a weekend. We talk tentatively, and I remark that his eyes are beautiful. Why does he hide them behind such heavy glasses? He dresses badly, with no love for his body, as though he were expressing a kind of contempt for it. His touch is soft, but he says it may take him time to become aroused. He has just left another woman and has trouble adjusting to my body. Once inside me though, he is full and alive, and I keep throbbing around him, aligned to him, and I say whatever comes into my mind— that I love him, that I never want him to leave. He tells me he loves me but, more importantly, that he trusts me. In these moments, consciously circumscribed, I believe him. One night, as I enter the bedroom, I imagine briefly that it is Christmas Eve and that the tree is trimmed downstairs and the presents wrapped and arranged for the morning.

When we meet a few months later though, there is difficulty. He tells me how he went to the house of a student to whom he is attracted and how he moved toward her, attracted, but she failed to respond. I don't know why he wants me to know this. In bed, I am easily aroused, but he loses his erection when he begins to enter. I feel vulnerable, rejected, then hurt and finally angry. I am the prisoner of these emotions, unable to help him or myself. He touches a level of longing in me which I do not understand and which frightens him. In a letter he says that he feels my vulnerability in a band of muscles around my chest, that I open too quickly, that I am demanding. We correspond about this failure, and intermittently about our lives. We remain uneasy friends, sometimes gentle toward our divergent aims, sometimes faintly incriminating.

I make love with a musician, who opens slowly, who says he feels confident with me, powerful, as he listens to me talk. I feel able to be foolish, to describe how, if I were a painter, I would paint his lamp, his table, how I would have to look at them for hours to know what it was I wanted to reveal. I talk hesitatingly, searching for the words to express my unformulated thoughts. He doesn't understand exactly, but he is fascinated, patient. I am aware of his gentleness, of the way in which he explores me, as though his penis were the extension of some friendly curiosity. He says I am smooth and soft inside. I say he feels like liquid gold.

For years I have thought that it was only women who have difficulty coming. Now I begin to notice the rhythms of different men, their individual manner of being, of touch, their pulsations and their release. One man, who is jumpy and anxious about foreplay, becomes possessed once he is inside. With him I feel drawn into a whirlwind. I feel a wilderness inside him, as if I were entering some dark forest, animated by brilliant birds. I give myself to his movement, rushing through flame to his fierce destination. He is one of the very few men with whom I spontaneously contract and this, idiosyncratically, in only one position. Slowly, I realize that each man speaks a different dialect, that I must learn each man's physical language, as a complex pattern of inflection, without which the flavor of meaning is entirely lost.

I begin to notice something I would call presence, the degree to which I feel a man inside me to be engaged or absorbed in what he is doing. For some men, I feel I am an envelope, a casing in which they deposit their seed, unaware of me as a particular woman, as though I were the occasion for a private fantasy to which they orchestrate their desire. There is an absolute difference between this kind of sexual expression and making love.

One man I know uses Vaseline Intensive Care lotion to lubricate the movements of his hand or mine on his penis. He also likes to make love in the living room in front of the fire. When I look into his eyes, though, fascinated by their utter blue, it makes him nervous. I also feel him receding from me as he is inside me, a diminishing or paling of need, which makes it difficult for him to reach the moment of climax. He does this by rubbing his penis against the upper part of the opening of my vagina, with a series of short, rapid strokes. He pulls back just before he ejaculates, as though coming and withdrawing were a single motion. He says I am responsive, and he likes that, but he doesn't feel romantic about me, doesn't love me. We offer each other comfort for a while and separate without pain.

Failures of passion, with which I am familiar in myself, baffle me in men. One man, who seems acutely sensitive to my body, to its flavor, its smells, who tells me that if I were to place my hand on his back in the dark that he would know who I was, who loves to massage my feet with his tongue, arousing me more than I ever could have imagined, inexplicably refuses to touch my breasts and labors toward a climax in which I do not participate. I concentrate too heavily on the slippage of his desire, anxious for him, unable to lose myself in the process. When he comes, it is a triumph for him, a pageant at which I am a spectator. I am a kind of cheerleader or fan section at a football game. This man, at another moment, giving me pleasure, soothing my labia with his tongue, butts his head against me, as though he wants to enter me with his whole body or to unlock the doors of birth and to reverse the irrevocable process of expulsion. At other times, he tells me he doesn't just want to make love with me, he wants to build a castle in my cunt. These intricacies excite and confuse me. I long for him without finding a key to his desire.

I have dinner with a friend who is married, who flirts with me, in whose conversation there is the sweet possibility of sex. We collude with the time, with the leisurely summer evening and with each other's anticipation. When he touches my hand, it is a pact, our bodies engaging with their own voices, apart from the light conversation we maintain through our drinks. In bed, he startles me by his difference. He is long and bony, his cock almost too large for me, probing me heavily, deeply. He asks if he is hurting me, and I say no. I am rather surprised by the sensation, don't know quite how to accommodate him, at which angle I am most at ease. I am trying him out. He is afraid of giving me pain, is even apologetic and asks for reassurance. When he comes, he wants to leave, uncomfortable spending the night. He is afraid I will be upset, but I'm not. I am curious, relaxed, interested. I remember the feel of him, and can identify him solely by his cock. Months later, when we seek each other out, he decides that he is responsible for making me come and touches me with the sophistication of the lover of many women. It feels to me, however, like a project, a task which he has set himself, and I don't like being watched. He is annoyed with me, enters me quickly, and moves too briefly for me to enjoy him.

Another man, tense, competitive, ambitious, will allow me to touch him with infinite slowness, inclining to my hand, smoothing himself against me with utter absorption. I am entranced by his sudden acquiescence to pleasure, his pliability, the ease with which our bodies curve to each other. He hesitates about entering me, but builds gradually to an intensity which I find rare. I feel that he is revealing himself, that he is allowing himself to be in me, and I am touching him, caressing him, pulsing to him, answering him, praising him with my smooth and flexible interior. I search for some words to tell him how I am moved and can only repeat his name over and over, as though it were a magical invocation, some kind of litany of pleasure or garland of flowers. We move like dancers, in a series of endlessly varied improvisations. We are composing together a rich music, to which we both respond. We feel its wake in the air long after we have parted.

I spend the night on impulse with a man who tells me that he is enjoying my company and invites me to his apartment to sleep. He is quiet as he smoothes my hair, moving his hands slowly down my shoulders, telling me that I am beautiful and unbuttoning my blouse. Then he shrugs and laughs and suggests that we both undress. In bed, he asks me what I want, easy, unhurried. I feel embarrassed because, never in my experience, has anyone said this to me. I say that I like what he is doing, and he moves down on me, opening me delicately, caressing me carefully. He is a gourmet, relishing my slippery oyster. But I begin to feel removed, wondering what I am doing with this stranger. He stops and asks again what I would like. I say I would like to talk, and we do, about his marriage, about mine, about the shifts and currents of our lives. Gradually, I begin to feel a passion for him, seeking his mouth, his tongue. When he slides into me, I hold him, wanting him in the full length of my canal. He moves without haste, pulling nearly out, rubbing the head of his penis against my opening, before plunging in again. We slip sideways, and then he positions me on top, so that I feel him sharply against my womb. Later, I ask him to come from behind, and he moves more and more urgently, until I feel the rush of darkness that accompanies my flight into pleasure, into the sudden clearing, the drop, the miraculous fall into a bed of flowers. We talk afterwards, randomly, of things we like, places we have lived, decisions we have made and unmade, until our passion resumes, and we move into each other again, this time savoring each flicker of pleasure, each recess of sensation. In the morning, he says he would like to enter me again, and I say yes.

Words, this man tells me, are refinements of gesture, a verbal choreography, from something more physical and ephemeral, like the movements of her teacher's hand in Helen Keller's palm. I think of passion as primary, in the way we describe colors as primary: red, blue, yellow, undiluted, intense. It is as real and unreal as dream. It opens me to a self which is unreachable by any other route. It is not like anything else, but rather the source of likeness, of animation, of all the flora and fauna of language.

There is also, in the body, a gestural memory, ghostly patternings, corresponding to the movements we have made, the pathways we have followed. At this mid-point in my life, my body is birth-patterned, remembering the mould of my daughter's head and limbs, as well as the shape and character of each man's body, each man's penis. Touch, as light and indestructible as flame, like the movement of wind and shadow over grass, both perceptible and imperceptible, is the atmosphere in which we live. To be immersed in this element is to live as easily as a fish, constantly caressed by the translucent medium of the sea.

There are men who have seemed luminous to me, whose presence, in some momentary aspect, is like a shaft of light from a door thrown open to the sun. This seems a form of arrival or annunciation. The expression of one man, when I touched him, would relax, would open, would promise abandon. I was moved by this alone, by the revelation of some kind of fragility, of vulnerability, accompanied by the trust that I would both recognize and protect it, as if I were to discover, walking alone in the woods, the first trillium. Making love with another man, whose energy I had found compelling, I became aware, one evening, of something like reserve, of a kind of gentleness, which had nothing to do with behavior or physical bearing. It was as though I had caught a glimpse of some wildness in him, like that of the birds he hunts or the white waters he canoes.

This man loves my breasts. While other men caress my breasts almost mechanically, in order to arouse me, knowing that this is recommended by the sex manuals, this man finds his own pleasure in mine. With him, I begin to notice a fine network of nerves, sending fiery currents from my nipples to my vulva. Once, as he held both my nipples in his mouth, pushing and pulling them with his tongue, the pulsing inside me suddenly burst into orgasm, surprising me with possibility. Only he touches this hidden route in my body, giving rise to astonished thoughts about the erotic bond between mothers and infants in breast feeding. On another occasion, as I kiss his penis, I touch myself, sliding him into me as I come, and we move in perfect accord to his orgasm, which releases me into another leap of pleasure, which feels like some pure note borne down the long throat of a golden trumpet. We have made love in summer in the fields under a clear country sky, in winter drinking champagne and listening to opera, on pillows borrowed from the sofa and rearranged before the fire. We have made love in brass beds and water beds, on automobile seats and garden seats, in kitchens and basements, on hiking trails and in duck blinds. At the level of desire, he feels to me like something not specifically human, like some principle of nature rather, something feral.

I am intrigued by the kind of knowledge revealed through these brief and intense connections. How much, I wonder, does the body know, that it speaks in accents so unfamiliar and oblique, that we ignore them as either untranslatable or meaningless? If we were compelled to know the world entirely through our senses, as I know the smell of one man's breath, the taste of another's sweat, how much more vulnerable would we be to its ravages, how much more intimate with its essential beauty, its exquisite sweetness?

I am drawn to a man whose eyes seem like a mosaic of blue tile. When I think of him, I think of Giotto's unearthly blue skies and haloes of gold leaf. I think of Peruvian cities, high in the Andes, where the air is sharp and clear, and the grass is long and green. I see in him a landscape of simple lines, suffused with light. Looking into his eyes is like looking into an ocean inlet, with white coral reefs and multicolored fish, or holding a shell to my ear for the distant sound of the sea. He tells me how he loves skin diving, how he spent one day being washed by a current in and out of a small bay in Hawaii, held fast and lazy by alternating bands of water, and how difficult, finally, it was to leave. When we make love for the first time, he talks continuously, his words like light on water, flickering, changing. He is beautiful and elusive, like some brilliantly patterned snake, at first indolent and relaxed, then muscular and taut. I am fascinated, but I cannot speak. What I want to say is scattered, like a spray of water against the sun, or the mythical shower of gold. In the morning, I look at him before he wakes up, fine-boned, strong, thinking of the men I have known with such shoulders, such fair skin. He turns slowly and draws me toward him. He starts talking, as yet half awake, with one arm around me, and comments "Here is my space," and then, as I am scanning my memory for this reference, adds easily, "Kingdoms are clay."

We spend a week together, falling into each other's rhythm: sleeping, waking, working, eating. Making love is part of this pattern. I imagine my nights and days alternating simply like the phases of the moon, from fullness to emptiness to fullness again. Passion, relaxation, energy, movement, touch. I feel the lines of his body through his clothes. Our last day together we drive to a farm house in the country. At the swimming hole, he walks out on a tree which has fallen across the water and sits in the crook of a branch among the newly green leaves. I follow him, and we talk about the places we have lived, California and Vermont. We talk about waterfalls, mountains and sun. Later, in bed, he tells me he wants to watch me come. At first, this makes me nervous, but as I begin to peak, I want him inside me, rippling and throbbing around him. It feels for a while like a change in my field of gravity, like some geological realignment, or shift in the continental plates which lie beneath the sea. As he continues to move in me, I feel that pleasure seduces us into knowledge of one another, of a kind that would allow us, if we were medievals, to hear the music of the spheres. Mortal and particular as we are, our images, like our cries, are earthly, human, but as real and beautiful as the sun outside, the summer day half gone, the space in which we move, easily, together, while Rome in Tiber melts, and pleasure answers pleasure.

# Furnace Creek
## Amber Coverdale Sumrall
### (for Dena)

We enter this opaque landscape together:
contours of bone fluted and weathered.
Moon floating like a sand dollar at midday.
Fallen ghost trees. Slivers of wind.

We find our way without trails or compass:
two women howling their heat,
tracks of crow etched on our faces,
pebbles like loose teeth in the mouth.

Deep in our bodies the last eggs drop
like doomed salmon into shallow creekbeds.
A faint red glow stains the canyon walls.
Vestige of blood. Instinct of membrane.

Coyotes laugh, step in our shadows,
the coral snake shaeds her skin on the sand.
We circle the deert licking old wounds,
underground springs surface as we walk.

Deep in the heart's dark grotto
we hold light and heat,
reflect like mirrors the blinding flash of spirit.
Fragments of desire. Cradles of bone.

All that touches us we take in
and when it is time we let it go,
return to our lives with nothing
we once thought we could never do without.

# Illness. Impotence. Infidelity. Not to Mention Intercourse.
## Excerpts from a Journal

## Nancy Mairs

**Friday, November 2, 1990.** Last night, after stretching, George and I made love on my exercise mat on the family-room floor. I can't think how many years it's been since we did anything quite so indecorous! Risky, since the children float in and out at will, but it was late and no one came to the open back door to discover us, bare-bottomed, humping and grunting and laughing, though I suppose our glee might have carried to the boys next door or the young couple and their eight dogs across the alley. How can he be wasting away, now, when we're happier than I ever dreamed we'd be? What good does it do for him to try to eat when he can't hang onto anything long enough to absorb any nourishment?

**Tuesday, November 6.** I've been terrifically hot since our encounter on the exercise mat—more so than George is up to. He's very sweet about kissing and stroking, but what I really want from him is penetration, and so I feel disappointed and also guilty, making him aware of his impotence as he wouldn't be if I were my usual compliant but cool self.

**Wednesday, November 7.** What George's illness represents for me, I see, is an infidelity: I am as jealous of it as I would be of another, more compelling, woman.

**Thursday, November 8.** Last night he initiated sex, to no avail for the third straight time. The night before, I'd stayed up late to avoid such a possibility, but last night I was tired and went to bed with him. Impotence has been so infrequently a problem that I figured as long as he was interested, he'd be fine. I had to get up last night and prowl around, and he must have waked early, as he does when he's worried, because I did, too. I'm feeling tired and edgy, but I keep telling myself that as long as I take my medication, I'll be all right.

**Sunday, November 11.** Damn. Damn. Damn. Damn. Another attempt, another failure: four in a row. I should have known better. I'd planned to stay up and read for a while after he went to bed, but then I thought, well, what if he *is* up to it and I'm not there? And indeed he embraced me passionately and I got very eager, but...I focus too much on penetration, I know, but damn it that's what I want from him. The rest I can take care of myself, certainly more efficiently and often more effectively.

Tonight I told him a little of what I've been feeling: fear that I'm somehow to blame but also—so much more acute and dreadful—that something is wrong with him. Yes, he says, the rectal discomfort may be to blame. And what the hell is causing that, anyway? Maybe after Tuesday's bowel x-ray we'll have a better idea.

God, I'm so sad. We went with Anne and Eric this weekend down to Rocky Point for Sean and Diana's wedding. Many pleasant moments. But I so wanted to make love—something I would have taken for granted in such a setting before—and instead he slept and I prowled. We may have had intercourse for the last time, and I didn't even bid it a proper goodbye.

**Tuesday, November 13.** Now he's sound asleep and I'm hoping the amitriptyline will kick in. I don't want to lie rigid beside his inert form and think about his limp cock, which seems to loom larger in my consciousness than anything else. The other day I connected this depression with the one I felt over Richard, but I didn't quite get to the point of seeing that the abandonment in both cases is *sexual*. "I no longer want to sleep with you," Richard said—and that's just what George's limp cock is saying now—and this rejection seems the deadliest.

**Wednesday, November 14.** As George wastes, I bloat, too weak to get any exercise anymore and unable to eat small enough portions to prevent weight gain. I'm seized by loathing for the roll of fat around my waist, my wrinkled sagging buttocks, my protruding belly. I'm also smoking more, even though I'm convinced that he no longer desires me not just because my body has grown disgusting but because I reek of cigarettes. But I can't bear the thought of going without them. I can hardly get through each day as it is. I say to myself that I'll shower and change clothes and use mouthwash more often, force myself outside again for every cigarette, but who am I kidding? The stench would cling, I'm sure. Am I really willing to give up sex for cigarettes? Seems like it.

**Monday, November 19.** The bowel x-ray revealed no problems—a sort of relief—and yet not, since there clearly *is* a problem and I, for one, would feel less distraught if it had an identity, a name, something that would enable me to define my relationship to it. When I talked to Dr. Jackson on Friday, he sounded puzzled and alarmed, especially when I told him about the impotence, and suggested a recurrence of melanoma either in the prostate area or in the spine. So first thing this morning we went to a urologist, who says that the prostate feels normal—another sort of relief. He prescribed a medication for the impotence, which may help in a couple of weeks, and that would be good, since a lot of my grief has focused on sexual loss.

Friday night we did achieve what might pass for intercourse, though nothing like what we're used to. George's cock is very large when fully erect, filling me and, just before ejaculation, pressing hard against the walls of my vagina—a sweet moment, sweeter than any orgasm—no other sensation substitutes. The thought that I may never feel it again fills me with despair. Saturday night we made love by candlelight, rubbing each other with baby oil, pleasurable but not fulfilling. No matter how I reason with myself, I read his limp cock as a reproach. Otherwise it's a symptom, which seems even worse. To increase the contact between us, I've been sleeping naked, as I haven't done in years, but as the weather turns cold, I don't suppose I'll be able to go on. I've always liked the idea of sleeping naked, but never the feeling.

**Wednesday, November 21.** Sometimes we lie in bed naked in each other's arms, and I run my hands down his back, cup them over his buttocks, kiss his nipples—actions that would once have raised and swelled his cock just to think of—and when he puts my hand on it, it seems to shrink, to withdraw, and my heart shrinks with it in pain and guilt and grief. Oh, I wish grief were something that could be *accomplished*, like some task, however strenuous, and not this prolonged hemorrhage of the spirit.

**Tuesday, November 27.** I'm old enough to know that the kind of pain I feel now can't possibly last, or it would kill me, and it doesn't. I wish that it had ten years ago. But it didn't, and now it's too late. To be spared *this* pain, anyway.

Last night George told me that he had an affair with an unidentified woman for two years. *Two years.* That seems to have struck me hardest of all: the durability. No fling, no passing fancy, but a sustained commitment to love another woman. Like me, he characterized her: smart, small-breasted! But not me. Not me at all. For two years, maybe—or more? He's hazy on dates. He ended it, he claims, something to do with his father's death, something to do with cancer. Nothing to do with me. For two years he lied to me consciously, purposefully, steadily. And ever since, really, in his silence.

I need to know who she is, but I don't think he'll ever tell me that. He still loves her. He is, I suppose, still loyal to her in a way that he hasn't been to me for many years. Not one of my friends, he says. Someone he's known a long time, long before she "seduced" him...I'm the one he's still with, anyway, the one who may get to help him die. Unless I can do it first.

I think of them together. Of her fingers unbuttoning his shirt, unzipping his trousers, holding his cock, guiding it into her. Of his mouth on her nipples, his sighs, the way his eyes shut and screw up as his cock swells and then spurts and he shouts and beats the pillow with his fist. Lying face to face (no smoker she, her breath always sweet), gazing, smiling. Not once. Not an isolated irresponsible uncontrollable burst of passion. Over and over again. For years.

**Sunday, December 2.** This morning while dressing I found myself rocking and moaning in grief—not over the affair but of the end of intercourse—and finally, when George came in an hour later, I was actually sobbing, real tears at last.

**Wednesday, December 5.** What, I begged him to tell me last night, could she provide him that I can't? That health and athleticism he acknowledged the first night we talked? Did she go down on him more gracefully, mount him, let him fuck her in the ass (no hemorrhoids for such a woman, I'm sure)? No, not sex, he insists. She was "too teeny" for sex to be very satisfying, even after the first time, when she "grabbed him by the pool" at her home and they tried it there but it "didn't work," even later with the help of pillows and whatever. "Well, you may not know this, but you're very large," say I, the woman with what one gynecologist labeled the world's longest vagina. "But I can think of a couple of guys I could fix her up with!" And he laughs, for the first time.

He clutches me sometimes, when he's weeping, and he tells me over and over that he loves me, but he doesn't touch or kiss me with passion any more. The medication the urologist prescribed should have worked by now if it was going to. I suppose we'll live together now as brother and sister. But, oh, I don't want to!

**Thursday, December 6.** Dr. Jackson says that the CAT scan shows a 6-cm mass in the left pelvis, perhaps attached to a loop of the small intestine. Possibly a lymphoma but more likely melanoma; if so, it could travel from the shoulder only via the bloodstream and so "seeds" of it must be everywhere. Tomorrow morning George will have a barium x-ray of the small intestine, and then Jackson will decide about surgery, followed by some sort of chemotherapy.

No surprise, of course, but horrible, horrible shock nonetheless. And outrage. What, for God's sake, is enough? Isn't multiple sclerosis enough? Isn't depression enough? Isn't adultery enough? Must there be cancer, too?

**Monday, December 10.** Yesterday morning George and Mum went shopping. In the afternoon Sean came by to take pictures of George and me. He'd been wanting to for a while, and now seemed the perfect time, before George grows any thinner and paler. His face looks suddenly old, the lines deeper, pouches under the eyes; and he's lost so much weight that the skin hangs in folds below his buttocks. He's being eaten faster than he can eat.

We make love a lot. No intercourse, of course—at the very mention his cock wilts and shrinks—but he seems to like having it rubbed with oil and sucked, even though he no longer ejaculates. He likes having his nipples rubbed and sucked, too, and I nurse at them with the erotic abandon of infancy. I'm growing freer in lovemaking—enjoy looking at him, so we keep a candle burning now—and so his impotence has been ironically enriching.

**Wednesday, December 12.** I feel so wretched that I might be the one dying.

My stomach churns with grief and too many cigarettes, my mouth tastes foul, I can't draw a full breath. I think back yearningly to the days—as recently as this summer—when I took George's energetic presence for granted, confident that he'd take care of me—bring me cokes and the *New York Times*, cut my toenails, pay our bills, fix the cooler, drive me wherever I needed to go—for the rest of my life. I even fantasized that a treatment for multiple sclerosis would be found so that life could be prolonged. What a ninny.

I've lost that man: the faithful, healthy, passionate husband of that edenic past, the one who'd drive his mouth down hard on mine, roll on top of me, plunge into me...

**Monday, December 17.** I can't help thinking, as I keep a bedside vigil, fending off visitors and listening to them sing his praises, how she got the good years and left me with this. She got him when he was still frisky—got all that lolling around the pool, drinking beers, good sex. I could still walk some in those days. I could still have a good time when I had anybody to have a good time with. Now I'm nearly helpless, and he's bailing out on me. "I'm sorry to add to your suffering," he just said to me sarcastically. And all I could say was, "You can't possibly add to my suffering, so don't worry about it."

I'm haunted by those wasted years. He kept it up with her until he thought the cancer had come back a second time. He kept his secret pact with her until he thought he was going to die. Now, "I'm sorry," he says over and over. I'm all yours, he's telling me. Here's my shriveled cock, my withered flanks, my cancerous guts. All for you, my darling. She wasn't so great in bed, he tells me. But maybe she'd be terrific at the bedside. Let's call her up and ask her to come over. She can listen to the pious visitors singing the praises of this perfect husband, this perfect father.

**Tuesday, December 25.** Part of my problem is probably that I'm having a period of sorts after about three months. They've been erratic since June, so menopause really seems to be setting in. I'm relieved, since my hands are getting too weak to handle the paraphernalia.

**Monday, January 7, 1991.** I've been trying to pretend that the events of the past few months haven't altered my feelings for George, but in fact they have. I still love him, but it's a disappointed love.

Perhaps the change began as soon as he started mentioning vague physical sensations. Complaint was so unlike him. But I seem to date it from that stony moment in a hotel bed in Massachusetts when he told me he'd heard what I had to say before and was sick of it. We'd just had sex, and I was feeling close enough to him to share the distress I've always felt when he behaves badly and then blames me for eliciting his bad behavior. Ironically, the issue was illness, although only a cold; he'd been particularly nasty and then accused me, as usual, of having trouble dealing with his being sick. As I certainly do—and no wonder, when I know what nastiness awaits me! But it took me a long time to recognize *his* responsibility in the matter, and he's trained me so well in self-blame that I really do have to discover it over and over.

It wasn't awfully long after that sudden chill—as though I had been shot off through the icy vacuum of space, totally out of the sphere of his warmth and light—that his impotence began. Is there a relationship here? Probably not. But the impotence has certainly contributed to my change of heart. I was accustomed to being desired. When I masturbate, I realize that, without penetration, he's no longer any use to me. True, he can make love to me without intercourse, but that only seems to make me feel sad and isolated afterward.

**Friday, January 18.** I'll go along fine for a few days—fussing over his food, telling him I love him, rubbing his back and even his wizened cock if he wants— and then suddenly, lying beside him as he snorts and twitches (drugged now or he doesn't sleep), I feel like throwing up. What a bastard he is, manipulating me all those years so that he could have his lover while he was healthy enough to enjoy her and returning to his nursey-wife now that he's too weak and impotent to satisfy a lover.

**Wednesday, January 23, 1991.** Back to Thomas-Davis this morning. God, am I sick of that place. First to the urologist, who prescribed an antibiotic in case the catheterization had caused prostatitis and something to increase urinary retention. It seems as though George needs one drug after another in order to function halfway normally. For impotence he could offer a penile implant, which would require more surgery, a self-injection before intercourse, or a suction device that removes air from the penis, allowing it to fill with blood and maintaining the erection with an elastic ring. George opted for the last, which is on order. I find the idea both ridiculous and repellent.

**Monday, February 25.** Lying in bed this morning, listening to George splash about in the bathroom, I was stabbed by the realization that some morning I'm going to wake up and know that I will never see or speak with him again, not that day, not ever. The thought wasn't new, but the clarity and poignancy were. This is really happening. George is really dying of cancer. Right now. If only he were running off with another woman, not with death, then even though I'd feel jealous, betrayed, heartbroken, abandoned, I'd know he still existed somewhere and I could hope that chance—however slim—might bring us together again. But *never*? How can I possibly deal with that?

**Wednesday, March 6, 1991.** Yesterday Cynthia told me something that rather charmed me. I was saying how depressed I feel about never having sexual intercourse again, since George's impotence persists, and after his death, even if I were a healthy woman, I could probably never hope to attract a sexual partner. (What's that statistic? Something like, after thirty a woman stands a greater chance of getting kidnapped by terrorists than she does of getting married. So how likely is a fifty-year-old to get laid?) Anyway, Cynthia said that a writer who taught here a while back, a close friend of hers though I hardly knew him, told her that he was so attracted to me that he kept his distance for fear of falling wildly in love! Of course, that was back when I was still walking and otherwise leading a pretty normal, if grueling, life. And if he had gotten to know me, he might well have found me as impossible to love as a good many others have. But I thought it sweet of her to offer that testimony to my attractiveness now that all my sense of it has vanished.

Friday, March 29. I've just been reading an old journal—the big black one Avram gave me twenty years ago—searching the years George first knew Sandra for evidence that he was already having an affair with her. All I found was ample evidence of my own affairs, consummated and unconsummated. Ten years of periodic eruptions of passionate longing for one man or woman after another: Avram, someone named Rick whom I don't even remember, Bruce (whose name appears only once, the brief affair having occurred during one of my many silent spells), Saul, Rob, Donald, Jon, Ramona, Jonas, Richard. And then blessed peace! Well, no, my life hasn't been exactly peaceful for the past ten years, but at least it hasn't been infected and sapped by sexual obsessions as it once was.

You'd think that reviewing my own faithlessness in this way would ease my anger at George for his, which seems really much milder and more wholesome, but it doesn't at all. My faithlessness did not merit George's faithlessness. Nor his, mine. The two are absolutely separate. Unconscionable both, but unconnected. And so my guilt, which is genuine, does not soften my anger, which is also genuine. It may, however, influence my forgiveness. It is unquestionably easier to forgive what one understands.

Anger is so tiresome, though. I'm mad at George about Sandra and even madder at him for having cancer and being impotent so that I'm always scared and sad. I'm mad at myself for having MS, which sucks up my energy so that I never get any decent work done. I'm mad at myself for continuing to eat even though I'm too weak to burn up calories any more so that I feel bloated and stupid. I'm mad that I didn't get a Guggenheim. I'm mad that my studio is a mess, filthy and cluttered, and I haven't the strength to clean it, and that the little heater isn't powerful enough to make it comfortable. I'm mad at the weather, which has been wet and unseasonably cold. I'm mad at the boys next door who have been blaring rock music and shouting at one another over it for hours. I'm mad at myself for letting all this shit get me down.

Tuesday, April 23. "So we've stopped being lovers," I pointed out to George as we sipped our iced tea, "and have become instead close friends, or siblings, occasionally mother and son." I could hear the disappointment in my own voice, but he seemed not to notice. All the same, I found myself trying to explain. "It's just that I seem to have taken my identity from being desired by you," I said to him. "And now I don't know how to organize myself. But I'll figure it out." Why do I always reassure him that whatever he's doing to me this time isn't really too much for me to bear? "I hope," I added, too softly for him to hear. I suppose I wanted, again, protestation, denial—*oh, but I do still desire you*—but all he said was, "Yes, you will." Why does he always accept my reassurances at face value? It doesn't occur to him that he might this time be hurting me beyond recovery. He's dying, for Christ's sake. That I may not survive.

**Tuesday, May 7.** Chemo starts again tomorrow, and again I dread it—having George retreat way beyond my reach. Why do I have the feeling he isn't doing well? He looks a little pale to me, seems forgetful, preoccupied, maybe lethargic—depressed, Anne thought this morning. Yet he's eating well and keeping active. Yesterday he was passionate, and last night we made love—no intercourse or ejaculation—but he was clearly eager and aroused. So maybe the signs I see reflect my own hysteria rather than his health. But no, he is changed and changing. I have to accept that—let it happen—without tormenting myself about the nature of the outcome, which I know, or the timing, which I don't.

**Wednesday, May 8.** No chemo after all—George's platelet count was much too low. And so my intuition was correct. We'll have to wait a couple of weeks and try again, putting it uncomfortably close to the England trip. Damn, I hope we don't lose that—dreaming of it has helped keep us going. This morning we also saw Orton and agreed to try the vacuum pump, which he'll order for us and maybe have by Friday. If so, with no chemo, we'll have the weekend for experimenting. I don't feel repelled by the idea as I once did. All these months of caring for and exploring George's body—gazing at it, stroking it with oil, mopping up its excreta—have made me more at home with it. And then, in the face of all those bad I's (Illness, Impotence, Infidelity), I yearn for the good I (Intercourse!), however we have to come by it.

**Monday, May 13.** George picked up the pump, which hadn't been ready Friday, so we'll give that a try some time. I seem to be in a nonlibidinous phase—I feel discouraged by the intransigence of the impotence and doubtful that the pump will work—maybe I'm just nervous. We haven't had intercourse for more than six months now, and George said the other day that he was having difficulty sustaining erections even before that—I feel ashamed that I didn't notice. Anyway, six months strikes me as pretty damned permanent. I wonder how common impotence is—I've never heard anyone refer to it, the way they might to their headaches or their bunions.

**Wednesday, June 19.** I can't achieve an orgasm any more, even masturbating, though I like the feel of his fingers and tongue on me. I have to fake desire all the time now, have to fake pleasure too, when all I really feel is disappointment and, in its wake, rage. I suppose that I'll feel sad and regretful that I wasted some of our precious time together on fury, but there doesn't seem to be any way around it, just to wait it out, knowing that it will pass, that I'll grow fond again, probably let him touch me again, even pretend to like it, until one day the whole cycle is cut off forever and I'm left alone all right with only my guilt and grief.

**Thursday, August 1.** George's impotence contributes, I think, to the sense that my life—in any terms that would enable an ordinary person to recognize it as a life—has ended and what I'm in now is a kind of trancelike afterlife. My body no longer functions as a source of pleasure. The simplest actions (keeping upright in my chair and typing this) drain me of energy and generally leave me frightened or furious or both.

**Wednesday, August 21.** It's George who doesn't want out. Why should he get melanoma? The interferon he's been taking for the past couple of months is destroying platelets and damaging liver function, so he'll have to stop for at least two weeks. As a comfort, if these cells are being destroyed, the bad ones may be also, Ralph says. But the truth is that keeping him alive means also killing him. He's an increasingly faded version of himself. I want to scream in mourning for our lost life. Sometimes I just wish the whole thing were over. The dread is so exhausting. And the grief. When it is, will I find the courage to follow him? A new book, *Final Exit*, published by the Hemlock Society is getting a lot of attention. I must get a copy.

**Friday, September 13.** INTERCOURSE! This morning George went over to Thomas-Davis and Dr. Orton injected some substance (Prostin, I think) into his penis. Then he came home and we fell into bed. Ooh it was lovely, just as lovely as I remembered. I could do it all day and all night. (Actually, I'm so weak now that I couldn't keep at it anything like so long.) Next week Orton will teach George to inject himself, and then maybe we can do it again. But even if we can't, at least we've done it once more.

**Tuesday, December 10.** Last night, preoccupied with gloomy thoughts, I was struggling out of my clothes when George showed up at my bedside with a "surprise." He'd slipped into his bathroom and given himself an injection without telling me. "What would you have done," I teased him this morning, "if I'd said I had a headache?" But of course I didn't say any such thing.

# I Miss Noisy Sex
## June Hudson

The loud groaning kind
Where sheets get tangled,
Lips chapped.

Messy sex
Like we used to have
When I wore jeans so tight
I couldn't sit down and
Danced barely balanced
In high heel shoes,

While whispering words
To favorite songs played loud,
Feeling the beat through
Our moving bodies held close.

Who turned the volume down?

# Postage Stamps
## Linda Norlander

I'm not sure what compelled me to book a bachelorette cabin on the *S/V Moira's Fate*, sailing from St. Maarten to Tortola. Perhaps it was the discovery that my husband Dougie was staying up into the early morning hours to write stories with lines like, "He thrust his throbbing member inside her wet, ruby red lips."

Perhaps it was son Jason's acerbic comment at breakfast that his sixteen-year-old girlfriend was "late." He said it in such a way to imply that somehow this was my fault.

Or maybe it had to do with being forty-five, sagging in the middle, and looking at a life filled with nothing more than fetching for a husband, a son, and a plodding boss.

The plane landed at Julianna Airport in St. Maarten at dusk. Already I felt guilty about leaving my family behind. While I waited for customs in the hot, sultry air, little bugs chewed on my ankles. I scratched and slapped, overcome with a lethargic kind of despondency. My vacation would be no vacation at all, just another chapter in the dull life of a nurse who has worked for a mumbling gynecologist for fifteen years, a mother who has raised a petulant, spoiled son, and a wife who hasn't had sex in two years.

The woman ahead of me smoked a cigarette to the very end, pulling on it so hard her cheeks caved in. When she was done, she flicked the butt onto the tarmac and muttered, "Goddamn customs. No wonder this country is so poor. Lazy sons of bitches."

"You've been here before?" I asked.

"I come here to gamble." Her complexion was of the grainy quality of someone who smoked, drank, and took in too much sun. She looked fifty and could have been thirty. Still, men appraised her as they lounged in the line.

My complexion, on the other hand, had the paleness of one who has spent too many hours in an examination room listening to a doctor talk to vaginas. No one paid any attention to me.

"I've never been out of Minnesota before," I remarked.

She looked at me as if I carried all my possessions in a shopping cart.

"You see," I continued as she stared, "I'm agoraphobic. I haven't been out of my living room for the past thirteen years."

"Oh?" She moved away.

The man in front of me turned around and grinned. He wore a beige-colored over-sized sport jacket and blue jeans. With his dark, smooth complexion, he could have been Jason's age.

"God, it's nice to be rid of that lady. Her smoke was getting into my eyes." Dark, glistening hair curled around his forehead like a halo.

I smiled at him. "I'm not really agoraphobic. I'm just dull."

"My father is captain of *Moira's Fate*. Do you want to share a cab to the dock?" He spoke with a slightly foreign accent—perhaps French.

"How did you know I was going on *Moira's Fate* ?"

He pointed at the brochure sticking out of my purse. "Don't believe what you read. The free rum swizzles are watered down, and the fresh fish come from a can."

"Great." Another reason I should have stayed home.

"My name is Cyrus." He extended his hand.

"I'm Alice."

He held my hand a long time. The warmth of his fingers shot straight to my heart. I found I was breathing through my mouth and staring at him.

"How old are you?" I didn't want to drop his hand, and I didn't want to know that he was seventeen.

His eyes sparkled. "Twenty-five."

He let go, turned, and stretched up on tiptoes to look for the head of the line. When he was finished, he hitched up close to me, close enough so I could smell the mintiness of his breath, and whispered, "See that man just ahead of us in the pink shirt?"

I nodded. The man was distinctive because of the wave of silver gray hair on his head, and because he was thin and close to seven feet tall.

"He's a communist revolutionary."

I burst out laughing. "He's a basketball player, Cyrus."

Cyrus shook his head. "No. I know him. His name is Che."

I shrugged. "Okay. And today, I'm twenty-five."

Cyrus again moved in close to me, his hazel eyes changing from brown to green. "I knew that."

My cheeks flushed, and I was overcome by shame. I should have been home, teaching Jason about birth control, instead of standing languidly next to this boy wondering what he would look like with his clothes off.

My bachelorette roommate in cabin 116 grasped my hand with a firm, warm handshake.

"My name is Gerianne. Glad to meet you. I'm a Lutheran minister on vacation."

Gerianne was an enormous woman who seemed unapologetic about either her size or her occupation. As soon as the bags arrived, she tugged herself into a pair of hot pink shorts, threw off her bra, and slipped a huge t-shirt on which said *Guess*. She danced out into the night. I crawled into bed for a dyspeptic sleep.

The next day after lunch, Gerianne grabbed me firmly by the elbow and ushered me to the top deck. The brightness of the sun whitewashed the entire area. Passengers lounged, soaking up the heat, oblivious to the crash of the ship through the swell. The canvas sails sang as the wind rushed by them. Gerianne sat me down next to her on a bench.

"I am content," she burped. "Nothing like a vacation away from everyone you know to really throw off those working blues."

"I've never stopped working long enough to throw off the blues." I replied. Or my bra for that matter.

"Well, God never said you couldn't have fun in this life." Gerianne smiled sleepily at me. Folding her arms, she tucked her three chins to her chest. In a moment, she dozed with a peaceful smile on her lips.

I tilted my head back and watched the rippling of the sails overhead. The constant beat of the music from the middle deck thumped in my head. I was surrounded by the smell of the sea and suntan lotion. Behind me, I heard the lyrical patois of the black crew bantering back and forth. I turned my head to see Zack, the highest ranking of the native crew pulling at one of the ropes that anchored the sail. His arm muscles bunched and glistened in the heat.

Something twisted inside me, a tingling feeling that I had long ago put away on a shelf. I felt a pressure in my chest and an inner warmth that spread all the way down my thighs. Zack saw me watching and winked slowly, holding his gaze on me long enough so I looked over my shoulder to see who he was really watching. No one was behind me. The tingling feeling crashed off its shelf, and I almost crashed off the bench. Gerianne snored gently beside me.

Watching Zack, a blush creeping up my cheeks, my head began to spin. When it felt like it was careening out of control, I stopped it abruptly by picturing the unused roll of postage stamps hidden at home in my top drawer with my support hose. The tingling stopped and my insides turned back to stone. I looked away from Zack and thought about the postage stamps.

When Dougie turned forty-two, he had a long, loud, and pitiful crisis. For six months he moped around the house reminding me that his life was half over and he'd never been successful at anything. My general feeling at the time was that he didn't have a prayer of doing any better in his second half if he didn't stop whining.

Being a good wife, and a good provider, though, I sympathized, and got a second job on weekends to pay for his therapy. During the worst of his pitiful period, he gave up sex. I didn't push him.

One day, he came home from group, announced that he was better and that he had a five-year plan for his life. I was overjoyed that he was better because in the meantime, the celibacy had reduced me to drooling over a pair of humping dogs across the street.

Perhaps I jumped poor Dougie too quickly that day. Perhaps I showered him with too much affection. Perhaps I should have asked Dougie first, but I was desperate. I wrestled him into the bedroom, locked the door, and all but threw him on the bed. Jason was out for the evening so I figured on hours of uninterrupted pleasure. At the time, I would have settled for five minutes of uninterrupted pleasure.

Dougie allowed himself to be pushed into bed, unclothed, and handled as if he were a rag doll. After a few minutes of trying to arouse him, I began to feel confused. What was wrong?

Then Dougie did the worst possible thing to me—he burst out in tears. "I'm no good, Alice—just no good."

Three weeks later, I tried again, this time with more tenderness and less velocity. The result was the same. I left the bedroom feeling defeated and unfulfilled. At least he didn't cry.

"I just need time."

After a few more months of celibacy, I noted that during ovulation time, when my hormones cried out, my hands broke out in a rash, and I spent a lot of time accidentally brushing against old Dr. Kidley. I knew I'd stepped over the edge when I fantasized about Dr. Kidley and me on one of his exam tables.

A urology clinic was located down the hall from Dr. Kidley. I knew the nurse, a sprightly gray-haired lady with the figure of a teenager. I caught her at coffee one morning.

"Does Dr. Ulna have to deal with men who...who have trouble in the sex department?" I blushed, embarrassed that I couldn't say "impotent" to her.

"You mean the ones whose cocks don't crow anymore?" Her eyes twinkled. I choked on my coffee.

"What...what does he do for them?"

She smiled and poured herself another half cup of the vile stuff that passed for decaffeinated. "He tells them to go home and do the postage stamp test."

"What?"

"Over ninety percent of impotency is mental, not physical. If it is in the head, during sleep the man will naturally get an erection. If he doesn't, it's a physiological problem. So he sends them to the post office for a roll of stamps, tells them to paste them around the penis before going to bed. If the roll is broken in the morning it means they had an erection. If not..."

"Oh."

I walked into the post office at noon feeling like a fourteen-year-old looking for condoms. When I purchased my roll of one-cent stamps—Dougie wasn't worth more expensive ones—I was sure everyone was watching.

That night, I told Dougie about the plan. His jaw dropped as I explained.

"You want me to put stamps *there*?"

It seemed less silly when Barbara had explained it. I nodded earnestly.

"Damn it, Alice! There's nothing wrong with me. I'm not the problem. You are."

"Me?"

"How can I feel turned on when you work all the time? You're not home when I need you. You don't take care of yourself, and you sleep with your mouth open..."

I didn't know that.

"...and I can't stand those wool socks you wear to bed. Furthermore, when you look at me like that, you remind me of my mother."

He stormed out of the house leaving me with a pretty useless roll of one-cent stamps. I stared at them for a long time trying to figure out how I could get them on him without him noticing. After thirty minutes of hard concentration, I burst into tears, tucked away the stamps, and wondered how long I could go without sex before my insides would dry up.

I didn't approach him again because I was afraid he'd say more nasty things about me like I smelled bad, was a lousy cook, and needed a haircut.

Dougie never once said he was sorry.

Watching Zack, comfortable in his masculinity, I wondered why I stuck with Dougie. I also wondered if Dougie had another woman.

"No," I said out loud. "Who would want him?"

Gerianne suddenly popped awake and pointed out that my thighs were turning scarlet.

"You need sunscreen or you'll spend the rest of this cruise in bed."

As I meandered through the lounging bodies on deck, I decided that I didn't need sunscreen as much as I needed sex. I walked by a couple who could have come out of a cartoon strip. The man had a Neanderthal face reminiscent of Fred Flintstone, and short, bandy legs. He lounged in a skimpy bikini swimsuit made out of green camouflage material. His female companion wore a matching bikini that covered very little of her skinny body. They were staring at each other with wet, vapid eyes.

I wanted to rip Neanderthal man away from his woman and force him into my cabin. I must have been staring because he looked at me bleary-eyed from too much morning gin, and winked. His front teeth were chipped. I didn't care.

I headed straight for the bar.

After a watered-down rum swizzle, I switched to beer, drinking two in rapid succession. Around me, people danced to the music, their bodies swaying and blending. On the deck, Gerianne bumped and twirled, her loose breasts like soft butter against the knit fabric of her shirt.

"Go for it, Gerianne," I said to myself, wishing I could dance. Instead, I ordered another beer. When I looked back, Gerianne was gone, replaced by a rangy, flat-chested girl. I was close to falling off the stool when Zack passed by. I took a deep breath, savoring his wake, the smell of sweat mingled with spice. His calf muscles, dark and solid, tightened with each step. I drank another beer.

The rocking of the ship was making me dizzy. It was time to go back to my bachelorette cabin and pass out.

As I slipped off the bar stool, Cyrus caught my arm.

"Come down below. I'll show you how the crew has to live around here."

"I think I'm going to fall on my face," I replied.

He steadied me as I swayed to and fro, gently nudging me toward the stairs. For such a skinny fellow, he had a steel grip. I bumped against him.

"Pardon me."

He kept me close, talking about mutiny. "I could be captain and you could be first mate."

I shook my head, "No. You can be captain and I can be passed out."

Below, we passed through an oak paneled corridor to a steel door painted with a sign, "No Passengers Beyond This Door."

Cyrus grasped the door handle and pushed it open.

"I can't go in there," I protested, resisting as he pulled my arm. "I'm a passenger."

"Nonsense. Don't you ever break rules?"

I shook my head and thought about it. I never walked when it said, "Don't Walk," never cheated on income taxes, and never stole toilet paper from Dr. Kidley's office.

God, what a life.

The door clanked behind us. Pipes lined the top and sides of the narrow hallway, rattling and hissing as they fed steam to the generators and water to the cabins. Underlying the noise of the pipes was a primal, rhythmic thumping of the engines, and an overpowering smell of diesel fuel.

Cyrus led me through the plumber's jungle, ducking under the low hanging pipes. I stayed close to him.

"Here," he whispered close to my ear, as we stopped by an oval-shaped door. "The black crew is crammed into little rooms like this one. The captain and his white boys get cabins up front. It's disgusting."

He unlatched the heavy steel door and pushed it open. Immediately, I smelled the warm humidity of human bodies. Sweat, perfume, suntan lotion.

I squinted into the dark little room, only big enough for a small bunk and a tiny closet. Something large and white moved on the bed. I stared for the longest time, trying to make sense of the picture as my eyes adjusted to the light coming in from the hallway.

The white mound was moving rhythmically back and forth while something dark on top of it grunted in time to the movement.

I blinked, my mouth open, as Gerianne and Zack coupled in a slow, lazy cadence. What would her congregation think about this?

I wanted to say, "Cyrus, let's get out of here," but my tongue became tangled. Instead of saying anything reasonable, I gasped, "Sex." It came out, "Thex."

Something inside me crumbled as the sounds of the engines, and the pipes, and the coupling overtook me. My legs turned rubbery. I couldn't take my eyes off the bed. The blood rushed to my head, thrashing against my temples.

Staggering, I fell against Cyrus, throwing my arms around his waist, desperately hoping he could hold me up.

"Sex," I choked, as we toppled together over the threshold onto the gritty metal floor of the cabin.

Gerianne's moan grew louder as Zack's hips pumped back and forth. I groped at Cyrus as the last vestiges of control left me. Without warning, I began pulling at his clothes, and smothering his smooth face with kisses.

"Sex," I wailed. Thunder crashed inside my head, and a "Don't Walk" sign flashed in angry red behind my eyelids.

Suddenly, Cyrus came alive beneath me. With effort, he pushed me away. I rolled to his side, onto the hardness of the floor, stunned.

Above us, Gerianne's moan changed to a higher pitched, "Huh, huh."

Cyrus inched away from me. I knew he was going to leave, to have me arrested, to have me removed from the ship. I opened my mouth to say, "I'm sorry." He stared at me, his cheeks dampened by my kisses, his dark hair falling into his eyes. I wanted to cry.

My chest was heaving, my body filled with shame. I gathered myself to crawl away. I would go topside and throw myself into the Caribbean. When I tried to move, though, I found that my legs were all tangled up in Gerianne's over-sized clothes. Even my getaway would be embarrassing. Overhead, the thumping from the bunk continued unabated.

Suddenly, Cyrus grinned. He no longer looked like a boy as his eyes turned a lazy brown color. Slowly, his long slender fingers touched my face, stroking my cheeks, outlining my lips.

"Sex?" he asked, in a raspy whisper as he moved his hand under my shirt and began caressing my breast.

I couldn't speak.

He undressed me to the sway of the ship, and the song of Zack and Gerianne in the bunk. When our bodies touched, he was oblivious to the softness of my belly, the striations of my stretch marks, the spider veins on my thighs.

We stayed in the cabin with Gerianne and Zack for a long, long time.

Only once did I think about Dougie, and that was when I saw that Cyrus could easily pass any postage stamp test.

Dougie could have his throbbing member, and wet, ruby red lips. Jason could have a pregnant girlfriend. Dr. Kidley could have his vaginas.

I had Cyrus, and I was truly on vacation.

# The Middle-Aged Blues Boogie
## (song lyrics)
### Gaye Todd Adegbalola

Well I was lookin' round and checking out
My very best friends
Seems that they'd all taken up with
Young, young men
Seems that when you reach around middle age
You don't want a final chapter
You want to write another page
I need a young man
To drive away my middle-aged blues

Well it seems like men my age
Are all married, boring, or tired
You got to find a young man
If you want to feel desired
Now some of my friends is worried
'bout what people may say
I say age ain't nothing but a number
The good Lord made it that way
I need a young man
To drive away my middle-aged blues

Well I'll forget about my arthritis, my backache, my lumbago
That young man makes me boogie at the horizontal disco
I'm cleaning out my closet, I'm no longer sentimental
Forget about experience, I'd rather have potential
I need a young man, to drive away my middle-aged blues
Well I don't need no reefer, I don't need no cocaine
All I need is a young man to drive me insane
I'm throwing away my dust mop
I got a brand new vacuum cleaner
I'm no longer taken for granted
My young man sucks it up sweeter
I need a young man to drive away my middle-aged blues

I say an old woman don't yell
An old woman don't tell
An old woman don't swell
And she's grateful as hell
I need a young, young man
Yeah—I need a young, young man
I need a young, young man
To drive away my middle-aged blues

I say age ain't nothing but a number
You know, age ain't nothing but a number
And like a rare wine
You don't get older
You just get better
Gimme a young, young man.

# A Tooth for Every Child
## Abigail Thomas

Louise, who is pushing down the tall grasses near the land of menopause, accepts an invitation from Mona, who is not that far behind. Mona could use the sight of Louise. "I need a drinking companion," she says. Louise can hear the twins wailing in the background.

"We don't drink anymore," Louise reminds her.

"But we can talk about it, can't we? Remember pink gins?"

"That wasn't us, Mona, pink gins. That was our grandmothers."

"Don't quibble. Just get off the bus at Concord. I'll pick you up."

"I'll come Friday. Thursday I've got my teeth."

The only man in Louise's life right now is her Chinese dentist. Her entire sex life consists of his warm fingers in her mouth, against her cheek. She thinks of them as ten slender separate animals, so dexterous is he. She is undergoing root canal, paying the coward's price for years of neglect. Every Thursday she settles herself in his chair and he sets up what he calls the rubber dam. Eyes closed, Louise imagines a tent stretched from tree to tree. Under this canopy he sets to work chipping and drilling, installing a system of levees and drains. He stuffs tendrils of guttapercha in the hollowed-out roots of her teeth and sets them on fire, reminding Louise of the decimation of the tropical rain forests. She imagines bright green parrots flying squawking out of her mouth, lizards running up the fingers of her dentist. Loves may come and loves may go but dental work goes on forever, thinks Louise.

"You owe me nine thousand dollars," says Dr. Chan.

"We're having a lot of work done," says Mona apologetically, as they pull off the country road and onto the rough dirt path that leads to the house Mona and Tony have built overlooking the lake.

"Aren't you embarrassed to be so successful?" asks Louise.

"It's not me, Louise. Blame Tony. All I've been recently is fertile. Wait till you see little Joe. He is anxious to see you."

Mona and Louise have been friends for thirty years. Louise had her babies first, four of them; she has been married twice, divorced twice. Her children have all grown up and gone except the baby, who at seventeen is in Italy this summer. Mona's first child, Joe, is five years old. She has twins, Ernie and Sue, eleven months. Louise wishes she had had her children later, when she knew better; Mona wishes she had done it when she was young. The two women are comfortable together, and Louise is planning to spend a week, playing with kids, sunning herself on the porch, reading.

Tony is off supervising the tennis court ("the tennis court?" Louise has repeated, incredulous), and Mona and she and little Joe are in the kitchen, Joe nestled in Louise's lap. Joe is learning about where babies come from. Mona is horrified to discover he thinks babies and peepee come from the same place, and Louise has taken it upon herself to explain about the three holes. A hole for peepee, a hole for poopoo, and the babyhole. "The babyhole is just for babies," Louise explains, proud of her succinctness. She had told her own children, years ago, that she had made them all by herself, out of a special kit. "What is the babyhole used for when there aren't any babies?" asks little Joe, not unreasonably. Louise looks mournfully at Mona. "Well, not really much of anything," she says, "in a bad year." Mona bursts out laughing and the two women cackle until their noses turn pink.

"The place is crawling with workmen," says Mona later. "You always wanted a guy who worked with his hands, remember? And the roofer is really quite choice. Fifty-three. Good hands."

"Do you talk like this in front of Tony?" asks Louise.

But it is the boy who catches Louise's eye first. Standing beside the path leading to the lake, he is bent over a snapping turtle the size of a Thanksgiving turkey. Louise doesn't know which to look at first, the long brown back of the boy or the spiky ridged shell of the turtle. So she stands there in the middle of the road looking from one to the other. Then the boy straightens up and turns toward Louise. "Oh my God," is what she says. She hopes he will think she is talking about the turtle.

"Ever seen one this big?" he asks, nudging the shell with the toe of one work-booted foot, and hitching his belt slightly so the hammer hangs down his left hip. His upper body is bare, his shoulders smooth and deeply muscled. His eyes and hair are almost black and he has a red bandanna tied around his head. He is smiling at her.

"Not for a long time." Louise notices the turtle's head come poking out of its shell. "Careful," she warns him, "He might bite you." She is a mother, first and foremost.

"Nah, he wouldn't dare. I'm so mean I have to sleep with one eye open so

I don't kick myself in the ass." He laughs, finding himself vastly entertaining. His teeth are remarkably white and there is a fine powdering of sawdust on his right cheekbone that she would like to brush off. "Don't you come too close, is all," he says to her. "This baby take you in his mouth no telling when he'd turn you loose." He grins at Louise who is oddly flustered. She feels fourteen years old. The boy shows no sign of boredom, of turning away from her, no sign of having anything better to do than to stand there and talk to her. She looks around to see who it is he is really talking to. Some young girl somewhere he is trying to impress.

"You up here for the whole summer?" he is asking her now. She shakes her head. "Friend of Mrs. Townshend's?" She nods. "Nice lady," the boy says, "very nice lady." He pauses. "So how long are you staying?"

"Just a week," she says. "I'm from New York."

"Figured that," he says, pulling a crumpled pack of Marlboros out of the back pocket of his jeans. "Smoke?" He offers her one.

"No, I quit. Three packs a day I used to do." Louise is bragging. She watches him cup his hands around the cigarette he is lighting, shake out the match and flick it in the dirt.

"No, I mean do you *smoke*," he says, making the quick sucking sounds of a joint.

"Oh, do I smoke. No," she says firmly. "I hate to smoke. I get paranoid."

He cocks his head to one side, "No kidding," he says. "Not me. Hey, know what I call 'paranoia'? Heightened awareness," and he cracks himself up again. He takes another drag and says after a moment's hesitation, "Would you like to see the countryside around here? I can take you for a drive later. That's my truck," he says proudly, pointing to a black Ford pick-up parked a little down the road. It has a bumper sticker that reads TOO CUTE TO STAY HOME.

In one of those moments Louise is famous for, when she decides to do something without thinking, "Yes," she says, "sure. Thank you very much." And then regrets it. "Well," she says, "see you," and hurries into her cabin where she goes directly to the bathroom and peers at herself in the mirror.

"What was he talking to?" she asks out loud.

"So when is he picking you up?" Mona asks. The twins are having lunch in their highchairs.

"I don't know," says Louise. "I ran away. I'm not going."

"Of course you're going," says Mona, cutting up a hot dog for the twins. "You're doing it for me," she says. "If you don't, we'll both get old. Now go sit out there on that porch and wait for him to tell you what time."

"I can't. I feel like an enormous piece of bait," says Louise. "I feel like a ridiculous elderly baby bird."

"Out," says Mona firmly. "I'm going to ask Bridget to clean in here and you have to be outside in the sun," she says, spooning mashed potato into Ernie's little mouth.

Louise sits tilted back in her chair. She has Auden face down in her lap, her own face is turned toward the sun. Her legs and feet are bare against the railing of the deck. The house is built on a wooded hill above a lake, and through the trees Louise can see water glittering in the sun. She has been remembering the first time a boy opened her clothes. It was 1957 or '58, she and Tommy Morell were leaning against the scaffolding of what was to become the Loeb Student Center in Washington Square. She was wearing a new blue coat from the now long defunct DePinna, it was freezing cold and they were standing out of the wind, kissing. She can remember today the taste of his mouth: decay and wintergreens. Every time somebody walked past, she would hide her face against his shoulder. And then she felt his hands on the front of her coat, the sensation taking a moment to travel through the many layers of her clothes, like light from a star, and his fingers were working at the buttons, the many small difficult buttons of this coat, and she was not pushing his hands away. Louise sighs. Amazing what else she has forgotten, but this scrap of memory is as real as yesterday. This morning.

Louise is deep in daydream when hammering begins under the porch, startling her. Sitting in her thin cotton dress, the hammering directly beneath feels particularly intimate. She hears murmuring of men's voices and the next thing she knows the boy has swung himself up over the railing, defying God knows what laws of physics, and is hunkering down next to her on the porch.

"So I'll pick you up at seven-thirty? I need to go home and get a shower first. Okay?"

"Well, sure," she says. "That's fine. Sure."

"See you later," and he grins and bounds back off the deck. His head reappears a moment later. "I'm Donny," he says. "You're...?"

"Louise."

"Just wear what you have on," advises Mona, after Louise has changed her clothes three times. "That nice dress that buttons down the front."

"You don't think I look as if I'm trying to look like Little Bo-Peep?"

"Louise, that's the last thing I'd say you looked like. You look fine. Really good, in fact. No wonder he asked you."

"Mona, what are we going to talk about? What am I going to say to this boy? I'm forty-fucking-six years old. I certainly can't talk about my kids. They're probably older than he is."

"I don't think you're going to be doing a whole lot of talking," says Mona. "I don't think talking is Donny's specialty."

Donny comes to the door to pick her up just like a real date. He is wearing a shirt tonight which has the odd effect of making him seem even younger. Louise feels unbearably awkward when he says hello to Mona, calls Tony "sir." Louise can't get out of there fast enough. "Take my sweater, Louise," calls Mona. "It's outside there on the rocker."

Donny opens the door of the truck and closes it behind her when she is safely inside. Then he runs around and hops up on the driver's side. "Do you have any idea how old I am?" asks Louise when they are both sitting in the truck. She feels she should get this over with right away.

"Well, I know you're older than me," Donny turns to look at her. "I figure you're twenty-eight or so." Twenty-eight or so? Dear God. Twenty-eight or so?

"Oh," says Louise, "How old are you?"

"I'll be twenty-one next month."

"You're twenty," says Louise, closing her eyes briefly. "You're twenty years old."

"Yeah, but I'll be twenty-one next month," he repeats, and turns the key in the ignition and the truck starts to vibrate pleasantly, reminding Louise, not surprisingly, of an enormously powerful animal just barely held in check. "Ready?" he asks.

She is looking at how loosely his hand rests on the stick shift. She nods, watching his hand tighten on the stick, the muscles in his arm bulging slightly as he puts the truck in first and they begin lurching down the steep path that leads to the highway.

"Wahoo!" he yells, thrusting his upper body half out the window, then he ducks back in and grins at Louise. "Couldn't help it," he says sheepishly. "I just feel good." She smiles at him.

Louise is now completely at ease. As soon as the truck started moving she felt something inside her click into place. She knows exactly who she is and what she is doing. She is a blonde-headed woman in the front seat of a moving vehicle, she is nobody's mother, nobody's former wife, nobody's anything. Louise is a girl again.

A mile down the highway Donny fishes around under his seat and comes up with a Sucrets box which he hands her. "Can you light me up the joint? Matches on the dash." Louise opens the box and picks the joint up. It is lying next to loose grass and on top of a bunch of rolling papers. Louise hasn't smoked a joint in a long time. The last time she did, she became convinced that she was about to become dinner: about to be minced, put in a cream sauce, and run under the broiler. She was at a party being given by her then-new husband's old friends.

"I don't really smoke," she begins, and then "Oh, what the hell," she says, shrugging, and lights the joint. "Maybe I've changed," she says, talking mostly to herself.

"Maybe the company has changed," says Donny, and she can't imagine what he thinks he means by that, but they are passing the joint back and forth and Louise is beginning to feel pretty good. Something lovely is happening deep in her throat, some awareness of throat-ness she has never experienced before. "God, I've got such an interesting *throat*," she says and Donny laughs.

"You're getting high," he says.

"I am?" Louise sits up straight.

"You okay? Feeling okay?"

"I think I feel good," she says, taking stock. "Yes," she announces rather formally, "I feel really quite good." Donny slows down and takes a right turn into what he calls a sandpit. It is a parking area off the road, behind a kind of berm. "Let's roll another," he says, proceeding to do so. Louise watches fascinated; she has always loved watching people use their hands. When he licks the paper to seal the cigarette she sees his tongue is pink. This kid's tongue is actually pink, oh Lordy Lordy, thinks Louise.

"Why don't you have a girlfriend?" she wants to know.

"I had a girlfriend. She moved out three months ago. She left me a note saying she was going to California." Donny snaps the Sucrets box shut now and looks for the matches.

"Oh. Crummy. Were you sad?"

"For a while. Thing that made it easier was she took my damn stereo. Hard to be sad and pissed at the same time. But yeah, we had some good times. Bummed me out she couldn't tell me to my face she was going."

"She probably wouldn't have been able to leave, then."

"Yeah. That's what she said in her note." He offers her the new joint to light but she shakes her head.

"What was her name?"

"Robin. But anybody asks me now how's Robin, know what I say? Robin who, I say. Robin who?" Donny laughs and then turns his head to look out the window. "Company," he says, as a red Toyota pulls in. "Let's go somewhere a little less public. Want to see the lake?"

"Sure," says Louise, "anything." What a nice state New Hampshire is to provide lakes and sandpits for its citizens to park in, Louise is thinking. They head off and stop along the way to see the school Donny was kicked out of. It is a plain, one-story brick building that Louise thinks privately looks pretty depressing, but Donny is driving around it slowly, almost lovingly. "You had a good time here?" she asks him.

"Yep. I had a good time here."

"How come they kicked you out?"

"Oh, this and that. I was a hot-head then, I guess. I'm a lot calmer now, though you might not believe it. Straightening myself out. Full time job in itself," he laughs. "Full time job in itself."

"I like hot-headed," says Louise. "I always did."

Donny, who has been circling the school building, pulls over to the far end of the lot and parks under a tree. He turns the engine off and they look at each other in the fading light of the summer evening; a little moon starts to show between the trees, a street light blinks on thirty feet away. He reaches quite frankly for her, or perhaps she reaches for him, but his hands are on her dress, the front of her dress at the buttons, and his dark head is against her neck, his breath everywhere. Her hands are in his hair, under his shirt, feeling the tight muscles of his belly above his belt. Fumbling. Then they are kissing, and because his window does not close completely, the truck fills with mosquitoes and they are kissing and slapping and slapping and cursing and laughing and kissing and kissing and kissing. Donny drags a blanket out from behind his seat and they stumble out of the truck and onto the grass and Louise is lying down under a million or so stars. "I wanted to fuck you the first time I saw you, to tell you the truth," Donny is whispering as he lowers his body down on hers.

They sleep in the truck that night, parked near the lake that seems to be everywhere. Or rather, Donny sleeps, his head in Louise's lap. Louise is awake all night, watching the woods drain of moonlight and fill up again slowly with a misty brightness that seems to rise from the ground. Donny's body is arranged somehow around the gearshift, his head and shoulders resting on Louise. He sleeps like a baby. She looks at his closed eyes, dark lashes, his straight black brows. His skin is beautiful, like silk. Dear God, how came this beautiful wild child to be asleep in my lap, thinks Louise. At six, she jiggles his shoulder. "Time to wake up," she says. "We've been gone all night."

"What if I refuse to take you back?" he asks sleepily. "Suppose I just decide to keep you?"

Mona is up, of course, when Louise gets in. The twins are out with Bridget; little Joe and Tony are down by the lake doing something with boats. "Don't let Tony see you," says Mona. "I told him you got in late last night. You know Tony." Tony has never approved of Louise, not since she asked him if she could up-end herself in his laundry hamper. "For the pheromones," she had explained, "It's been so long since the last good kiss." Louise had read somewhere that women who lived without the company of men were apt to age more quickly.

"Why can't she just ride the subway at rush hour?" Tony had asked irritably. "Plenty of nice hair tonic and body sweat in there. Why does it have to be my laundry?"

"Come on, Tony, it's just your gym socks. Be a sport," Mona had said.

"So?" says Mona now, pouring two cups of coffee. "Or don't I really want to know?"

"I'll say one word," says Louise, "to satisfy your morbid curiosity because I know it's on your mind. Hung."

"Comme zee horse?" Mona is leaning forward.

"Comme zee horse."

"Ahhhh."

"And you know what else? I like him, I actually like him. He's working so hard to grow up. His girlfriend left him and he had to move back with his parents because he couldn't afford the rent by himself. He works his ass off. I like him."

"Yeah? Well, great, but don't start taking this seriously."

"He's picking me up again tonight. You know what? Staying up all night makes me feel young again, isn't that weird? I haven't been this tired since I was young."

"Go lie down. I'll wake you up at lunch."

"Mona? I loved not talking about my kids. It was like being twenty myself, you know? It was like not having a tail I had to fit everywhere. I'm never going to tell anyone about my kids again."

"Louise, you're delirious. Go upstairs and lie down."

"Good night."

"Louise?" calls Mona, as Louise disappears up the stairs. "You're being careful? I'm not talking about babies, you know what I'm talking about."

Louise's head appears around the corner. "Mona," she says, "what could be safer than a twenty-year-old carpenter from New Hampshire?"

Two days later Donny takes off work. "I've got vacation time coming," he says. "I'm taking you four-wheeling. That is if you want to drive around with me for a few days."

Mona is worried. "I hope you're not taking this seriously," she keeps saying. "I know how you can get, Louise, and I don't want you to get involved with a twenty-year-old boy who lives with his parents."

"Come on, Mona, I haven't had this much fun in my whole life," says Louise. "I'm twenty years old myself this week. The last time I was twenty I had two children and an ex-husband in the making."

Mona's expression relaxes. "All right, but I don't want to hear a word of complaint out of you for eighteen months and I hope you have plenty of raw meat for the trip."

Louise feels like a summer house this kid has broken into, pushing his way through doors that haven't been opened in years, snapping up blinds, windows, pulling dust covers off furniture, shaking rugs, curtains, bounding on the beds. A fine, honorable old house, and he appreciates the way it has been made, the way it has lasted, the strength of its structure, noble old dimensions. It has been a long time since Louise was put to such good use.

"What's the longest you've ever gone without making love?" she asks him. He thinks for a second.

"Fifteen years," he answers.

She loves his raw energy, and the lavish way he squanders it on pointless undertakings, impossible feats, such as driving the truck directly up the steep wooded side of a mountain whenever he thinks he spies faint tracks. (Louise sees only dense woods.) He screeches the truck to a stop, leaps down to lock the front wheels, jumps back inside to do something sexy to the gears, pausing to kiss Louise for five minutes, and then he coaxes, bullies, cajoles the truck off the road and into the trees. Louise loves it. She loves everything about him by now. She loves the muscles in his shoulders, the veins in his forearms. "I like how you touch me," he whispers. She wants him to explain everything he knows, the difference between a dug and an artesian well, how to build a ladder, hang a door, put a roof on. "You're really interested?" he asks her. "You really want to know?" She nods. "The plumb-line is God," he begins, gravely.

Louise is as close to carefree as she has ever been. There is nothing behind her, her past is not part of this trip, and nothing in front but a dashboard full of music and the open road. They like the same music, sing the same songs. Stevie Ray Vaughan, The Georgia Satellites, Tom Petty and the Heartbreakers. "Break Down" is their favorite song and they blast it all week, yelling it out the windows, singing it to each other in the truck, "Break down, go ahead and give it to me," and then they collapse laughing, this forty-six-year-old woman and this twenty-year-old boy, who are having the time of their lives. They rent a room in a motel when they get tired of fighting off the mosquitoes. Louise uses her Visa card expecting any minute the long arm of the law to grab her by the collar, bring her to her senses. Donny is bent over the register saying, "You want an address?" and Louise hears the manager saying, "Oh, just put anything," with a knowing snicker. For just a second, she feels gawky, naked. How many good years does she have left, she wonders, before she appears pathetic. Right now she can still get away with it, but fifty approaches, the hill she will one day be over is looming in the distance. So when the manager shows them the room and it contains two double-decker beds, one cot, and a king-size four poster, Louise rubs her hands together largely for his benefit and says, "Good. We can really use the room."

They order Chinese take-out that night from an improbable place down the road and Louise bites down into something hard in her mooshoo pork. Spitting it into her hand she sees it is a human tooth. She hurries into the bathroom and locks the door. "You all right in there?" asks Donny, knocking. It is Louise's tooth, her temporary cap, and she rinses it off and jams it back in her mouth praying to God it will stay. "Donny," she says, coming out of the bathroom, "I've got to tell you how old I am. Guess what, I'm forty-six." He doesn't seem particularly interested. "I'm forty-six, did you hear me?"

"Yeah?" He is lying down on the big bed, his hands behind his head. "So?"

"And what's more I have four kids and three of them are older than you and I have two grandchildren on top of that." Louise seems out of breath all of a sudden. He just looks at her.

"Come here," he says. She goes there. He grabs her hand. "I guess that makes me some kind of motherfucker," he says with a lazy grin, pulling her down on the bed. "Stick with me, I won't let you get old," he says, into her hair. "But

I am old," she wants to moan, "I already am old."

"Why are a woman's breasts always softest in the evening?" he wants to know, pulling her toward him.

Louise is awake all night. "You can't kiss all the time," a friend of hers once said, by way of explaining her having picked up a few words of Italian one summer. "You can't kiss all the time." Louise thinks she knows this, she knows it is time to go back to the grown-ups, back to New York, her office. Back to real life. This isn't real life, this relationship relies too heavily on rock 'n' roll and the open road. Real life is not this dream come true, it is long winter nights with nothing to talk about. You can't kiss all the time. "I'll build you a house," Donny said yesterday. "Stay. I'll build you a house."

He knows before she tells him that she is going home. He is quiet all morning, sullen even. "What's the matter?" she asks but he shakes off her hand.

"You're leaving."

"But I'm coming back. I'm coming back for your birthday."

"But you're leaving, right?"

She nods.

"Well, I'm bummed."

She tells him about the office, the mail, her apartment, bills unpaid, her daughter coming home from Europe soon.

"What do you want for your birthday?" she asks him.

"You."

"You've got me. What else?"

"More of you."

"You've got me. What else?"

"Am I asking too much?"

Back in New York, Louise is lonelier than she expected to be. New York is gritty, dirty, sad. Her apartment is so empty, quiet. Louise is of an age now when most of the men in her life are former lovers who fly in from nowhere for a couple of days every six years or so; they sit on her chairs, eat at her table, sleep in her bed, and when they leave they leave a kind of half-life behind, an absence so palpable it is almost a presence. The furniture rebukes Louise on these occasions. "So where'd he go?" asks the white sofa, the pink chair. The bed. But Donny has never been here, so she has to conjure up his memory out of whole cloth, so to speak, and she misses him more than she thought she would.

In fact, she talks of little else. She is as apt to pull pictures of Donny out of her wallet as of her grandsons. "You're in luck," she might have said a month ago. "I have fifty-three new pictures of my grandsons." Now she takes seven photographs out of her wallet, they are all of Donny, and she lays them out on the table like a row of solitaire. "So," she says, to anyone who will listen. "You know that poem by Auden? 'Lay your sleeping head my love'?" Her friends are respectful, for the most part silent. They let her play it out.

"Do we sleep with the young to stay young ourselves or just to lie down next to all that beauty?" Louise wants to know. Mona is irritated. They are together in Riverside park with the kids. Joe is in the sandbox, Mona and Louise are pushing the twins in the little swings. "Neither," says Mona. "How should I know?" she snaps. Then more gently, "To lie down next to all that beauty."

"I knew it," says Louise, hopping. "I knew it!"

"I'm worried about you," says Mona. "I mean I hope you're not being faithful to him or anything."

Louise bursts out laughing. "Come on, Mona. Who am I going to go out with? The drycleaner?"

"I'm just concerned you might get hurt. You let your emotions get involved."

"Well, of course I let my emotions get involved. What the hell is the point if you don't let your emotions get involved? But it's not like going out for ice cream and coming home and saying 'Gee, I wish I hadn't had that ice cream.' I liked the kid. I loved the kid, if you want to know."

"Just what I was afraid of. And I certainly don't think you should go back up there for his birthday. Enough is enough."

"I promised him I'd go. I promised him."

But Louise has not heard from Donny, and though she has left messages with his mother (an exquisitely humiliating experience) he has not returned her calls. The night before she is supposed to get on the bus she finally gets him on the phone. She does not want to keep her end of the bargain and wind up sitting on a suitcase in the parking lot at Concord waiting for Godot. It is a bad connection and she can barely hear him, and she has to keep repeating "What?" into the telephone like an old woman with an ear trumpet.

"Are we still on for tomorrow?" she shouts, although she already knows the answer.

"Things have changed around here," Donny says. His voice sounds so foreign, so young.

"So do you still want me to come up tomorrow?" Louise is amazed at how painful this is.

"I guess now is not a good time," he says but she can barely hear him. "What?"

"No," he says. "Not this time."

"Well, Happy Birthday to you," she says, hanging up the phone.

"Would you mind removing your lipstick," asks Dr. Chan, handing Louise a tissue. He always makes this request, but Louise wears it to his office just the same. She likes to look her best for the dentist. Dr. Chan wears his hair cut short except for three very long, very skinny braids, and Louise has always been too shy to inquire as to their significance.

"Today we put in your permanent tooth," says Dr. Chan, setting out his instruments, mixing his little pots of cement.

"That's good," says Louise, "because this one fell out over the summer and I had to put it back myself. 'A tooth for every child,'" she adds, but Dr. Chan does not ask after her meaning.

She settles back in her chair. The land of menopause stretches out behind her closed lids, as Dr. Chan easily removes the temporary cap. It seems to be a quiet place, resembling a kind of savannah. There are mountains in the distance. There doesn't appear to be much activity beyond a certain amount of flank-nuzzling, as far as Louise can tell. But who knows? She has heard some odd cries at night, down by the waterhole.

# Giving the Cat Your Tongue
## Deborah Shouse

I never wanted to own a cat. I just liked the comfort of a sleek black creature curled opposite me as I sat on the patio editing my work.

"Silent presence," I explained to Jeffrey.

"Is that like 'quiet gifts'?" Jeffrey asked, using his index finger to redistribute the ice in his Diet Pepsi.

The cat stirred, blinking its fierce yellow eyes. Jeffrey made a meowing sound as he lounged against the sliding glass door, dressed, as usual, in practically nothing.

"Jeffrey, remember the neighbors." I pointed to old lady Nadle pruning her rose bushes in the next yard. But Jeffrey merely flexed a tricep, popped the band of his navy blue briefs, and put a tender hand on my breast.

"I'm working," I said.

Jeffrey retreated to the mimosa tree at the opposite end of the patio. He raised his face to the sky, as if posing. His body was firm from working out, and lithe from dancing at the club. I tried not to think about how beautiful he was.

"Of course," my friend Clara said when the subject of Jeffrey came up, "who isn't beautiful at 21?"

Jeffrey watched me as he drank his cola. I did not try to push my frazzled hair into place, or hold my chin so the wrinkles didn't show. Jeffrey had convinced me age was something to be cherished and admired.

"And you believed that?" Clara had shaken her head at my naivete.

Jeffrey rippled his chest muscles. Despite the impossible golden color of his skin, I returned to chapter five. I was concerned about the sudden change in Margot, a secondary character. Margot was supposed be aloof, independent, with a sense of malicious mystery. But somehow, in chapter five she had turned sweet and gauzy. She was stealing the pages from the heroine Daphne, plus she was flirting with Hector. I could either abandon my outline and give Margot free reign, or take my red pen and send her to a nunnery.

I sipped my tepid coffee and addressed the sleeping cat. "What do you think?"

"Now you're giving that cat your tongue," Jeffrey said, pouring his ice onto a petunia, "when I could make far better use of it."

Clara was amazed when I told her how freely Jeffrey discussed sex.

"I'd never be caught with a man twenty-five years younger than I am," Clara said. "I can't believe you actually let someone move in with you."

I was as surprised as Clara. I had always kept my lovers separate, apart from my house. Jeffrey sneaked up on me. He overwhelmed me with his admiration. He disarmed me with his sensuality. I knew one night he would disappear with whoever stuffed the hundred dollar bill down his crotch. But somehow, I didn't care.

Jeffrey walked over and massaged the ridge of my shoulders.

"Omelet for breakfast?" he asked.

"Fine," I answered.

With my red pen I dressed Margot in something more conservative. The cat arched his back, turned twice in the chair, and curled into a ball.

Jeffrey brought me hot coffee.

"What's happening with Hector?" he asked. Hector was Jeffrey's favorite character: strong, powerful and devastating to women.

"Margot is flirting with him."

"That Daphne's a piece of fluff. Hector would be happier with Margot." Jeffrey did a knee bend. He assumed he was my inspiration for Hector. But I'd loved my character long before I met Jeffrey.

Jeffrey stroked my face. Even his fingers were well proportioned, long but not too delicate. He knelt down and kissed my knee cap. I saw Mrs. Nadle practically straddling a rose bush for a closer look.

"I've got to finish this, Jeffrey."

"Apres eggs, then," he said.

While I tamed Margot, I wondered how anyone as agreeable as Jeffrey could stand me. Long years of independent living had made me willful and inflexible.

I had never asked Jeffrey to move in. He followed me home from the bookstore that day, drank a Coke, and then traced each line, stroked each grey hair, admired each imperfection with a loving hand. He adopted me. He ignored my defensiveness, paid me too much for rent and cooked too many omelets.

"You're making it up," Clara said, when I told her about Jeffrey.

"Come see for yourself," I replied. Clara wrote romances, but she wouldn't believe in anything that wasn't straight from the pen. She was suspicious of all real life affection.

The cat jumped onto my chair. I scratched him under the chin, then gently shoved him away. His bold beauty pleased me, but I preferred him at a distance.

"Breakfast." Jeffrey came to the door wearing one of my old aprons.

The table was set, the toast lightly buttered, the eggs were just gooey enough.

Jeffrey looked at me as he ate his toast.

"Wet t-shirt contest at the club tonight," he said. "I won't get to dance much. I'll probably only get a hundred in tips. Maybe I'll call in sick. Then you and I could go out for a change." His eyes were green and gold, like autumn meadows. I watched him lick a smear of butter from his little finger.

"You should go to work. Later on, you might need the hundred." I was amazed at the cash women gave, just to get their hands near Jeffrey.

While I finished my coffee, Jeffrey cleared the table.

"Come on." He took my arm.

"Sex in the afternoon," Clara had squealed. "Only teenagers do that."

"Just don't call me between three and five," I told her.

Afterwards, Jeffrey curled into sleep. I kissed the elegant lines of his cheeks, and brushed his hair off his forehead.

"Don't you worry when he's at that club? Aren't you scared he's with other people?" Clara asked.

But I never worried. When Jeffrey was away, my time stretched out as it always had. I thought of him as someone who came into my life, soft and simple as the cat. Already he was almost too close. Already he was sitting on my chair.

Jeffrey stirred, and I covered him with the satin sheet. Jeffrey was flattered I had written his eyes onto Hector. Now Hector walked on Jeffrey's wonderful firm legs, and combed his hair away from his forehead, like Jeffrey did.

I dressed, and went out to the patio to reread chapter five. Margot still puzzled me. What caused her to abandon her independent pose, and throw herself at the dashing Hector? What caused Hector to respond?

From nowhere, the cat appeared and claimed his place. His tongue flicked at sleek fur, a rhythmic rubbing, caressing of flanks. As I read about Hector, I thought of the sleeping boy in my bed.

I knew he would leave soon. He needed the reckless pulse of the young against him. I was too solid, too bound to house and book. Without meaning to, I would somehow push him away.

Clara would be delighted. "It was just a silly fling," she would say. Old Lady Nadle would bring the last of her roses to comfort me.

I would work on the patio, with just the cat for companion. The petunias would shrivel; the maple leaves would litter the ground with their gold. I'd sit at the table, drinking tepid coffee, shaping my world with a red pen. And if my voice cracked when I read the love scene between Hector and Margot, only the sleeping cat would know.

# Love Bite
## Susan B. McIver

Tomás and I fell in love with the same woman. At the time I was a Presbyterian, a closeted lesbian, and an academic. Tomás was a neutered tabby-Siamese cross with no religious affiliation. I was early middle age. Tomás was old.

I met Sheelah one evening when I was a participant in a panel discussion on women in academe. Afterwards she came to argue a point with me. She was tall, graceful, and flamboyant both in manner and dress. Jangly silver jewelry dangled from her ears and wrists. Her silk lavender blouse was unbuttoned to mid-chest revealing hints of perky, free breasts. Her purple slacks were tucked into the tops of knee-high leather boots. I had on my pillar of the community blue suit. Tomás met Sheelah when she walked through our front door. He wore his usual gray-brown and white striped fur coverall.

I knew Sheelah four months before I fell in love. Tomás needed three minutes. The results were the same: we were both besotted.

When she moved in, Tomás forsook my lap to lie in hers and purr seductively. In treasured moments he would stretch across her bosom and while resting his head on her shoulder, contemplate the wonders of her ear lobe. At other times he would simply follow her around the house in anticipation of rubbing rapturously against her legs.

Tomás's whiskers, which had begun to droop Kung Fu style with age, resumed their youthful stiffness. Nothing about me drooped either. I was as deliciously delirious as the cat.

My hormone-driven body craved Sheelah. The smallest touch ignited the flames of our consuming passion. We found ecstasy in every embrace. Tomás watched with jaded eyes. When our fevered thrashing had ceased, he would steal into our love nest and stretch lengthwise along Sheelah's naked body. If he couldn't participate, he would at least bask in the afterglow.

As frequently happens in *ménage à trois* arrangements, jealousy arrived on a galloping stead. Tomás and I were not jealous of the attention the other one received from Sheelah, nor, as far as I could tell, was Sheelah jealous of the few times Tomás and I still exchanged pleasantries. BUT I was green jealous of Sheelah having bewitched Tomás. That special spot in my heart reserved for my beloved cat ached with betrayal and loss.

A year passed and then almost another. The vapors of amorous stupor continued to hang heavy upon me. While dressing in the morning, I would put my arms around Sheelah's neck and drape myself along her sleek, languid body. I had to capture the feel and scent of her to sustain me through the workday.

While we were out for the day, Tomás would wait with characteristic feline patience in the front window. When we returned in the evening, I would be torn between my desire for Sheelah that demanded satiation and my boiling jealousy that Tomás always greeted her first.

One Sunday afternoon Tomás perched on the dresser, while Sheelah and I made love on our bed. We sipped wine and nibbled each other: the tease of a tooth, the touch of a tongue. We were lusty and carefree.

I engaged Sheelah in a round of play-wrestling. Being the stronger she quickly pinned me flat on my back with hands outstretched over my head. Suddenly her look of triumph turned to total astonishment a fraction of a second before she screamed in pain. Tomás had bitten her bare bottom.

I leapt from the bed and embraced Tomás. Clutching him tightly, I danced with joy. As I nuzzled my face against his head, repeatedly kissing his ears, I told him what a brave cat he was to have rescued me.

Meanwhile Sheelah nursed her wounds. Shortly thereafter she left.

Now, I am no longer a Presbyterian, closeted, nor an academic. I am truly middle aged and Tomás is no more. I miss him.

# The Loneliness of the Middle-Aged Woman

## Susan Moon

I've been thinking a lot about loneliness lately. To be blunt, I *am* lonely. It's taboo, to admit to being lonely, especially for a single middle-aged woman. It makes people feel uncomfortable, afraid you expect them to do something about it. It's humiliating, like being the only girl in the dorm without a date on Saturday night. You're supposed to hide in your room, so at least nobody *knows* you don't have a date—you're not supposed to trail up and down the halls in your bathrobe and slippers, looking forlorn. (Not that people have Saturday night dates any more, or even bathrobes and slippers.) A down-and-out man in a country song proclaims, "The only friends I've got left are lonely women and bad booze." We are presumed to be desperate.

But how could I be lonely? My life is full of people: I have wonderful friends. I'm close to my family—parents, children, siblings, nieces, nephews— if you can call two or three thousand miles close. These days, my loneliness has to do with the fact that I don't have a mate at the moment, and my children have recently grown up and left home.

There's a sense of shame about being lonely—a feeling that there must be something terribly wrong with me or I wouldn't be single. Or, more subtly, there must be something terribly wrong with me or I wouldn't *mind* being single. I know that my character defects—big mole on my cheek, I talk in the movies, my houseplants die—are not really monstrous. I *was* married, long ago, and I've been in love several times since. I tell myself there are reasons other than unlovability that I'm alone. I have sent away people who loved me; I've loved people who were, finally, unavailable. I've been beset by those twin demons that get you coming and going: fear of intimacy, fear of abandonment. And there are all the outer explanations—the demographics: not enough men to go around, especially for my height, age, and educational level.

Married friends try to comfort me by saying: *Oh, but remember how much worse it is to be lonely when you're In A Relationship.* Or they say: *I love it when Jack goes to conferences and I can read in bed.*

But they know as well as I do that there's a deep need to be intimately connected with another person. After all, they're together, aren't they? They could get divorced if they really wanted to read in bed. Adam and Eve had each other. So did Gertrude and Alice. That's the way it's supposed to be, so why should I pretend not to mind? I've heard there are people who prefer the single life, and I suppose there must be a few, but I don't know any of them personally. All of the single people I know would rather have a partner.

I don't go around feeling sorry for myself all the time. I enjoy my independence, I love reading in bed, I like being able to decide to have popcorn for dinner. But when an earthquake wakes me up in the middle of the night, I want somebody to grab onto. The bottom line is that I don't want to die alone, although I guess dying is the one thing I'm going to have to do alone no matter what.

I don't just lie around waiting for a knight in shining armor to call me up on the telephone, either. I circulate. I go to wine and cheese benefits, and I hike with the Solo Sierrans. My friends try to help me out by inviting me over for brunch on the rare occasion that an eligible bachelor swims into their ken. I even placed a classified ad in a local paper. "But what about AIDS?" asked my mother when I told her. "What *about* it?" I said. "I don't think you get AIDS from reading the *Bay Guardian*."

I "went out for coffee" with the three men whose letters I liked best. They were nice. They were not the dregs of society after all, at least not any more than I. They knew people I knew, they lived in my world: a recently divorced environmental lawyer who liked to hike, a naval engineer who baked his own bread, a computer programmer who played Hungarian music on the violin.

I went to a cafe to meet one of them. I was a few minutes late, and a strange man was standing by the entrance, shifting his weight from one foot to another, looking up and down the street. "Sharon?" he said, as I approached.

"No, it's Susan," I answered. "I'm sorry I'm late." We sat down and ordered coffee and dessert. He talked about fishing, and wanted to know when I'd been on my last scuba diving trip. About the time my cheesecake came ("You're going to eat *that*?"), we realized we were the wrong people for each other, and on further investigation we found his Sharon and my computer programmer waiting for us outside the door. After a couple of dates, the computer programmer and I turned out to be the wrong people for each other, too, and I wouldn't put any money on Sharon and the scuba diver either. It makes a funny story, but how would you feel if this was the way you were spending the evenings of your middle age? Even *one* evening feels like too much time while it's happening.

I keep forgetting how old I am. Sometimes I'll encounter an attractive man without a wedding ring, and when he tells me about his backpacking trip in the Dolomites, saying "I" not "we," I start to perk up. He says he's a child of the sixties, and I say, "Me, too," meaning I came of age in the sixties, but then I suddenly realize he means he was *born* in the sixties.

To go through the courting process in one's forties—what torture. It's a terrifying prospect to get to know somebody from scratch who himself has old habits, a lifestyle, a dependent parent, who has to watch his cholesterol, who has back trouble, who will only travel by United Airlines in order to earn mileage plus credits, who snores, has hemorrhoids, child support payments, favorite television programs, an exercise routine that can't be altered. A used person. And I'm not too pristine myself. It's hard enough just getting used to riding in the car with such a person (his seat belts are broken, and he accelerates in jerks), to say nothing of taking off your clothes and getting into bed with him and asking him whether he wants you to put the condom on him or whether he likes to do it himself.

Less frightening is the prospect of getting together with someone you already know from the past. People go to reunions for this. At my twenty-fifth college reunion, a nice man whom I vaguely remembered greeted me enthusiastically, reminding me that we were both in "Playboy of the Western World" in our sophomore year. He wasn't the playboy and I wasn't Pegeen Mike, or I'd be telling a different story, I suppose. We were townsfolk. He told me he'd pined for me all during sophomore year but was too shy to ask me out. Alas, I would have been happy to go. If he'd asked me, we might be celebrating our twenty-fifth wedding anniversary about now. But he's married to somebody else. It seemed they all were, at the reunion.

Of course people *do* get divorced, but if a man who is old enough for me gets divorced, there's not time for me to meet him and marry him, because he probably got divorced in order to marry somebody he's already having an affair with, or else he got divorced because he's having a midlife crisis and wants to get together with a woman in her twenties. Or else I'm too tall.

My therapist: "When you're ready for it it will happen."

A Zen teacher: "When you don't care any more, it will happen."

An old friend: "You must not want to get married, because if you did, you would have."

A possible boyfriend, rejecting me: "You want a relationship too badly."

Another possible boyfriend, rejecting me: "You don't want a relationship badly enough."

I'm anxious about getting old. After menopause, women tend to become invisible in our society. Standing in line at the post office, for example, it's hard to distinguish one gray-haired old lady from another, unless it's your own mother. I figure I better find myself a partner before I pass into that shadowy realm. In fact I've already started that journey: men pay less attention to me than they used to—men who don't know me yet—even though I'm more interesting now than I was when they were more interested in me. Attracting strange men is not a goal in itself, mind you, it's just a sign.

The worst of it is that I'm sick and tired of thinking about it. I want to turn off the radar. I'm tired of planning my vacations and recreational activities to include the most openings for meeting a mate. Tired of being afraid of waking up in the middle of the night, older and lonelier, less and less bendable, surer and surer there will never be anyone beside me.

How much longer can I keep this up? Shave the legs, put on the contact lenses, sign up for another set of West Coast swing dance classes. And smile.

Maybe I'll just go over to my friend Bill's house. He's gay, but he loves me. He'll cook us a good vegetarian supper, we'll take his dog Park to the dog park, talk about books and music, we'll laugh a lot, lie on his bed and watch an old movie on the VCR. When I come home again I can read in bed. It would be a perfect evening if only I didn't have some other idea of what I want.

But maybe that's good enough.

# Angst
## Jennifer Stone

I'm running out of men who knew me when. You know, when I was thin and desirable and presentable and worth the effort. Remember Henry Miller's line: "An old cunt is a dead loss."

"No dear, an old dick is a dead loss," says the man seated across from me at the breakfast table, smiling like the satyr he'd like to be.

Oh that, as if that were all! It's not about *that* all the time, I tell him. (*Are* men as obsessed with getting it up as they seem to be? Is that really their measure of manhood?) For me it's the lonely thing. It's thinking that *I* am the only one who will never leave me. (Sometimes that's a great thought!)

I thought that if I got married I would never be lonely. And married was the loneliest I got—being without the one you're with. Sometimes sex is as close as men get. Closeness, intimacy, sometimes it's all so tiring. When I was young I took the sex in place of affection. But my feelings were hurt and when my emotions were blunted the orgasm wouldn't come. Masochism? Maybe. Psychological pout? I tried to keep things simple. I told myself, an orgasm a day keeps the psychiatrist at bay.

But orgasms are a dime a dozen now. All that really keeps me alive is knowing someone cares whether I live or die. I want to believe that men and women grow more alike as they age. He doesn't always give me what I want. Who could? (Well, I could, but that's another dimension.) With him, it's knowing he knew me when. We were tear-gassed together! We're pieces of the same history. Fragments of an age. When I'm feeling frail, he gives me confidence. He reflects my existential aura, helps me do battle with my dragon, my fear of being all I am. He celebrates my accomplishments, my hero's journey, my grandiose schemes. I need him to take away my doubt and come to the party with me. In the early days, he even read my reviews to his friends. His favorite was: "She's so down to earth, you have to take your shoes off to read her."

He's as good as it gets. Not like the male chauvinist prig before him, the one

I thought had changed. I can't help but regret the shipwreck of that affair, the one that promised peace, the one that rekindled with a kinder gentler intimacy because we'd hurt each other in the past. This time around, I thought, we will be tolerant and humorous. Surely the time has come to forgive. We know the gentleman with the scythe is sitting at the breakfast table with us, sharing our prunes. This time we will be refined and affectionate. We will protect each other's solitude and maintain a mutual front before the onslaught from without. Rapport will replace romance and our world-weary warmth will hold hands by the hearth...and other Hallmark cards.

It's a movie myth—that age softens, ripens, mellows. (G. B. Shaw's Captain Shotover in *Heartbreak House* called it, "The sweetness of the fruit that's going rotten.") I suppose some soften, some turn to stone. I asked myself why he should be the one to surface after all these years. Even back then, we didn't have much in common, except we were so much alike. Looking back at all those alcoholic spasms we called love affairs in the days of the flowers and the funk, I think we came together because we were, in some way, closet Victorians trying to come out. Once he upstaged me beyond my wildest dreams—became more myself than I am. But life came along and pickled him. I tried to love a pickle and he wouldn't let me. He just sat and glared. Who said, "Men don't have to leave, they've already left"?

Desperate for guidance, I went to a feminist seminar, cheerfully titled a Feminar. The question posed: "Is sexual intimacy possible without a dominance/ submission paradigm!" Not at my house that week. Over coffee I tried to practice intimacy the New Age way. (One New World Order deserves another, but I wish to Goddess they'd find a new post-modern phrase for this phase of fascist fragmentation.)

I began by telling this man I loved to distraction, that it's patriarchy which separates us. Patriarchy forbids sharing and closeness. Real men don't give themselves away.

"Intimacy!" he yells. "Intimacy is everywhere, and much of it is violent and abusive." I show him Susan Howe's book *My Emily Dickinson*. Howe writes that the sad riddle of the world is that sadism breaks down barriers between isolate souls. I ask him if that's why he's yelling at me, because violence forces reaction?

He tells me I need taking down a peg or two. I am overconfident, he says. He insists I *don't listen*. (He's right about that. If I listen, I feel betrayed. Bad faith is the lot of lovers?) He is phallocentric to a fault. Suddenly pissed, he tells me I don't even understand my own sexual response. Tells me clitoral stimulation is an infantile form of sexual activity, and that the only mature female response can be had *in depth*...

Stunned, I decide not to tell him how many years it took me to learn how to adjust my own sexual needs to his and to other males who think they know what they're doing. Even today, many women struggle to get their sexual needs met, simply because so many men still believe sex is an athletic affair, rather than a comfort zone. I look at this jockocrat and say simply that the clitoris is analogous to the penis. No go. He puts his trust in the main thrust, etc. We get into a fight over the issue of female genital mutilation (excision of the clitoris and other genital tissue) in forty African and Arab countries. I yell that he can't get it up without an argument and he dismisses my references books: *The Hite Report*, Phyllis Chesler's *About Men*, Nawal El Saadawi's *The Hidden Face of Eve*, and so many others. He tells me my sources are tainted, second rate. He will not take knowledge at my hands.

He will not learn of me. That would be against his religion. He is orthodox. His power comes from withholding. He will stick to his guns, whatever I say. He has read his Nietzsche!

I tell myself that one curmudgeon deserves another. I tell him that we don't need to win anymore. We're old and wise. He shrugs this off. My existential angst threatens his nihilistic nausea. I insist there's space for both. Duality is destiny! Why, I ask him, why can't you make the "yes, and" adjustment, instead of always saying "no, but"? When you say no to my reality, is it because it threatens your own? I need you to care or my courage fails. I put my hands on his shoulders and ask him what the world would be like if men believed in women.

He is not user friendly. The fascist fun has just begun. I must go along with his mythos or he will not sleep with me. (I used to believe in the truth, until I found out what it was.) If I throw stones at his glass ass, I will lose him. Flustered by lust and hope, I do what I did in the beginning.

When I learned to love, male arousal was sacrosanct. I read my D.H. Lawrence. I did as I was told. I worshipped in his temple because I thought that would lead him to mine. I believed the erotic was romantic and that sexual liberation would open the door to the rose garden.

As I grew older, I learned to love myself. The door to the rose garden became red when I found the rose of Gertrude Stein. "Civilization begins with a rose," wrote Gertrude. Gertrude's rose is a clitoris, the rosebud, the heart of the matter. It is the metaphor for her art. Woman's sexuality is biological fact and part of primal elder religious faith. It is the "curse" of patriarchy. (Between 80 and 90 million women on the globe have suffered genital mutilation, so deep is the fear of female sexuality.)

I turn to the man of the moment, the cheerful one who still sits at the breakfast table with me. I ask him, "What would happen on earth if men and women revered a female principle, in fact and fiction? What if we worshipped not only the phallic pillar, the tree of life, but the...?"

He puts away his dishes as he says, "I know what's going to happen to me if I don't get out of your revolving door...I'm not going to get any work done today."

# Gentleman Friend
## Lisa Vice

**M**y mother's leaning against the kitchen counter with the groceries half put away reading "Something for Everybody"—this magazine they sell up at Purtlebaugh's Grocery. People put ads in there when they want to sell stuff they don't need anymore: old tires, used frigidaires, baby cribs.

I'm sitting at the kitchen table doing my math. "Listen to this," she says. "Lost eighty-five pounds. Selling my whole wardrobe. Size forty. What size do you figure she is now? A thirty?"

"You sound like one of these problems I've got to figure out."

"My little book worm. For pity's sake," she says, shoving the cans of soup up on the shelf. "It's Friday night. You're probably the only kid in town doing homework."

"It's real hard. You try it."

I tell her the problem I'm trying to figure out. "From a point on a straight road, John and Fred ride their bicycles in opposite directions. John rides ten miles per hour. Fred rides at twelve miles per hour."

"O.K., O.K.," she says, slamming the cupboard. "That's enough to give me a headache for the rest of my life."

She sits down at the table with one of her highballs and a box of crackers. I draw a chart like the one in the book. How many hours will go by for John and Fred to end up being fifty miles apart? I can't imagine riding my bike for fifty miles. The furthest I ever got was five miles. My legs hurt so bad I had to walk half way home.

My mother starts laughing and laughing. She's laughing so hard she's got tears running down her cheeks.

"What's the big joke?"

She smacks herself on the thigh, gasping. When she catches her breath, she reads it to me. "Wedding gown. Size fourteen. Worn only once." She starts laughing again.

"What's so funny about that?"

"Well, what'd she expect? To wear it every day? Put it on to take the trash out in? Wear it to work?" She swirls the ice cubes around in her glass and takes a swig. "Picture how desperate you'd have to be to buy yourself a used wedding dress."

She flips to the ads in back where people want to find each other and go out on dates. She's always trying to figure out if there's anybody for her to write to.

"Here's a doozy," she says. "Looking for a Christian family man. Now what kind of moron would advertise for that? Just go to any church if that's what you want. There's plenty of 'em lining the back pews."

"Retired fellow," she reads. "Don't drink or smoke. Looking for that special someone. Bet he's a real barrel of laughs. Probably thinks your feet'll fall off if you go dancing."

"Ruthie," she says, talking to herself the way she does. "It's Friday night. What would you like to do? I ought to stick my own ad in here. That's one way to get me a date."

"It'd be some total stranger."

"So?"

"Wouldn't you be scared?"

"Of what?"

"I dunno. Just scared."

"You watch too many of them late night movies."

"Well. You never know."

"He'd have to write me a letter first. Some ax murderer's not going to go through all that trouble just to lure me out of the house." She takes my pencil and starts filling out the squares on the form that's on the back. I read it upside down. 'Widow seeks gentleman friend,' her ad says.

"Gentleman friend?"

"Well. I can't exactly say boyfriend. Me here with more grey hairs than I can count. What else am I supposed to call it?"

"I'm home," my mother hollers, standing with the back door open letting the wind blow leaves right in. "Did I get any mail today?" She flings her car keys on the kitchen table and unzips her skirt, wiggling her hips till it slides down her legs and falls to the floor. She yanks her blouse off over her head before she even finished unbuttoning it. What she means is did anybody answer her ad. Even though there's nothing but junk mail, she looks through it real careful to be sure I didn't miss anything. Then she stands at the sink in her slip running cold water over her clothes—a black skirt and a white blouse with a floppy red bow she calls her Dairy Hut Get-up. She scrubs at the pink and brown stains from where the ice cream and syrups dripped down the front.

"Don't ask me why I bother with this. It's not like the morons who come

162

to get an ice cream would notice. But old Finicky Fowler's got an eagle eye." The way she always talks about her boss, I figure all he does is follow her around breathing down her neck looking for an excuse to fire her.

All during supper, she talks about what kind of guys might answer her ad. "Maybe there'll be one that looks like Paul Newman," she says, closing her eyes and holding her palm over her heart like she's about to swoon. Later, we turn the TV on and my mother lies on the davenport flipping through a magazine. She stops at a story called "September Eve." There's a picture of a blonde lady leaning back against a dark-haired man in a blue sweater. The lady's eyes are half-closed.

She throws the magazine on the coffee table. "Every night I sit here like some nun," she says.

I get the Chocolate Dream Bars I made after school and carry them in to her. "Ta da!"

She sits up and pats the cushion beside her. After a while she lets me brush her hair. When I take the bobby pins out, it falls down her back like syrup.

"You find any gray hairs, you know what to do."

"I don't see any," I tell her, even though there are a whole bunch of thick white hairs in the back. I can't stand yanking them out.

I lift her hair and pull the brush through in long strokes. While I'm brushing I can see Mr. and Mrs. Reeb from across the street sitting on their davenport watching their TV. I can see the blue light flickering across their faces as they stare straight ahead. I think about everybody, all up and down the streets of the town of Windfall, sitting side by side in front of their TVs. I don't know why, I can't explain it, but thinking about that makes me cry. I have to blink my eyes like crazy so my mother won't notice.

"Just tell me one thing." She grabs my hand to make me quit brushing. "Just tell me now. Is it my imagination, or is every single man in the whole God dammed state of Indiana already taken?"

When the letter comes, it's a long white envelope with her name and address printed on the front in red pencil. She stands in the middle of the kitchen with her lips moving as she reads it silently to herself. Her face is pale, the soft hairs on her cheeks have flecks of face powder on them. When I was little, I used to put my hands on either side of her face and give her a kiss. I can still remember the taste of her lipstick and how her cheeks felt like peaches.

"He put in his phone number. Give me a ring, he wrote, and signed his name. Bus Arnold. What kind of man calls himself Bus?"

After supper, while I'm doing the dishes, she takes one of her bubble baths. She keeps the door open so she can talk to me when I'm not running the water. "I have never once in my life called a man up on the telephone," she says. She acts like her hand'll shrivel up and fall off if she does. Even though the dishes are clean, I fool around with the suds, letting the cups fall like space capsules landing in the ocean.

"What am I supposed to do?" She sloshes the wash rag. Steam is thick on the windows making drops of water streak down the dark glass. I stand on tip toe and wipe it away. My own face looks back at me, like I'm some stranger peeping in the window.

When my father first died, my mother always said we'd lost him when strangers asked. Whenever she said that it felt like he was just down in the cellar, hiding behind the mildewed boxes of photographs and old clothes, waiting for us to find him so he could jump out and say, "You're it."

When my mother comes out of the bathroom with her house coat on she starts pacing back and forth, her slippers making sticky sounds on the linoleum. Finally she says she'll talk to this Bus Arnold if I dial his number. As soon as it rings, I hand her the receiver. While they talk, she twirls the black phone cord around and around her elbow. When she hangs up, she does a little tap dance across the kitchen.

"What'd he say?"

"He wants me to go have supper with him at Meryl's Highdecker. He says he just loves going out to eat."

The next day, she comes home with a brand new dress, this black sheath dress that zips up the back. It has scalloped edges around the neck and six tiny pearl buttons down the front. "It was on sale," she says, like she's apologizing.

On Friday night, she spreads her clothes out on the bed. Her white slip, clean underwear, stockings, her black dress. I watch her powder herself all over and put her clothes on. She stares in the mirror, dabbing her cheeks with rouge.

"He *is* some total stranger," she says. She looks at the back of her head in the mirror, jabbing the bobby pins in. She groans and snaps her purse open. She puts on more lipstick and blots it with a tissue. "I can't do it," she says, crumpling the tissue up and flinging it in the direction of her wastepaper basket. "I can't go out with somebody I've never laid eyes on." She kicks her shoes off and throws herself on the bed.

"He'll be here in five minutes," I say. "You want me to turn out the lights?"

She lies perfectly still, staring up at the light fixture like it's some crystal ball. "I'll tell you what," she smiles. "Let's lock the door and go upstairs. I can get a good look at him before I go anywhere."

We crouch in the dark, our eyes on the driveway. When the blue station wagon turns onto our street, we both hold our breath. The door opens and Bus Arnold, a skinny old hunched up man with thick white hair, gets out. He has a red and black checked hunting jacket on. When my mother lets her breath out, she sounds like a beach ball going flat.

"He's an old coot," she says, letting go of the curtain and sitting back on her heels. There's a loud knock on the front door.

"I'm not answering it," she says.

Bus Arnold is knocking and knocking.

"Go tell him I got sick." Her whisper smells like toothpaste and cigarettes.

I don't say anything.

"Well, all right. He'll get the hint eventually. Unzip me, will you?" She turns her back to me. I pull the zipper down and she steps out of her dress and lays it carefully on the end of my bed. Bus Arnold is tapping on the window.

"I ain't about to go out with somebody that's old enough to be my own father. Not when Mr. Right's out there waiting for me." She stretches out on my bed, her stockings rustling under her slip. She seems to shimmer and glow in the dark room, her long legs glistening like marble polished smooth.

# Three Conversations
## Martha Gies

**G**ladys handed Nan several pamphlets in a plain brown mailing envelope. "They tell the facts of life. You read them," her mother said, "and then we'll talk about it." The brown envelope had been lying in Gladys's bottom dresser drawer, beneath a tumble of slips with broken straps and sun halters with gardening stains. Nan, then eleven, had already studied the pamphlets half a dozen times in secret. She doubted much of what they said. Specifically, she doubted how so particular an activity could be called "the facts of life." But Gladys never mentioned the pamphlets again.

Nan heard her mother's scream after she had already gone upstairs to bed. She was home from Stanford, spending Christmas break in the big country house she'd grown up in.

She opened her eyes and held her breath, waiting for something to follow that piercing wail. The house was silent. She swung her legs out of bed, fumbled for her robe and hurried downstairs, keeping a firm grip on the polished banister. She found her mother in the bathroom off the master bedroom, sitting in a dry tub. Gladys wore a peach-colored knit suit and she was sobbing. In one hand she held a highball, in the other a lit cigarette.

"I'm sick. My head clangs. I'm cold."

"Do you want to get out of the bathtub and get in bed where it's warm?"

"No. Just put one of those towels over me, would you?"

"Do you want your bathrobe?"

"I'm fine," she said. Tears ran down her face. "Just put a towel on my legs."

Nan covered Gladys's knees with a big bath towel and laid another one around her shoulders like a cape. "Better?"

"My head hurts. The nerve down my left leg hurts. My shoulders are stiff. I feel nauseous."

"You don't eat anything."

"I don't care about food," Gladys sobbed.

"You have to eat."

"I would like another drink."

Nan took the glass out of her mother's hand. "What are you drinking?"

"Tequila. I drank up everything else."

"Maybe it's time for coffee."

Gladys shook her head and sobbed. "I'm thinking about going to bed with Ruben."

"What?"

"Just get me a drink."

In the kitchen, Nan rinsed her mother's glass, filled it with ice, and poured tequila. Her mother's late-night confession made Nan feel conspiratorial. She got another glass out of the cupboard for herself.

When she got back to the bathroom, Gladys was calmer, though her face was streaked and puffy. She was forty-two and very pretty. "Thank you," she said to Nan.

Nan turned on the little lamps on either side of the mirror, switched off the bright overhead light, folded the bath mat into a cushion, and sat on the edge of the tub, facing Gladys.

"Okay, so you're planning on going to bed with Ruben."

"I'm not planning it. I think about it all the time."

"That can't be right. You weren't thinking about it yesterday."

"I thought about it tonight when I danced with him."

Nan had been bopping around the living room to an Ike and Tina Turner record, the volume turned as high as it would go without distortion, when a car had pulled off the county road into their gravel driveway. Two men came to the door: Horace, the balding manager of their family farm, bulky in his big winter jacket; and Ruben, the handsome labor contractor and prosperous owner of three trucks. They were stopping by on their way home. Nan had turned the music down; Gladys had insisted on pouring drinks.

"Skip's only been dead three months," Gladys said. "What would he think of me?" She swigged her drink as if bracing herself for that verdict.

"It doesn't mean you don't love Daddy."

"I can't sleep with Ruben!"

"I guess you can if you want to." Nan lit one of her mother's cigarettes.

"I don't *want* to. I don't want to feel this way. I had twenty years of marriage to a wonderful man. He was wonderful in bed. That should be enough."

"I don't find Ruben that attractive." Nan couldn't quite reach her mother's ashtray, so she used the washbowl near her elbow.

"He's not attractive." Gladys stared at the burgundy terry cloth covering her knees. "Oh, well, of course he's attractive," she said. "I don't know. He watched me when we danced. I like his voice. I know he's young."

"Mother, what you're feeling is natural. It means you're alive." Skip had been the central focus of Gladys's life for twenty years. Possibly she'd never thought about another man.

"What are you talking about? It's not natural. He's the labor contractor. Skip would be ashamed. I'm ashamed. What was Ruben even doing here?"

"He was dancing with you. He was with Horace. Horace just stopped by to wish you Merry Christmas. You mixed them drinks and asked Ruben to dance."

"Ruben doesn't mean anything to me. I shouldn't have these feelings. I miss having a man."

"Well, I think it's natural."

"I suppose you'd sleep with Ruben."

"As a matter of fact, I would not sleep with Ruben. But not for the reasons you think."

"But you'd sleep with a Mexican."

"I'm the one who brought a black man home last Christmas, remember?" That had not gone over well with her father.

"I don't think that's funny," Gladys said.

"Neither did he. Neither did I. We thought of ourselves as on the cutting edge of the civil rights movement."

"Very funny. You're going to have a rude awakening some day."

"I have a rude awakening every week. I look forward to them."

"I don't know what's going to happen to me."

"Maybe you should get out of that bathtub."

"I'm sick. I think I'll just stay here."

"Do you want an aspirin?"

"I want a cigarette."

"You want Ruben." Nan lit a cigarette and handed it to Gladys. "You want Ruben, the hired labor contractor, a mere employee of your famous late husband. And you want him in bed."

Gladys nodded, sleepily. "Just once."

"Just once?"

"I think that would help."

"Help you feel better."

"Yes." Gladys laid her head back against the porcelain, snuggling down lower in the tub.

Nan slipped the cigarette from her mother's hand and then the glass. She sat on the edge of the tub, sipping tequila. The whole household was turned upside down since her father died. So much for the tight control he had kept on everything.

Gladys stirred. "If I could sleep with Ruben," she said, "I could get out of the bathtub."

The year Nan and Phil divorced, Nan left San Francisco where she had been assistant director at a private medical clinic. She bought a used Dodge pickup and retreated to a log cabin in the foothills of the Cascade Mountains. It was 1974, five years after the conversation in the bathtub. Nan wrote Gladys, inviting her up to spend a week in the back woods, and offering to meet her in town and drive her up the abandoned logging road. Gladys wrote back she'd get there herself.

Nan heard Gladys's car coming from a long way off. It was a warm September day. She stood out by the little road and watched her mother slowly maneuver a new Oldsmobile Tornado over jagged rock. When Gladys came alongside Nan, she stopped and lowered the automatic window.

"You're crazy to bring that big car in here," Nan said, leaning in to kiss her mother.

"Is there a place to park or shall I just abandon it?"

Nan directed her to a wide spot up ahead. "It will be safe. Nobody gets back in this far."

Gladys parked the car and stepped out. She was wearing a rust-colored ultra suede coat and ivory pumps.

"I hope you brought some other shoes," Nan said.

"Boy, and I thought Baja was remote," Gladys said, making her way across the rocky, pitted road.

Nan took Gladys up to the little cabin, which was outfitted with an iron cot, an Ashley wood burning stove and several of Nan's books—*Walden, The Autobiography of a Yogi*, Rodale's *Encyclopedia of Organic Gardening*, and *The Tassajara Bread Book*. There was a sink, but no running water. Nan burned kerosene and carried water from the spring.

Gladys seated herself at the wooden table beneath the window. "Well, this is austere."

Nan stood in front of her mother with a bowl of hard boiled eggs. "I thought we might take a picnic up to the waterfall, if that sounds good to you."

"Great."

Nan set the bowl down near Gladys. "You could help with the egg salad."

Gladys cracked an egg on the edge of the table. "What do you do for plumbing?" she asked.

"There's an outhouse."

"That's picturesque. Do you have some place for me to put the shells?"

Nan placed two squares of paper towel in front of her mother.

"Do you have a radio?"

"I don't want a radio. I came up here to get away from noise."

"How will you know if a storm is coming?"

"I'm not going to worry about it." Nan was brewing coffee on the Coleman stove, and when it began to perk she turned it down low.

"I hope you're not going to try to spend the winter up here!"

"Tell me about Mexico," Nan suggested.

"At least you might have gone to a commune," Gladys said.

"Mother, please."

"Alright, Nan. I just don't like to see you all alone."

"I didn't want to see myself all alone either," Nan said. "I got married, remember?"

Gladys bounced a peeled egg into the bowl. "I'm sorry about whatever happened between you and Phil."

"You'd be amazed how many men leave their wives when they finish med school," Nan said, feeling miserable. "I'm part of a trend. I'm a statistical probability."

"Maybe it can still be fixed."

"I don't think so," Nan said. "I'm not the great all-sacrificing wife that you were."

Gladys folded the paper towel around the egg shells. "What do you want me to do with these eggs?"

Nan moved the bowl of eggs to the counter and began mashing them with a fork.

"What do you do for refrigeration?"

"I keep a spring box down at the creek." Nan forked mayonnaise into the eggs. "You about ready?"

Gladys got up from the table and changed into a pair of flat shoes with laces. She put on the suede coat, and picked up her ivory leather handbag. "There are other men out there besides Philip Green," she said.

"Mom, let's just forget it." Nan spread egg salad onto whole wheat bread, then wrapped the sandwiches and nestled them in a small day pack. "You're not going to need your purse. Why don't you leave it in the cabin?"

"Oh, well," Gladys said. She positioned the handbag over her shoulder and followed Nan to the door. They stepped off the low wooden porch onto dry leaves. Nan started out toward the logging road, which would take them up to the waterfall.

"I guess I told you in my postcard that I met this man," Gladys said.

Nan slipped her arms through the straps of her small day pack. In the woods she liked her hands free. "All you said was he owned the resort where you stayed."

"One morning he sent a *mariachi* band to my room. Nine o'clock in the morning, here are all these men in black pants and vests with gold braid, playing trumpets just outside my door."

"Will I get a chance to meet him?"

"I don't know if he'd ever come up here. What would he do up here? He'd be bored. Besides, everybody would treat him like a Mexican."

"He *is* a Mexican."

170

"You know what I mean. Miguel is the former Lieutenant Governor of the Federal District. I take it the current administration doesn't like him, because he moved to Baja and bought this resort."

"Is he a Communist?"

"I never thought about it."

"You know, they actually let Communists have government jobs in Mexico."

"You don't have to lecture me, Nanette. I know they do."

The woods were silent. It was slow going over the rocks, but it was the only way to reach the trailhead. Sharp stones pressed into the soles of Nan's hiking boots. The road climbed through the cool forest of old Douglas Fir and Western Hemlock, fern, salal and huckleberries. When Gladys stopped to smoke a cigarette, she pulled a photograph from her handbag.

Nan studied the photograph. Miguel was seated with Gladys at a white table. Behind them were two palm trees and the sea. He looked like a Latin Bing Crosby and Gladys, in a white lace cocktail dress and sunglasses, could have been Dorothy Lamour. "*Road to Baja*," Nan said.

Gladys laughed and ground out her cigarette under her shoe.

"This way," Nan said. She steered Gladys off the road onto a faint and narrow path. They heard the roar of the waterfall before they saw it. Nan let her mother go ahead. The trail led to a clearing, and then they were standing at the edge of the little canyon. Directly across the canyon, the creek plunged a hundred feet into a circular green pool and sent mist rolling up the moss-covered rock walls around it.

"My God!" Gladys said. "It's something, isn't it?"

"It doesn't show up on the maps." Nan spread a cloth on the ground and patted it in invitation for her mother to sit.

"You've become pretty much a recluse."

The thermos hissed when Nan twisted the cap off the hot coffee.

"Well, I never want to interfere in the life of my child. If you enjoy living this way, that's all that's important."

Nan poured out two cups of coffee, and for a moment they sat in silence, taking little hot sips.

"Miguel and I were walking along the beach one day. It was the hottest part of the day, but we hadn't taken a siesta. No one else was on the beach. We were walking along the water line and carrying our shoes. When we started back up the beach, the sand was so hot I didn't think I could stand it. Miguel took the sandals out of my hand and knelt down to put them on my feet. He was fastening my sandal strap. I looked down at his back and I realized I was in love."

Nan handed half of an egg salad sandwich to her mother. In front of her, across the little canyon, tumbled the white strip of water, vertical and energetic. In her mind, Nan saw the other scene: the searing coast, her mother's hand on

Miguel's shoulder for balance, the sun in his eyes as he looked up at her. Behind them lay a blue lid of water, flat and consuming.

"So you're going back to Mexico."

"I fly out of Portland tomorrow."

"I thought you were spending the week here!"

"I'm sorry. I thought I wrote that."

Nan sighed and bit into her sandwich. The Mexican coastal scene glowed in her mind like the after image of a photo flash.

Eleven years later, Nan checked into a suite on the Oregon coast. She was late: Gladys had arrived the night before.

"I'm sorry about the schedule screw up," Nan said. Gladys sat on the bed, spraying a drying solution over a fresh manicure; Nan leaned down and kissed the top of her head. "They changed the date of the site visit, but didn't tell us until the last minute."

"Don't worry about it," Gladys said. "I've been rereading *The Sun Also Rises*."

Nan took a handful of pants, bras and slips out of her suitcase and put them in the drawer Gladys had left for her. "Half of the clinic's funding depends on that site visit."

"No problem. We have dinner reservations for eight o'clock."

At the restaurant, Gladys ordered razor clams. "Whenever I eat them I think of that summer we spent in a beach house at Waldport while Skip studied for the Bar."

"I remember that. Every morning at low tide, Daddy routed us kids out of bed to go clam digging. It took me years to figure out what the two of you were up to as soon as we left the house."

Gladys laughed. "You remember living on clams the whole six weeks? I learned to cook them every way in the book."

Behind her mother, a man dined alone. He had a beautiful profile, but he was obese. A silver-handled cane protruded from the empty chair beside him. He seemed to be staring at Nan whenever she looked up.

They were drinking coffee when Gladys suddenly said, "I know I'll never go to bed with a man again."

"Now why are you saying that?" Nan hadn't been with a man in over two years. She spent all her time writing grants for the clinic.

"I've thought about it. I'm pretty certain."

"You might marry again," Nan insisted. She looked at her mother, fifty-eight now, her blue dress and auburn hair, a rinse, no doubt, but attractive. Nan had her work, which consumed her; what did her mother have?

"For a long time, I thought I would move to Mexico and marry Miguel. Maybe I should have."

"I thought you were going to."

172

"He wanted to, but then we argued about a prenuptial agreement. I insisted on having one."

"What was the big deal? He had more money than you did anyway."

"Oh, I'm sure he did. He owned property all over Baja."

The obese man was signaling the waiter for his check. "See that man back there?" Nan asked.

Her mother dropped her eyes to the table, waited a moment, and then shifted around extra casually in her chair. "Senator Borkland," she said when she turned back. "Majority leader during the late sixties. He's been retired for ten years."

"Am I supposed to know him or something?"

"He and his wife were at our house for a couple of parties years ago, when Skip was alive."

"Anyway, Kathy's mother got married again when she was sixty-eight. She met a man at the racetrack. At Bay Meadows."

"Thoroughbreds or harness racing?"

"Harness races."

"That's not me."

"Mother, you don't know who you're going to meet. You might feel differently next year, or five years from now."

"I'm not going to argue about it. I'm saying I *know*."

"Well, I wish you wouldn't say it." Nan caught the waiter's eye. He paused at their table, and she ordered brandy.

"Bring me a brandy, too," Gladys told the waiter.

When he left, Gladys said, "The point is, I'm not young anymore."

"But you're alive."

"You don't know what it's like, Nan. When you're thirty-seven men still look at you. I'm fifty-eight years old. Men don't look at you when you're fifty-eight."

How could men "not look at" her mother? What gave them the right? The table appeared as a still life: damp circles imprinted the white linen, the U. S. Navy-cut teaspoons lay overturned, lipstick smeared the coffee cups. Nan took in her mother's pearl ring, the fresh pink nail polish, the chalky grey shingled walls. From behind a swinging door, she heard the rattle of silverware and a woman ask a man for cream.

"Your life doesn't depend on men's desire," Nan said violently.

The waiter, making an exaggerated show of not hearing any of the conversation, set two tumblers of hot water in front of them, each holding a cocked brandy snifter. He left quickly.

Nan leaned forward. "Do you remember when I first learned about sex?"

"Not really," Gladys said. "But I guess I must have told you something about menstruation."

"You gave me these pamphlets to read. One was called 'The Facts of Life.' Remember?"

"Vaguely."

"Actually, I read it before you ever gave it to me. I found it underneath a bunch of those halters that you wore for gardening, the kind with the wires running up the front."

"I wish you'd stay out of my drawers."

"Mother, that was twenty-five years ago."

"So what about the pamphlet?"

"Actually, there were several. But this one title made it sound like the key to the universe."

Senator Borkland rose to his feet. He wore a dark, expensive suit. He reached for the silver-handled cane and leaned on it heavily. As he passed their table, he looked appraisingly at Nan.

"Good evening, Senator," her mother said.

Nan saw his face assume the politician's mask. "Pleasure to see you, Gladys. This your daughter?" He winked at Nan.

"Nan, you've met Senator Borkland, haven't you? This is Nanette."

"Beautiful girl. Beautiful."

Nan was afraid the old bastard would try to join them. She nodded briefly and turned back to her mother, away from the man's expectant look. "We're about through here, aren't we, Mother?" She brought her napkin to the table.

"Pleased to have two beautiful women join me for a nightcap."

"Perhaps we'll see you later, Senator," Gladys said.

He bowed slightly, straightened, turned and left.

"I don't have any interest in going," Gladys whispered to Nan.

"God, I don't either," Nan said. She inhaled from her brandy snifter and felt her eyes burn.

"Good," Gladys said. "Then let's just enjoy ourselves. So what about this pamphlet?"

"All it talked about was sexual intercourse."

"So?"

"Well, there's a hell of a lot more to life than sexual intercourse."

"Name something," Gladys said, deadpan.

"Oh, for Chrissakes, Mother."

"I'm joking."

Behind her, Nan heard a limping footfall and the blows of a cane, powerful on the polished wooden floor. She felt a rising anger, an irrational desire to run after the old Senator and knock his cane out from under him. She took a swallow of brandy, squeezing her eyes tight against the fumes.

When she opened her eyes, she saw Gladys's snifter raised expectantly. "It was a joke, honey. Here, let's toast your work."

# What Can You Do About Love
## Naomi Feigelson Chase

**M**y daughter and I often discuss what we refer to as "your love life." We talk about sex, about love, about "relationships." When we do, it seems our roles are reversed. She gives me advice. That's because at forty-seven, it's strange to be dating. Everyone I know who is forty-six or more and dating thinks so too. It's a sign of an unstable world. "God's not in his heaven," I tell Rebecca.

"Her heaven," she reminds me.

That's another sign. At her age, I didn't believe in God, but the God I didn't believe in was a man. At her age, we discussed kissing on the first date. Now everyone asks, What about sex on the first date? What about drugs on the first date?

"What about spontaneity?" a friend asked me.

"What about aesthetics," I said.

"Thank god, I thought you were going to say 'morality.' I thought you were going to say 'respect.'"

What about morality? What about respect?

Janice is still dating at sixty. But she says she's through with men. Married and divorced twice, she sounds angry and afraid.

She rests her case on the ground of male ineptness.

"You know," she says, "men think they just have to stick it in and everything's fine. Or they just mess around a little bit with their left hand and everything's fine."

Janice says when she wants human contact she gets a massage.

"Every day?" I ask.

Evidently once a week is enough.

That's like my favorite line from "Annie Hall," from the scene with the split screen. Woody Allen says to his shrink, "She never wants to have sex. Three times a week."

And Annie is saying to her shrink, "He wants to have sex all the time. Three times a week."

"Nobody sleeps together anymore," Jerry said when I told him Lucy and Jim hadn't slept together for a year.

"But they've only been married two years," I said, "and already they're getting divorced."

"They're just a la mode, dearie," he answered, lunching with me in the Atrium Club, an unlit cigarette between his teeth to keep him from smoking. "Chic. If they hadn't slept together at all, they might not be splitting."

"You're too sophisticated," I said. "And they're not English. They're not the Harold Nicolsons. Or Leonard and Virginia Woolf. And they're both heterosexual. At least I think they are."

Jerry was disdainful. "You're such an old-fashioned girl," he said. "I'm not talking heterosexual. I'm talking celibacy. I've been celibate two years now."

It surprised me to hear that. "What about Karen?" I asked. "Don't you live with her?"

"Live, yes. Sleep, no. I've no desire. I've told her, 'Have a fling if you like. Just don't tell me about it.'"

"And how does Karen feel about that?" I asked.

He ignored my question. "Really, Lila, you'd be better off like me. Celibacy's 'in.' You should try it."

"I'll think about it," I said, but I was dubious. Jerry put out his unlit cigarette and reached for the check.

"If you're celibate, what do you do about love?" I asked.

"Love," he said, "what does anyone do about love?"

Alice is very upset about the sex-abuse scandals, kids in day care centers, two-, three-, four-year-olds, babies. First in California, now in New York. Even the Minneapolis theater where she once worked. It's true, it's all over the place.

Alice wants to know why it's happening now.

I tell her it's always happened. Not that it's any comfort. It's just today, nothing sacred is sacred. Nothing profane is private. Look at Virginia Woolf. Her uncle abused her as a child and maybe it made her crazy. And everyone knows about it.

Look at Lucy. Lucy's uncle forced her to have sex with him for twelve years, from the time she was four. Her mother's brother. When her parents found out, they were furious with Lucy. It makes me sick. It made Lucy sick.

I told Max I was going to put an ad in the Personal columns. He said it's dangerous going out with people you don't know. His cousin once picked up a guy and had sex with him and then they went to his sister's house to get something to eat. When they walked into the kitchen, the guy went crazy. Chopped Max's cousin up with a cleaver. He nearly died.

When my father asked me why I was divorcing Ben, I said I couldn't talk to him or sleep with him anymore.

"Well, sleep in another room," my father said.

"What do you think I'm going to get Pat for our anniversary?" Maddie asked me, after she told me he was sick in bed.

"A pornographic TV movie," I answered.

"How did you know?" She seemed surprised and disappointed I had guessed.

"I'm a writer. That's how I'd write it."

When I told Max, he laughed. "One day they hired me and Craig to clean their apartment and we decided to turn the mattress. We found three porno books, you wouldn't believe it. All of women's boobs."

"I hate that word."

"Which word?"

"You know which word. And you must have been expecting to find something like that if you turned over the mattress."

"We were."

Celia got Dan a gift for their fifteenth anniversary, a new bed with mirrors on the ceiling. I told her it sounded like their marriage was improving. She said it was. The only other person I ever knew with mirrors over her bed was Caryl Dee, the nightclub singer. I always wondered if that was narcissistic or pornographic. Celia says it's love.

Lucy called me up the other night, hysterical. She said, "We've only been separated three days and already Jim's sleeping with some other woman."

I said, "But Lucy, you asked him to leave. You said your marriage was impossible."

"But I always thought he'd come to his senses and beg me to come back."

"But you don't want him back."

"Yes, I do," she said. "I want him back."

Two weeks ago I went out with a man I liked and we had a wonderful time. He wrote me a note telling me what a wonderful time he had. I asked Dan what I should do about it.

"Don't sit by the phone," he suggested.

Ted used to count the number of times we'd slept together. He'd say, "I figure we've slept together 370 times" or "470 times," or when we'd been married twelve years he said that was 4,380 days and if we averaged every three nights we'd be up to 1,460 times.

I loved him but I couldn't stand the counting.

He said, "You knew when you married me I was a number cruncher."

After he died, nights I would get in bed with a glass of gin and my notebook and count the number of days he'd been dead. I can't remember when I stopped counting.

"There wasn't much going on in Mobile," Max said, "but there was this really attractive guy and we used to fool around a lot. Everybody fooled around a lot, whether they were gay or not. He used to do some trapping. Sometimes I'd go with him, just to go for a walk in the woods. It sure wasn't because of the trapping. And we had some pretty hot sex, but he just used to shoot off like a pistol. He couldn't wait.

"Well, he got married after I moved away and a couple of years ago I heard his wife killed him. Either shot him or stabbed him in the back. I always wondered if it was because he came so fast."

Max and I never talk about sex. I mean, I listen to his stories about all his affairs—"affairettes," he calls them—but we never talk about what they mean. I want to ask him, Is it just sex? Don't you really want friendship? Don't you really want love? Why are we so afraid to talk about love?

Ted was an ever-ready battery and a terrific lover besides. Except when he was drunk. Which was often. Then he got belligerent. And mean. "C'mon," he'd say. "Let's fuck."

"That sounds like the punch line of a lousy joke," I'd tell him. But he didn't laugh. He'd threaten to leave. Then he'd pass out. I'd end up sleeping on the couch.

It was just before the poetry reading, about two seconds after he said hello, that Jim told me why he left Lucy.

"I told her there was something fundamental missing. She just got up and left."

"What is it? What do you think is fundamental?"

"I don't know," Jim said. "That's part of the problem."

"What's part of the problem?"

"That we don't know. That we all go around ad-libbing our lives. I'll tell you one thing, though. It's not sex. It's what comes before sex."

"Maybe it's chemistry," I said.

"Maybe." He paused. "You know how with some people there's just this attraction. You either have it or you don't."

"Maybe it's friendship."

"I don't know. Maybe it's love. Maybe that's what it is."

He didn't sound sure. But at least he was trying.

Why is everyone so confused about love? Even the *New York Times* tries to explain it. The *Times* quotes a Yale psychologist who says romance is not so important as sharing ideas and ideals. Sex is not so important either. What is important is how equal the love is.

One "eminent psychoanalyst," Dr. Otto Kernberg, opts for sexual passion, according to the *Times*. "An internal wildness" is what preserves a marriage, Kernberg says.

He describes a pathology of love, a continuum ranging from narcissism to mature romantic love. The latter is a very complex emotion. In achieving it, mystery is more important than orgasm. Mystery leads to transcendence, even though transcendence, he warns, has its perils.

That's where I stopped reading. I think Jim put it better when he said we're all ad-libbing.

I'm on an alphabet kick. What begins with L besides Love? Loss. Loneliness. When I told that to Rebecca, she said, "Lemons. Latkes."

"Nobody needs a daughter who's a smart-ass," I said. "You should feel sorry for me. I'm your mother."

"I do feel sorry for you, but you don't really need it. You feel sorry enough for yourself. One of us has to keep on going. How about L for Life. Levity."

# Celibacy at 50
## Or the Week All My Old Lovers Return
## And a New Movie Opens in Japan

### Claire Braz-Valentine

Old lovers call me, one after the other,
missing me,
wanting to see me,
be with me,
touch me,
love me.

I am confused.
What's happening here?

Flowers arrive and chocolates,
cards in the mail.
Even my ex-husband gets in the act,
gets a divorce and calls me.
Would I consider perhaps dinner,
a lunch—well then just a snack maybe.

I am confused.
What's happening here?

Men begin to stop by,
just happen to be in the neighborhood.
The phone rings over and over.
How about a weekend away?
A movie...a cup of coffee...some drinks.
a walk by the beach...

What's happening here?

I list all their names
and try to remember
things about them,
to remember when we were together
and why we parted.
I am afraid to answer my phone
or even look in the mailbox.
Should I see them?
If so which one?
Should I see all of them?
Maybe put them in a room together,
let them talk it out.
Find out what's happening here.

I can't make a decision
and I dream of hiding in a closet
wearing a nun's habit.

On the seventh day
an old friend calls
and when he tells me what he tells me
all my questions are answered.

"He's back," he said. "Read the paper.
The front page. He's back and he's better than ever.
I wanted to be the first to tell you.
Godzilla lives!"

GODZILLA LIVES

Evolved from the volcano where I thought they had killed him,
refreshed as if from a five year sauna,
trimmed down and mad as hell,
ready to fight a genetic mutant rose bush,
with fangs,
who goes by the name of Violante.

Well now,
Godzy baby,
my choice is made.

You are back in my life,
big and burly and so full of yourself,
with a mind of your own,
and so politically correct.

You will stomp down streets
and flash your little pointy teeth
with your full green lips snarling,
so righteously pissed off
about nuclear warfare and Trident II missiles.
You are my man of action
like no other.

With just the right devil may care air about you,
and that sexy swish in your seductive scaly tail,
oh the delicious gentle dangerous power in you.
How could anyone compare?

That night I dream of a lover
burly and dark,
brave and gentle,
wild and lonely.
His skin is green.
And he doesn't wear a deodorant.
His flesh is cool to the touch.

Oh Godzilla, I just can't help but love you.
I forgive you your sins.
Of stepping on cars,
and walking though bridges,
and even your rotten table manners,
and the fact that my family thinks
you're funny looking.
I forgive you for letting me think
you were gone forever.
Godzilla, you are the one I've been waiting for.
I will meet you anywhere, any time,
no questions asked.
I'll even pay for the drinks.

Welcome back Godzilla.
What's happening baby?

You are my monster.
I am your woman.

# The Black Madonna
## Maria Bruno

The idea of menopause has always bothered me. In my Sicilian family when the women reach menopause they start to shrink, wear black and grow mustaches. Suddenly they're keeping plastic on the lamp shades and dressing like little gnomes, with black scarves and widows' dresses and orthopedic shoes with the sides slit to let their corns breathe. The women pace the house, stopping at the thermostat to ask, "Is it hot in here, or is it me?" They huddle at kitchen tables and whisper, dipping crusts of white bread into cups of thick Maxwell House coffee. They take on an aura of mystery. My Grandma D'Angelo once told me about this coven of Sicilian witches called La Strega who had a potion for everything, which involved some bizarre rituals with lizards and plum tomatoes, and the nasal hair of local Mafioso. I often thought my grandmother and my aunts and even my mother looked like little witches, straight from a La Strega meeting, huddled over their bread and coffee, holding their large black purses in their laps, close to their hearts. They were always surrounded by food: large cans of olive oil decorated with indecipherable script I could not translate looming over bowls of freshly cut pasta, which ofttimes looked to me, a superstitious child, like mounds of yellow snakes. Thick red sauces bubbled on the stoves in silver pots, the steam rising like old souls to the ceilings. Sometimes old age seemed a mystery to me, something strange and wonderful and powerful. The women would gather at funerals and hush and moan and finger their rosaries and comment on the condition of the corpse and what the widow would stand to inherit. They could size up the mortician and the dead man's assets without missing a cue; it was phenomenal the way they understood a good embalming job, not to mention money and inheritance. They would nod in approval, or shake their heads and say, "Did you see his lips? He never had lips like that. She should have called her cousin Guido. Who's her broker anyway?"

It was only when my gynecologist told me I was pre-menopausal that I remembered the mustaches and my ever-shrinking aunts, Rosie and Philomena, always hemming their dresses, as I towered above them in my new found height. As my doctor talked to me about bloating and heavy periods and hot flashes, all I could think about was me dressed in a little black dress with matching orthopedic shoes, bending over with a razor blade to slit the leather. I thought of my mustache sprouting overnight like one of those slow motion nature films you see on public television. "And of course your eggs are old," said the doctor, interrupting my reverie. I looked up, my mouth wide open, thinking about all those Shrinking Man movies I saw in the Fifties and how the cat always cornered the tiny victim in a doll's house. "Old?" I asked, still trying to focus my attention.

"You're probably not going to have any more children, are you? So not to worry."

"Maybe you've made a mistake," I blurted, panicking. I tried to think of all the reasons I could be bloated. Water retention, bad sushi, a visitation from an incubus. I saw that in a Barbara Hershey movie once. This incubus made some sporadic night visits, tossed her around, and impregnated her with the future anti-Christ who eventually grows up and works for the CIA, Latin America division. I touched my stomach waiting for a stiletto-toed kick. It felt large and round and it gurgled, just as if I were gestating some small sea mammal. That's it. I had had a close encounter of the first kind with a radical extraterrestrial Save the Whales coalition, who had a bizarre tabloid plot to repopulate the planet using *in vitro* fertilization on human subjects. This wasn't menopause at all. This had intergalactic ramifications. This was prime time; this was Oprah, Geraldo, maybe even Kitty Kelley.

"When was the last time you had intercourse?" he asked matter-of-factly as if he were asking my shoe size.

I held up two fingers.

"Two months," he said, scratching the information onto a pink form.

"Years," I said softly. "Two years."

He looked up and into my eyes for the first time.

"Years," he said, crossing out his scribbled annotation.

Menopause, I thought. Men, oh, pause. I had already paused big time. I was hoping things would warm up any time soon, and now this news: unwanted facial hair, old eggs, a uterine aquarium fit for endangered species. Not to mention the fashion risks involved in looking like an Italian widow.

"You really should be thinking about taking it out," he said, clicking his Cross pen.

"Taking what out?" I asked. I was thinking about Barbara Hershey doing a crazed lambada in Peruvian alpaca while her son looked on.

"Your uterus. You don't need it anymore," he said, smiling and patting me on the shoulder. He left the room.

"Why not take my vagina too?" I said after him. "I'm not using that either!" I struggled to get out of the stirrups.

"This isn't a fatal condition," I argued out loud, as I plunged a finger through my pantyhose. So I had a few old eggs, a fibroid or two, and I could possibly be featured on the UFO segment of "Unsolved Mysteries." Life as I knew it wasn't over. It wasn't as if I had to go straight home and start clipping coupons for "Attends" from the weekly shopping guide. I couldn't even remember why I had chosen celibacy anyway. I knew it had something to do with the string of bad luck I had had with men after my divorce. There were of course the men my age who wanted a woman to be "sporty." They wanted me to kayak down Number 5 rivers in the Royal Gorge, or bicycle to Niagara Falls in spandex, or powerwalk the Appalachian Trail. Too many of them had seen those Mickey Rourke movies where he didn't wash his hair and wanted to experiment with ice cubes, vegetables, and doggie commands. The even kinkier ones had seen one too many talk shows and decided since this was the Nineties, sex could be good in inversion boots or during the spin cycle. The yuppified soon became boring, steeped in spring water, balsamic vinegar, and free range chickens wanting antiseptic sex at Club Med. Much to my chagrin, the best lover of them all, my last relationship before the hiatus, had voted for Reagan twice. I decided it was politically incorrect to experience another right wing orgasm even if I did see a white light and heard God. So I called it quits. While I still had reasonably young eggs. While red was my color of choice. While dust still collected on my lamp shades.

But when I exited the doctor's office things rapidly changed. By the time I had signaled a taxi, I was literally on the prowl. I was ready. Okay, I thought. I'll kayak. You want kayak, you've got it. My middle name was "Whitewater" from then on. I was willing to try spandex. Nikes. Those narrow bike seats you wince at when you think of them. And even though, according to "A Current Affair," there's a serial killer stalking the Appalachian Trail killing unsuspecting couples as we speak, just see if I turn down a powerwalk proposition. I'd be willing to experiment with a zucchini or a cucumber, perhaps, if they haven't been left in the garden too long. I draw the line at leashes and dog obedience training, but he doesn't have to wash that oil pomade out of his hair if he doesn't want to. There was no chance I'd see a white light and hear God with a George Bush aficionado—at best I could expect an all expenses paid astral projection of John Sununu—so I assumed I could remain politically correct even in my most desperate of times.

I decided to go to Madame Lucia Sophia, the resident psychic in my old neighborhood. She was legendary in my familial circles; women especially spoke her name in hushes, as if the mere articulation could stir some cosmic upheaval. Madame Lucia Sophia did all of her work in bed, the bed she had taken to twenty-five years ago when she thought she was dying. She gave readings while her clients, mostly Sicilians in the neighborhood, sat at the foot of her bed, sneaking the enveloped payment underneath the horsehair blanket. It was said you could just take two steps into her bedroom and she could tell all about you, what was to happen, who had placed a curse on you, how much it would cost to lift it. She knew spells, and how to make potions, how to make men love you, how to seek proper revenge. She wore a black dress, and a black wool scarf tied in a big knot underneath her chin, even in the summer when the room grew hot with her relatives attending to her every need.

"Francesca," she said planting two kisses on my cheeks. "You look well." I sat next to the bed.

"Thank you Madame Lucia Sophia. That's not what my doctor says."

"Doctors! What do they know?" she said, waving her hands in the air like a magician. "Give me your hands, Francesca."

There was a palpable silence.

"Ah," she whispered raspily. "Ah."

"What is it Madame Lucia Sophia?"

"Antoinette," she yelled, "light two candles at the Holy Virgin. Say Francesca Ricotta three times and then two Hail Marys."

"Yes, Grandma," Antoinette answered, scurrying to the mini shrine next to the window, lighting the votives with a disposable Bic.

I began to get worried. What had she seen? Old eggs? Stomach bloat? Satan's spawn offering aid to the Contras? I frowned.

She held my hands tightly. For a moment she looked odd, ethereal, like one of those talk show channelers whose faces contort into New Guinea tribal masks. Her voice changed too. "Ah," she roared, like some mega-hero circa 4000 B.C., "ah!" She never let go of my hands.

Suddenly I felt a white heat surrounding me. Was it global warming or was it me? I began to feel woozy, almost drugged. A fury of images sped into my vision: Johnny LaPaglia in his inversion boots hanging from the ceiling, all bat-faced and flushed with his nostrils flaring. "Come on, Frankie," he said, "strap yourself in." When I wouldn't, his penis appeared, half pachyderm, half iguana, summoning me to follow the gravitational pull. Suddenly I saw Joey Benvenutti setting the Kenmore on spin, lifting me into position above the agitator, the next best thing to a whiter wash. The sudsy expanse became a Number 5 river in the mountainous Royal Gorge, the Colorado water whipping my face, the whirl-pool spinning furiously until I tumble like Alice into a dark Palermo cavern where a coven of Sicilian witches are plucking nose hairs from half drugged mafioso. I'm wearing a black dress and knotted scarf and black shoes; my corns ache. "Bloat? Hot flashes? Irregular menses? Step this way," they say in unison, stroking the soft fur above their lips. A large crone hands me a glass of green liquid. "Drink this," she says. I do, carefully surveying at first, for anything reminiscent of nasal sloughings. The crone points to a large mirror. I walk up to it. No longer womb-weary, I loom large, the Women's Singles Kayak Olympic Champion. The image undulates and I appear powerful, dressed in athletic spandex, Nikes, wrist and ankle weights—I'm making a citizen's arrest on the Appalachian Trail, singlehandedly disarming the serial killer who looks suspiciously like an unwashed Mickey Rourke, Vitalis and all. For a moment I see Barbara Hershey playing me in a subject for reenactment on "America's Most Wanted." She's holding up some handcuffs, a dog leash, two overgrown zucchinis. Another flash of white light blinds me. In that instant, I see the Holy Virgin, the Black Madonna, straight from Tarpeni, in a black robe, complete with a moon shaped aura, toe bells, and what appears to be marinara dripping from her open palms. I kneel at her feet. I know at last I'll have what I am looking for. I look up; she is a Da Vinci. Instead of the silver heart pierced with bloodied swords that has always been a symbol of her eminence, she's carrying a large black purse next to her heart brimming with grains, garlic, sweet basil. At her feet lay a scythe. She seems awfully quiet. I twitch. What? Say something. Anything. What about world peace? Hunger? Mario Cuomo? Remember Bernadette? Lourdes? The time you appeared on that canoli in Bensonhurst? Give me a sign, Blessed Virgin. A small sign. Maybe a sealed envelope I can open in the year 2000. More silence. I trace my fingers over the scythe; it vibrates, as does the earth around it. My fingers tingle with the power. Finally, a flutter of blue doves circle her head. "Women are the real mysteries," she said cryptically and disappeared. And suddenly my eggs don't seem so old, my waistband loosens its vicelike grip; no more visions of Third World antichrists bearing my surname doing "The Forbidden Dance" for the Pentagon. Instead of Roses, I smell pesto.

"Francesca?" said Madame Lucia Sophia. "Francesca?"

"Yes?" I stammered, still feeling the heat.

"You're squeezing my hands, Bambina," she said, soothingly. I let go. "Go simmer these with some plum tomatoes, imported, not domestic," she whispered raspily, retrieving a small cloth sack from beneath the blanket. "Say four Hail Marys and light a red candle over the steam. Soon you will have your answers."

"Will it work?" I asked, still dazed.

"Ivana Trump asked me the very same thing just last week," Madame Lucia Sophia laughed, waving me away with one swoop of her hand.

Later that day, I answered the door. There was a time when I didn't answer the door for unexpected visitors: the uniformed Girl Scouts pushing Thin Mints and shortbread, Indian Guides hawking raffle tickets for sides of beef, the Jehovah Witnesses offering *The Watchtower* and armageddon for one quarter and fifteen minutes of my time. Then there's the newly formed Christopher Columbus Defense Fund headed by one of the DeBlasi twins in the neighborhood, the same boys who once, in a perpetual seventh grade drug sniffing haze, mistakenly identified the Nina, Pinta, and the Santa Maria as street hustlers working the sidewalk in front of their cousin Mikey's delicatessen. There's always a succession of men at my door: one who wants to side my house with aluminum, another wants to sweep my chimney, sell me light bulbs, backyard ceramic Madonnas, salvation. Then, of course, there's the Kirby man. He comes every year trying to sell me his Kirby, with its fifty nifty vacuum cleaner attachments. He always arrives in an old Malibu Classic and leaps up my stairs two at a time. He stands at my door in a too tight gabardine suit, a white button-down shirt and a metallic necktie, looking like something out of "Robocop," half man, half machine, with $1,200.00 worth of metal slung over his shoulders. He looks wild, disjointed, ready to fight dirt and oppression anywhere, ready to make my life complete.

That day, after I made the sauce Madame Lucia Sophia had suggested and lit the red candle and said the Hail Marys, I stood in the kitchen swirling the red sauce with a wooden spoon. When I was through, the Kirby man arrived and I let him in. I had very distinct reasons. At forty-three, I am one of those women *USA Today* has categorized as having about as much chance of getting married again as getting shot by an Arab terrorist, contracting hoof and mouth disease, or seeing Elvis and Mayor LaGuardia appearing live at Radio City Music Hall with the Rockettes.

That day he looked oddly familiar.

"Don't I know you?" I asked, while he set his equipment on my living room carpet. I could smell the sauce brewing in the kitchen.

"Maybe. Maybe not," he said, deliberately ambiguous.

I didn't care that he poured dirt, sludge, coal chips on my carpet. He smashed the alien particles into the open weave, his black stilettoes moving in a circular motion. There wasn't anything the Kirby man couldn't do. Plush. Shag. Sculptured weave. His machine swept away dog hair, Dorito chips, kitty litter, stray buttons, rotten eggs, unpopped kernels of corn, the kind Orville Redenbacher would call Old Maids. He worked feverishly, sweeping, swirling, smiling, often slicking back his oily brush cut with his free hand. "Don't I know you?" I asked again, marveling at his Godlike precision. The vacuum cleaner purred with delight. He stood close to me and I could hear his heart, a well tuned machine, beating rapidly. "Aren't you from Richmond Hill? Lenny Patriarcha? You fixed cars?"

"Whatever you want," he whispered blowing a rush of hot air onto my neck.

"I want you to sweep me away," I whispered back. He placed the attachment in my hand. I came alive. I did the carpet, baseboards, lined curtains, venetian blinds, cat hair from throw pillows. He held my hand as I glided through the room. I decided I had to have it all. "I know you," I said, trying to remember. We whirled in unison, dusting elephants with raised trunks, the plastic Madonna suctioned to the TV, the crucifix on the wall, the fabric lamp shades. "You really ought to get plastic for these," he said breathily, adjusting the suction on the hose. I trembled. He was something familiar I couldn't shake, like a bad dream, a black ride, a dark angel—a door-to-door Desperado who pedals something

Everywoman needs.

"Take it all," he cooed, nibbling at my neck. And I did. All $1,200.00 worth.

"Do you have something on the stove?" he asked as I was writing the check.

I could hear it bubbling as I entered the kitchen. The deep red, almost purple sauce flowed over the tall silver pot into a growing puddle on the floor. I took it off the burner and it kept bubbling as if it had a mind of its own. The kitchen was hot. I fanned my flushed face with a potholder. The red liquid swirled, spilling over, spattering my bare legs, making me wince. The sauce roared, and I could hear generations of the La Strega Sisters collecting body hairs from Brando look-a-likes, unafraid. I looked into the pot and saw generations of kitchens with women whispering in black dresses, seated at enamel tables, holding their large purses next to their large hearts, drinking that thick coffee, smiling those Da Vinci smiles.

I heard the door slam. I ran to the window, exhausted, spattered with sauce. I cradled my new machine; it was still running.

He slid into the car, stuffing the sales receipt and the check in the overhead visor, elated over my purchase. He blew me a final kiss as I watched his Malibu Classic sputter down the street to the next driveway. I turned the machine OFF, just as he disappeared forever into another home, lugging his wares behind him.

# Sleeping with Soldiers
## (an excerpt)
## Rosemary Daniell

I met Raymond as we both stood among the crowd in a gay disco that jostled and hooted beneath the stage during a "buns" contest—a chorus line of jockey-shorted or G-string-clad contestants who pranced backward across the stage, jiggling their backsides. As the applause melted, he took my elbow, asked if I'd like to dance. I looked up, way up, into liquid black eyes fringed by long sooty lashes. As we moved around the floor, it was as though all the grace in the world had magically flown into his lanky six-foot body. Following him left me breathless but exhilarated. "I'm twenty-eight," he confided over breakfast at a fast-food spot after the disco had closed at three. "How old are you?" "Thirty-six," I lied, easily lopping off six of my forty-two years. "And at my age, I don't go out with anyone over three times unless there's a chance of a long-term relationship. And just now, I think that would have to mean someone with money." "Don't worry 'bout it," he said to my surprise, "I've got thirty thou in a trust fund."

By the time I found out he was actually eighteen and unemployed—indeed, was back in high school after an abortive stint in the army—we had already slept together several times. On the most recent occasion, I had admired, like a seamstress admiring a fine piece of shirring, the puckered scar from navel to groin ("Kidney surgery—if I ever have to go through *that* again, I'll just kill myself") that marked his otherwise China-silken body. He had burrowed into me, holding my wrists to the pillow as Mother's Finest sang, "Tie Your Mother Down" from the FM radio. "That reminds me," he blurted into my ear, "I'm not really twenty-eight like you thought..."

Since I now knew his true age, I invited him to sit outside on the porch when he stopped by after his high school classes. I wanted to avoid the wrestling match toward my bed, the teasing and pleading and nipping that made him seem like a cute but annoying puppy, that would inevitably take place if I asked him inside.

Determined to redirect my emotions toward the maternal—feeling, since I was older, responsible for both our sexual impulses—I listened supportively—all the while, admiring his black-lashed eyes, set like gigantic onyxes within his eggshell face, his perfect Grecian profile—as he talked about school, his "other" girl-friends, and repeatedly, his problems with his engineer father, his straitlaced mother, his preppy siblings. An orchid in a field of crabgrass, I thought. I had once given him a ride to his parents' house in the suburbs. He had directed me to an ugly, sprawling split-level on a vast but shrubless lawn. A graying crew-cut man in a droopy sport shirt had stared warily at me from over his power mower, a woman with a crimped beauty-parlor wave, a red-and-white-checked apron around her puffy middle, had stepped out into the carport to see who had arrived. "I sleep in a room off the kitchen," Raymond had told me. "It's sort of like I'm not really part of the family. In fact, I used to think—to wish—I was adopted."

He was different from them, he said—he wanted to travel, do things, meet people, maybe even become a male model, or go on the stage. He had run away to New York once, he told me, where he had hung out around Times Square, performed in a couple of porn films—from his exhibitionistic dancing, his fancy fucking, this was easy to imagine. Finally, he had been picked up by "a man in a black leather coat—the only man I ever fell in love with. We lived together at his apartment; he bought me a coat just like his—that black one I have now. Then one day, he ran out into the street, got hit by a cab..."

Like his fantasy finances, his imagined thirty thousand dollars, Raymond's past was an extravagance, a creation, as was his personal style. He dressed with a flash, a flair, common to Savannah blacks and gays, yet rare in straight white Southerners. Sometimes he duded himself up in a black leather jacket with a tiger painted on the back, black leather pants, black leather wristbands studded in steel. Other times he affected a three-piece mint-green suit—"Don't I look like one of the bro's?" he asked proudly. In his vest pocket, he stashed a half-pint bottle of Maddog 20-20 from which he occasionally swigged as I primly sipped Bloody Marys or gimlets over lunch in middle-class restaurants.

"Where did you get *him*?" Anne asked when I met her at a Savannah airport with Raymond in tow. He was walking ahead of us, carrying her bags, dressed in the black leather jacket, the steel-studded black wristbands, his glistening black waves slicked back in a satiny ducktail. I could tell she wondered if he was dangerous. "But really, he reminds me of a motherless puppy," she laughed after he had eagerly shaken her hand, jumped out of the car at a downtown intersection, and, waving good-bye over and over, had loped backward down the sidewalk like a gangly black Labrador retriever.

"You're just like an actress—you get right down on his level," accused another woman visitor after going dancing with us. "Well, of course!" I said, amazed that she found anything unusual in my behavior, in my consorting with an eighteen-year-old. "You don't expect *him* to get on *my* level, do you?"

Indeed, right then, maturity meant sadness, the past, to me. Pleasure was my primary value—and Raymond was by far the best dancer in Savannah, moving through strobe lights like liquid mercury, leaving me too breathless to live in any but the present moment.

# HE 2-104: A True Planetary Nebula in the Making

## Gloria Vando

On the universal clock, Sagan tells us,
we are only moments old. And this
new crab-like discovery in Centaurus,
though older by far, is but
an adolescent going through a vital
if brief stage in the evolution
of interacting stars. I see it
starting its sidereal trek
through midlife, glowingly complex—
"a pulsating red giant" with a "small
hot companion" in tow—and think
of you and me that night in August
speeding across Texas in your red
Mustang convertible, enveloped in dust
and fumes, aiming for a motel bed,
settling instead for the backseat of the car,
arms and legs flailing in all directions,

but mostly toward heaven—and now
this cool red dude winking at me
through the centuries as if to say
*I know, I know,* sidling in closer
to his sidekick, shedding his garments,
shaking off dust, encircling
her small girth with a high-density
lasso of himself, high-velocity
sparks shooting from her ringed
body like crazy legs and arms until
at last, he's got his hot companion
in a classic hold and slowly,
in ecstasy, they take wing and
blaze as one across the Southern skies—
no longer crab, but butterfly.

# First
## Eva Shaderowfsky

The ride to Fred's place in New Jersey was too long. A drop of sweat tickled its way down her side and another itched between her breasts.

Damn the air conditioner. Why did it have to give out the first hot day in June!

Just two hours ago, after Jack left for work, she had bathed, shaved her legs and underarms, washed her hair, put on her beige silk and lace underpants and camisole, a black polished cotton skirt and a white on white patterned blouse.

Shouldn't have worn a bra. It'll leave marks.

Her stomach did a flip thinking of him. He seemed surprised when she called.

She missed the turn off. Fifteen minutes later, she was back in the same place.

He'll think I chickened out.

The apartment house was red brick, like the one she had lived in as a child. She knew she would be too nervous to feel much today. A body of fifty to bring to a first-time lover—marks, scars, roughenings, dimplings.

But he's fifty-six, he must have them, too. I know better than that. It's different for him. He was with that young woman at the party.

When she parked the car, her skirt was stuck to the backs of her thighs and the blouse glued between her shoulder blades.

OK. This is it.

She rolled up the windows and got out. Suddenly, she was dizzy. Leaning against the car, she took several deep breaths of muggy air. Her stomach heaved and she sat down on the car seat with her legs still outside.

"Beth, what is it?"

She looked up and there he was. He must have been waiting. Her stomach hurt.

"Oh, hi," she said and tried to smile.

"You look really pale. Let's go inside. I'll get you some cold soda."

"I think I've just got to sit here for a second. I'll be better in a couple of minutes," she smiled wanly.

"I'll be right back. I'll get some coke. It'll make you better. Always works for me when it's so hot."

He strode off. She leaned over, staring at the gray asphalt, her stomach pressed tightly against her thighs. A wave of nausea was building.

Jesus! Now I'm going to throw up!

She rocked back and forth, head down, holding her knees. The asphalt had an intricate pattern of cracks. The lines blurred and moved. Her thighs felt prickly and a cold, moist film covered her forehead and upper lip. The wave receded.

"Here. Have some ginger ale. That's all I have, but it's cold. Just take a few sips."

"Thanks." She pressed the can against her warm cheek.

I must look awful.

Her stomach turned. Her insides rumbled.

Got to go to the bathroom. Now. I wish I was dead. "I think I've got to go to the bathroom."

"Right. Come on. Let me give you a hand." He took her by the arm.

"Sorry about this."

He held onto her elbow as they walked into the smoke-mirrored lobby and she saw herself, ashen and dumpy. Her white blouse was wrinkled and her skirt hung in uneven folds, like a rag.

Too bad. But I've really got to go.

His apartment was cold, almost icy, from air conditioning. He led the way to the bathroom. "Take your time. You'll feel better soon. Do you think it's from something you ate?"

"I don't know. Maybe it's the heat." Maybe I'm scared. Maybe it's menopause. "Sorry. Thanks," she said and closed the bathroom door.

I'll probably die here. And I hardly know him. Came on to me for one hour New Year's and here I am. I'll die of the shits in this man's bathroom. Some kind of wry justice. He'll have to call the police, they'll call Jack....Won't he be surprised!

She took the plastic wastebasket and positioned it under her face as she sat down on the toilet. Doubled over, clutching her aching sides, she rocked.

I can't go here. It's too quiet for God's sake!

With that, she let go. She felt like laughing as the smell hit her.

Awful! Nauseous. It won't come up. Stink up his house. Hope he has some Lysol. And a windowless bathroom, too!

She listened to the ventilating fan. Then flushed. I'll probably have to clean the toilet.

She looked around for a toilet brush.

I won't fuck him today, that's for sure. More. Stomach doesn't hurt as much. Seems to be passing through. That's me. Passing through. Just to screw. With you.

"Beth? How's it going?" through the door, nose into the crack.

It's going. How? Can he smell it? "Pretty good. I'll be out in a while." And I guess I will. "Do you mind if I bathe here?"

"Sure, go ahead. On second thought, I'm not so sure I'd sit in that tub. I just take showers. Maybe you could take a shower?"

I could. "Okay. Thanks."

"I'll hand you a clean towel."

"No, don't bother. Just hang it on the handle. Okay?"

"All right."

"Thanks."

Better and better. In every way. Face is so hot. My cheeks are burning. Flush the toilet. My skirt is wrinkled. And the shirt, too. Take them off. Got no clothes to change into.

She stood up and looked in the mirror over the sink.

Oh, no! I didn't see that. That old woman looks like a sick monkey.

She looked in the tub.

Hair in the drain. Water on the brain. Not cleaning his mess. Do single women live longer than married women? The article said men live longer if they're married. Obviously. They've got someone to wait on them. Like me.

She turned on the shower, cold, then hot, almost right, and stepped into the tub on the rubber mat.

Hate to see what that looks like underneath. Won't clean that either.

She let her head hang as the water hit the back of her head and poured down both cheeks. Slowly, she turned twice around under the spray and then stood, letting the water hit her face. The air felt cool as she stepped out of the tub.

I think I feel better. Damn! Forgot to get the towel.

The mirror was steamed. She unlocked the door, opened it a crack and saw one of his legs beyond the livingroom doorway.

"Better?" he yelled.

"Yes, thanks! Be out soon!" she said with a cheerful lilt.

As she dried her body and her hair, she felt chilled. Her clothes hanging on the door hook were still damp. She used his Arrid Extra Dry, some baby powder, then pulled his fine-toothed comb through the wet tangle of gray hair. She wiped the steam and runnels of water off the mirror.

Not so bad. Could be worse. My hair will dry kinky which makes it look grayer. And I'm so pale! Lipstick? Pocketbook. In the livingroom?

She didn't remember where. She looked at the bathroom door.

I didn't see that robe before. A kimono. White L's on brown.

She took the robe from under her clothes and put it on. The cotton felt good on her skin and warmed her. On tiptoes, she saw that it reached just below her knees and closed around her middle well enough.

I'll never make it as a geisha, but I'm okay. I'll be all right.

It was time to leave the bathroom. She put her hand on the doorknob, turned it and walked into the cool of the apartment.

# Based on Experience
## Candida Lawrence

When I opened my eyes, the dream was waiting, as distinct as a photograph I could trace with a finger. I knew it was a dream because when I turned over, the photograph grew smaller and its edges curled up. The backs of my knees were damp and there were cool beads dotting my stomach. I stared out the window at the dripping yellow blossoms of the acacia tree. I opened my mouth and cautiously let air slide into my lungs. As usual, I was brine-packed, crowded by coast fog, but this morning it didn't matter because I would be on the road by noon. Still, getting ready to enter my dream would be more pleasant if the sun were shining.

I wanted to call my daughter and tell her where I was going, but then I would have to explain about the dream and how imagination wasn't enough if you were a writer. You had to have experience. I couldn't be sure enough about details, spotty even in the best of dreams, and that's why I was going. I could hear that cool, young, almost patronizing voice suggesting that jealousy was making me a bit irrational and asking wasn't it silly? She would remind me that what Karl and I had wasn't exactly a one-night thing after nineteen years and ask why couldn't I put my mind on what was in the typewriter and let the foolish man have his fun as long as he loved me as much as he obviously did. Ignoring the part about imagination not being enough.

I pulled myself from bed and walked stiffly through the moist livingroom. I opened the door and saw the dog. Oh God, I'd forgotten. I might be gone two or three days and I couldn't delay the dream with a visit to the kennel. That wasn't part of it. I'd have to cover the beautiful tan leather in the back seat of Karl's car with a soft cotton sheet and hope that scratch marks would come off with Armoral. It was disturbing to think of these details, and how odd "the dog" and "daughter" sounded in my head, as though they didn't have names, names I had bestowed myself and used often, even to strangers.

After a second cup of coffee, I stepped into the shower stall and lifted my face to the warm water. I knew the first thing I had to do was look through the closet for black garments which would absorb the full moon and stars shining on Karl's desert garden. Karl and the woman would be white and I wondered if there was any color in the dream. I couldn't remember but didn't insist on a memory of something which was past and future, all around me. I knew the dream existed in the night and I would stand on the edge until it was time for it to happen.

The ring of the telephone drifted into the water. I turned the knobs and dried myself slowly, hearing and not understanding. The ringing stopped and started again. It would be Karl telling me the airplane hadn't crashed, it was hot (over 100 degrees), he missed me, and asking how was the car? I picked up the receiver and told him I was glad he was safe, sorry it was so hot, and yes I was just out of the shower and would go to my typewriter soon and was writing so much that I might pull the phone and he said fine, go to it, baby, I love you.

The drawstring of my black cotton pants scraped my stomach and as I fastened the frogs on my coolie jacket, it amused me to think that they'd better croak now because soon it would be too hot for frogs.

I covered my typewriter with a pink and orange scarf, carefully tucking the silk edges around and under its body to discourage ants and spiders. On a three by five lined card, I wrote down the three tasks for the morning:

1. Remember key to Karl's desert house.
2. Go to bank and buy $150 in traveller's checks.
3. Get gas.

I packed a small canvas suitcase with toiletry pouch and a change of clothes. The clothes I folded into the psychedelic-patterned case were pink. I knew I would not want to wear black when I had left the dream.

Getting ready to leave was easy, requiring only skills and knowledge on automatic. I did not water the garden for it didn't seem to me that time would be passing in any ordinary sense. I closed the windows and locked the door, as I always did when I left the house. The bank and gas station performed perfectly when I said "I want $150 in traveller's checks—in twenties plus a ten" and "Fill it with Regular, please." I wrote a check for the bank and paid for the gas with a traveller's check.

Everything was in order and nothing was out of order. The dog lay quietly on the pale-green cotton flannel. The landscape in front and to the sides was unalarming. There were curved hills, jutting oak trees and telephone poles, then flatness and heat. There were many cars and then few. The highway had two white lines or one. The speedometer said fifty-five or sixty-five and every few hours there was a picture of a gas tank in the upper left-hand corner of the dashboard which flashed a yellow light. It flashed intermittently at first, and then grew brighter and stayed on. This was machine talk and scarcely interrupted my necessary concentration on the dream. I always stopped at the next gas station, said "Fill it with Regular and check the oil," gave the dog water in a red plastic bowl, and went to the bathroom. Each time I sat on the toilet, the dream picture went blank and I hurried back to the car.

Karl's automobile didn't know how to cause trouble. The gasket never blew, the radiator kept its temperature, the oil level remained constant, the window buttons raised or lowered glass when a finger pushed, and there was always water to squirt on the windshield when bugs splattered yellow spokes of light from a black center. In the door pocket there were useful maps, but I already knew I had to go south for a while and then east. There was no need to unfold paper and look at lines and numbers. In the spacious glove compartment were tapes of three kinds: ten Spanish language cassettes of graded difficulty, four cassettes on How-To-Be-A-Successful-Salesman, and three exquisite samples of seventeenth and eighteenth century music.

I inserted "Hits of the 1720s" as soon as I started my journey. I played one side and then the other. I wanted Pachelbel's Canon, which paced my dream, but listened to Albinoni, Bach, Handel and the rest, even the side which had no Pachelbel. I liked to wait thirty-five minutes for the eight notes which told everything, excluding only terror. Six hundred miles, ten hours of Pachelbel on the half-hour, and when I parked the car on a side street two blocks from Karl's house, I waited for the notes to curl up against silence before I punched out the tape and placed it carefully in the plastic box with the hinged cover.

Before turning off the engine, I pushed each window button until the smooth electric power had pulled down four sheets of glass to a halfway point, enough to let in the hot night air, yet keep a dog from jumping out and following me. The orange-blossom scent was heavy now and insistent, unlike the dry, lifting delicacy of my April visit. I pulled a black chiffon scarf from the glove compartment and wrapped it around my light brown hair, pulling the bangs off my forehead, tucking each hair under. My hand brushed a gold earring, hesitated, then swiftly removed the loops and placed them in a tray above the dashboard. The dog's cold wet nose froze a spot on my arm. I rubbed the soft ears, and shivered. There had been nothing in the dream about a car or a dog or walking to the house or using the key which now gleamed in my hand, catching all the light from the moon which was suddenly all around and inside the car. The moon was in it, but I was still outside.

I knew that if I continued to sit, I would begin to think and would miss the entrance. I opened the heavy door and stepped out. The dog jumped into the front seat and tried to get out. I closed the door, slowly pushing the heaviness against the furry chest. The nose poked through the open window and I kissed it and whispered "Stay."

I stood in the shadow of white-flowering oleander. I felt light and lithe, not at all tired. Through the thin soles of my black canvas shoes, I could feel the press of rough pebbles, black now on the edge of moonlight, but I remembered their daylight color, a rusty mauve, and so light in weight that they bounced when you walked on them.

I walked swiftly towards Karl's street, careful always to remain in the shadow of oleander and olive trees. The house was not yet visible, but I knew that straight ahead one more block, and over one, his corner lot with high white walls on three sides would suddenly be, abruptly, there—white walls with black cypress sentries and iron mandala decoration—and that I would have to go first to the front to see how many cars were in the driveway.

The moonlight was making my black cotton shine and the eight notes began again in my head. The roar of tires and motors on the freeway filled the spaces. I hoped I could step into the dream soon because it was wrong to have noise in the spaces. And foolish of Karl to have bought so close to traffic. There were no dogs in his neighborhood and no one could see behind the walls. There were mailboxes outside the walls but no one ever saw his neighbor taking mail out of a box or said hello how are you, isn't it hot? Everyone lived somewhere else most of the time.

When I stood beside the white wall, I could hear rhythmic splashing in the swimming pool and knew he was doing his aerobic laps. As I walked close to the white stucco, the fear came and I knew I was entering the dream. The key in my hand was wet and cold. I saw two cars under the grape trellis, the light in the kitchen, and beyond the living room, visible through one of the slender windows on either side of front door, two white bodies bending over the plastic covering of the pool. The beautiful first of eight was sounding now and silence before the next. My fingers spread to clasp the doorknob. I watched my wrist turn. There had been nothing about a key in the dream, and after pushing the door open, I dropped it in the corner. It stood upright in the deep pile carpet, like a tiny silver statue.

The woman was standing beside the pool and with quick, short-range movements, she picked up a white towel and wine glass. She watched Karl as he adjusted the plastic cover and then she turned and began walking towards the sliding door of the living room. She stepped tidily, efficiently, her dark cap of hair bent to one side into the towel held in her hand.

And now in the dream there would be Karl's words and two breasts with dark nipples hanging down, swaying above the black triangle tucked between short white legs.

"Lock the door, will you?" he called out.

I had to wait for the dream. I couldn't go down the hall to Karl's bedroom until the glass door began to slide and the notes began again, but there was no difficulty in trusting. The fear, the music, the picture, all were combining, rehearsed and familiar, but this time real.

The door squeaked and a white leg appeared. Now I could walk on carpets to the golden chair in the corner of his room. There were never any footstep sounds in his house. It was not possible to know of an approach or a departure.

In the dream I had known about the lack of footsteps and how dark it was behind the golden chair, out of the path of moonlight which illumined the Super-King waterbed.

I crouched in the darkness, waiting. There was a sound of shower water and showers were not in the dream. I twitched and sought the notes. Had the dream ended early? If it abandoned me, should I confront them when they emerged? Should I lie on the bed in my black clothes and watch their naked faces? Laugh? Should I pretend to have a knife or a gun and spring from behind the chair? Shower and freeway noise, huge in my head and in the room, absurd sound sucking breath from my throat.

And then the silence again, a silence between and behind the notes. Karl was naked, just as I had seen him in the dream, and he lay down on his back, groaning, his fingers twiddling with the black hairs and flesh between his legs. He pulled and twisted and stared at it. The woman would now walk quickly to the other side of the bed and lie down. Yes, she was walking quickly and she lay down on her side, curled towards his body, but not touching him. She plumped the pillow under her short black hair. He turned away from her and one hand lifted in the moonlight, came down on her white thigh, patted, and she lifted a knee. The hand disappeared between her legs. They lay still.

The dream was all around me and the music was streaming through my body, high in my head, low in thighs and the place where Karl had been so many times. He sat up and straddled the woman, pulling her small hips under him, aiming. He looked down at himself, at the place where he would enter. The woman watched his face and did not smile, her breasts parted from each other.

I watched from the dream. Tiny golden bristles on the back of the chair cut into my hot cheek. He moved with the notes and the folds of his stomach leaked drops of perspiration onto her whiteness. The woman closed her eyes. He was much older than she. Faster and faster and then he cried out, a high wailing moan and "O-O-O baby, bab-e-e" and fell on her.

The noise from the freeway and far, far away, the violins fading in the distance. I had to get up and get out of his room. Quickly! They must not see me...must not...why had I come here? I forced myself to think about the house, the hallway, the carpet. About sleep, and when was it deep? The moon. How long would it shine into the room? Could I wait? The heat. Over a hundred he had said.

I began to crawl, keeping my head below the level of the bed. There was a monstrous fish picture hanging on the wall and he seemed to be watching me and speaking in bubbles. I stopped each time I thought I heard the soft slurp of moving, shifting gallons of warm water. When I reached the hallway, I stood up and without looking back, ran past the spare bedroom, around the corner, and out the front door.

I left it open, and later on, I wondered if they had quarreled about that, and if they ever had words.

# Sssh, We'll Talk Later

## Ginny MacKenzie

"Is everything satisfactory?" a pink-cheeked tuxed waiter puffs into David's ear without acknowledging Susan. "Does madam just love the cake?"

"It's quite worthy of the Plaza," Susan answers, reassuring him so that he unclasps his hands from their prayer position, drops them to his sides, and spreads his feet into an at-rest position, making him part of the celebration—for the moment. The Swedish chocolate cake topped with yellow icing and heart-shaped strawberries is for Susan's fortieth birthday. David, a successful artist and her husband of nearly twenty years, has staged the night right down to the location of the table, near the harpist, in the back. Pulling at her skirt, gathering it from between her knees, she smoothes the wrinkles out to the sides, as though, there, they'll be invisible. She's unsure if she's feeling warm, itchy, or simply exposed. Beside them, the harpist, looking cool and statuesque, adjusts her hands around her instrument. She wears a dark green dress and velvet camisole. An antique-looking brooch pinned to a large lapel leads into her cleavage, reflecting an intimate red glow onto the neck of the harp. If only right and wrong were as easily distinguished, she thinks, disengaging from the harpist, and from David. It must be right to want to know she can get what she wants herself, to know she's enough. She thinks of the cigarette smoke circling the neighboring table, free, capable of rising to great heights. She wants to be like that. She promises herself that tonight she'll tell David she wants a divorce.

"Go on, lovely, make a wish," David says. He's chirping already, Susan thinks; soon he'll be the sloppy drunk again. To be out of this stuffy restaurant, standing under the slice of new moon, refreshed, away from David's declarations of love for her while sleeping with half of the women artists in New York City. Joanne Vinte for one—everyone at his gallery knew about her. They'd meet there and massage each other's shoulders under Picasso's erotic prints. Susan's theory is that artists paint passion into their art to keep people from noticing the lack of morality in their lives.

Susan knows David isn't entirely to blame for their less-than-passionate sex life. Even alone, she hates being naked. Her chest is a roadmap of scars—pink, red, brown—depending on their age. A bad aorta. Although her health is fully restored, her reaction to the brutality she views in the mirror every morning sometimes brings her, sobbing, to her knees. She makes love in her blouse, or nightgown. Once, in bed, when she was naked, David ran his finger over a scar under her left breast and kissed it. She'd thought him crazy. But times like that, she loved him more than all his paintings put together.

Last September Susan's mother died of a cancer that ravaged her body and left her thin as paper, a wrinkle in the bed. She'd been at her bedside when she died. The veins in her mother's neck, which had been pumping memories into her consciousness and causing small exhalations of non-sequiturs like, "such a lovely girl," and "be, Susan, just be," stopped pulsing. David said her mother had been part angel for months, and Susan had felt grateful to have him then. Sometimes she is afraid that without him she may curl up and die, like a leaf, or like her mother.

Can she leave David just because he's unfaithful, just because she wants to "be, just be," she wonders as she plunges her fork into a fat heart-shaped strawberry. When he's involved with painting, she truly loves him—dark, brooding, romantic, dragging them both on vacations to Maine for "better light, to paint in the white north light." The aurora borealis freezes the emotions in his subjects, he says; he can capture people in moments of crisis: a young man running to a drowning child, a woman arriving at her dying father's bedside, separations that remain with you long after you've left the paintings.

"Suze, the waiter thinks something is wrong. Blow out the candles."

"I'm deciding what to wish. All those candles! Two would have been enough, one for each decade with you. In fact, one candle, one for this perfect day, would have been enough." Her deceit saddens her.

"You're so fragile, Susan, and so untouchable. I don't know how to touch you. I never have."

This kind of talk makes her nervous; she thinks he might be on to her. Twisting around in the red-cushioned chair, her hips stiff with lies, she pulls her skirt up above her knees, as if more air on her thighs will propel her up, with the smoke—to caress the smooth marble columns, to wrap them in fingers of inspiration, up and up, like a mountain goat ascending into the pure invigorating air at the pinnacle.

"Come on," David offers. "We'll blow together."

It is more than the smoke from the candles that surrounds them; the two chimneys puffing away at the next table and looking wealthy enough to buy new lungs are watching, directing all their smoke at the objects of their vicariousness. On Susan's exhale, the cake grows dark. David claps. The chimneys coo.

"Thank you." Susan feels foolish and dishonest but returns the smiles of the woman with the perfectly coiffed white hair and her flushed mate. Maybe now they'll go home, she hopes.

It's hard to leave someone, anyone, she thinks, especially after so many years. It takes a certain fearlessness to face the truth. Susan wonders if she has it. Her grandmother, Holly, believed religion was truth. Hymns like "The Old Rugged Cross" and "Come Walk with Me" rose like spirits from her piano. Holly's living room lent itself to excess—hot and overlit, covered in blue and white gardenia wallpaper. Presbyterian, Susan had called it. The house even smelled of sickly-sweet flowers, mixed with the odor of Vicks. It was brick, damp all year round, and when Holly wasn't feverishly playing the piano, she could often be found in bed with a cold.

Once when Susan was eight and delivering medicine to her, Holly got up and shoved her into the closet, locked the door, and whispered through the keyhole, "It's good, dear, stay in there, you'll be safe." Most of the northeast had turned dark at midday because of a fire raging across Canada. It had blackened the sun and Holly believed the end of the world had come. She believed she was saving her granddaughter. Years later Susan wondered if she had stood passively in that dark vertical tomb as if she were on the porch, or if she had pounded on the door, screaming at Holly to let her out. The answer was hidden in her unconscious somewhere between her first period and her first boyfriend's hard-on pressing against her leg. All were experiences that left her feeling frightened and excited; all were doors that opened to possibility. She does remember that when she turned the doorknob inside Holly's closet and pushed, the lock sprung and she faced Holly triumphantly, as if risen from the dead. Sex too proved to be a power no one could lock up and was sweeter than she imagined.

"I know this is a lousy time to talk about this, Suze," David says. "But I can't stand it anymore." His voice sounds distant, as if it is coming from the past. It seems to require great effort on his part—jagged and high-pitched alternately, like a teenager's.

The chimneys had lingered over their dessert just long enough to see the extinguished candles, and left, and now the new quiet feels frightening to Susan, as if their presence had been staving off something awful. The harpist is leaning attentively into her strings. Susan's throat is raw from smoke. She wants to disappear into the field of strawberries in front of her, drown in the layer of Swedish chocolate so she won't have to tell David she wants her freedom.

"Suze, my moth, I'm so glad you're enjoying your birthday; I wanted it to be perfect. But I really need to talk to you. I've been putting it off, searching for the right time, but no matter when I do it, it'll be hard." David was squirming in his seat like a six-year-old. "I don't want to spoil things for you tonight, but I need to talk to you. I've met someone, a woman..."

As if wearing tight pants and not a skirt, she feels cramped, constricted; her throat swells, nearly closing off. "David, you're always meeting women. I really don't want to hear this. I'm tired. Maybe we should go home." She wants to be a child sitting with her mother watching the snails criss-cross the garage windows, making elaborate icy designs in mid-summer. Back then, the two of them would stare at the glassy landscape and count all those paths until they lost track. Susan feels as if it has taken her a lifetime of wrong turns only to arrive at this blank slate.

"Hold on a bit, Suze."

"I want to leave. Now!"

"I've met another woman," David says, looking insistent. "Did you hear me? I've been seeing her for some time."

She looks at David: no remorse seems present in his eyes.

"What's the big deal, Susan, we haven't been sleeping together for years—you don't love me."

Just like him to blame her, she thinks, just like her to take it. She should have suspected this. "Break it off with her, David."

"I can't."

"You can. We can work it out."

"It's too late. I can't. I waited until I knew it was serious before I told you." Standing up, he pulls out her chair. She feels his hand awkwardly supporting her back. "Sssh, we'll talk later," he says, making it sound more like a threat than a promise.

The restaurant looks enormous to her as she walks ahead of David. Voices from neighboring tables are echoes; the waiter, a priest taking confessions. "Will there be anything else?" The waiter's voice comes from within the confessional. She feels too weak to make it to the door, a whole country away. She remembers a game she played with friends on her backporch steps with small painted stones. White side up meant marry, black side up meant had a baby, and offsides...offsides...of course, divorce.

What feels unbearable to her now is her sense of being temporary in the world. Her live-in lover believes she is truth, says he loves only her but, to her, everyone has a secret they're waiting to spring on her. She carries her house with her now, under her arms, to avoid arousing suspicions.

# Hyacinth Bath Salts
## Constance Hester

After the dissolution of my marriage,
I collected
An extra toothbrush
in a cardboard box
with a cellophane window,
A flower-scented douche,
A contraceptive foam,
A sexy, backless
black dress
of silky crepe,
A lacy white nightgown
embroidered with delicate
pink flowers,
A rosy envelope
of hyacinth bath salts.
Tucked them away
In a bedroom drawer
Then waited.
It's been ten years.
I just finished menopause,

Threw away the foam.
On New Year's Eve -
Tried on the black dress -
Too tight.
Shoved it into
The Goodwill bag.
My son used the extra toothbrush,
When he visited at Christmas.
Last week I used up
The bath salts.
It's a hot night,
Think I'll sleep
In the white nightgown.
The flower-scented douche
Is still in the drawer.

# Luck with Ponies
## Thea Caplan

One freezing day in February he came back, looking a lot older than she remembered, waltzed up the front sidewalk, up the veranda, loaded down by Safeway bags stuffed with what she later learned were thousand dollar bills.

"I'm here," he called out, setting down the plastic bags on the living room bureau. He surveyed the room. It looked like it had been waiting for him. The gleaming mahogany coffee table with its glass top that he had loved putting his feet up on, especially when drinking beer. Over the stone fireplace the oil painting of the boy and the dog hunting still startled him, a boy so young to be out running alone in the woods, with a rifle. The onyx and silver-plated ashtray his brother had stolen from a theatre in Buffalo and smuggled over the border stood beside the tall fern, where it always had. All those Sundays butting out in that ashtray, ignoring Nancy's yelling to empty the stinking mess for chrissakes. Once the goddamn thing overflowed, hell to pay; it burned a doozey of a hole in the carpet. He bent over to smell the ashtray. It didn't smell at all, no trace of tobacco, no assault of disinfectant. At least a faint smudge of grease on the back of the sofa where he'd rested his head had survived. Bill was surprised she'd let that go; the dark stain, an ugly reminder of him. He ran his finger along the top of the phonograph (his mother-in-law's, surely a bona fide antique by now) that had, according to Nancy, instigated a lapse of etiquette one night allowing him to have her on the light green couch, without the slip covers. The rose-colored chair, his grandmother's, still looked out of place, he'd never get used to that damn chair. The room seemed to mock him. Gone ten years and the fern that they bought one Sunday at Henry's the Chinese grocer was sprouting new leaves. He looked under the couch and was disappointed—although not surprised—no dust balls. The newspapers strewn on the couch, though, looked like his messing. You'd think he'd been gone only a week. The stairs creaked.

Someone was coming down the stairs.

What do you say to a woman you walked out on ten years ago, telling her you were going to get a newspaper?

Nancy stood in the archway to the living room, her arms crossed. He looked her over. She looked pretty decent. A little thicker in the waist, and her hair more auburn than it should be, but decent. Legs still graceful and subtly muscled. He wondered if she still went dancing.

"You left the front door unlocked," he said.

She nodded. He wished she'd stop staring at his belly hanging over his belt.

So he's back, Nancy thought. *He's in my living room.* What almost flew out of her mouth made her giggle. *Got your newspaper, have you?* but she caught herself. Other than hurting Bill, what was the point? She no longer dreamed of Lucy and shoving a pillow down that non-stop mouth. But here she was, finally, face-to-face with her tormentor, the bastard responsible for publicly humiliating her. Other people went for counselling, had a fight on the front lawn. Her marriage hadn't even been worth fighting for. "Think I'll get a newspaper," was all she was good for. It was *his* fault the neighbors had whispered, "What could have been so bad?" scrutinizing her, her groceries at the check-out, her visitors, her bags of dry cleaning. Tim's math teacher telling him that there's a reason for everything and asking how his mother was. Three, four in the morning, a raspy voice on the phone suggesting kinky sex, she must want it bad. Then, into her foggy ear, describing her choices.

Here was her chance to hit back, reduce Bill to his pitiful self. From her bedroom window she'd seen him: a drab figure with a snow-crusted head, drifting up her walkway. Suddenly, she felt exhausted, defeated by a lack of enthusiasm. She had carried her anger so long she felt young and numb now without it.

When, Nancy wondered, had the anger left? That was the sort of thing you noticed, it didn't disappear overnight. But she couldn't locate when. It seemed to her it had always been there, choking her, laughing at her in the sheen of the kettle, and now, suddenly it was gone.

"How are you?" Nancy asked.

"Not bad for an old geezer." He followed her eyes straying out the leaded window. He found himself wanting to tell her that Lucy's hair turned a brassy orange under the California sun. He didn't think Nancy'd appreciate him going off at the mouth. Didn't look like Nancy was much interested in *anything* he had to say.

"Uh hah," she said.

He knew he had hurt her deeply, taking off like that, never calling. But he hadn't neglected her. You had to give him that. Even though it had been Lucy who persuaded him (the woman had a heart of gold!) to leave Nancy every-thing—the house, mortgage-free; the boat; and all his Bell stocks. Every six months he had sent Nancy a seven-thousand-dollar money order, increasing it five per cent a year, inflation. Hadn't missed one payment.

"What brings you here?" Hell, she sounded like her daughter Katherine, bottom-lining it.

"Why are you laughing?"

"I'm not laughing. I don't *mean* to laugh," Nancy said through pursed lips.

Bill didn't know why he was back. Last Tuesday he'd woken up and said aloud, *I wonder how Nancy is?* That morning he bought an airplane ticket. He left Lucy a note on the fridge saying he had business out east. Back in a couple of days. Lucy was off at a spa in New Mexico, he'd lost the phone number.

"It's crazy, Nancy, but I was wondering how you were."

"Well, I'm fine. There's your answer."

"You look fine." He felt his head nodding energetically.

Nancy was grateful when his head stopped scrambling like a turkey. She took a small step toward him. "Actually," she said, "there's something I want to ask you." After getting over the initial shock of his walking out (once the first bank draft came she knew he hadn't been kidnapped or murdered, that he had left her), she had wondered when she was making dinner for the kids, helping Tim fill out his college application, what Bill had taken with him—other than Lucy, whom she had known about for years. Every suit and tie left behind in his closet, even his arch supports. His fishing lures in the tackle box, he could have slipped one or two in an envelope, mailed them to himself. How could a person up and leave like that? Even a year after he'd left she would race home from the gift shop and check to see if he had taken his Cross pen or his sunglasses, or had slipped a photograph of Katherine or Tim from the album. "When you left, what did you take with you?" she asked.

Her face was as blank as an envelope. For the first time Nancy looked him in the eye.

"I don't remember."

"Try."

"Just some cash I'd saved. I didn't touch our bank accounts," he said quickly.

"I know that."

"I don't think I took anything."

She looked at him with something close to, to—was that admiration in her eyes?

"Nothing?" she asked.

"Just the clothes on my back," he said, instantly sorry. It made him sound desperate to get out, and he hadn't been. "I like to travel light," he said, knowing too late he was not amusing her.

She shook her head slowly, murmured, "Nothing." It was inconceivable to her. A man doesn't live twenty years in a house and leave everything, *everything* behind.

Bill watched Nancy licking her lips. He'd told the truth yet she didn't seem appreciative. He wondered why she wanted to know so badly but knew she'd clam up if asked.

Lately, he seemed to have lost interest in everything. Last week at the race track, he slept through Strike The Gold's spectacular finish. He woke up to hollering, bodies ripping the air, an elbow knifing his ear. Some idiot slapped him on the shoulder. "Wake up, BUDDY!" Everywhere he went he was either getting screamed at, bumped, or hit. In Safeway's parking lot six months ago his leg was crushed between two cars. Later, at the hospital, Lucy's wailing, "Oh my GAWD, Bill. Your leg! Your leg!" blotted out the orthopod's explanation of emergency surgery. After Bill scribbled his signature on the consent form, he pretended to pass out but that only revved Lucy up. Her shrieking blasted through the Emergency Department. He could hear it now, piercing, commanding, making him nauseated as hell. Bill knew better than to try to silence Lucy.

The pin in his leg ached. He wasn't used to trudging through snow. He popped another Tylenol. His feet tingled and were cold, numb.

Maybe he was having a heart attack. Lucy once said that the feet were the mirror of the soul. But she had been into Shiatsu then, and had a lot to say about feet.

Maybe he was getting old. He longed for a little quiet, ambiguity. Lucy, he had learned, was right about everything. She just was. He'd always marvelled at this flawless, seemingly effortless, probably innate ability. For ten years and two months he'd barely had to think. Now, watching Nancy straighten her collar, he wondered, How could it be—that at sixty-one years of age—he knew nothing?

"There's something I want to ask you," he said following Nancy into the kitchen, trying to sound off-hand. "How long did you search for me?" The thought of her trying in vain to track him down still thrilled him. A long silence filled the room, and Bill breathed deeply, surprised by an overwhelming calmness and a staggering interest to hear Nancy's answer.

She waved her hand vaguely. "I never looked for you."

He felt as if he'd been hit in the stomach with a baseball bat. He concentrated on getting air flowing down his windpipe.

"Say that again?"

"I never looked for you."

"*You never tried to track me down?*" He leaned heavily against the stove.

"If you mean did I hire a detective or something like that, no. I called the police, of course, and reported you missing. They did an investigation and said there was no sign of foul play. They figured you took off with Lucy. I was in shock. After the first money order I was furious. Humiliated. I'd rather you'd been murdered. Lying in a ditch somewhere, my name on your lips."

"You didn't search for me," Bill said, hypnotized by the pale skin of Nancy's throat. He was out of patience; he needed to hear the sad details of her fruitless searching for him—the door slammings, the dead-ends, the cold trails burning with dedication.

Nancy dropped two tea bags into a tea pot.

"Steep for a bit," she said.

"Weren't you curious about where I'd gone?" Bill asked, hoping to stimulate an angry (anything!) rendering of her hunting him down.

"Yes, I guess I was," Nancy said.

In these ten years his wife had developed a polished cool. Almost convincing. Bill suspected that he still knew Nancy better than anyone else. She poured an astonishing amount of rum into the tea pot.

"The house looks good, Nancy, you kept it up." Talking about her home always had a way of putting Nancy in a better mood.

"I've always liked this house," she said.

"I see you got the porch redone."

"And the roof too. You don't mind?" she asked quietly.

He looked at her steadily. The sarcasm was new. It *was* sarcasm, wasn't it? Now Nancy was running a hand through her hair, looking out the window at the bird bath. Her calm was unnerving. Best to play it straight, he reasoned.

"You've done a good job," he said. He walked over to the fireplace. On the mantle was a photograph of Tim, all grown, sitting on a rock. "How's Tim?" When he'd left Tim was twelve, battling pimples, shutting himself in his bedroom, listening to rock music and staring at the light fixture.

"Much as you'd expect," she answered. "He's not a bad kid."

Bill was taken aback. He had hoped to knock Nancy off balance, expose her jangled nerves, show her she couldn't pull off this cool-as-a-cucumber act with him. He knew all about Tim. Chanting like a fool in the mountains, Hare Krishna! Hare Krishna! Then finally coming to his senses and escaping. The vision of Tim wheeling through the Rockies in a red Mustang excited him, but he knew Nancy—if she would admit it—would prefer Tim safe in his group, gazing and chanting under the moon.

Nancy thought of Tim, sweet Tim, a dreamer with a lovely, almost soprano voice. Although his last letter was somewhat jumbled, she deciphered that he had left the Hare Krishna in October and was driving through the Rockies to Banff, Canada, in a used red Mustang convertible. She could picture him, camping on a glacier in a thermal pup tent, singing. Their daughter Katherine, on the other hand, was enough to send anybody off the deep end. She was a tough young woman baffled by emotions which she held at arm's length. Katherine taught family law, and consulted on a few cases, battered women mostly, and was very busy. Although she lived only two subway stops away, Nancy hardly saw her. Sometimes Katherine called at ten or eleven at night, huffing into the phone, "How are you, Ma?" and Nancy knew she was doing sit-ups with the phone neatly wedged between her shoulder and ear. Katherine was twenty-eight with a stomach hard as oak.

"I've seen Kathy," Bill said.

Above the rim of the tea cup, Nancy's eyes blazed. "When did you see Katherine?"

"She took me to the Faculty Club yesterday for lunch, insisted on ordering. The sweetest, juiciest lobster tails I've ever had."

"Then you got your update from her."

Nancy was tougher than he imagined. He thought of the nights when he had come home late, Nancy sitting in the breakfast nook, in the dark, drinking tea. He would sit with her and have a cup. She never asked him where he'd been, he volunteered it—out drinking with his sales manager, Garth, or one of the other salesmen. She'd nod, her eyes low, as if praying he'd skip the lies. She'd banter about the latest household catastrophe, how the plumbing had backed up, or the new lilac bush had died. He would promise he'd take care of everything, and he did. A small price to pay, for a while.

"I have something to show you," Bill said, walking out of the kitchen. In the living room, he lifted one of the Safeway bags off the bureau. A few bills fell onto the floor.

Nancy didn't move. "Is it hot?"

"Nancy." She'd never complained before when he'd won at the ponies.

"You're not in some kind of trouble, are you?"

"Can't I do something nice?"

"You could have sent another bank draft. *That* would have been nice."

He should've just sent Nancy the money, maybe half—his horse had won by a nose. "I'm sorry I left you like that," he said. "It was a reckless, thoughtless thing, disappearing." But Lucy wouldn't have waited forever. What would have been the point in telling Nancy? She'd have gotten hysterical, begged him to stay, promised she'd change. Anyway, Lucy was the woman for him. She was the sexiest woman he'd known, and he'd known women.

"It was a crummy thing to do. But it's water under the bridge now," Nancy said in the same dull tone she had used with Tim and Kathy when it was too close to dinner for a snack.

"Don't misunderstand. I'm not sorry I *left*. I'm sorry I left *like that*."

"I understood what you meant," Nancy said. "And I'm not surprised that you're sorry—about how you left, that is. What I couldn't believe was how gutless you were. I gave you more credit than that." She reached for a Safeway bag. "You know, I don't think I've seen a thousand dollar bill before." Nancy held a bill up to the light. "It's not even pretty," she said. "Mud-purple. How much money is in here?" She rummaged in the shopping bag. "Maybe I'll buy something ridiculous. An emerald necklace." She whispered, "I've never admitted this: I've always wanted an emerald necklace. Did you know that, Bill?"

Hearing her say his name jolted him. "Bill"—it fluttered in his hand. He didn't think she realized she'd said it.

"Hawaii, what about Hawaii? Float around the pool under a striped umbrella and have handsome Hawaiians serve me piña coladas. Oh, I'm being silly, I know," Nancy said. "Maybe I should just have my teeth fixed. This bloody overbite. Imagine, braces at my age!"

She sounded like a teenager.

Nancy looked up at him, laughing. "Hey, Bill! What do you think? Is there enough money in those bags to do all three? *Go* to Hawaii *wearing* the emerald necklace *after* I got my teeth fixed?"

Nancy's face was flushed, her grey eyes turned a devilish, shimmering green. She twirled around in the bay window, her madras skirt bouncing off her knees.

He wondered what she would look like naked. Bill heard himself say, "We could go to Hawaii together." Shut up, he told himself. Shut the fuck up. He heaved into his grandmother's chair. It creaked obscenely. Outside, beyond the leaded glass, the snow swirled. A white-out. Driving would be dangerous; the rental car, a bland Ford, wouldn't make the Bathurst Street hill. Bathurst was the only way out of their cul-de-sac. He could go down the hill, south, out of his way, but he was afraid he'd lose control of the car down the icy grade.

Bill jumped when the telephone rang. Nancy straightened her skirt, lifted the receiver.

"Hello Ma," Nancy heard.

"Is that you Katherine?" There was no huffing or puffing.

Katherine sounded offended. "Of course, it's Thursday."

Right, Katherine always phoned on Thursdays. "Well, I didn't hear any huffing."

"Mother?"

"Usually when you call you're puffing away, working on those stomach muscles."

"You know I don't have time to go to the Y."

"I know."

"What's up?" Katherine asked.

As if she didn't know. Lobster tails. Nancy squelched saying, *I've never stepped foot in your Faculty Club.* She waited for Katherine to confess. The rum soothed her stomach. After a few moments, she said more generously than Katherine deserved, "He told me you saw him."

"You spoke to him?"

"Actually, he's here and he asked me to go to Hawaii with him."

Katherine yelped, she actually yelped.

Nancy couldn't believe how much fun she was having. "He walked in with bags of money, the ponies. Anyway, it's mine and I've always wanted an emerald necklace—"

"You'd go to Hawaii with him?"

"I'll have to get a new bathing suit, something black and simple. A V-neck would be nice." It would be a lark, going off to Hawaii with Bill. They'd always adored a beach.

"Mother!" Poor Katherine, sounding all worked up. "Take the emerald necklace, it's a good investment. But Hawaii?" Katherine cleared her throat, summoned up her lawyer-voice. "Let's be reasonable here. You want to get back at Lucy. I understand that. But think, mother. Think. You'd have to..."

"Did you know that tea with rum is delicious?"

Katherine yelled, "Where's your pride?"

Nancy sipped her tea. The rum was divinely mellow.

"Mother! I can't talk to you!"

When Nancy heard the dial tone she was elated. Imagine, ruffling Katherine's feathers so much she hung up on her! A hot toddy or two isn't such a bad thing, she mused.

Bill's shoulders seemed to have caved in since she last looked. "Are you tired of Lucy?" Brazen, but what the hell, she was curious.

"I...ah...I wanted to see you." When she didn't respond, he asked quietly, "Nancy, are you seeing someone?"

Nancy laughed. "Nothing to write home about." Noticing Bill wince, she added, "I don't take that stuff seriously. Really." Now he looked puzzled. "After you left, Bill, I surprised myself, had little flings on those buying trips to New York. The wedding bands and the smudgy photographs of children in their wallets horrified and excited me. The pleasure some of the men took in pleasing me—that was a wonderful surprise. I'll always be grateful to two or three of them. But underneath all the packaging, the sex, men were pretty much the same; trying to steal bases, doing as little as they could get away with, and when they did do something, hip hip hurrah! Men make women nags. Who needed it? I realized I didn't have to put up with dirty socks on the bed, sour-tasting tobacco mouths, the lying—at least not on a permanent basis. I could come and go. See a man when I wanted to. And as I got older—lucky for me—men weren't that picky. Even the younger ones. I know it sounds cynical, but what does it matter who you're with? There's an interchangeable quality to men. Did you know that, Bill?"

A yellow glaze spread over his eyes. Bill kept staring at her.

Pain cut through Bill's chest; breathing was dangerous.

Nancy saw Bill's torso shudder, collapse in spasms. She watched him, curled like a sea shell, leave the living room. She heard the faint thud of his boots on the hardwood. Nancy felt a sweep of wind on her toes, clean, tingling.

Bill, wading through the darkening snow, admitted, finally, that ten years ago he had fled Nancy's indifference, her strength. Sustained all these years by fantasies of Nancy—grim, blotchy-faced, relentlessly searching for him. And he knew that nobody but Lucy would ever hound him to death.

Later, after Nancy watched David Letterman, when she shut off the light in the front hall, her eye caught something on the floor. Crouching in the dark, she reached under the radiator, drawing a glove, soft and warm. Nancy recognized the smell. It consumed her, that sweet, voluptuous smell of tobacco and sweat which used to bother her so much.

# Carrots
## Victoria Branch

The first time the man of Veronica's dreams came to her house to go horse-back riding, she thought she had everything he could possibly desire. She'd stocked up on Anchor Steam beer for before and after the ride. For dinner, she'd selected the two biggest Dungeness crabs she could find and baked sourdough rolls from scratch with her own wild yeast starter. The patio where they would eat was full of flowers—two afternoons' worth of planting petunias, tuberose begonias, impatiens and star jasmine in glazed Mexican pots. Veronica had been meaning to do that for ages, of course, but home improvements were always more fun when company was coming and Fred was the first sexually attractive man to visit in three years.

The horses belonged to Veronica's neighbors, who encouraged her to ride as frequently as possible because the animals needed the exercise. Veronica had permission to invite her friends along too, but until Fred came into her life, she'd never wanted to do that.

They met at a Co-dependents Anonymous meeting in the Valley. It was Veronica's first and she'd only gone because she'd read somewhere that celibate people were afraid of intimacy and she wanted to prove to herself that wasn't so. The instant she saw beautiful blue-eyed Fred in the doorway, Veronica signalled her willingness to relate by removing the mirror-coated sunglasses she'd had on since her arrival.

Although there were plenty of empty seats in the room, Fred took the folding chair next to Veronica's. During the meeting, he sighed a lot and bumped her several times with his elbow. Veronica enjoyed these intimacies so much that she returned the following week for more. This time Fred smiled as he took the place beside her. He favored her by bumping her knee. He also "shared" with the group that he was an obstetrician and in the process of breaking up with someone he never should have allowed himself to get involved with in the first place. Now that he'd found the courage to do what he should have done months before, the only thing Fred said he regretted was losing access to his ex-lover's horses.

"There are horses where I live," Veronica said after the meeting. "You can ride with me any time you want."

In reply, Fred scooped her into a full-body press and whispered in her ear, "I've been wanting to do this all week."

The following Sunday afternoon, Fred arrived at Veronica's house wearing tight jeans, a cornflower blue T-shirt that matched his eyes and a scowl he attributed to a difficult night.

"At the hospital?"

"No," he said. "The woman I broke up with just kicked the shit out of me."

Veronica handed Fred a beer and showed him into her backyard. Ignoring the freshly potted flowers, he made a beeline for the hammock at the edge of the lawn.

"I'll be better company if I can take a nap," he said and promptly fell asleep.

When her guest stirred two hours later, Veronica hurried to his side.

"What can I get you now?" she asked. "Another beer? A snack maybe, before we ride?"

Fred stretched and laced his fingers in the rope webbing above his head. Arching his back, he licked his lips and sighed.

"You know what I really want?"

Veronica moistened her own lips and leaned in closer.

"Tell me."

Fred closed his eyes. "I was just thinking it might be nice if you..."

"If I?"

"If you had some carrots for the horses."

The riders watched the sunset and the rise of the full moon from the sandstone ridge above Veronica's house. Once she forgave herself for not having carrots on hand, she realized that everything about the occasion was exactly as she'd hoped it would be: the horses lively, the chaparral fragrant, the evening clear and still.

Later, after she and Fred had demolished their crabs and torn their rolls and littered the patio with shells and breadcrumbs, they lay side by side in the hammock, suspended in jasmine-scented air.

"Has it really been three years?" Fred asked.

"More like three and a half," she said, "but I'm not shut down completely. I'm very good to myself, if you know what I mean."

His teeth flashed in the moonlight. "Thank you for your honesty."

"Well, I'm sure I don't shock you. After all, you're a doctor."

"True. And I'd like to have a chance to be sexual with you sometime, too."

"Oh, goodie."

Veronica turned her face toward Fred for the kiss she thought was coming next, but her guest said he had to be going. At the door, he nuzzled her neck. "I'll be calling you very soon."

That night, Veronica had trouble sleeping. When she heard crockery clattering on her patio, her first thought was that Fred had come back to "be sexual," but instead there was a four-point buck on her lawn, sleek as a silver statue. It hesitated outside her window before crashing off into the brush.

In the morning, Veronica discovered that a few of the petunias were gone and two of the pots were broken. She did the necessary cleaning up, and then went shopping for new underwear, condoms and lubricant, sheets and pillowcases, and even four new pillows. It was only a matter of hours, she thought, before she'd be wearing that lingerie, piling those pillows beneath her hips and bucking the beautiful blue-eyed doctor from there to eternity by the light of her bedside oil lamp. And on the way home she made a point of stopping at the market to pick up a large cellophane bag of carrots for the horses.

A week went by. The buck returned and consumed the rest of the petunias. The next week, he ate the begonias. The third week, in the dark of the moon, he cleaned out the impatiens and jasmine. Eighty-five dollars worth of flowers, gone just like that, but Veronica thought the sight of the deer was worth it. She only wished she could have seen him in the company of beautiful Fred.

Exactly a lunar month after his first visit, Fred called and said, "What's new?"

It was the day after Veronica had abandoned hope of hearing from him again and the only response she could think to make was that she now had carrots for the horses.

"You know," she said, "just in case you ever plan to come riding again."

"I'd love to, but it sounds like you're mad."

"No, I'm not. I'm just..."

"Just what?"

"Well, if you had a patient and you put her feet in the stirrups and spread her knees and then walked out of the room saying you'd be back very soon and left her like that for a month, how would she feel? That's sort of how I've been feeling."

Fred laughed and quickly apologized. He told Veronica that he found her most attractive and that he'd been using her in his sexual fantasies ever since they'd met. However, he explained, he really wasn't ready to get involved with anyone so soon after his last relationship.

"If I have to choose between having sex with you and having you for a friend, I really want to have you for a friend. For now, anyway, if that's okay."

Probably because of the "for now," Veronica said that it was, and Fred came over the following evening. After another sunset-moonrise ride to the top of the ridge, she suggested a dip in her neighbors' swimming pool.

"I didn't bring anything to swim in."

"That's okay," she said. "Nobody's home and I promise not to look at you if you don't look at me."

Veronica plunged into the water and swam to the shallow end. When she didn't hear Fred behind her, she turned around and saw that he was hanging by his arms from the diving board. He undulated there, another silver stag in the moonlight, while she breast-stroked back to the deep end and did her best not to stare.

"Isn't this erotic as hell?" he said.

"Why do you think I'm swimming so hard?"

She was in the middle of a lap when Fred surfaced right under her, causing a collision.

"Do you really have to swim that hard?"

He's like the deer, she thought, bold enough to go for the flowers, but if I make the slightest move, he'll bolt.

"You're the one who wanted to be friends," she said. "I'm just trying to respect your space."

"You should do whatever *you* want to do, Veronica."

She loved the way he said her name. She loved the simple, solid sound of his.

"Fred," she said. "Fred. You know, it's been so long since I've been with a man, I can't do anything until I know I'm wanted."

He held out his arms. "Don't you know when you're wanted?"

Veronica did. She rushed into Fred's embrace and blissfully finger-combed his dripping hair.

"Jesus, I've wanted this since I first saw you and you've known it since then, too."

But Fred didn't meet Veronica's eyes or her lips. "I'm not feeling very sexual right now," he said.

She froze, fearing that the slightest motion from her would send him bounding naked into the chaparral.

"Fred, you don't have to do anything. I'm not going to make any demands on you. I'm just glad you're in my life."

He sighed then and slid his hands across the small of Veronica's back, down over her rump and between her thighs, which he began tugging apart as he lifted her. She ended up with her legs wrapped around Fred's waist, her breasts right in his face, and her heart pounding hard as hoofbeats.

Then, just as suddenly as he'd raised her, Fred lowered Veronica again but now he had an erection and he closed her thighs around it. He's tapered, she thought, just like a carrot and just the right size for me, too. Yet Fred still didn't kiss her and Veronica started to shiver.

"You're cold?"

"I don't understand. Parts of me are burning up."

But her teeth chattered and goosebumps studded her arms. Veronica thought she'd get warmer if she swam for a bit but when that didn't help, she went back to her house to take a hot shower. She left the bathroom door ajar. When she emerged in her bathrobe, she found Fred lying on the living room sofa. He was fully dressed and his eyes were closed.

"You can sleep here if you want to. I won't bother you."

Fred looked up, then used the ties of Veronica's sash to pull her down beside him.

"I couldn't do that," he said. "I'd bother you."

"It wouldn't be bother. You're so beautiful."

"I won't ever leave if you tell me that."

"You're beautiful. You're beautiful. You're beautiful. You're beautiful."

"So are you," Fred said, but he left soon after that anyway.

July passed. And August. No deer. No Fred. Veronica missed them both. To attract the deer, she knew she could pot more flowers, but it was Fred she longed to feed, if only she knew what blossom he craved.

Eventually he arranged another riding date for a Sunday afternoon in September. That morning he called Veronica to advise of a slight complication. Her name was Rose and she was a naturopathic doctor from out of town who was visiting his department at the hospital for the day. Though he didn't actually come out and say so, Fred gave Veronica the distinct impression that Rose, an expert rider, would have nowhere to go and nothing to do for the evening if he didn't bring her along.

"Well, bring her," Veronica said. After months of wondering where she stood in Fred's life, she felt that she'd just been promoted. All at once, she was the one he was bringing his colleagues home to. No telling what he'd do next. And as if he'd been reading her mind, Fred uttered the magic words, "I really do love you, Veronica."

The sky was a dirty yellow and the horses were sluggish going up the ridge. Veronica had taken the slowest mount, so she had plenty of opportunity to admire Rose's seat and observe the way Fred rode alongside, bumping his knee against hers now and then.

Veronica adjusted her sunglasses and apologized for the way the smog had ruined their view.

Rose turned in her saddle. She was young and blonde and the jeans she'd borrowed from Veronica fit as if they'd been sewn on.

"It doesn't matter," Rose said. "I've seen it clear. I've been in L.A. for a month now."

"I thought you two just met today."

"Oh no. I've been helping Fred catch babies all week."

Back at the house, Veronica offered to make a stir-fry but Fred insisted on going after take-out food. While he was off on his errand, Rose showered and changed into the gauzy floral print dress she'd been wearing when she arrived. She helped set the table on the patio, humming and dancing as she worked. Veronica opened a bottle of wine, put one of her favorite samba tapes on the stereo and, after dinner, turned the music loud so they could all dance on the lawn. Together, the women tugged Fred onto the grass but he said, "I'd rather watch," and climbed into the hammock.

Veronica was afraid he'd go to sleep again but instead he covered his face with his hands and from the heaving movement of his shoulders, she could tell that he was sobbing. Unsure again of her status, she immediately beckoned Rose.

The younger woman was very professional in the way she got into the hammock and cradled Fred's head on her breast. Veronica climbed in, too. She took Fred's feet into her lap. They were cold and limp as crabmeat and she tried to warm them while Rose stroked his heart chakra upwards and encouraged him to speak. Fred said nothing but one of the dead crustaceans in Veronica's hands gave a violent twitch.

"Does that mean you want me to leave?" she asked.

"Please," Fred said. Then he slumped down deeper into lovely Rose's garden of gauze.

Veronica retreated to the kitchen, did the dishes, made a pot of tea from homegrown mint, and carried mugs out to her guests. Fred didn't acknowledge her but Rose said, "This is very nice. I hope you're as good to yourself as you are to your company."

"I do my best," Veronica said.

Back in the house, she turned the tape over and put out the lights. Unable to think of anything more she could do for her guests, Veronica retired to her bedroom, lit the oil lamp, lay back on her pillows and wondered what she should do with herself for the rest of the night. She was too spaced from the wine to think clearly and much too confused to sleep.

If she was truly Fred's friend, then why couldn't he talk while she was there? If he really loved her like he'd said, then why didn't he let her comfort him? If he didn't want to get involved with anyone yet, what was he doing opening his heart to this Rose? And why had he made it sound as if Rose didn't live in L.A. when she did and that he'd only just met her that day when they'd already spent more time together in the past week than he'd spent with Veronica all summer long? It didn't make sense, but she realized that nothing else about Fred's behavior up to then had either.

Veronica turned out the lamp and surrendered the man of her dreams to the younger, prettier woman. Looking out at the lawn, she realized that she hadn't seen the deer lately either but that was to be expected because she was all out of flowers.

Still, Veronica reminded herself, she wasn't shut down completely. As a matter of fact, she could still do her best to be good to herself. And though her guests would soon be leaving, she had a lot of nice new underwear, new pillows, plenty of lubricant, and even, in the bottom of the refrigerator, an entire unopened bag of perfectly tapered carrots.

# Sunday Night Sauna
## Irene Marcuse

Do all men have hairy asses? Stick their heads first
under the shower? I used to know these answers, but
I've sort of fallen into being a virgin again. Like I used to
sort of fall into bed. With a man. Many beds.
Mostly they are circumcised. Circumspect. But not the one
I married. Unmarried.
I remember that men have longer arm bones with leaner muscles
and more hair. They reach for you, and you fit together.
All men have narrow hips. Sometimes they shave at night
before going to bed not alone. This is sexy.
So is the smell of aftershave, not too strong, in an elevator.
Or on an airplane, I've always wanted to do it. It.
The ultimate euphemism: What we do with down there. What
do we do? I forget. Times have changed. I fell out.
Forgot how to do what you didn't used to have to know how to
do. It. Just Do It. Now it's an ad for running shoes.
Yeah—and they used to be sneakers, in and out of bed, but
now you need rubbers. Now you need to run.
It's still easy to look, pretend I'm not but my mouth smiles,
my thighs remember. Sigh. Size, yes, size is good.
If I had the opportunity, I'd have sex again. Either
it's there or it's not. So what do I do?
Smoke a cigarette—instead, not after. Eat something sweet,
ummm, ice cream. Lick the spoon.

# The Bargain
## Lynn Kanter

I try to memorize the details so that later I can spread them out, sift them through my fingers like stones, examine each one. After all, I never thought this could happen. I never dreamed I would find myself in this cherished place again, and certainly not with her.

Here are some of the things I'd forgotten: The way her skin feels electric, rippling with heat beneath the surface. The way her heart beats through the smooth, private flesh along her ribs. The way my touch can send blood coursing to her face. The way the sharp catch of her breath stabs me with sweetness. The way it feels to sit across the room from her. The way the air crashes against me like waves when she moves.

I can't believe I gave all this up for him.

He has beautiful hands: strong, square, with blunt fingers and a sprinkling of dark hair. On billboards, in magazines, on the sides of buses, his hands hold beer cans, shaving products, power tools. On TV screens his hands write with a fountain pen, clinch business deals, display a sandwich that another man, in another shot, will eat.

As long as his hands look good he can go to the studio scruffy, hungover, unshaven, but he does not. He works out. He dresses well. He trains for each job: no drinking, no late nights. His hands have bought us our house, clothes for our three children, vacations in Mexico. They are precious, an investment. He would risk almost anything to avoid damaging them.

Here are some of the things he cannot do with his hands: He can't wash dishes. He can't fix the kids' bikes. He can't pick berries. He can't light the grill. He can't garden. He can't scrub the sink. He can't paint the dog house. He can't change a tire.

He cannot reach me. He cannot move me.

I learned early on that life is a trade-off. Give something up, get something in return. Sometimes what you get is more valuable than what you lost. Usually you can't tell until it's too late. I was never surprised to find that life wasn't fair, that people weren't decent, that the home team rarely won. It's a beggar's market, I always say. You make what bargains you can.

I never bargained on this. Her body is still smooth and firm, like a young girl's. She has no brown, down-turned nipples, no silvery stretch marks, no scars. Of course, she has no children, no hungry husband hanging on her for sustenance.

I knew her body once, so long ago it was another life. We went to the woods that afternoon—there were still woods around here then. In a clearing she spread out an old blue blanket of her mother's. We didn't mind that it was rough, that it smelled of dust. We lay on our sides and ate sandwiches, drank Cokes out of thick glass bottles.

After lunch she braided my hair. I gathered hers into a French twist. We were too old for such games, but we didn't care. It was a glorious day. The next morning we would graduate from high school. That evening we would go out with our friends and spend the night in dimly lit rooms, calibrating just how far our panting boyfriends could go. We thought the future held no surprises for us, but we were wrong.

I pinned up her glossy black hair. Slow-moving sunlight illuminated the back of her neck. I saw how soft her skin was, how it sparkled with tiny golden hairs that were invisible in any other light. As if she were a fawn, I reached out to stroke her.

It was all as simple as gravity. Soon I was touching her in ways I had never touched anyone, not even myself. Her hands moved over me slowly, with assurance, as if they had been there before. Evening shadows stretched across us. Our cries sent birds flapping into the air.

Afterwards I was mute. She laughed, kissed me on the lips, combed out my braid with her fingers. It was then I realized she did not possess the heavy human spirit with which I was to plod through life. She would fly, and I could never follow.

I worked at the dime store, dated briefly, then married my husband, the man with the beautiful hands. Many years later we went to a formal party at the home of his agent. It was there I tried my first artichoke. I nibbled the delicate flesh and then I had to sit down and fan my face. I couldn't believe that none of the sophisticated people at the party had noticed: the artichoke tasted like a woman. It was the taste I had been craving all my life.

There were no women's bookstores when I was young, no resource centers, no restaurants. Not in my little town. There was only a bar, with painted windows and no sign, hidden behind the furniture factory.

I did not want that. I wanted children, a house, respectability. I wanted to go to church on Sunday, to have the minister nod benignly at me and my brood. For that I was willing to give up all the smooth shoulders, all the ragged sighs, all the tender breasts, all the trembling thighs. She had made me roll like the ocean, I knew that. But it was a trade-off. I thought I could afford it.

I was surprised and flattered when she called. It didn't seem possible that she remembered me.

Our little town is no longer considered separate, but a suburb of the larger city to the south where my husband sells his hands. She was visiting the city on business, but she booked a room for herself here, at the homely old motel near the Dairy Queen.

Of course there was nowhere to sit in those rooms, there never had been. We perched on the bed like schoolgirls and chattered about where the years had taken us.

She did some job with computers, something I didn't understand. I had forgotten how her eyes are flecked with gold. I had forgotten how our hands are the same size. I had forgotten how a body can hunger. I had forgotten all of that, but she reminded me.

My husband and I have twenty-three years together. I would do anything for him, and I have. We share a history, a family, a lovely house. But the only place I have ever known that I was home is in this woman's hands.

A moan escapes me and she laughs with delight, moving more slowly to prolong the pleasure. She lives in a city where women walk together in daylight, where love carries no price. Tomorrow she will leave and I will not follow.

After all, this is the life I have chosen. It is the bargain I struck. I clinched the deal. I offered my hand.

# It Is a Question of Timing
## Judith W. Steinbergh

And when as a young girl, I wanted to put your hand on my breast, your hair was too long and people gaped at you even in Harvard Square. And when you left school and begged me to come along like a gypsy on a Harley, I fled to my dorm at Wellesley and crossed my legs. And when you pulled up, a year later, with a full brown beard and a Mexican dress for me, I was away healthy at camp with twelve ten-year-olds who thought I was Mother Superior, stable as Gibraltar, I lectured you, trying to rid you of your shrinks, your demons, intense as I could be for a day at a time, until I started to giggle, horrified you'd discover the real me. Oh your hand was strong by the wide Susquehanna and your voice saying your poems was deeper than your years. Now you arrive, left by your wife and kids, to me, left as a wife with my kids, charming in your Pakistani coat, your fluid Spanish, your rakish hat, the crowsfeet warming your eyes, your voice resonant as night, your laugh a comet. How have you come at the perfect time, at the sun's eclipse, taking my breath like an orange moon rising? How have you come in the month-long blizzard to wrap yourself around my children on their sled? How have you stayed with your white wine buried in snow outside my window, my raw hands warming under your fleecy coat, our foreheads rubbing away their creases, and finally, after twenty years, our tongues.

# Fires of Autumn
## Lea Wood


Saturday, five-fifteen p.m. I knock on the door. It opens and a face looks out. "I'm early," I say, walking in. "Shall I go out and come back later?"

"Get out and don't darken my door for another half hour," he says, with sweeping out-the-door gestures.

We laugh and embrace. Whenever I come, we have some kind of joke going with the door. Sometimes he answers the knock with "Who's there?"

"The bill collector," I say, or the name of a character in a play we're doing.

"I'm not here—nobody home."

"Okay, Nobody—let me in." He opens the door but hides behind it while I pretend to look for him. He's 63 and I'm 65, but the children in us are delighted with the game.

In the apartment kitchen little piles of chopped onions, peppers, cabbage, carrots and mushrooms are heaped on the cutting board; on the stove some brown rice is steaming. Aaron returns to the garlic he's mincing, as I lean against the refrigerator and listen to him talk about our reader's theater projects.

"I talked to Dellums's secretary about the play, but you'd better sit down to hear the bad news." He looks serious. I think he's kidding, until he firmly sits me down at the table and picks up some notes. "She got the play," he reads. "She loves the play." Long pause, looking up. "She thinks it's very clever." He pockets the notes and returns to the chopping board.

"Some bad news!" I laugh. The play dramatizes how a National Health Service, described in Dellums's Congressional Bill, could function in people's lives. A working couple—Aaron and I—take this role and I get to live the fantasy of being married to him. They have a son in medical school; I work in a nursing home; Aaron and I replay our fictional past through a young couple facing bills for a premature baby. The cast takes three couples. I wrote it because Aaron asked me if I would. He was so excited that such legislation existed and wanted to spread the word in an interesting way. Now he beams in telling me these nice words about the play, which, though I wrote it, is in all respects "our play." While working on it, I'd try scenes out with him. His criticisms were spare, and gentle. "Hmmm. Don't you think that sounds a bit soap opera?" It was the part between him and me.

"It does?" I took another look, winced, and rewrote the scene. From his own experience he could tell me about the hazards of being a tool and die maker working with machines for the part on worker safety. We sit down to dinner, Aaron pushing the clutter of cassette tapes, political notices, and junk mail out of the way. He sets down a big wooden salad bowl, steaming with enough rice and vegetables for four people, and a small china bowl for me. He owns barely enough dishes. When I empty my bowl, I pass it to him for a refill. It seems very proletariat—and romantic. Comfortable. It fits a self I am with Aaron—one that feels like most of my real self, one that I like.

As we eat, we listen to the news. My attention weaves in and out of the radio broadcast because when I'm with Aaron, he fills most of my mind. News of a demonstration at Rocky Flats nuclear weapons plant in Colorado captures my attention, reminding me of how we met.

He was leaning against the hood of a car in a parking lot in downtown Santa Cruz, his gray head a standout in a throng of mostly students. My daughter had dropped me off, and as I shouldered my backpack, scanning the lot for my affinity group, he caught my eye. He looked like an old revolutionary: faded blue corduroys, arms folded across his chest. A mane of hair swept back from a peak to a ragged cut in back that looked as if he'd cut it himself. Slavic cheekbones set off his craggy face, prominent nose. The youthful crowd swirled about him in the bright August sunshine, carrying banners feltpenned on cardboards, lugging backpacks, shouting to friends.

I felt irresistibly drawn to him. A peer in an action like this? I approached him like an iron filing to a magnet.

He smiled at my "Hi!," his eyes flashing an intense blue.

"What's your group?" I asked, reaching for a quick handle of contact.

"Solar Cruzers," smiling at the name. "You in this, too?"

I nodded. "We call ours Mother's Helpers. Where're you from?"

"Can't you tell? Brooklyn. Only been here a couple of months."

"Ever done this sort of thing before?" I ask him.

He shook his head.

"Me either."

Jean, in my affinity group, hailed me to pack in for the drive down to San Luis Obispo.

"See you in jail!" my colleague in protest called after me. We had committed ourselves to civil disobedience against the Diablo Canyon nuclear power plant.

In the protest that hot August Hiroshima Day, Aaron had been an occupier, trespassing on the land of the power plant; I had been a blockader, stopping workers' cars at the gate. Afterwards, with nearly five hundred others, we spent three days locked up in two wings of a prison gymnasium.

Back home we explored our new relationship. In the first weeks each encounter started with a dialogue of eyes asking the unspoken questions: "Is he—is she—still interested?" "Will she—will he—be The One?" And each time the first answer was affirmed in our eyes, leaving hope for the second. An affair at our ages did not have to lead to marriage. He had been widowed, left with three children; I had been twice divorced, raised one child.

The Abalone Alliance, umbrella for the California anti-nuke groups, decided on a demonstration trial in San Luis Obispo of twenty participants from the 484 arrested. Aaron and I were asked to take part, to commit ourselves for the six weeks the trial was expected to take. The idea, of course, was to put nuclear power on trial. I was excited to be involved, but to share the experience with Aaron was a bonus. I wondered about the living arrangements.

After the first day's session, we dropped in at the headquarters of the local anti-nuclear group to wait for someone who dealt with housing. I wandered around looking over the posters and notices while Aaron sat down with a newspaper.

"Hey, Lea!"

I turned around to see Jean, whom I had come to know and admire during our lock-in.

"Tell me—are you and Aaron sleeping together?"

I gasped; felt myself blush all over. The forthrightness of her generation about matters of sex was not part of mine.

"Good grief!" I exclaimed, looking around, wondering if anyone had overheard so shocking a question. The few others scattered about seemed to be paying us no attention; Aaron didn't even look up from his paper.

I fairly swept her out the back door into the yard. "Well, sort of," I answered her question. "Why?"

"I need to know because Dave and I have been offered a tiny cottage on the edge of town and there's room for two more—except they would have to sleep together in a loft."

"Oh!" I said, thinking that my hopes had been answered. "Sorry I got so freaked." We laughed. "Sounds wonderful! Thanks!"

So that was the other level of the trial, our nights together as well as the days in the courtroom. It was like being married, the honeymoon phase.

We lost the cottage at the Thanksgiving break in the trial, but Jean and Dave found another home for the four of us at the edge of one of the town's volcanic hills.

Given the choice of a room in the house or a tiny camper in the driveway, we took the camper. It was like a vacation cottage; in the midst of the courtroom ritual I thought of our coming home to it. We called it "home." When the trial ended for the day, we ranged through a grocery for food and prepared dinner together. Aaron loved shopping, liked to cook; I could do without either, but with him it was fun. Our major staple was potatoes, baked or boiled, heaped with yogurt.

I was already aware of the alone time he seemed to need, and left him to take care of laundry, go to the post office, stop by the drugstore. During lunch time he liked to read in the city's library, and I often sat in the back seat of my Volkswagen bug with my portable typewriter on my lap, banging out press releases or personal letters. In the courtroom we didn't always sit together. I took notes for the lawyers, stole glances at him in the unfamiliar brown suit, yellow shirt, a tie! I'd think about being in his arms each night, remember waking up to him, close, warm, and dearer with each day.

One rainy weekend near the end of the trial, we sat across the camper table from each other, rain beading down the windows, drumming a metallic tattoo on the roof. He was engrossed in a newspaper and I was reading a book, but kept glancing at him over the covers, my heart yearning. What was in our future? In four months he had never said he loved me in so many words, but his look was often a caress. Surely, these weeks showed that we could live together harmoniously.

I could not keep it inside any longer; I didn't care if I was the first to say the words. I went over and stood at his side.

"Aaron," I said, my throat choking. "I have to tell you."

He looked up from the paper with those blue eyes, so intensely alive.

"Tell me what?" he asked, in that resonant voice, moving his knee from under the table for me to sit on.

"That I love you so much. You've made me so happy." I put my cheek against his.

"Fine," he replied. "But saying it doesn't necessarily mean much."

I was taken aback. "What do you mean?"

"It's easy to say 'I love you.'" He almost sneered the words. "What really matters is how you show it."

"Well, sure," I agreed, "but it's nice to say it, too." I waited for him to say it, but he didn't.

"Love," he almost spat the word. "What do people mean by it?"

"Well," I mused. "The Japanese don't even have a word for it. But," I added reasonably, "we're not Japanese. What about our experience here, living together as we have—what has it meant to you?"

"It's been nice," he said.

"Nice! Is that all?"

"What else?" He seemed genuinely puzzled. "Don't you think it's been nice?"

"So much more!" I protested.

On the day of sentencing, Aaron put on his worn blue corduroys and jogging shoes, leaving the polished leathers in the closet.

"Today I'm going as myself," he said gruffly, in answer to my raised eyebrows.

Our lawyers had told us that if we took a two-year probation, our sentences, which could be six months max and a $500 fine, would be suspended.

Aaron stood before the judge in his aging corduroys, his crooked haircut, his slightly stooped figure and asked for time to consider the probation until January when the rest of the defendants would appear.

"Denied."

"Then I'm not signing it."

The Judge went on reading as if he understood quite the contrary.

Aaron interrupted him. "I said, I'm not signing the probation," he repeated, his voice edged with anger.

The Judge looked up. "Then you will start serving sentence January 15th."

After a parting shot about the justice of a trial in which none of our expert witnesses were allowed to testify, Aaron walked back to his seat.

I looked over and tears blurred the room. Only he and two other women turned down probation. After a few minutes, he came over to sit next to me and I pressed his hand.

"I felt like a whipped dog up there," he muttered. "I just couldn't stand it. I couldn't sign for probation feeling like that."

But Aaron's punishment was temporarily suspended by an appeal to continue testing the defenses of the anti-nuclear movement.

Back home, we resumed our established two nights a week, though I kept yearning for seven, or at least Sundays, too.

"Hey, nine o'clock!" Aaron says, standing up and stretching. "And I've got a great idea!" His eyes are flashing and I think I know what the idea is.

"To get an ice cream," I say.

"A whole gallon!"

Aaron lives on Social Security, its benefits shrunk by an early retirement, but we are both children of the Thirties Depression and thrift is ingrained. I love it that we have so much fun doing the simplest things. We usually walk the mile across the bridge to Thrifty Drug where the price is the lowest in town.

"Let's take the car," I say. "I spent the whole day hiking and my feet are sore. Besides, I don't want you wasting your energy at this hour of the night."

After the ice cream, I'm looking ahead to what I've looked forward to since the last time we were together in our private space. We see each other in class; there are times we rehearse or read a play before a community group, but it's the alone time together that I live for. No doubt the years-long absence of an intimate relationship and the way Aaron makes up for it is the reason for my craving.

This affair is so different from any other. I was married twice, had lovers in youth and mid-life and seldom felt cheated in sex. Yet Aaron uncovered inhibitions, nudity for one, and dissolved them with his own naturalness. I don't have to worry about contraception—or trying to get pregnant! I find it strange to be able to accept my old body, when I hadn't much liked my young one. I can still be surprised at what I see in a mirror because of my interior view.

In Aaron's room we start taking off our clothes. I am quick, draping mine over a chair while he's by the closet hanging his up. The light from a single bulb up in the ceiling glares, bright and uncompromising, but the glare no longer bothers me. I dash for the bed, a single-size mattress on the floor with its red blanket cover and squeal at the coldness of the sheets.

I lie with the covers drawn to my neck and watch him. He walks to the window and puts his glasses on the sill. I look at his aging body, a bit thick around the waist, stooped in the shoulders, but oh, beloved. He switches off the glaring bulb and approaches the bed. I move over to give him room. He slips his arm under my head and we bask in the wonderful warmth.

How to tell of love-making, so interior an experience. We make an ecstasy for each other, wordless, the body speaking the caring, the giving and receiving that flows between us. I am touched at the way Aaron enhances sex for me, making an art of loving, heightening my sense of self as a desired woman. He also makes sex fun. I could not have believed at thirty that beyond sixty could be like this, the best sexual experience of my life.

So I ask myself why can't I be content with not living with him since we have this wonder. To bring up the subject is to ask for personal disaster. I don't want to make waves that will spoil the time we have. I look at it as talking out our differences; he feels criticized. Yet we come from such different backgrounds; there are bound to be misunderstandings.

I feel the need for him to be part of my everyday life: waking to him every morning, knowing he's in the house somewhere or returning home. The separateness makes me feel as if I have two lives and that I'm always saying goodbye to one of them.

From time to time the yearning for more wholeness boils up. The subject usually creates a freeze. If I am ill-advised enough to bring it up during one of our two nights together, I sleep with an iceberg and must wait for a thaw. He finally breaks the silence—often not until the next of our nights—with "This way we can stay friends!" Yet there was a time when he said he might want to live with someone again, so I'm checking.

Sundays are hardest. I wake up knowing that another goodbye will be soon, but postpone the thought in the delicious nearness of him. Mornings seem to bring out his political side, and he harangues about our social ills while I mostly revel in the sound of his voice, the feel of his arm around me.

While we're getting dressed, I decide to try him about Sundays. "Aaron, if there's a march for labor or peace on Sunday we always go. So come on. Why not other Sundays?"

I feel him closing off.

"I told you." He's irritated. "I need to do my laundry, catch up on my reading, clean the apartment."

I wonder why he can't do this on Saturday. "For me, Sunday is a special togetherness kind of day," I tell him, wanting him to understand how I feel about it. "I feel lonelier on Sundays."

"Well, that's your problem," he says bluntly. "I thought you were an independent woman with your own life; that's what attracted me to you."

I understand about the space; he needs more of it than me. I also believe the best relationships are those where each has separate interests but I feel I can practice the theory better if we live with each other. I do go off on hikes with the Sierra Club, take an active part in a Unitarian Fellowship, go folk dancing, write for a local paper, but I miss him, wish that he wanted to go on the hikes and the dances with me. I am still too emotionally needy to fulfill myself in a separate life. I grew up in a social space that decreed a man as the focus of a woman's life. I did not yet see this as a shadow kind of existence.

When the appeal of our trial was denied, we were called back to San Luis Obispo. Three years had softened the punishment. The ninety days were pared down to thirty, the fine to $300.

At the jail window we handed our papers to the young woman behind the glass enclosure, who studied them, and sighed.

"You owe a $300 fine?"

"It says we can do it with jail," Aaron said.

"Wait a minute." She took the papers into a back room.

A uniformed young man appeared with our papers in hand. "I can't do anything about these," he said.

"Why not?" I asked.

"You're not in my computer anymore."

"We were in the trial—" Aaron started.

"That cost the county a lot of money; we don't want to spend any more on it," he answered, but in a friendly tone.

In spite of our commonalities, Aaron and I did not live happily ever after. Through eight years of two nights a week our interests together grew less, our differences more. Near the end we were down to movies, peace marches and sex.

The crash came after seven weeks of togetherness in Europe, where I was trying to market a screenplay about Emma Goldman. In spite of the guidance of a local filmmaker and the interest of Liv Ullman which opened many doors, I could not find a producer willing to take it on and was advised to try Europe where studios were more open to radical subjects.

I was able to manage a house trade near London to help with finances. But I also wanted to go to Spain, France and Italy where we'd have to depend on cheap hotels and youth hostels. Aaron was not as enthusiastic as I hoped, but he did put aside his reluctance and agreed to go with me. What to me was a joy at the prospect of being with him for weeks was to him a deep unease which I did not see until the ragged end.

He often remarked to friends that he and I stayed together as long as we had because we didn't live with each other. "It wouldn't have lasted two weeks!" he'd exclaim.

As a traveling companion, Aaron was a mix of patient support for what I was trying to do, a comfort to sleep with, and a pain in most other ways. If we decided to dine out he checked prices in place after place, and then bitterly criticized the choice he finally made. We both liked best to buy food at open markets and mostly subsisted on buns, fruit and cheese.

Our last city was Vienna. I just wanted to enjoy the city of Mozart, my favorite composer. Aaron had business of his own there, so it was a mutual decision. A trail of possibilities for my script led to interviews with directors, agents and collaterals, but nothing was definite. I was usually told that the story was "too American."

After shabby hotels and hostel dorms, we finally stayed in our very own room of a beautiful big hostel. I was ecstatic over it, but Aaron wasn't. The worst quarrel we ever had erupted when I expressed a wish to change our plans. We'd hardly been in Vienna two days before Aaron wanted to leave, and reluctantly, I agreed. We had the great luck to hear Mozart's Requiem in the fabulous Karlskirche, but I'd not have inflicted an opera on him. After we made reservations on a Friday afternoon to fly out Monday, I found out that "Abduction from the Seralgio" would play the night after we left. The travel office was closed over the weekend, but to miss such an experience at the very opera house where it was first performed seemed a wrenching—and needless—deprivation. There must be a way!

When I voiced my anguish, Aaron exploded. How could I ask such a thing? He was desperate to get back; the trip had cost so much money and he hadn't gotten that much pleasure from it; I was selfish and childish to even *think* of changing the plans for an opera!

"You've no *right* to think of it!" he added.

Wait a minute! Now he was over the border. In the angry exchange, I believe I told him, among other things, that I could live without him.

"So stay!" he shot back. "I'll go back by myself!"

I was tempted to let him. Yet, I thought of his patience about following up my contacts, listening to my frets about them, just being there for me for the most part, and much as I wanted to let him go back alone, I could not.

Talk was spare between us from then on. When, home at last, we met after a few intervening days at a Christmas Fair, Aaron spoke to me tight-lipped and briefly, then left. I ran after him.

"You didn't say anything about tonight."

He looked at me and there was no caress in his eyes now. "I think we need a vacation from each other."

"You think so?" I answered, feeling a little twist in my heart region. "How long?"

"Two months?"

"Two months!"

"Yeah, then we'll see."

But it was over. I wanted to reconcile, to make up somehow, even though in a deeper place I felt hopeless about us. I had to pass through various phases of numbness, anger, and grief to come out whole again and to the decision that ours was a relationship that had run its course.

But my 60s had been full of unique political action, creative opportunity and sexual love. They were treasured years, especially Aaron's part in them.

# Good News
## Regina deCormier-Shekerjian

Afternoon sun of late October
blazes in the fist of chrysanthemums
by the kitchen door and in the woods
a loud clamor of light echoes the cry
of ducks flying south. She squints
against the sun, and brings the axe

down. A clean split. She smiles
at the good-sized pile of oak and apple
neatly stacked. David worries about her
needlessly, she thinks; at sixty-seven
she can still manage—yes,
she still works three days a week as an apostle
for nuclear disarmament, cleans the house, cooks,
continues to spy on the world and gossip
its news, as Yeats did, she whispers, and
she will split the wood
cleanly, she hopes, for a long time yet.

She carries an armload of fragrant wood
into the house. It is almost time for tea
and David is coming with two friends. No
melancholy angels, no nattering pedants
today, thank god. She has bought scones
and Seville marmalade. She has moved the table
to the window. She brings plates, fragile
cups, chrysanthemums flecked with light,
a bottle of 15-year-old scotch...

*Tea laced with a good scotch*
*civilizes winter*...Five long years

and she can still hear Richard's voice
bounding about in the corners
of all these rooms, tenor shrapnel of wit,
and love, polyphonic
in memory. She bends, and touches
the wood to life—and
                                          desire
leaps—without warning—

       naked, in an apricot sun,
       she is drowning
       in a storm of tides, a Catherine Wheel
       of lights spinning, whirling—

shaken, she moves to the window,
and watches light slowly
silence itself in the woods...it was
forty years ago, in Florence, a room
with a fire, another October, another
Richard...

Hurry, David, hurry, she whispers. I have
news, good news; the good
news is—everything is mysterious, and

remains mysterious.

# A Season for Sex
## Gail Weber

On this autumn day, I sit down to write about women's sexuality at menopause, and I am finding it difficult to do this from an academic, disinterested and dispassionate perspective. Issues about women, sexuality and life transitions such as menopause are an important part of my work and my life at this time.

Thoughts on autumn...It is rich in color and in texture and there is a sadness about it. There is a beauty in its variability, one day cold and crisp, the next wet and dark. And then, suddenly a day of such brilliant sunshine that it is enough to warm your heart, quicken your step and make you feel that you will indeed live forever.

Is this the autumn of my life, rich in color and texture with a hint of sadness? Is this the autumn of my sexuality after the heat of summer?

Thoughts on 1990. What a year, what a decade, what a generation! Did time used to go so fast? Did things used to change so quickly and so dramatically? Since my adulthood, we have seen a social and sexual upheaval, a women's movement, the wall has come tumbling down, Meech Lake failed, the NDP won in Ontario. Things change, life happens. It may be confusing to be a teenager today, but it is just as puzzling to figure out how to be a woman today when you are 50, single and sexual.

As a woman who grew up in the '40s and '50s, married in the '60s, got "liberated" in the '70s, and spent the '80s trying to figure it all out, I question where I am now as women in terms of my sexuality in these "golden years."

Women of my vintage who were adolescent in the '50s grew up with enormous social prohibitions about our sexuality. It was not okay to be sexual before marriage, and afterwards, we were not to initiate sex, take too active a role or enjoy it too much. How could you with all that guilt! Female sexuality was narrowly defined; you had to be with one man, never a woman, in marriage, monogamous, in bed, at night, lights out, in the male "superior" position. And all of this was to be forever and ever.

What goes around comes around. Even after the pill and a "sexual revolution" the old taboos that prohibited our sexuality as children and adolescents come back to haunt us. Somehow sex and seniority do not seem to mix. We never see older women in films or on television being sexual without looking ridiculous or embarrassing. We as a generation have been restricted to two sexual identities—in our youth we're portrayed as pure and virginal and as adults with sexual desire we're seen as whores. We have been taught that sex in midlife is okay, if you don't look your age, and sex in later life is really strange.

I think about seeing the movie "The Graduate" back in the late '60s or early '70s and identifying with the young couple who overcame enormous obstacles, married and lived happily ever after. I saw it again several years ago and found, much to my delight, that I understood and was moved by Mrs. Robinson's plight. "So here's to you, Mrs. Robinson," I judged you too harshly from the narrow perspective of my youth. There has been change, personal and societal, and these changes say something about being a woman, sexuality, aging and changing times. I am sorry Mrs. Robinson, I did not know your pain.

It seems strange that just when some women finally get to a point in their lives when they feel a sense of personal independence and autonomy, and may want to express this new-found self in a sexual way, they invariably face one of life's ironic twists. Here she is finally free from concern about birth control and the kids barging in, and yes, you guessed it, her partner of some 25-30 years is finding that he is too tired, uninterested or has slowed down in his sexual responsiveness. This is referred to as the "cross over effect." Talk about bad planning. Whoever designed us must have figured that we would be long dead before we had to worry about such problems.

Another of life's hard ironies. While I write about celebrating our sexuality, I feel the shadow of death of 14 young women in Montreal just a year ago. It is with us, it always will be. We may celebrate our sexuality and our feelings of female solidarity but until we, as women, are safe from the associations of sexuality and violence, we must be forever vigilant and not forget the dangerous side of sexuality and being women.

Janine O'Leary Cobb in a recent speech described sexuality as a process that continues throughout the life cycle. Sexuality goes beyond sexual activity. "...it is the look, smell, taste and feel of being a woman" and is more about how we feel about ourselves than it is about "being sexy" or involved in sexual activity.

She explored the thought that women's sexuality has, through time, been defined for us by men "who cannot imagine sexuality except at the service of penetration." Now, this penetration she describes may be necessary from an evolutionary point of view, but it certainly misses the point about women's sexuality. The intercourse imperative we have been socialized to accept as the norm is a narrow, constricted one that does not serve women well in later life or at any time in life.

Sexuality can be expressed in a myriad of ways. We need to create a broader definition of sexuality that expresses itself through life in different ways. The image of sexuality as a moving stream is an apt one for it describes how sexuality flows through our lives. As young girls, it is narrow, and as we reach maturity it widens, is full and spilling over. As we age, it may narrow again but it never stops flowing.

Let us celebrate our sexuality by exploring how it changes, both qualitatively and quantitatively at the time of menopause and midlife. Menopause has been referred to as "The Change of Life" and yet we know that all of life is involved with change. From our birth until our last breath, we are aging and changing. Women's lives are biologically and socially involved with change.

The physical changes that take place in our bodies around the time of menopause are difficult to separate from the physical changes of aging. After all, 50 years of wear and tear takes its toll in fatigue, poor health and stress-related illnesses. The use of alcohol and coffee, and the effects of certain medications (such as tranquilizers, antihistamines and blood pressure drugs) affect sexuality, usually in a negative way. We know that good nutrition, adequate exercise and a reduction in stress result in good health which is reflected in our sexuality.

The specific physical differences that may affect sexuality are genital changes due to a decrease in the production of estrogen. These changes are relatively easy to deal with.

With menopause, there is a thinning of the vaginal walls, a loss of vaginal elasticity, a shortening of the vagina and a decrease in vaginal lubrication. All of this sounds pretty grim, but in fact, these changes do not create problems for most women. A longer and slower period of foreplay, with the goal of pleasuring and not performance, is important.

Vaginal lubricants in the form of massage oils, saliva, vegetable oils, or KY Jelly can be lovingly incorporated into lovemaking with or without a partner. If the vaginal changes are severe, the use of a prescribed estrogen cream may be helpful for a period of time.

Around the time of menopause, the clitoris becomes larger and more exposed. Direct stimulation may be uncomfortable and so lubrication is important. As well, clear communication with a partner about what feels good and what does not is, as always, important.

Some of the pharmaceutical and medical literature on hormone replacement therapy (HRT) would have us believe that the use of HRT will keep us "young and sexy forever." However, it does not affect our libido or our ability to be aroused except insofar as it does relieve hot flashes and severe vaginal dryness.

Women as well as men may notice in the middle years and beyond that the quality and quantity of orgasmic experiences change. Some women report that orgasms are less intense, less frequent and take longer to achieve. More creative forms of lovemaking, unhurried, leisurely and playful are important. Sometimes "sexual burnout" can be a problem and perhaps the relationship itself needs replenishment. Other women find that they become orgasmic for the first time in midlife and later life and are "turned on" most of the time. It is difficult to sort out social versus biological factors. However, it has been suggested that there is a shift in the estrogen/androgen ratio at menopause. With a decrease in estrogen, the effect of the male hormone, testosterone, present in both men and women, is more evident in women and accounts for an increase in libido at midlife. Perhaps when we are more mature, more self-assured and confident about who we are and less influenced by social prohibitions, we are better able to express ourselves freely and genuinely. Perhaps it is the feeling that "at last, these years are mine and I can do as I please with my life."

The quality of the sexual experience changes as does everything else. We know we are in midlife when we don't look in the mirror as much, we start to read the obituaries and even "a quickie" takes 45 minutes.

Women I see in counselling and in education/support groups give voice to the great individuality and variability in their experience of sexuality at midlife. There may be an increase in sexual fantasies and in desire or there may be a marked decrease in interest. They may experience a change in orgasmic experience or a change in sexual orientation. Our sexuality is not separate from the rest of our lives.

In the final analysis, we likely do not know all the factors that account for changes in sexuality at midlife. It is a complex issue and needs to be studied more. And the data must come from women themselves and their experiences.

Social factors that affect sexuality at midlife involve societal attitudes of ageism, sexism, homophobia and a resurgence of puritanical thinking.

Women are seen as somewhat "deficient" if we do not live up to an idealized mass cultural image of youthful sexuality. Because we're surrounded by these powerful images, it's an uphill battle to be different. We internalize these harsh societal judgements and berate ourselves for our grey hair and extra weight. Our need to look like the stereotypical females in the beer commercials keeps the gyms and cosmetic industries booming in spite of recessions. It is often difficult to accept ourselves as aging and changing.

Today, women work at home and in the work place to a greater degree than ever before. This may offer middle-class women greater independence but being "superwoman" is hard on us. All women pay a price both physically and sexually for our double days of work. We suffer more than ever before from chronic fatigue-like syndromes.

Poor and immigrant women who work in factories, clean homes and toil in low paying, undervalued jobs struggle even more. Fatigue, poor nutrition and inadequate medical care take their toll on our lives. To be poor and 50 and to feel that we can never be as the media dictates, is to suffer a massive cultural denial of our womanhood.

In our society, heterosexual women typically have been partnered with men who are older. As a result many women at midlife are often widows and alone. Or alone as a result of his midlife madness which has him running off with a socially sanctioned younger woman. The worst part of this scenario is that we are subtly blamed for his "sexual boredom." His sexual inadequacies are somehow our fault. It's the old blame-the-victim routine.

In looking for ways to express our sexuality at this stage in life we can happily give up our prohibiting notions about age, race, religion and gender in seeking a partner. It is not uncommon for women to come out at midlife and enjoy a lesbian relationship which offers sexuality, companionship and understanding. Our knowledge of lesbian sexuality at midlife is scant but we do know that despite rampant homophobia there is more support for women who choose to lead an unconventional life.

The social and cultural constraints on our sexuality are great. We are told to "act your age" and to "use it or lose it." And as if all this were not enough to fret about, we now have to concern ourselves with the very real problems of sexually transmitted diseases.

Masturbation or self pleasuring may be an alternative to having a partner. With a partner, it is certainly an important aspect of lovemaking. Celibacy may be appropriate for periods of time or as a life commitment. There are many ways to express our sexuality and this is a choice that we make.

Psychological factors which affect us are the internalization of social labels such as "aging dyke," "dirty old lady," or the idea that we are too fat, too old, too whatever for loving. Negative judgements about our age probably affect our experience of sexuality more than all the hormones and glands in the world.

Our capacity for sexual enjoyment is dependent on our biological inheritance, our childhood upbringing and our life experiences. All of these factors come into play long before we come into menopause.

In spite of all the cultural and psychological factors that affect us at midlife, for many women it is a time of great emotional growth and liberation. Menopause is one of those marker events that gives us the opportunity to take stock, reaffirm where we are and make changes. It is a time of renewal. As we change at midlife there is the same opportunity for a renewal in our sexuality.

The good news is that there is sexuality after menopause. The sexuality of youth, of middle age and of later life is not the same and is not to be compared. If we try to hang onto the spring, we miss the summer. Each phase and stage of our lives and our sexuality is unique and perfect...like the changing seasons.

So, if indeed this is the autumn of my sexuality, rich in color and in texture, variable and with a hint of sadness, then let it be. I will hope to be ever open to the winter. But not just yet. I am still enjoying playing in the leaves.

# Fulfilling Fantasies at 68
## Corinne Davis

Most of my life I honestly believed "nice girls don't." It took me 48 years to experience orgasm, admit my sexuality and define sex as a passionate but normal human activity separate from guilt, inhibitions and society's speculations. I had been married to my second husband 28 years when I ventured outside my sexually disastrous marriage to find incredible, sensual sex with a massage partner I met at church camp.

Today at 68, I am 48 years into my second marriage and have five marvelous lovers ages 35, 37, 37, 46, and 49! They are all men I met through two free want ads netting me 71 and 49 replies respectively. I do not discuss my age and could pass for my mid-fifties but I weigh 185 pounds and am pleasant but not sensational looking. All the men are professionals, have incredible backgrounds and high incomes, are bright and both married and single.

I don't believe men are hung up on young women. I specified men over 55 and my replies ranged from ages 23-60 with the majority in the 25-35 year range.

Twelve years of celibacy in my marriage finally helped me realize only I can fulfill my needs or even admit they exist. Other personal considerations make it impossible to leave a marriage which works for me in most other areas. I decided to seize the day, take a risk and see what happened. I found out I get what I want and what I need at least two-thirds of the time. That beats the law of averages.

Do I feel wicked or immoral? Absolutely not! To hear a man praise my "lush body," "big, beautiful breasts," or "warmth and openness" is heady stuff after decades of hurtful jokes regarding my frigidity, headaches or disinterest in sex.

I feel valued and appreciated by men who are successful, sexy and adoring. If relationships come and go as they must, I have delightful memories of elegant hotels and fabulous restaurants where my partners have listened, asked my advice and made me feel like a total and complete woman. I feel elated when lovers tell me how my attitudes have made positive changes in their own code of living and marriages.

To find good sex, a woman has to feel entitled to sexual fulfillment and to act in a positive way to make it happen. Want ads have worked well for me as I work in a profession where one doesn't see men often and I have limited access to meeting people.

You need to be clear about what you are seeking. Don't expect to receive cards, letters, gifts or romance. Don't anticipate seeing him oftener than agreed. Don't expect more than friendship and great sex. And above all, don't think sex will be more than loving pleasure with someone you like or that it will last forever. Nothing does.

But if you learn the rules, sex can be fantastic, wild, adventurous, warm and totally satisfying with a wide variety of terrific men who really want to please you. When I first rebuffed a 22-year-old man I met at church camp, he stated "That's your prejudice, not mine!"

The men who have answered my ads have been exceptional men who liked the idea of a woman who was educated, intelligent, literate, traveled, stable, and financially independent. They are hard-working, brilliant men who give so much energy to their careers, they want a relationship which is non-demanding, safe, discreet, and sexually uninhibited. These are my priorities, also.

Why would any exciting, handsome, successful man answer an anonymous ad? The reasons vary but frequently they had sensational sex as an adolescent with an older female mentor or find an older woman "a real turn-on."

Some men simply don't want to risk constant phone calls, demands and interruptions from a partner. Others have wives who are emotionally or physically ill or a disinterested partner. Because I am a married woman, married men feel I'm safe. Mostly, men are seeking an intelligent woman, a non-dependent partner and sexual variety.

What does one say to intrigue a stranger? Be sincere and honest. My headline "Afternoon Delight" clearly set the tone for a purely sexual relationship. The text stated "Professional woman in celibate marriage seeks partner for fun and games. Must be gentle, passionate, healthy, discreet, uninhibited, happy with himself, non-smoker, moderate drinker, no drugs." Be clear about your demands and try to have a different angle. Mine was "seeking a non-committed relationship without future expectations." I am not seeking love or romance. My goal is solely fantastic sex with men I really like.

What do you deserve from your lovers? Respect for your preferences and limits is foremost. I need gentleness, warmth, leisurely lovemaking, privacy in pleasant surroundings, a clean, well-groomed partner, safe sex using condoms and a mutually exciting experience.

When you actually meet a man for the first appraisal, don't apologize or be ashamed. Meet in a public place using an anonymous name. Be sure to use a post office box and reserve your phone number or address for a future meeting. Be honest and open. Pay your share of the initial bill for lunch or dinner.

Fantasy is the secret of all good sex. Sex in strange places is a real turn-on to most lovers. An irrepressible streak of wickedness led me to having sex on a satin comforter in a tree, in a darkened auditorium in an erotic art museum, on a kitchen table and other exciting but private places sparking incredible sex for both of us.

How does a woman who's never had good sex learn? I learned of my right to live my life completely through a number of growth experiences including encounter groups, a woman's support group for pre-orgasmic women (Lonnie Barbach, our co-leader, did her doctoral thesis, "For Yourself," on our group) at our university medical school's sexuality clinic and through various group nudity activities where I learned to love my middle-aged, overweight body.

When you actually end up in bed, accept your body without apology or embarrassment. I have a friend who initiated her incredibly diverse love life in her 50s after undergoing a double mastectomy and breast implants. Her current lovers range from 25-65 years of age and include a male transvestite who usually wears women's attire but is a handsome, bright, attractive man!

Don't apologize for human needs. Men take lust for granted. It's time women acknowledge it as a normal drive. Initiate new sexual activities often. This will enhance and expand your joy.

Ask your partner for what you want and give him feedback. Ask him what feels good or pleases him. Be adventurous. Read books and magazines to expand your knowledge and pleasure.

Don't discount an older lover. An erection or ejaculation isn't vital to a loving, satisfying experience. Many men can be marvelous lovers with tactile pleasuring or oral sex and remember, we all have bad days. Not every time will be a five-star experience.

When I think of my friends, many of whom have not even had coffee with a man in 15-20 years, I feel sad that they prefer celibacy to bucking the system and enjoying a warm, mutually exciting sexual relationship.

They feel nice women only have sex with someone they love. They have never experienced the pure exhilaration of great, total erotic sex purely for fun. What a loss! These same women automatically refuse dinner invitations from strangers, knowing ahead of time "I don't see any future in him."

Certainly there are times when I have been rejected or I have found no mutual chemistry in a new man. However, it has more often been a matter of limiting my lovers to my availability. In return for risking, I have found enormous joy and sharing with very special human beings whose needs have closely paralleled my own.

I would certainly encourage every vital woman to enjoy sex, sex, sex. It's available to all of us if we reach out!

# Sestina for Indian Summer
## Enid Shomer

October, and the kudzu still spreads
the pines and oaks with green
skirts wide as tents, still pairs
shack and shrub in the false-
harmony, still resists the shave
of autumn's cool blade. Wait

for me like that. Wait
like heat rising under a spread
wing, like the cautious glide of a shaver
over skin or the slow greening
of bronze. Time is a false
bottomed chest, a basket of pears

that never ripens, a clock pared
down to a single *tick*. Wait
as the orchard did, its false
rigging of blossoms spread
windward, then snagged on the green
slope where today tractors shave

the dropped leaves to dust. Say *a close shave*,
meaning you escaped a dangerous pair:
proximity and severance, green
belief and the final *no*. Wait
somewhere between the two, spreading
the words apart the way waterfalls

chisel through stone. The false
colors of autumn are summer's shavings,
bits of sun and lake spread
in the trees, fluttering above the pair
of lovers who recur but do not last. Wait
until they're replaced by the green

thrust of the kudzu, that greenery
that does not flame before it falls.
Seasons always bring the pasts we waited
for, when the calendar was shaved
to a strip narrow as a paring
of light glimpsed through a lover's spread

hand. We were the green pair who spread
the season thin, waiting and counting on
autumn's sheaves. We were the false summer.

# Dance Steps
## Tema Nason

She's waiting. He's twenty-five minutes late when he rings the bell. She presses the buzzer. His feet climb the long flight of stairs in this brownstone row house in steady cadence. She swiftly calculates how long it will take him to reach the top, and just as he approaches the door, she opens it so that he won't have to knock. It's been two weeks.

He enters, shyly brushes her slightly rouged cheek, or her lips sometimes, and smiles wryly, a smile that suggests, Well, I'm here again, as though a part of him resists coming. He's a large man, big chested, but there's an emptiness about his arms—they swing aimlessly as he ambles in. Then, as usual, he seats himself in the hard maple chair that she found at a church auction for two dollars; it came from their Sunday school, and the writing arm is scratched and etched by years of students who probably slouched uncomfortably as he does now. She always selects the armchair opposite him, a folding outdoor chair with wooden slats and tubular legs and a red pillow that hides a broken slat. While he has carefully chosen the classroom chair, she has just as carefully made a choice; she will not start out by lounging on the studio bed discreetly covered with a purple batik spread and Marimekko pillows tossed about with planned abandon. He selects asceticism; she hovers between degrees of sensuality.

Outside the shrieks of sirens; inside she offers him Bolla. White or red? She's taken to keeping wine around, several kinds—though for herself she would not. She's not a solitary drinker...not yet.

"Well, so how are you?" He speaks with the slightest lisp.

"All right."

He displays his youth before her in this large room with the three tall bay windows; she has made it her own by covering the walls with good prints and the assorted notes on white index cards she writes to herself and posts on the bulletin board near her desk:

Give Michael heavy beard.

Mildred wears size 10 1/2 shoes, teased hair.

Steiglitz on a 1919 Marin painting: "to paint disorder under a big order."
WRITE A PROSE THAT'S EXPOSED AND GNARLED LIKE THE
ROOTS OF A CENTURY-OLD OAK—TOUGH, TENACIOUS, RESIL-
IENT AND INEVITABLE.

He is garbed in male plumage; tight jeans that outline his crotch and the buttocks that have elicited her compliments and caressing hands. In the warmer weather when they met, he sported an open shirt, open enough to reveal his hairy chest; on colder days like today a handsome turtleneck (this one's a Gauguin purple striped punctiliously in golds) that frames his Slavic features and curly hair. Once, glancing out the window—he's always fifteen to twenty minutes late, never more or less—she saw him as he paused outside, reached into his pocket, and combed his hair. But today he has added a new note, a beret.

They talk amiably; he offers a rambling account of a recent perplexing conversation with an acquaintance of his, and he pauses between sentences to examine its implications, then about a book he's reading (Kierkegaard is his current god). Sometimes about his boss and petty office politics and his dissatisfactions. Or a rejected manuscript for her, though she's the more reticent because there are certain subjects she'd rather stay away from—her ex-husband, her continuing misery, her grown children who present her with growing problems daily as though cold offerings on a stainless steel platter were the nexus for their familial connections. No, these are not subjects to discuss with him, she's decided, because they are so painful for her, but even more so, because they would bore him and how can an older woman hope to keep her young lover through sad tales and ennui? She can't afford a bad performance. The play would close.

So she conjures up funny anecdotes, offers her painfully accreted wisdom (if asked) and converses wittily, sagaciously, insightfully about feminist fiction and the diabolics of publishing, and her work—yes, the novel is going well, she says today—another day, she says no, the novel is not going well, not at all—these are subjects that will not depress or bore him. The woman writer. Does he speak of her to his business friends—somewhat the way one displays an exotic shawl? A find in a secondhand shop? *By the way, I'm having an affair with a writer...older woman...attractive in a tired way...knows a lot of writers.* He might be a name dropper, though of that she's not certain. They've always been alone together, never going out with friends, his or hers. Somehow they've just settled into this pattern.

All is proceeding as usual. More wine is offered; he accepts. After enough wine and conversation, he will make some move or gesture that now indicates he's ready. Sometimes he moves from the schoolboy chair casually—as though he really happened to rise to stretch—arching his back in a feline sway—or to examine once again that marvelous woodcut of Emily Dickinson and happening to sit down on the studio couch. Sometimes he stretches out on the small oriental on the floor, though it's too small for his six feet, slipping off his Danish clogs, or hiking boots, or tasseled loafers, or Italian white and brown shoes with stacked heels. He never says, come here. He never spontaneously reaches out his arms to her, or says, "Hey, you look terrific in that outfit!" though he must realize she's taken special care in dressing and perfuming. She's even begun treating her calloused heels with pumice because he once mentioned liking soft feet, something about a childhood fetish with his mother.

No, without a word, he will assume position two. Now the next move is always hers: she moves closer so that she's within reaching distance—if he wants to reach her. If he chooses the studio couch, then she pulls her chair closer to it, close enough so that she can place her unslippered feet on the bed. Slowly he will massage them reaching higher and higher up her legs. Or else she lowers herself next to him on the floor (thank God for yoga), though the rug is too small and threadbare to be either roomy or comfortable.

Once she's made it possible for him to reach her without stretching, then their lovemaking begins. Begins and buds and blossoms. They're silent, she because he is. Sometimes he grunts...and she's amused...the writer in her must describe it truthfully...grunts as though...constipated. Other men she's been with yipe or sob or roar with pleasure. But he grunts.

Sounds aside, the lovemaking is marvelous and he knows it and so does she. Last time, afterwards, he said to her—it was the only time he ever spoke afterwards—"Thanks, that was a gift."

Was that your farewell gift to me, she wondered? For he went on to tell her he was about to leave the city, taking another job in a small town, west, about four hours away. He had never mentioned the possibility before. Taken so by surprise, she almost blurted out, perhaps I can drive out and visit you. But she checked herself in time, she realized she had to wait to be asked. It had become a ritualized dance—comic, yes—and such a move would have been out of order, introducing another step. Can you picture Laurel and Hardy changing their routine—Laurel's sly smirk or Hardy bopping him over the head with his bowler? Impossible! The very essence of ritual is that you make no change. That is its magnetism.

After forty-five minutes now of desultory conversation, she babbling on about Virginia Woolf and her remarkable relationship with Leonard, they're still in first position, though usually by now, they've flowed to the second. At the moment she's trying also to balance the wineglass on her left palm as she goes on to relate what happened yesterday at the periodontist's. "He's such a business man, he's talking with his broker in between drilling! 'Rinse!' he orders me as he picks up the phone. When he looks in my mouth, I'm sure he sees only money."

He laughs, this time a short polite one, and when she offers him more wine, he gestures, no more. And he never gets up from the schoolboy chair, only shifting uneasily, perching first on one buttock, then the other.

This dance does have its funny moments, she reflects wryly.

He must be keeping an eye on the old pendulum clock on the antique chest (another church bargain) because precisely in an hour he plants his hands on his thighs. "Well, I guess I'd better get along...snow warnings for later y'know..." and his square hand with the short clean fingernails and the fine tufts of hair on the second joint jabs towards the windows colored by pewter skies as though they were already blurred with white flakes.

"Yes, of course," she replies mechanically. He *is* being sensible. Correctly so. No use taking chances driving into the mountains. From the closet she fetches his blue ski jacket plump with down and the new navy beret and hands them to him. Once he's snugly buttoned inside, he brushes her cheek, missing her lips, and mumbles, see you soon. She pats his shoulder.

Inside the room, the resonance of silence as she listens to his footsteps on the stairs descending...leaving, leaving her alone. She hears the latch snap as the heavy front door closes.

She rushes to the closet, tears her coat from the hanger and plunges down the stairs, still struggling with one sleeve, and outside. Bare-armed trees are moving and swaying as the snowstorm whips in with a keening sound. His Mustang is just pulling away from the curb; with his eyes on the rearview mirror, jauntily he waves.

"I hate you!" she shrieks into the wind, her face contorting as her breath is flung back into her throat. "Do you hear me? Do you hear me? You bastard!"

Strands of dark hair caught by the wind wrap around her face like a veil, while playfully he signals with his hand, Goodbye, Goodbye.

# 40 Years Later

## Phyllis Koestenbaum

When we embraced this time, I felt that embrace, one particular embrace, after running to meet each other from opposite ends of a Brooklyn subway platform after being apart two or three months. Whether or not he is the same man he was 40 years ago, to me he is. After drinking Calistogas in the museum cafeteria to moisten our dry mouths, we walked to the Russian restaurant he knew about and ordered the same lunch: rather I ordered what he'd ordered, but the meats—salmon, trout, white fish—were too salty, so after eating some I offered him the rest. I am not the girl I was. We both drank iced Russian tea. The waiter told me Russian tea is black tea with whole currants for sweetness. We held each other before we left the restaurant and walked hand in hand like sweethearts on the walk back to the museum, where he picked up his car for the drive to New Haven for his *Waste Land* seminar (did I really introduce him to Eliot?) He looked at me in the restaurant mirror, "to remember you from all angles," he said. "It would have been a tough marriage, for *you*, tough for *you*," he explained. Has anyone but this man ever imagined my life? On the phone the next day I questioned him about grief—did he feel any, not 40 years ago, I know about his grief 40 years ago, yesterday's. Yes, of course he felt grief, and he revised his opinion of the success of the marriage that never took place: it would have had a chance. To assuage my pain, I asked him about his, and I did feel better. His wife doesn't know we met or that we write and talk on the phone. She knows he wrote to me and that I answered, but not that there are letters now and exchanged poems now and regular phone calls now. I was hurt by a husband's infidelity. Am I flirting with what I condemned him for?

# To My Middle-Aged Sisters
## Chris Karras

After I received a flier inviting me to a forum called "Seasons of Life: A Celebration of Women's Sexuality" in Toronto, I quipped in a letter to the woman I knew to be the keynote speaker that I wouldn't come unless the graphics included at least one lusty-looking woman, pushing sixty, posing in a *Depend* undergarment (for light to moderate incontinence), and not one woman there would shudder and say: "Now that's disgusting!"

I knew, of course, it wasn't that kind of a forum, but had it focused on Desire and Erotica instead of on the larger context of Sexuality, my guess is that, even among the broadminded, the implications of a leaky bladder concurrent with an unabashedly lustful pose would have evoked gut-reactions of self-loathing, self-censure, and revulsion for the older woman who might still feel like doing it.

Ever since a friend of mine gushed unexpectedly one day, I have been prepared. There's a package of absorbent *Depends* tucked away high up in my closet just in case. But am I to shelve my sexuality and its byproduct, sexual activity and desire, the day I might have to haul a diaper off my closet shelf?

For me it's no small feat to talk about sex, let alone write about it. To appreciate my coming out like this you need to know where I am coming from.

I am conventional and straight, have a German Catholic/Protestant family background, and have been monogamous for the last thirty-seven years, having been legally married to the same man all this time. I am coming from a place of limited sexual experience; what could I possibly have to say about midlife sexuality that couldn't be put on the back of a postage stamp?

Well, plenty!

Considering the number done on me by Church, State, and Sigmund Freud, as well as by significant women in my early life, I am talking nothing less than transformation. That I got from there to here in full possession of my sexuality is cause for celebration.

In spite of attempts made to stifle the experience of pleasure, I do know what an orgasm is, although it's irrelevant to me just exactly where it comes from: vagina, clitoris, G-spot or brain cells. Any woman knows that this is something for the learned male sexologists to decide, who, after all, know so much more about our sexuality than we do!

When I was born, Freud was still alive, exerting a powerful cultural influence on my society, engaging the intelligentsia in ways that few had done before. After his death in 1939, German society became even more deeply infused and highly charged with the religion of psychoanalysis, and there followed much "mind-fucking" (thank you, Fritz Perls, for this contribution to our language!). It became almost common knowledge that dreams were all sexually loaded; that women had penis envy and were incomplete men; that our wombs were a source of trouble and neurosis. Later, Carl Gustav Jung came forward with a few possibly valid points, and some of us talked about archetypes, the anima and the animus, and psychological complexes, getting a little relief from the Freudian focus.

My mother, an artist and intellectual, went for Sigmund Freud in a big way, theoretically. My mother refined and sublimated her sexual energies into art, culture, and literature. She detested sex and mostly abstained from it. When she became a widow at forty-four, after fifteen years of marriage, a union she had entered as a virgin after a strict Catholic upbringing, she remained celibate and effortlessly abstinent (so she claimed) until her death forty years later.

Her influence on me was considerable, but not as much as that of my paternal grandmother who had taken care of me as a child. Grandmother did not give a damn about the sublimation theory of Freud and believed instead in a simple, two-part body-split, known as The Great Divide: the upper body was good; the lower, bad. To keep my hands from touching my genitals, accidentally or intentionally, I had to sleep with my arms out, over the bedcovers.

At age eleven I went to a boarding school run by Protestant sisters. My budding sensuality and sexuality were driven systematically underground and spiritualized as far away from carnal sin as Protestant Christianity could push them, that is until legal sex for purposes of procreation ("be fruitful and multiply") would make my sexual services legitimate and I would be called upon to service one man for life, in exchange for room and board. It was called marriage.

My first solitary sexual experience came during my stay at boarding school, and I did nothing to bring it about. I was awakened one night from my sleep by an unexpected, pleasurable sensation, a faint orgasm, just in time to catch the aftershocks. I was twelve, and I was stunned: how could something so electrically charged come from such a place? It was nothing short of a miracle. I put the whole thing down to what felt like a very full bladder; I peed, and established my cause-and-effect theory. From then on, I drank lots of water at night before going to bed. Sometimes it worked; sometimes not. I told no one.

How I got from there to here, to midlife sexuality, is a long story, one that would do any therapist proud. By my late thirties or thereabouts, I finally got it right, thanks to my partner, who had been raised by a mother who originated from an entirely different culture, and had none of my hangups. We had met early in life; my husband understood the inhibiting influences of my childhood on my sexuality; he knew my mother. Our relationship, warm and intimate, eventually freed me from conditioned sexual restraints. It was then that my anger at those who had imposed their limiting, restricting teachings on me, both personal and societal, turned into sympathy and sorrow over their irrecoupable loss of a full and vibrant femininity and sexuality, all of which had been there just for the asking.

Now, at fifty-seven, a full three years since my last menstrual period, I experience my sexuality as a free-flowing constant that informs my life and relationships with an uninhibited, spirited energy. Sometimes it is directed toward my fifty-eight-year-old partner, when he is up to it; sometimes toward my two daughters and three grandchildren with affection; sometimes toward my women friends with resonance and humor; and sometimes toward a self-defining center of my psyche. My sexuality is no more separable from me than is my breath. Nor does it need validation through reflection in others' eyes. Past the age of sexual assessment and evaluation, based on my sexiness or desirability, I am no longer object, but subject. To become aware of this shift is liberating.

There are days, weeks, even months when my mind is focused intensely on an idea, a problem, a project, or an inner question, leaving me convinced that sexual tension has gone completely from my aging body and I may never have to face the possibility of getting ready for love-making by peeling myself out of *Depend* underwear instead of lingerie. But I know well that the time will come when sex will be on my mind again in such concentration that I could do with a three-day passionate love-in with the right person who, after brief reflection, continues to be my marriage partner. Monogamy did not always come easy to me. As sexual rhythms go, we were more out of sync than in. For years I lagged behind; now he does. Nothing lasts forever. We have periodically moved in and out of intimacy—gaining distance, shrinking it, then gaining it again. Whenever there exists a failure of communication, it is at the junction of feelings. Although we both speak English, you wouldn't think it's the same language.

Having arrived at the upper limit of midlife with the sexuality intact, I get amusing mixed messages from mainstream society about what my correct sexual behavior now ought to be. One message is contained in the crass dictum of "use it or lose it" (not at all my experience); the other, in the popular (mis)perception that I am effectively de-sexed and devoid of sensuality, now that my reproductive life is over.

There is another message: although I had best stay sexually active during and after my menopause for the sake of my mental and physical health and be regular about it so as not to lose it, the subtext of that benevolent medical prescription is written entirely for the benefit of my husband's sexual well-being.

Once, my husband and I, busy with moving house and changing our lifestyle, hadn't had time to make love in several months. When we finally noticed how the months had gone by, neither of us seemed to have suffered any serious ill effects, physical or mental, from this situational dry spell.

Because we had moved, I needed to find a new family doctor. For lack of a woman doctor, I saw Dr. F, young and male. At the end of the consultation and examination he inquired about frequency of intercourse. I did not tell him the truth. He might have concluded I was withholding, or frigid, or had no libido, or that we had marriage problems. To get him off my back, I picked a number I felt would seem plausible. Knowing that newlyweds made love two to three times per week, if not more, and I wanted to be normal, I calculated quickly and said: "Oh, two to three times a month." After twenty-five years of marriage that sounded normal to me. He looked at me incredulously and said: "But, Mrs. Karras, is that enough for...your husband?"

When my granddaughter asked me a few years ago: "Nanny, do you and Grandpa still fool around?" I answered without hesitation: "Occasionally, Asha, occasionally." And that is how it is today, occasionally. Neither of us feels we have to service the other. Yet, the perception in society of the sexual act as a service is as persistent as patriarchy. Or should I say because of patriarchy?

As the fear of women's untamable sexuality grows, uppity feminists will continue to experience deliberate as well as unconscious misinterpretations and degradation of our sexuality ("Can't seem to castrate those bitches no matter what we do!").

It seems to be an affront, if not a severe shock, to the mainstream culture that we define ourselves, celebrate our sexuality and sensuality at any age in spite of physical and metaphorical castration (how many unnecessary hysterectomies are performed on menopausal women?). That we find our sexuality reflected in our affections, our friendships, our humor, our voices, and our shining eyes. That we dare write about it.

# White Eggplant
## Elizabeth Searle

ince she's not in a hurry—not ever, anymore—Lydia Zimmer takes time to read the signs. Loose Carrots, Cherry Tomatoes, Pickling Cukes. She nods, stopping her cart by a bin. Purple Top Turnips, Lemon Curd. And she squints, her eyes in the mornings clear but dry. California Seedless. Another cart pushes around her, a young mother with wild unbrushed hair, or maybe it's supposed to look that way.

"Ex*cuse*," the mother mutters over her bare shoulder.

"Accuse me," Lydia murmurs back, gripping the handle of her cart with both hands, her fingerbones aching. Bare-armed and bare-legged and smelling frankly of sweat, the mother noses her own cart between the Loose Carrots and the Curd. Supermarket lights drain her white-blond hair of shine and color. Her blond fuzzy-headed baby is whimpering. Its hair, too, looks dyed. And could that be a thin cigarette in its lips?

"Hush up." The mother halts her cart. Sniffling, the baby twists in its plastic seat to stare back at Lydia: wide-eyed, wet-eyed. "Just you wait, you." Abruptly, the mother turns heel, her hair vanishing like a bushy tail. Her sweat scent hovers. Lydia feels herself stiffen, eye to eye with the baby boy. His cigarette stick bobs. His whimper jars the fluorescent supermarket stillness.

Usually, Lydia loves shopping alone. The smell of cheese and apples, the company of mute food. Thirty some years ago, she'd leave the kids with Sid and sneak off on weeknights, lingering a bit even then, when she had to be back by nine to herd the kids into bed, Sid konked out on the couch. His snores sounded vigorous, impatient.

*Lyd*, he'd always say, chopping short her mother's lilting name. Lyd and Sid, he liked to introduce them, as if she were jaunty and full of fun too, as if she weren't, in fact, a true Lydia. Tending her African Violets, settling into long intent Scrabble matches with her dear mother, dead now, her one worthy opponent. The two of them would bow over the board, seemingly tense. Secretly serene.

*Look alive, Lyd,* Sid was always saying in his last year, when he'd tag along to the supermarket, startling her from her trances. We haven't got, he'd claim, all day.

"Lah-*ee*—" the baby is telling her now, insisting. He waves his stick in one chubby fist, conducting himself, trying to conduct her too. Nine a.m. or so, the other aisles near empty. Lydia looks down and picks at a filmy plastic bag, inching apart the layers, thin as onion skin. But strong, stretchable.

She lifts a head of lettuce, Iceberg—pleasantly frosty and light. Her knees ache. A garden: that's what she'll never get, up on the 33rd floor. Just three furry Africans. Lights hum now like the sun lamp she switches on once a day for them. Her shy Vies.

"Lah-*leee*—"

Lydia looks up to see the baby hurl his cigarette into the Loose Carrots. No smoke. A lollipop, was it? Sucked and abandoned. He squashes his wet lips together, stares defiantly from the stick to Lydia. Sighing, she squints beyond his fuzzy head. Yes: his mother paws through the frozen meat, bent in her halter top, her shoulder blades curved. Firm flesh, savagely tan. Lydia had hurried past Meat and its brutal signs.

Hog Maws, Bottom Round Rump Roast.

The baby gulps a mouthful of nothing. As Lydia begins maneuvering her cart around him, he lets loose a hungry howl. The metal bars of his cart seem to vibrate: a zoo cage. Lydia's head hums. Simulated African sun, a mere ghost of the real thing. Poor things. No wonder their purple has dulled to lavender, an old lady color, pretty and pale, the sort Lydia wears but never did like.

She eases to a stop. His howl strains to reach her, a few feet behind her, but she studies her head of lettuce. Blinks, her lids sticking. Is she going to eat this? Ever? She works her jaw. The whole idea of chewing seems impossibly strenuous. She blinks again, a faint burn in her eyes. He half chokes on a throatful of tears.

Swaying with her next step, an unexpected sway, Lydia pictures the bushy-haired young mother bent over an open fire, tearing meat with her teeth, chewing it up and spitting it out into her baby's gaping mouth. At the old supper table, Lydia used to slice the children's meat, chew her own. At the other end, Sid would bend over his plate. Careful to keep his mouth closed, for her. My, how he loved his Sunday Roast. How he tried, in his last years, to keep chewing it, shifting his teeth. Funny thing, she doesn't miss them much, her own. Secretly, inside her mouth, her tongue touches her upper plate. It sticks.

Lettuce, shredded wheat, milk to soften the shredded wheat. Lydia peers again into her cart, squinting through the boy's last sputters. She shuffles forward another step, slow to lift her feet in her heavy rubber-soled shoes. A dirty brown root confronts her: ham-sized, chopped off at both ends. In the earth, it would plunge and plunge. Above its bin hangs a helpful sign: Peel and Boil.

Lydia blinks to wet her eyes, blur the words. Too many today. Only hours before, hadn't her breakfast box tried to tell her, persuade her that she might want to melt cheese and tuna fish—tuna!—over a square of shredded wheat? A Tasty Treat!

"Lah-*leee*—" he squawls, freshly inspired. His mother is stalking back towards the cart, wielding a Family Pack of raw pork. Her skin tan, the pork pale. Her job to feed him, thank the Lord. Lydia licks her lips, a quick lizard flick of her tongue. What she does these days instead of smiling, in public.

"—up, I said hush up or I'll smack you— Want me t' smack you?"

Yes, presumably. A small sound in the vast near-empty market. As if to make up for the disappointing smallness of the smack, the boy gives a hoarse shuddering sob that tightens Lydia's shoulders, sets a crick in her neck as she starts to turn her head, then stops herself, picturing his hot red face streaming. Wanting to touch that fresh wetness and yet at the same time glad she doesn't have to.

Red meat. She bows over her cart, shuffles forward, shivering under her blue cotton dress. Her flesh feels, these days, like a form of cloth: another thin inadequate covering. The straps of her brassiere bite into her ribs, the cups only half filled. It's her bones that ache these days. Not her flesh so much, anymore.

"—*lee*— Wan *Leee*—"

Lydia stops to rub her arms. Iceberg, Let us. Too cold in here to think of salad. Something hot, instead. Chopped vegetables simmering together in her old iron pot. That makes sense, doesn't it? Even in summer? The kid stops sobbing— another pop stuffed in his mouth, no doubt. Fluorescent lights resume their comforting hum. Lydia bends into Idaho's Finest, her hidden nipples tingling. Faintly, strangely. Stew, she thinks. Along with the word, she grips a potato. Hefts it, solid and dusty. Hold it, Lyd. Please hold it? Sid's slow wheedling salesman voice, the roast and onion smell on his breath and sometimes, hushing him, she'd take it in her hands. Swollen and crinkly smooth, a rich dark purple, her favorite color. In a way, she liked it better in her hands, where she could touch it, stroke it, take her time.

She sets the potato gently in the cart, on the plastic baby seat beside the Iceberg head. No bag; she doesn't want to bag it, poor thing. But she squints down at it and the lettuce together, something missing.

"Scuse us, dear!" Another Mother For Peace bends over Lydia's cart, grips two potatoes in one knuckly hand. Her t-shirt stretches on her broad back, the bright yellow words plain to see, no bra straps digging into her shoulders. Her hair hangs down, straight and brown. Another Mother. Lydia feels her cart jostle as this Mother straightens, her unbound breasts swinging. Flesh melons. Her chunky brown-haired daughter watches Lydia watch. Lydia's breasts were more like peaches, really, not much bigger than that. Steadying herself, Lydia blinks at the potato, its pinched underworld eyes.

"—*me* one too!" Gracelessly, Another Mother's daughter bends over Lydia's cart, her t-shirt shouting its own slogan in electric green letters. Save The Earth. "Please Mama—?"

The girl's plump elbow pokes Lydia's bony forearm. Lydia stiffens as if one of her own had bolted out of the aisle and jumped her the way kids do, hungry for hugs, young and wild all over again. As if Sid hadn't been enough of a handful. Lydia clicks her tongue, remembering potato eyes gone wild, a sack of potatoes she'd bought and forgotten and one morning Sid had burst into the bathroom when she was in the tub, waving a monstrous potato head, its green roots vibrating like tentacles. She'd shrieked, splashed.

Then, even worse—Lydia watches the Earth girl reach out, straining her whole body, fumbling in the bin for the biggest ones—then there was the time with the pumpkin, canned pumpkin for a pie, quarter of a can left. Stupidly, she'd forgotten it in the back of the fridge, months maybe, Thanksgiving to Christmas. Christmas morning in front of everyone she'd unwrapped a second gift from Sid, a can, the pumpkin can, a lid scotch-taped back on top of it and an odd sour smell wafting up from it, and the kids all gathered round as she peeled it open. The girls had shrieked too, louder than her, though they didn't know yet what it looked like: the orange moldy mushroom thrusting up to the rim of the can and Sid laughing so hard his bald head turned its richest shade of red-purple and for two days, even after a bouquet of white violets, she wouldn't speak to him, couldn't smile.

'Til now, thirty some years later. At least Lydia starts to, her lips twitching. Earth girl straightens and glances at her, struggling to hold two potatoes in one hand. Sid Jr. and Sid and the girls had all stared so eagerly, their eyes wet with laughter. And what was wrong with her, what was so closed-up and shy, that she couldn't smile when they all wanted her to? Just like her poor mother, another Lydia.

Another Mother begins to pull away, slow as a train. Lydia's cart rattles, the handle jarring her lower ribs. Her heart.

"Mama, you bumped her!" The daughter's voice pipes up, and Lydia presses her lips into a tight quavery line, swaying. Can't take a joke, Sid had said, hurt in his way. A dirty joke, she'd answered in her mother's voice. Soft and yet not, not at all.

"You bumped that La-dy!" Beside Lydia, the brown-haired daughter stands on tiptoe, her adult-sized glasses sliding down her nose. "Say you're *sorry*, Mama." She exaggerates a nagging grown-up tone, armed with a potato in each fist. "*Ma*ma?"

Lydia's hands tighten again on the cart handle, greasy plastic pressing her fingerbones.

"—So sorry, ma'm." Another Mother sighs, side-glancing at her daughter.

Lydia gives them both a brief dismissive nod. A denim knapsack bobs on the Mother's shoulder as she pushes her cart forward, wearily. The daughter imitates her heavy tread, adding her own smug sway. Side by side, they turn a corner: yellow Peace, electric green Earth.

Lydia too takes a shuffling step, ready to follow the blue at a safe distance, out of Vegetables. Worn blue knapsack. Lydia stops, sucks in her breath. No weight dangles from her own elbow. Had she set it down somewhere, back before the loose carrots, the pickling cukes? Her shiny black purse? She blinks and her eyelids almost stick together, so dry.

"Make way—" sings a low husky voice, a teenage black boy, a bag boy Lydia's seen before. Hasn't she? He jostles her cart, but gently, wheeling a tray of plastic berry baskets. He nods. Strawberries, yes. Their juice, their sweet heady smell, much fainter now than ever before. "Make way plea-ease—"

Must everyone, these days, give the same sly half-mocking emphasis to the dearest old words? Sorry, please.

" 'Cuse me," Lydia rasps, her tongue all at once dry, and she half shuffles half staggers forward, forgetting to turn. She leans on her cart, staring down into it. Shredded wheat, lettuce, potato. How do they, did they, ever connect?

Peel & Boil.

But what? Like a rowboat running ashore, her cart bumps into a last Vegetable bin, refrigerated. A rear wall bin, lit up white. She squints, starts to back away. That's when she sees them. Arranged in a row above the Avacados. When she sees them, she stops. Stops moving, breathing.

White Eggplant.

Slowly, two times, she reads those two words. Those letters. Scrabble squares, meaningless in themselves. Refusing to connect, make sense. She moves her eyes back down to the eggplants, set out in a row alone, arranged on their shredded green cellophane like Easter eggs, outer space eggs. Something from another world, all white. They glow in their skins.

Slowly, Lydia Zimmer bends forward over her cart. She reaches out as if this is the last reach she'll ever attempt. She touches the eggplant as if it's the last thing she'll ever touch, the last she'd ever want to touch, hold.

Straightening up with effort, her head humming louder than the lights, she cradles the eggplant in both hands, strokes it like a breast in silk. That same weight. Years ago, in secret, she used to stroke her own full breasts in her nursing nightgown. Never again would she feel that swollen softness. But this in its way is better, perfect. On this eggplant, the silk is the flesh, one and the same. Its texture is slippery smooth yet not slippery at all. Oily yet not that, either. Lush. Silk made flesh. She can almost hear, almost feel the dense squishy mass of seeds inside, perfectly sealed. She keeps stroking the skin, shining it, drinking in with her eyes its creamy white sheen. Her knees wobble.

A stem presses through Lydia's dress, pokes her stomach just above her sunken navel, the stem prickly where it was chopped from the vine.

Might become a vegetable, they said of Sid after his last attack, as if nothing could be worse. And when, instead, he died, it was seen as a blessing. A vegetable, other old ladies say, their voices quivering. But, funny thing, Lydia Zimmer wouldn't mind, not really, not if she could become this vegetable, this eggplant, purest white.

Even harsh supermarket lights can't diminish its color, a white utterly unlike the yellowish white of Lydia's hair, drained of natural brown. No, this white is a color all its own, as rich as the deep purple of a regular eggplant. A color Lydia once loved, long ago, a word she once loved, secretly, one that began with the sound but not the letter O.

Oh, Lydia mouths in surprise. Mild surprise. All at once she is sitting on the supermarket floor by the sticky rubber wheels of her cart, leaning against the refrigerated cool of the rear wall bin. A relief to her kneebones, her ankle bones. And since she has—as Sid used to say, when he'd gotten skinny and old himself— no butt left, her tail bone presses the cold hard floor. Too much trouble to pull herself up. She'd have to let go and she never wants to let go of it, this beautiful thing she's found at last.

Above her, the bag boy bends in his white smock, his motion brushing her skin, his brown face gleaming. The whites of his eyes gleam too, painfully expectant. Like Sid's oldest face, those last months when she'd inch out into the waiting room after talking to the doctor alone. He'd stare up at her, wanting her to tell him, as she always did, that he was going to be all right.

Peace, please. The bag boy seems to be speaking but she can't tell what he's saying. It's as if she doesn't have her hearing aid on, but of course she does.

Oh, she mouths again, this time to herself, still stroking the rich white skin, richer than any purple. How satisfying it is to hold, this shape: oval and yet not, its curves not evenly balanced. Its curves too smooth to be called lumps. Pear-shaped, yes, only more so. Rounder, fuller on top. A shape all its own, lopsided and whole. Oh...Burr...something. She lowers her eyes and the white blurs. Oh, Burr and then a name, a name that could be both a man's and a woman's. Lunar white, moon grown. Cool plush dust on her fingertips. Oh, Burr—

Above her, hopelessly blurred, Another Mother waves something shiny and black and square. The brown-haired Earth daughter is bouncing on her toes, her glasses agleam like the boy's eyes. A harder meaner gleam. She points her fat finger at Lydia Zimmer. How rude to point when everyone's staring at her already, aren't they? Lydia blinks, feels on her dry cheek a slight delicious trickle.

Another Mother hands the shiny square to the boy, holding it by its straps, trying to tell him something but he won't listen as he should. He turns instead to Lydia, bends so close she catches a whiff of his spicy sweat. He's hugging the black square to his chest and speaking again, enunciating clearly, his thick-lipped mouth opening like a baby bird's. Can't he see she's through with that, she's done all that? Can't he see?

Skin and bones, all that's left. She lowers her eyes. Its flesh, so much thicker than her own, has begun to grow warm in her hands. Her cold hands. Oh, Burr, Oh, Burr. She squeezes shut her eyes, feels another soothing trickle. She licks her lips, tastes salt, hot liquid salt and she licks again, feeding herself now, only herself. She presses it close to her stomach, low in her lap, thinking: Jean, Gene. And she clicks her tongue, secretly pleased, not caring how it connects, if it connects. Someone touches her shoulder but she has no intention of moving. She keeps hold of it, stroking its smooth cool sealed-up softness. Why rush? She's got, finally got—they can't take it—all day.

# Love Lines

## Karen Alkalay-Gut

When we were first married, Dave and I spent a lot of our time together telling each other jokes. Most people at that stage, I suppose, reveal all their terrible secrets, discuss their hidden dreams, and analyze their most intimate aspirations, but we were very tired of all that, weary with past tragedies, and wanted this marriage to be a new start, a clean beginning. So we spent our evenings in bed, trying to top the previous guffaw, choking out limericks between giggles, and stumping each other with more and more weird and raucous riddles.

The result of that honeymoon is that we began to communicate secretly with punch lines. I mean we could let each other know about entire states of mind with a single phrase, a phrase that would be entirely foreign to anyone not clued in. Even our best friends couldn't understand what we were talking about, and even now it is hard for me to describe it without a rather long example. Like this:

A man is walking down the street and he sees a big neon sign that says "Ultramodern Whore House." Attracted by the novelty, he goes up to the metal door, and reads the sign over the slot. "Ultramodern Whore House—deposit fifty cents." Fascinated by the idea, he deposits his fifty cents and the door swings open. In front of him lies a long dim corridor. He walks through and finds another door with a sign: "Ultramodern Whore House—deposit one dollar." He pays, the door opens onto a red carpeted spiral staircase and he races to the top, getting more and more excited with each step. At the head of the stairs is another door with another sign: "Deposit $5." The man isn't even thinking anymore—he's so involved in the experience he doesn't pay attention to the fiver he drops in the slot—and just anticipates the opening of the door. There he sees a long corridor, with velvet wallpaper and gas lighting. He races down the corridor to the door at the end, deposits the ten dollars required, pushes open the door, and finds an even more elegant—marble—staircase. He goes down the staircase, pays the $25 to the automatic door, and when he pushes through, finds himself on the street. In front of him a big neon sign flashes, "Ultramodern Whore House—

You've Just Been Screwed."

Lisa is sitting in my kitchen, head down, weeping into her folded arms. She is worn out with telling me about her lover who convinced her to leave her husband, and then, when she was alone, poor, and utterly dependent on him, dumped her. Dave walks in the room, is shocked and moved by her appearance. "What happened?" he whispers. "Ultramodern Whore House," I answer, and he nods.

"You see," I tell Lisa, a few months later, when she is now on to another man, and she asks how Dave understood so quickly about her sad love affair, "You don't have to know all about a person's past or his history—you just need to share a language."

Lisa has been giving me the old story about how this time she and her lover are going to tell each other everything, and that way, if they know all about each other, there won't be any more surprises.

Dave leans forward with a serious, fatherly expression. "Let me tell you about my aunt Molly. After thirty years together, she turned to her husband one day and said, 'Jake, if something happened to me, would you remarry?' Jake was shocked. 'What kind of question is that? You're in perfectly good health, why should we have to think about things like that?' 'I know, Jake, but just tell me, would you marry again?'

"Jake was silent for a long time, and then he stroked his chin, 'After all, if you go, I would still be here...Yes, I suppose I would.'

"Molly went back to her knitting, and Jake went back to his paper, and then suddenly she said, 'You think you'd move her into this house, Jake?'

"'What are you talking about? You're alive and well! What is all this conjecturing?' 'Come on Jake, tell me.'

"Once again he was silent, contemplative. Finally, he said, 'Why not? I mean, it would be my house then, and we've had such good times here together, I'd want to stay here.'

"Molly nodded. After a few minutes, she started again, 'What about our bed? Would you sleep with your new wife in our bed?'

"'After all, I'm used to the bed,' he said after a long time.

"'On our sheets? Would you use our sheets?'

"'What is this nonsense, Molly? You're here with me, right now. What is this game of "ifs"?'

"'Just suppose, Jake...Would you use our sheets?'

"Jake sighed, 'I suppose...'

"'What about swimming, Jake? Would you take her to the same lake where we swim together?'

"'Molly, please...All right, I'm an old man, I wouldn't want to change my habits...I'd probably go to the same place with her.'

"'And golf? Would you play golf with her, too?'

270

"'I've always played golf...why should I stop?'

"'With my clubs? Would you give her my clubs?'

"'No. Not that. Definitely not.'

"'Why not?'

"'She's left-handed.'"

Lisa laughs, but I can see she doesn't understand what Dave wants from her. When he leaves to play basketball, she asks me, "Doesn't it bother you that you never sit down and discuss things all the way through, from start to finish, work things out?"

"Oh, we understand each other completely," I answer.

"What if something comes out of his past, something that you didn't know about, because you've never bothered to talk to each other, and it changes your future?"

"I think I know the general outlines of everything. Maybe not the details, but what I know is good enough..."

"And your marriage? Is it as fresh and happy as when you first met?"

I am reminded of another joke. The honeymoon couple are walking down the street and she slips, and he lifts her up gently, murmuring, "My poor dear, did you hurt yourself?" A decade later, they are walking down the street and she slips and he says, "You okay?" Years after that she slips again, and he looks down at her with a disgusted expression, "Look where you're going, you old bag!" I don't say anything to Lisa.

We have been married for five years. We met when our spouses ran off with each other. Both of us were shattered then, confused. I hadn't known that my husband was playing around, even though, as a psychologist, he used to stress the importance of openness in a relationship. I looked up the Wronged Husband then because I thought it would give me a clue to what had happened, would tell me whether there was a chance that all would be well again, that he would come back to me, that the whole thing was a mistake.

What I found was a man who refused to discuss the matter, a dead end. "What happened between my wife, or ex-wife, and myself," he said, "is between us. I don't mind talking to you about myself now, about you, about our future, but let's not get to know each other by comparing dates and suspicions."

Still, when we began seeing each other, people said it was a mutual sympathy association, that we were licking each other's wounds. It was normal, they said, but of course it couldn't last.

When I moved into his apartment, even my sister came to give me her advice. "Why do you need to remind him of his past? Start somewhere else like normal people!"

"Look, I like the apartment," I said. "It's beautiful, practical, well thought-out, in the kind of simple, elegant taste that I've always admired but could never put together. I'm not only going to move in, I'm also not going to change a single thing in it."

"What if she comes back to him?"

"She'll find us if we move too."

"Do you know what his ex-wife looks like, how gorgeous she is? Why give him ways to compare you two?" I'm one of those plump red-cheeked blondes—the kind that were in style during the Depression. My predecessor passes for a Vogue model. I do not like to be reminded of that contrast.

"Like my favorite cigarette," he said when I confronted him with my fear. "Round and firm and fully-packed. Besides, I need something to hold onto now, after years of groping for her in bed. Never could find her—she was always hiding in the folds of the sheet."

Last year I had a mastectomy. "Not so round any more," I pouted when I woke up.

"Don't worry, Amazon," he purred. "Windshield wipers aren't what they used to be either."

The anesthesia had probably not worn off, because I couldn't figure out what he meant, and before I could ask I dropped off again.

That night I woke up alone in my room. The silence was frightening, and I wanted to ring for the nurse—just to cheer myself up—but I didn't have the nerve. Suddenly the joke came back to me: The institutionalized man was up for review by the asylum board. They were pretty sure he was sane, but decided to ask him one final association question. "What does a luscious woman, naked from the waist up, remind you of?" "Windshield wipers," he answered, and they sent him right back to the ward. On the way back, the attendant turned to him, "Why did you say that? You almost got out! How could a woman's breasts possibly remind you of windshield wipers?" "Oh, you know," the patient said, moving his head from side to side, "Kiss...kiss...kiss...kiss."

"Windshield wipers don't make that noise any more," Dave once pointed out to me, as we were sitting in the rain in a car full of people, and he began to explain the difference between the old engine vacuum wipers and the new electric ones. "What's he talking about?" Lisa asked me, looking at him worriedly. "Private joke," I answered.

So I got used to having one breast. "Easier with a shoulder bag," Dave whispered to me as we were walking down the street. "One day I'm going to switch them on you," I hissed back, "the way Marty Feldman switched his hump from side to side in 'Young Frankenstein.' "

After work one day, I went to the plastic surgeon to discuss reconstructive surgery. I was beginning to feel good—thinking about wearing see-through nightgowns and parading around naked again—and then I came home to find a Vogue model sitting on the sofa.

Dave was in the kitchen making coffee. "I'm Rita," she said, as she extended a very poised hand to me, and I thought she was going to add, "I've come home now."

In the kitchen I asked Dave if I should leave. "Why—are you left handed?" He kissed my left hand, then my right, and then turned the palms up and kissed them. Then he sniffed them. "Antiseptic soap...You've been to the doctor...What does he say?"

"I'm on for next month."

"Sorry, Rita," Dave said as he re-entered the living room with his arm around me. "We can't have that coffee. The three of us have to celebrate with champagne...my wife's going to get a new breast!" Then he turned to me, "Does that mean I'll be able to keep the prosthesis with me all the time in my briefcase?"

Rita turned slightly away—whether from disappointment or disgust I couldn't tell. "Let me go out for the champagne," I said.

There must be a limit to my masochism, I think, on my way home from the liquor store. I go to get champagne for my husband and his ex-wife, who, apparently, may soon be my ex-husband's ex-wife, and leave the two of them alone together to work up an appetite. By the time I get back to my own door, I am overwhelmed by remorse and fear. Dizzy with the confusion, one hand clutching the champagne, I fumble in my purse for my key to the apartment. "Hey, Old Bag." Dave opens the door and kisses me. "You don't have to look for change. This isn't an ultra-modern whore house."

# Reconstruction
## Hannah Wilson

Years ago, when she thought that all she had to worry about was money, Leona invested three months of child-support payments in a real-estate course. Selling real estate, she could be home when her children got out of school, stay with them when they got sick. Friends told her she could find a man selling houses, some sad but good soul, his divorce not yet cold, his next hot meal uncertain.

The men she met seemed as vacant as the houses they wandered aimlessly through, puzzled where the coffee table had gone, but when she sold enough to join the Million-Dollar Club, Leona looked back and thought real estate had been a good choice. She had managed to get home to console Jan and Ted through chicken pox and friends' squabbles, and she survived what to her was the most distasteful part of the work, all the deception—fresh paint that concealed leaks, cheap carpeting that hid buckling floorboards.

A week after her fifty-third birthday, when she had to have first one, then her other breast removed, she told the doctor she didn't want implants. Assuming that she would get prostheses, he wrote her a prescription so that her insurance would cover the cost, but she never ordered them. Her friends admired her daring, and warmed by their admiration, she thought of herself as bold, not mutilated. "After all," she kept repeating, "they're the easiest appendages to lose."

So a dozen years later, when she caught herself turning over and tucking a pillow under her chest in bed, when she hugged a friend or held a grandchild and realized she was aching for her own answering softness, she felt betrayed. Last week, on the anniversary of her surgery, she stood in the Y shower room, wrapped in a towel but feeling naked to the bone, and gave up. "Enough," she thought. "I'm almost sixty-six years old. I'm an old house. I could use some remodeling."

From the front doorway, Leona could see the beam from the halogen lamp Burt had saved for six months to buy. She went into the dining room and sat down across the table from where he sat, the lamp shining over his shoulder. He was squinting into the back of an old, gold pocket watch, a jeweler's loupe in one eye.

"Burt, I just told a plastic surgeon that you wouldn't marry me unless I had breasts."

"That's nice."

"You're not listening. Take that thing out and listen to me."

"Leona," he said, still bent over the watch, "I don't listen with my eyes—"

She slapped her palm flat on the table. Miniature screws and stems from his tool case somersaulted into each other's velvet compartments. He took out the loupe.

"What did you say about a doctor?"

"I said, I told a doctor you wouldn't marry me unless I had breasts."

"We are married."

Just like Burt, she thought, to state the obvious. Early in their life together, she had distrusted his patience and accused him of being indifferent to outcomes...

"The doctor said the surgery at my age was chancy, my skin is too dry, my heart risky...how he would know, I don't know, he never even listened. He asked me why, after all these years..." Leona got up to put a light under the kettle.

"And?"

She answered from the kitchen, "That's when I said you wouldn't marry me." She went back into the dining room and bent to kiss the top of his head, smooth as her grandmother's red-oak darning egg. "I thought it was the only thing he would understand."

"And?"

"He said go home and think about it for a week." When she heard the water boiling, she went back into the kitchen to brew tea, and then brought her china teapot to the table.

"So why did you go to the doctor?"

For days before she made the appointment, after her noon swim she had lingered like a voyeur in the showers. When she leaned to rinse shampoo out of her hair, she would angle her head so that she could look at the women's breasts. She glanced quickly over the very young, those pubescent mounds too tender to last. She couldn't remember when hers had been that tentative.

*The hospital counselor had given her a pair of nubile falsies to take home. "These might make you feel better when the bandages come off." At home, with Jan watching, she tucked them inside a T-shirt. Jan hooted, turned Leona around to face the mirror, and then they both laughed so hard Ted came upstairs. He had to ask whether they were laughing or crying. Leona looked like a carnival photo, a head tucked on top of a cardboard figure—her body could have been the Bionic Woman's or Richard Nixon's, it was so clearly not hers.*

In the shower, Leona looked the longest at middle-aged women's breasts, trying to remember the droop of her own. Had she been as uneven as that woman? Maybe she should ask the surgeon for unevenness, the way dentists make false teeth seem real by molding irregularities. When there was no one left to look at and her skin was puckering, Leona would turn off the water, all her insides alive to imagined touch, and walk to her locker, her shoulders back as if they were carrying weight.

"I don't know," she began to answer Burt. "I thought maybe before I die, I'd like to be whole again. What if some archeologist digs me up and thinks I'm a freak?"

"So instead they'll think you're some mutation, that humans began to grow silicone," Burt said. "What's the half-life of that stuff, a trillion years?"

"I knew I shouldn't have told you."

"What, are you going to make me feel guilty now because I think you have a cockeyed idea?"

"Okay, truce," Leona said. "Don't make me feel foolish." She drummed her fingers while she talked. "I don't know, I don't know why now, but I have this terrible urge to swish around." She stopped drumming and skimmed her hand like a feather floating over the table. "I want to turn sideways and see cloth drape out over my chest instead of hang straight like a starched curtain."

Burt looked at her the way he looked at watches whose breakdown he couldn't diagnose. Then he turned off his lamp and got up to add water to the teapot.

Two days after her appointment with the surgeon, on a morning she was supposed to volunteer at the library, she drove to a new mall that had a reputable foundation shop and where it was unlikely she'd run into anyone she knew. Inside the shop, she stood fingering some bras on the sale rack, a white sports bra, a black lace, then turned and said to the young saleswoman, "I'd like to try out a pair of prostheses. I'd pay for their use, of course..."

The woman seemed dumbfounded by the request. "I'm afraid we don't...I could show you some over-the-counter molded forms."

Leona envisioned herself draped over the counter, her bosom lying cold against the glass while this young woman sculpted flesh-toned styrofoam under her. "Well, I'm thinking of reconstruction and I want something to help me imagine..."

"Why don't you step into the dressing room."

Patricia—"Just call me Trish"—brought Leona a half dozen models, from Sweet Springtime to Autumn Fullness, and fit them into a beige lace bra. Her cold hands chilled Leona's skin when she reached inside the bra to adjust the forms, reminding Leona of every technician who had ever administered her mammograms.

*Leona volunteered to go with Jan when she went for a base-line mammogram, as if Leona's presence could warm the slab on which her daughter's breasts would be slapped, loosen the screws over the plastic plate pressing them flat.*

*"Mom, I'm a big girl, you don't need to take time off for that. You're not worried are you? I'm not."*

*Leona had trouble catching her breath that week, had trouble not calling Jan every night, until finally Jan called her.*

*"Everything's fine. And listen, if some day it isn't, I'll be okay. I'll be just like you, okay?"*

"This is the last model we have," Trish said, holding out yet another half-moon, "our most expensive but most popular. It has more give..."

It was like all the others, some designer's fantasy of a mass-produced woman. Leona shrugged and Trish began gathering the forms, checking sizes like a salesperson re-boxing shoes that didn't fit.

"How long has it been?"

"Twelve, almost thirteen years." Trish looked so pained that Leona added, "That's encouraging. I'm safe."

"We have a set that came in this morning for a woman who's built like you, narrow shoulders, long waisted. She doesn't know they're here yet. Would you like just to try them?"

The prostheses were so heavy that at first Leona thought she couldn't hold her shoulders upright. Trish explained that they had to have sufficient weight to ride right, that "We just get used to carrying around our own weight and hardly notice it—like the farmer who lifts a calf every morning and one day hoists up this three-hundred pound heifer..." Leona stared at her, "...or something." But after Leona put her clothes on over the false breasts and walked around the shop, she began adjusting to their heft. She would have to remember to ask the doctor if she should do special exercises to get used to wearing implants.

"Let me wear them today," Leona proposed. "I've showered this morning..." Trish looked embarrassed. "I'll leave you my purse. There's my driver's license, car keys, credit cards, pictures of my grandchildren, my senior-citizen's bus pass, punch card at the video store..." Trish looked more embarrassed. "I'll come back for all that."

"Oh, I trust you. It's not that. It's...do you know how much trouble I could get into?"

"Of course I do," Leona said. "You could lose your job."

Patricia reached inside Leona's blouse to tighten one of the bra straps. "Call at 3:00, so I don't worry. We close at 5:30."

Leona had enough time to get to the library, but she cringed at the thought of people staring. In long check-out lines, at neighborhood improvement meetings, whenever she got fidgety at gatherings, Leona played a guessing game with herself, "One in nine, one in nine, whose breast is missing, just like mine?" She didn't want to play "it" this morning, and she didn't want to go home where Burt could see her.

She drove back towards town as if on automatic pilot, as if, her body an imitation of itself B.C., Before Cancer, her brain was also miming the past, until she found herself in her old neighborhood. She had stayed on in the small yellow house after the divorce, with its fenced yard for the dog, the roses she had planted bare-root, children's friends up and down the block, and the realty office within a mile. After her first sales, she became known in the neighborhood, the way a doctor or plumber might become known. People in sudden distress called Leona—a marriage neither partner had realized was about to implode, sudden loss of work, a death no one had been willing to plan for...

It helped Leona to get involved with other people's problems. It kept her from feeling ashamed that she was profiting from their grief, and, after her surgery, from realizing her own.

She drove into the mini-mall and bought a frozen yogurt, walking around while she licked it. Maples had been planted along the curbs, and pyracantha in the center of the parking lot. It was defeat that moved Leona out of the neighborhood. She could admit that now. She had helped organize a group opposed to re-zoning the corner for a mall—residents and small business-owners, the PTA, and a philatelists' club that met in the back room of the small pharmacy on the corner.

In the midst of the zoning fight, she learned she had cancer. Leona had anticipated that cancer would inspire her with existential freedom. Instead, she grew timid, like someone who checks to be sure she hasn't forgotten her keys, and then immediately re-checks.

The couple who owned the realty agency where she leased space, where she got her turn at listings, where she had built up a following, grew more and more nervous about her involvement in the zoning fight, especially when she was chosen spokesperson. They were afraid that if Leona painted the agency anti-development, they'd lose their large commercial clients. She begged off from testifying before the Zoning Commission and City Council, saying she didn't have the energy. She was the first in line for flu shots and stopped going downhill skiing. She met Jan and Ted's demands with weakened resistance. She couldn't risk any more.

So others testified, gathered petitions, but three years later, the corner was re-zoned. When they installed the floodlights, Leona moved, unwilling to face one more daily reminder of loss. Burt said if they'd won the fight, he might not have met her, but Leona shrugged that off. After the cancer she had given up playing "what if's." But she did meet him the day she was giving out her cards to people who would soon be dislocated by the mall.

Between the pharmacy and a dry goods store a dim walkway led to an insurance office and two repair shops, one for small appliances, the other Burt's cage. Leona couldn't imagine how anybody ever found either one. Burt was sitting behind the bars, a loupe in one eye when she went in. By then, she knew that none of the tenants owned their own space, but she thought they might want to get together to buy another building in the neighborhood. They didn't. In his closet-shop, looking at delicate watches for small-boned wrists, the kind her far-sighted eyes could no longer read, she remembered her father's pocket watch sitting in her top bureau drawer. She brought it in the next day to ask if it could be put into running order. Perhaps he could put a pin on the back.

Burt cleaned it. "That's all it needed, why did you let it sit so long?"

"Well, I didn't...That's my business."

"Dust ruins things. It's a gem of craftsmanship; it will run longer than you. Too bad about its face."

"Thanks for the prediction."

"All the truly beautiful things in this world should outlast us. What's wrong with that?" he said, like someone who wants to encourage a discussion.

"What's wrong with the face?" Leona used to trace the second hand with her finger while her father tried to teach her to tell time.

"Roman numerals. Trying to be something it isn't. It's a watch, not a sun-dial. No one tells time in Latin, it's—"

"Okay, okay, I get the point. How much do I owe you?"

"You asked." He held the watch up, a few inches from Leona's jacket. "Want to pin it on?"

Burt had attached a short braid of gold to the watch, with a plain gold bar backing a pin at the chain's other end. When it was pinned and dangling from her jacket, Leona could raise its face to read it. She felt time beating through her. She thought, consciously for the first time since her surgery, I will live years and years, and then this will bob from a grown grandchild's jacket.

She wrote him a check and turned. The shop was so small she had to back a step towards the cage to open the door. She could see him looking at the check.

"Ms. Fredericks...Leona, would you like to walk down to the ice-cream parlor before the bull-dozers get it? I'll treat you to a soda."

Leona took her hand off the doorknob, unbuttoned her coat, put her hands in her pockets and said, "Three years ago, I had a bi-lateral mastectomy. All I've got left is skin. If you hope that every walk down the street is the first block on the long road to coupled happiness, you might want to re-consider."

She watched him put her check in a drawer, then sweep filings of metal into an envelope. "I missed lunch today. What I want is a strawberry malt. Want to come?"

She had gone back to work the summer after the surgery. Her male colleagues, like horses with blinders on, looked everywhere but at her chest when they talked to her. She went out a few times more with the man she had been dating, but when her scars healed he stammered and sobbed, "I feel like a louse, but..." The worst time with anyone new was when she sensed they would soon become intimate, when she would have to decide whether to tell him beforehand or let him discover what she was missing. Once she took a man's hand and traced it over her chest while she still had her camisole on. He was so startled that, like a child looking for a surprise he's sure is there, he picked up her shirt and peeked.

After the fourth such encounter, she greeted each new potential lover with the announcement she made to Burt. Few came back a second time, none a third. After dinner with friends, some wine, maybe a show, she fell into the habit of satisfying herself in bed under a warm comforter. Sometimes watching an erotic scene in a film, she experienced a vicarious arousal when the woman's breasts were bared, caressed, kissed, and later that night, she would stroke her scars.

The first time she and Burt made love, he caressed her scars so long she thought he hadn't understood that she had lost sensation there. She tried to move his hand, but he persisted and then moved hers to his head, and whispered, "You become the expert in phrenology and I'll become one in rib-ology. We'll write an article on symbiotic knobs for the New England Journal."

It had been years since Leona giggled during sex. Laughter loosed a passion in her that she thought had atrophied, and when Burt massaged and kissed and tongued her belly, her inner thighs, she could feel pulses from her amputated breasts, and then, her arms and legs around him, her chest tight against his, she reached a climax so deep and sustained she thought hours had gone by.

She walked back across the mall towards the phone booth. She ought to call Burt, to apologize for lying about him to the doctor. Then she thought that she'd buy him a plant instead. As she approached the garden shop, she saw her figure reflected in the glass doors, a vaguely familiar shape that, from one angle looked like an old friend until the angle widened. She turned her head, uneasy with that stranger in the door.

Inside, she browsed a long while, buying plant food and a bonsai—a flowering plum—for Burt, and a half-dozen pink roses for Trish. At the counter, she picked up cards for the gifts.

Back in the car, she considered how to spend the few hours before 5:00. No point in going into a dark theater. She could drive to the park and walk around the lake, but she'd had her full of swishing, and the weight of the prostheses was making her shoulders ache. How much do implants weigh, she wondered?

She pulled out of her angled slot and drove towards the mall exit, still uncertain where she would go but more aware now that her shoulders hurt. In the seconds that she reached inside her blouse to massage where the bra straps were cutting her, a woman laden with boxes stumbled off the curb in front of Leona's car. Leona hit her brakes hard but without both hands on the wheel couldn't control the skid, swerved to her left and circled to a stop. No one was hurt—Leona didn't count scrapes on the woman's knees and hands—but the clerk from the yogurt shop and the manager of the supermarket and three drivers nearby clustered first over the downed woman and then at Leona's car.

"Are you sure you're not shaken up?" the manager kept shouting, as though she were deaf as well as old. "We could call 911, take you to a clinic close-by for a quick check."

Leona heard her mother: "Always wear clean underwear. You never know when you'll get into an accident."

"Would you like us to call someone?" The man would not stop. "Is there a husband? A daughter? We could send a car for them."

Leona finally shook him off, got back in the car and headed for the freeway, away from those well-meaning hoverers. What if they had called Burt, or worse, Jan?

Leona got a sick feeling in her stomach thinking that if Jan saw her now, her daughter would believe that all these years Leona had lied to her. And in a way, she had. She had done the right thing for the wrong reason. It was right to refuse to hide what happened, to refuse to wear under or over her skin something that others expected but that offered her nothing of herself. But it was wrong to muddle her refusal with the absence of grief. In some skewed way, that grief, swelling inside her, had pushed her to the surgeon. She was like people who dig up the scattered bones of their martyrs to place them in graves where survivors can mourn them, trying to resurrect her old self in order to bury it.

It was 3:00. By the time Leona stopped to call Trish, she could just about be back at the shop. She was weary of carrying these false breasts around. She wanted to get them off and feel her own skin against her shirt, to parade her flat chest like the front of those sandwich boards men used to wear to advertise neighborhood stores: Celebrate the Organic.

Back in the shop's dressing room, while Trish waited on another customer, Leona took off the bra and rubbed her sore shoulders. Dressed again, she sat on the stool there in the booth to write Trish a note. She set it next to the roses on the shelf. She re-wrapped and boxed the prostheses. And then, she took out the second card from her purse, the one she had picked up for Burt. In her straightforward hand, she wrote in large black letters, "Inspected by Leona," and slipped that card deep inside the tissue paper surrounding the prostheses. Trish was still busy when Leona set the box alongside the roses, left the shop and went home.

# Vermeer at a First Class Fuck Palace in Versailles

## Laurel Speer

It's early morning in this first class hotel
in Versailles. Not exactly the elegance
of the Hall of Mirrors, so close by, or Marie An's
public bed (the one where she had to lie, while
the crowd milled), but nice enough to have chairs
and diaphanous white curtains behind drapes
that are pulled back and secured.

You are standing naked before the morning sun coming
through, while I lie propped on pillows against
a headboard sipping iced orange juice. I'm struck
by how little you have to offer: short, a thick trunk,
legs that are chunks, a belly that protrudes and drops
to an apron of fat, big, pendulous breasts with nipples
that have fallen down and to the side, so the mouth
must search for them in passion, the fingers locate
and place them between lips; sharp chin, hair to shoulders,
loose and rather fine, lacking body as they might say,
swirling your face, hiding, revealing as you move, entirely
too young a style for your age, which is, after all, nearly 50.
And yet so many have been drawn to penetrate
the mystery of your heaviness—I not least
among them. You could be viewed as the ultimate
Baroque in thick, gilded frame, a monumental painting
of some classical subject that takes puzzling, so busy
is it with plot and fleshy, naked, louche women.
You have nothing of the clean lines of the real classical

with its imposition of the Appolonian purity of line, form
and materials—or even its later perversion on overblown
subjects and figures. You predate all this. You are
far less artful, far more elemental, less ornamental,
moving back in time to the mounds of earth that draw us
by their rich, heady smells to fall on our faces
and embrace the promise of harvest and receptivity.

The night before, sipping wine at a meal far too elegant
for our tastes, you have puzzled your physical self,
saying how chunky and fat, always too heavy and ugly
you've been by any public standards, so how could you
think well of yourself, always struggling and wishing
to be other than you are? And yet how puzzling that never
has there been a time when your adult body didn't draw those
who needed to sink themselves in your plenty.

As I have done and do here lying long, well-muscled and lean
between sheets in Versailles watching you in silhouette
before the curtain with sunlight outlining, but never
defining your pulling so many to your center.

# The Eleanor Roosevelt Erotic Letter Writing Club

## Portia Cornell

When Gillian turned 50, she and her lover parted; her lover, to the West Coast, to join a women's psychic healing group, to deal with her breast cancer, and Gillian to Cape Cod, to fulfill her lifelong dream, to write a novel.

She sold the rear seat of her car to her mechanic for $25.

"Why are you doing this?" she asked Gillian.

"I need a van," Gillian replied.

She piled what remained of her belongings after the tag sale into her van. Her dog climbed in and lay panting anxiously on the passenger's seat. They made an unaccustomed stop at McDonald's for two hamburgers, one for Gillian and one for the dog.

"It's clams from now on," she told the dog as she turned onto the highway. Four hours later Gillian was crying as they sped past scrub pine up Rt. 6 to the tip of Cape Cod.

Her new landlady greeted her beside a tiny gray cottage that looked out over the dunes. Gillian settled herself at the window with her typewriter and began writing without unpacking. The dog sniffed around the three rooms, then lay down to sleep.

It was summer. Afternoons, Gillian went to Herring Cove Beach to watch women. Usually some were topless, a feature of this beach Gillian enjoyed.

Once she went to the Pied Piper Women's Dance Bar but she felt like she was in an aquarium, swaying, staring at the ceiling and not touching anyone. She swam through the crowd, jumped on her bicycle and pedaled home. She convinced herself that she didn't want a relationship, anyhow. Relationships were too encumbering. They pulled her away from herself. She was afraid to get involved with anyone. She just wanted to write.

By November, the tourists were gone. Herring Cove beach was home to squabbling gulls. The wind lifted the water in great gray hooks that dug at the beach, eroding the sand up to the dunes.

Gillian sat at her desk and stared at the sharp tan edge where dune met sky wondering if it was time to take a trip to the post office. This was her middle of the day routine. In the morning she did yoga and in the afternoon she ran on the beach. At night, in bed, she made up stories for herself of mermaids emerging from the sea to make love with her. She enacted the love scene and when she came, she rolled over with a sigh and fell asleep, often to wake in the night to re-enact the same scene.

Maybe there'll be a letter from my ex-lover or a friend, she thought. The dog whined. She rubbed her behind her ear. She pulled on her down jacket, her wool hat that covered her mouth, her lavender and white striped mittens, and rode her bike to the post office.

Three fishermen were discussing whether the storm was going to hit the cape or veer out to sea while Gillian collected her mail. No letters. Only holiday catalogues. She threw them in the trash bin. Pedalling home, head down against the damp wind, Gillian thought: I'm going to start a letter writing club.

By the time she tucked her bicycle under the porch, she had polished the concept into an erotic letter writing club.

She thought: there must be women out there, like myself, in love with the written word, yet lonely. Women, aware of the hazards of relationships, still yearning. The problem was simple. She wanted a love relationship guaranteed not to distract her from her mission of writing her novel. She would need rules to insure that her club worked the way she wanted it to.

She typed:

1. You can write anything you want in your letter.
2. Names and contents of letters are confidential.
3. You are not obligated to reply or continue a correspondence.
4. Correspondence with several members is encouraged.
5. No phone calls, photos, or personal contact between club members.
6. No faxing.

She decided to call it the "Eleanor Roosevelt Erotic Letter Writing Club." She would market it by trying it out on friends. Their response would tell her whether it would fly.

After two weeks she received her first response.

> Dear Gillian,
>
> Thank you for inviting me to join the Eleanor Roosevelt Erotic Letter Writing Club. My life is very tied up since I became aware of my addictions. I go to 12-step meetings every night. Sex is one of my addictions. Your club would disturb my serenity.
>
> In the name of the higher power,
> Anne

A week later she got:

> Dear Gil,
>
> Your club exploits women as sex objects. Also I would like to bring to your attention that there is real danger that it could be co-opted by the patriarchy. How would you know if it wasn't a man writing to you, disguised under a woman's name?
>
> In sisterhood,
>
> Jane

Gillian's hand went limp. Jane's letter floated onto the floor.

The next one said:

> The Buddha says we are love, that suffering comes from desire. Meditation is the way to end all desire. Therefore, meditate.

I wonder who sent this? thought Gillian, turning the envelope over. She picked up another.

Karen wrote:

> Gilly, get with the action. No one writes letters anymore. I don't even read. This is the music-video age.
>
> Do you dig it?
>
> Karen

Gillian folded Karen's letter into a plane and sailed it into the kitchen where it landed on a bowl of steaming oatmeal.

"I guess I don't know the women of the '90s," said Gillian, and went to eat her oatmeal. The dog sat beside her, watching the spoon travel from bowl to mouth.

The letter that came the following day was also disheartening:

> Dearest Gil,
>
> Like Virginia Woolf, you are fortunate to have a room of your own. Follow her example. Work. Don't distract yourself. When you publish your novel you'll get your fan letters.
>
> Your college roommate,
>
> Sarah

After all our talks about the problems of women artists, how they need to relate, as well as create, and she says *work*, thought Gillian, crushing the letter into a ball and tossing it at the wastebasket.

The next day dawned unusually balmy for December. Bright white gulls soared overhead like winged angels bearing tidings of joy. Gillian leapt out the post office door, froze and read:

> Sarah told me about the club when we broke up. I'm on a new path. Your erotic letter writing club can save me from the damnation of the no boundary relationships I always end up in. It will keep me on my path. Sign me up, my darling. Sign me up for the gold card membership.
>
> Gratefully,
>
> Lonnie

"Whoopie," shouted Gillian.

"Keeyew," screeched the gulls on high.

Breathless from the rapid ride home, she wrote:

>Dear Lonnie,
>
>Knowing there exists a woman such as you fills me with desire. I imagine your eyes, your lips. I long to see dreams in your eyes, words on your lips, my hands on your soft furry parts.

She signed it, folded it along with the club rules, and put it in a bright fuchsia envelope, lingering with her tongue on the seal. She pedaled rapidly to the post office groaning with pleasure as she lifted the labia of the waiting mailbox and slipped her message in. As she picked up her day's mail, she noted an airmail envelope amidst her unsolicited junk mail. Postmark: Denmark.

"Multi-national already," she congratulated herself, and waited to get home to read:

>Dear Gillian:
>
>A lesbian hitch hiker gave me your address. She said you have a club in America we have not in our country. In the lowlands there is much freedom. In lesbian relationships we have what we call the sadomasochism. I am a well educated woman. To all the time wear the black leather pants, and yell swears during sex, makes the boredom. Do you know the writer George Sand? Can you send me romantic letters like she wrote, American style.
>
>I lie upon my pillow, waiting for your letter of love,
>
>Jeanne.

Humming happily, Gillian wrote:

>I dream of you Jeannie, with your light brown hair, floating like a zephyr through the morning air...Mine eyes have seen the glory of your coming, Halleluia...The bombs bursting in air give proof through the night that you are there.

She folded a copy of Lonnie's address in with the Club Rules, and inserted it into a fresh fuchsia envelope.

"Now, back to my novel."

Letting the dog out the door, she went to work. Late that night she rose from her desk, gazed at the moon folded in fog, fell into bed spent and contented.

From that day on there were always letters from members of the Club waiting for her. She corresponded with some, referred the rest to each other. She lost track of the club's membership, but that didn't matter.

In three months she completed her novel, dedicating it to the Eleanor Roosevelt Erotic Letter Writing Club. Through a friend, she found an agent in New York City named Mary Shallot.

One morning, she left the dog at her landlady's and boarded the 6am off-Cape bus. She wore a navy blue wool coat purchased at Ruthie's Boutique & Thrift Shop, and cradled her newborn manuscript in her arms.

Climbing the steps of the IRT subway at 59th and Lexington, Gillian dodged descending human traffic. She slid into the doorway of Bloomies, hugging her manuscript to her chest, and stared across the street at the rising rows of square pink windows reflecting the movement of clouds across the sky.

The street sign flashed WALK. She obeyed, crossing Lexington and the green marble lobby into the elevator where she stood in a clump of strangers, staring at her shoes.

Ding. She was at floor 23.

Mary Shallot wore a gray pin-striped suit and bifocals that she looked up and over when something in Gillian's novel amused her.

Gillian smiled back nervously.

She finished the manuscript and said,

"There is a problem with my getting this published for you."

"My syntax is poor, I know," responded Gillian quickly.

"It's not that."

"You don't like it?"

"I think it's terrific. It's imaginative. It's funny. It's just what lesbians love to read."

Mary Shallot rose.

"It's also," she walked to Gillian's chair, "interesting," and placed her hand on Gillian's shoulder, "like you."

Gillian looked up and asked, "You just don't think you can find a publisher?"

"That's not the problem," said Mary. "The problem is I'd have to quit The Club to become your agent."

"The club?" asked Gillian, puzzled.

"The Club is important to me," said Mary, looking out the window. Gillian's gaze followed and she saw the blue windows of Bloomies reflecting the faceless pink windows of the building they were in.

"Before The Club I couldn't work. I was too busy with relationships. I was either breaking up or in love. It was an emotional roller coaster. I had no creative juice left. When I found The Club, all that stopped and I could do my work."

"The Club," said Gillian hunching into herself. "You mean the Eleanor Roosevelt Erotic Letter Writing Club, don't you?"

"That's the one," said Mary, laughing. "The one you dedicated your book to. Obviously we are both members. Obviously we cannot have personal contact. Whoever conceived of that club was brilliant. Solves a myriad of problems for women writers."

Mary Shallot walked back to her desk, sat down, and stared intently at Gillian.

"You wouldn't want to get back on the emotional roller coaster either, I suspect."

Gillian felt dizzy. She reached for her manuscript. She got Mary's hand. It warmed her cold fingers.

"I wish you the best of luck," said Mary. "You've got a winner there."

Gillian walked out and descended alone in the elevator. It made a soft swish as it stopped and the doors silently opened.

"Winner?" puzzled Gillian, as she walked into the green marble lobby, her manuscript tucked under her arm.

"I guess that's you, babe," she muttered.

She passed a large green trash barrel. It said, KEEP NEW YORK CLEAN. Resisting the urge to drop her novel, she walked on.

# It Is a Very Good Year
## Ayofemi Folayan

I have had an incredibly hard time writing this piece. In some ways that doesn't make any sense, because I am an out and proud lesbian, excited to have reached the age of forty. Yet there is some internal wall that stops words and feelings from emerging onto paper. The process of acknowledging where I am in my life as a lesbian has forced me to look back over where I have been and to deal again with old pain. Coming out for me was more than stepping out of the closet and declaring myself a lesbian. First I had to figure out that I *was* a lesbian.

Today there is a visible lesbian community. Here in Los Angeles, there is a monthly Lesbian Writers Series and four bookstores which carry a range of lesbian titles. The June Mazer Collection archives lesbian materials. *The Lesbian News*, published now for fifteen years, advertises therapists, chiropractors, and real estate agents, all of whom provide services as and for lesbians. There are several women's bars and even recovery programs where lesbians are welcomed.

It wasn't always so. The word *lesbian* didn't exist publicly when I was first coming out. There was no affirmation that other women shared the emotions that churned inside me. The community was underground, seeking each other out through codes and signals, meeting in bars and at private parties. *Everyone* was closeted at work or school. Black women, in particular, didn't use the word lesbian to describe themselves. It was a word I associated with characters in books, not real people.

There is a Frank Sinatra song that goes, "When I was seventeen, it was a very good year..." Well, when I was seventeen, I had no clue that it could be a very good year. I had just been released from a psychiatric facility after eight weeks of intensive psychotherapy and drug therapy. I had been admitted to this hospital by my parents after they discovered me making love with my best girlfriend from high school.

I didn't even know the word *lesbian* yet. I didn't hear that label for another eleven years. I didn't understand what I was feeling or experiencing as a lesbian.

Like most adolescents, I was propelled to sexual activity by confusing emotional and physiological signals I could neither define nor explain.

Back then it would have been impossible for me to imagine my life today, living openly as a lesbian. It was 1967, well before Stonewall, before women's music festivals or women's liberation became visible. The assumption was that a female would finish high school, get married and settle down as a happy homemaker. There were even contests, sponsored by the Betty Crocker Company, about becoming "A Better Homemaker of Tomorrow."

I grew up in the strict fundamentalist Pentecostal Church. My grandmother, grandfather, two uncles and a cousin were all ordained ministers. My social life was defined by the limits of a full calendar of church activities, including choir, Bible study and youth group. Then, at fourteen, I saw my first movie, an action forbidden by the tenets of my church. I was so enthralled by the film, "Dr. Zhivago," I returned to see it thirteen times! I kept waiting for the lightning to strike, but all I experienced was the joy of a really romantic love story. I reasoned that if the church could be so wrong about something like movies, I could begin to question other doctrines.

Sex as a concept was a "black hole" to me: highly charged and totally incomprehensible. While I had crushes on my girlfriends, it never occurred to me that there could be any sexual content to those feelings. When I was around boys I was mostly bored, unless we were intellectually matched. By the time I found myself "practicing for dates with boys" with my girlfriends, it was still not clear to me that those feelings could exist in a context of their own.

As our rehearsals progressed beyond kissing to other sexual activities, such as petting, I became less and less interested in the "real" performance. I was thoroughly inebriated by the heady wine of my increasing passion. Yet, I would not have defined any of our activity as sexual, because I did not have the context of lesbian to define it.

I was crushed by the indictment of my family, my church and the community around me, which called me a pervert. I submitted to their external pressures to conform, to be "normal." After my psychiatric imprisonment, I hid in a disguise of heterosexuality to avoid the punishment that had been so swiftly dispensed. While I proceeded to get married and have children, there was a part of me that resisted, that struggled to stay alive.

While married, I continued to have "affairs" with women who were as confused as I. We each thought we were "the only one" and that somehow we had been fortunate to stumble upon each other. Even after I had been involved with four or five women, it still did not occur to me that I was a lesbian or that these feelings I had for women had any validity.

I often say that it is surprising to me when I meet a lesbian from some small town in Iowa. "How did she know that she was a lesbian?" I ask myself. I struggled so hard to come to terms with my identity as a lesbian, partially because

I had no community to reflect and validate me. After two marriages and two children failed to convince me that I could fit into the heterosexual mold, I moved to Los Angeles at the age of twenty-three.

There I came into contact with a lesbian community: women who called themselves lesbians, who wore jeans and Birkenstocks and carried backpacks, who congregated at women's bars. Over the next few years, just being around these women who were lesbians produced a major transformation in me. I went to concerts and dances, sang in the Los Angeles Women's Community Chorus (which welcomed all women of whatever sexual orientation), and gorged myself on a mental diet of lesbian books.

I didn't "come out" until the Briggs Initiative, a referendum on the California ballot in 1978 that threatened to attack homosexual teachers and anyone who supported their right to teach. I was so personally outraged by the homophobia explicit in this potential law that I worked actively on the campaign which successfully defeated the initiative. In a sense, I leapt out of the closet, never to return.

Since then, my individual evolution has drawn on that core assumption that I am a lesbian. Politically, that has meant a commitment to ending all forms of oppression and to improving the quality of life on our planet. I think it is important at this point in my life for me to continue to encourage women who are struggling with coming out issues today, in the persistent context of homophobic oppression. Personally, that has meant taking my full identity with me wherever I am. Sometimes that has made members of the various communities I am part of, such as the black community, the disabled community, and the politically progressive community, uncomfortable.

The journey I took to reach a clear and calm acceptance of myself means never looking back with some sentimental confusion about the past, never apologizing, never again suffocating in the cloud of ignorance that surrounded me as a young lesbian. In the words of the Judy Small song, "I'm going to keep on walking forward, never turning back, never turning back!"

# Office Visit
## Trudy Riley

I shift my body so that I can show Dr. Stevens the exact spot where the pain starts. There is a fair amount of body to get around, which doesn't bother me one bit except at times like these, when I have to get in a position that nobody gets in anyway. If my regular doctor were here I would reach for her hand and put it over just the right area but she's off having another baby and I am left with this young man who is looking at my contortions with disinterest. "I'm going to make it," I say, hoping he has a sense of humor. I press the skin on the left side of my back below my ribs. "There, right there!" I am triumphant.

From six feet away he tells me that area is called the flank.

It's a nice name. I think of the silky sides of horses. "Well it hurts," I tell him, " 'specially when I press."

He looks at the spot I am pointing to and furrows his brow. He is thinking, taking a breath, letting me know that any moment he is going to make a long-distance diagnosis.

I'm not very good at waiting so I reminisce about the time when doctors weren't afraid to touch people. When I was a kid Doctor Bradley would touch my belly—palpating it was called. He had a nice touch, firm but gentle, with a little magic mixed in. When I grew up I'd heard about doctors that lingered a bit too long over the breasts and other private parts. Well I'd been lucky. I'd always had confident, well-behaved hands reading my ills. But for about the last ten years my doctors have stood across the room and talked *at* me. Maybe they have lost the talent of listening to the body with their hands. But maybe it's not that at all. Maybe the idea of touching such a large, aging woman is something they don't want to do.

I wonder at this because I have grown so fond of my body with its pendulous breasts and rounded belly. There are these striated marks running down my middle. Sometimes I imagine I can tell which ones belong to the time Christie made her home in there and which ones came along with David. Every mark is not totally pleasant. There are those varicose veins from standing too many years at Macy's selling handbags. And I suppose my feet aren't the prettiest things in the world. But I see them as deserving of a great deal of sympathy and respect because they wouldn't be that way if I hadn't had to squeeze them into high heels for so many years.

I bring my mind back into the room and study this serious man, fresh from his training, who wears his over-sized white coat like armor. I am sure he is not about to appreciate this road map of a well-used body. He is standing there now, bright brown eyes staring at the area above my rump.

This has gone on long enough, I figure, so I press again and say, "Ouch," and give an exaggerated wince. I think that if I add a little drama to the situation he will get that I have a problem that I expect him to solve.

"If it's in that area," he says, "it's neuromuscular and nothing to worry about." He is picking up my chart and about to leave.

"Wait!" I yell, letting the beige hospital gown fall over my white cotton britches. I raise myself up to full height. I am determined to give the message that all one hundred and eighty pounds of me, from the top of my recently home-permed head to my size nine feet, need to be taken seriously. "Neuromuscular or not it is interfering with my life!"

He turns his back and rifles though my medical chart. My guess is he's looking for my most recent blood test, not because that would be related to my complaint, but because it is something to do. Blood tests are in now—read the blood not the body. But I'll give him a little credit because he murmurs into the chart, "And when is that?"

"When I have an orgasm." I say this loud and add, "Which is often."

He turns and looks at me in a way which makes me feel like he believes I am no longer entitled.

"And of course when I have them they go on such a long time." I let go of a wistful sigh and put my hand to my forehead as though it is all wondrous and exhausting. "Wave after wave, if you know what I mean." I watch him intently to see if he does. I think not. His stance tells me he is about to turn back to the chart. "It wasn't always that way, you know." I feel as though I am conducting a strange sit-in. I park myself in the only chair in the office, a plastic job that looks made for thin, short people like the doctor who is now looking at me with a hint of discomfort. I take some pleasure in that and decide I will stay here and barrage him with my sexual life until I am taken seriously. "Like I was saying, I didn't even have my first one 'til I was twenty-six and that was with this fellow named George who had just come back from France and knew a thing or two."

He faces me. He seems annoyed. It is hard to tell with this man. The only give-away is two spots under his cheekbones that are turning red. "I don't think there is any point in..."

I interrupt. It no longer matters to me what he is going to say because I know, whatever it is, it will be an attempt to dismiss me. "You know, at the time, I didn't realize that first orgasm was just a puny little thing compared to what happens to me now!"

"Yes, well, Mrs..." He looks back to the chart. "Mrs. Keegan." He is turning pages now. Just in case he's doing that blood test stuff again I reach under my gown, press the place and say, "Ouch!" He looks at me.

"It's still there," I say, hoping a little humor will help.

He sighs. "How long have you had it?"

"About two weeks and that's two weeks longer than either Susan or I can stand."

For a moment he looks surprised but recovers quickly.

"You know I really didn't have many of these powerful orgasms until I met Susan. I think it's feeling so valued and, of course, trust is part of it. Those things are important, don't you think?"

Resigned, he approaches me and places his fingers over the place I have pointed to. His touch is more decisive than I would have expected. Only the expression on his face, as he lists the tests he plans to order, gives away that he feels he has been wandering around in the land of the inappropriate.

I wonder if he is thinking about two middle-aged, ample ladies bouncing around on a lumpy bed. You got it wrong I want to say to this man who stands so rigid in his body, it's not like that at all. It is moist and leisurely and oh so loving—and our skin. They probably don't mention in medical school how soft the skin becomes with age, how it surrenders to the touch. How there's no hurry to do anything. Whole conversations can happen in the joy of that warm, liquid time. Sometimes we giggle like girls at a slumber party. Other times we shed a few tears at the wonder of creating such a safe, happy place for ourselves on the Deluxe Serta mattress that was the first thing we bought together.

He is leaning over a small counter and writing furiously. I have the impulse to keep talking until he looks at me like I have a life but an inside voice that is smarter than I am says, "Not possible," and adds, "Quit while you're ahead."

He hands me a number of slips in various colors and tells me the nurse will give me instructions. He is brisk now, heading for the door, white coat flapping.

"The nerve of that man trying to brush you off. If I'd been there he wouldn't have gotten off so easy." It is Susan, being fierce.

"I know. You would have lectured him about why he chose his profession if he couldn't treat people like human beings. You probably would have ended up quoting...what's that oath they take?"

"Hippocratic," she laughs then and adds, "Of course I would have. He deserves nothing less."

I watch her as she moves from the kitchen to the dining room placing steaming bowls on the table. She is wearing a blue caftan, there are big silver hoops in her ears, she has pinned her hair up. She manages to hold all that long grey-brown hair in one giant hairpin with only a few wisps coming down at the back of her neck. It is such a vulnerable place, her neck, that I want to bound off the couch and kiss it, but I don't because she is one hundred percent involved in getting dinner on the table and when she's concentrating on something her whole body is into just that.

I ask if I can help but the only thing left to do is light the candles. I think that we are really out of an earlier time with our candlelit dinners every night. Sometimes when we don't want to talk much we put on a little Cole Porter. I console myself with the fact that some of our tastes may be right out of the fifties but our menu is not.

"A feast of complex carbohydrates," she announces as she offers me a generous helping of brown rice. There is tofu in a tomato, rosemary and onion sauce and broccoli that is such a deep velvety green it looks unreal.

"This will spice it up a little," I say, pouring each of us a glass of white wine. My usual limit is one but tonight I may have two. It has been a hard day.

We get to talking about the past. Tonight we remember when we thought the best thing in the world for us was red meat. We talk about the dim restaurants with maroon-padded booths that we frequented with husbands sometimes, lovers at others. There was something quiet and intimate about those places, not like the trendy place we were taken to recently with floor-to-ceiling windows and no sound proofing and a lot of shiny metal and plastic. While our friend raved I leaned toward Susan and said, "It's like having dinner on a sun porch."

After dinner I do the dishes and Susan works on her computer. She started writing short stories about three years ago. She is not discouraged by rejection slips. When she gets one she talks to it. "Just wait," she says, "I'm getting better every day," and tosses it into a box that is filling up pretty fast.

I am tired so I go to bed. I take the latest P.D. James mystery with me but I don't read it. Instead I pull the quilt up to my neck and think about the events of the day.

Sometime later when she joins me I enfold her in my arms. She reaches around and smoothes the place where the pain is.

"Press, a little," I say.

"I don't want to hurt you."

"Just press, you won't."

"Harder." I reach around and push on her fingers as hard as I can. "I don't think it's there anymore," I say, smiling into the darkness. I try again. "It's gone! It must just have been..." We say the word, "neuromuscular," in unison.

We are joyous with relief. I reach for Susan with even more enthusiasm than usual and whisper, "You know what I'd like to do tonight that would be different?"

"No, what?" Her whisper tickles my ear.

"Let's bounce around a little, just for the hell of it."

# No Words for It
## Tilly Washburn Shaw

Such very old women.

At meals in the retirement home
they would make a signal others didn't see
then one would excuse herself
and a moment later the other
follow suit. This was how
they arranged to meet daily
for a moment down the hall
in front of one of their doors
and embrace. Unimaginable,
such a tender, lingering kiss
from two such very old women.

My mother snorted in the telling.
She was 88 and they were acting like schoolgirls,
ought to pull themselves together.

At this end of their lives—85 and 83—
their minds hardly reached anymore
to the rest of us, their ports of entry
closed to the large print and
louder voices with which we
pressed them. It was easier finally
just to give up on words
and loosen hold.

They had no other place to go to.
It couldn't happen in a bedroom,
needed to be done in the open
so as to mean right and put at a distance
the mind's other thoughts.

Untroubled about whom they loved
since life left them but a handful
of persons, they took whatever offered itself
and opened their needy hearts
humble and greedy both. You might
think it matter-of-fact but it was also romantic:
dreams hopelessly mixed in with needs
the way probably it always is.
My mother ended her story with
a surge of impatience: adolescent
crushes at their age! The others
followed her of course into laughter
eager to push away deeper
yearnings they were all now too old
and close to wanting
to avow.

# Deep Time
## Elisabeth Boone

W hen Clara left Max after three decades, Zoe suggested a face lift. "You'll feel
better about yourself, Clara, take it from me!" Zoe's cosmetic surgery last
year left her looking rather like a kewpie doll—at the time Clara thought of a line
from a travel journal, *Restoration is the curse of the Mayan ruins.*

"Oh I don't know, Zoe, I kind of feel it's a losing process so why not relax
and enjoy it?"

"But you're *not* enjoying it," Zoe pointed out.

This was so. The Age Spectre had been stalking Clara for some years but
she'd always supposed she'd grow old along with Max who was a comfortable
five years ahead of her. Clara had been with Max thirty-one years, long enough
to get thoroughly tired of dead animals around the house.

Taxidermy, Max liked to say, was a unique and original art—and every
artist had a right to hang his work in his own home. Over the mantel hung a six-
foot marlin exquisitely airbrushed down to the inside of its mouth; a raccoon
looked out of a nest on a corner table; a squirrel nibbled at a nut on the dining
room buffet. Max's pride and joy was the brown Kodiak bear standing in the
front hall. The hunter who'd bagged this prize died of a heart attack while Max
was still working on it; his widow bestowed it on the artist—no fool she.

Clara knew Max's dream had always been to create displays for one of the
great science museums and so she held her peace; but who wants to live in a
mausoleum?

All winter Clara had been working around Madison for the Prairie Pinch-
Hit Agency. This snowy January morning she was starting a new job near the
apartment she shared with Zoe. Reception work at the Bio-Energetic Center. She
thought it might have something to do with electronics.

"Faith healing?"

"Some might call it that," Jim Pollock said, unnervingly handsome, tall and
thin with curly grey hair and Paul Newman eyes. "Any M.D. knows you can't
get well without it, think of placebos."

But Clara thought of voodoo rites, of Phillipine surgeons removing psychic appendices on kitchen tables.

"Very interesting," she said diplomatically. After all, it was only for three months, and he wasn't hard to look at.

"God, Clara! Is it laying on of hands?" groaned Zoe.

"It seems more like laying *off* of hands. He doesn't touch people at all, Zoe, he says there's an energy field around them and he works on that."

"Well...that sounds harmless enough," Zoe frowned.

"It's mindfuck, mother!" cried Barbara from her campus office in Cincinnati.

"Oh, Barbie, he's a gentle person, I think he means well."

"Ma," Barbara snapped, "all those people are bad news! Don't mess with them—ask for a transfer."

But Clara decided to mess with them anyway. Working at the Center was more interesting than her other jobs, and she liked Jim Pollock.

"Good morning, Bio-Energetic Center, Clara speaking, may I help you?"

"Hey, I hope so. These last two weeks there's been this radio playing in my head, you know? It's driving me nuts, I gotta find out where the off-switch is."

"That fella?" said Jim after seeing the scruffy young man at noon. "He just got tuned to the wrong frequency. It's like getting PTL when you want MTV, he'll be all right."

The woman in the doorway was fortysomething with eye makeup reminiscent of Mac's raccoon.

"Say, you're new aren't you? Where's Stephanie?" She flounced in and sat down smoothing tight blonde curls, crossing plumpish legs.

"Stephanie's on maternity leave, I'm Clara. You're Mrs. Trappel?"

"In *spades*!" Mrs. Trappel leaned across the desk conspiratorially. "I'm after his hormones."

"Excuse me?"

"Well, you know, whatever the hell makes him so radiant," Mrs. Trappel said, waving toward Jim's office behind her. "So fucking *young*."

"Good morning, my dear," said Jim, breezing through the open door. "Come in and let's have a look at your fucking aura. Would you like some fucking tea?"

Of the many things Clara felt nostalgic for—Eleanor Roosevelt, soda fountains, boogie woogie—she missed most of all her body of thirty years ago. Each morning stepping out of the shower she contemplated flesh once firm and fertile eroding into Saharan sands. Somehow she couldn't get used to her present reflection: what *had been* seemed the normal state of things and what *was now* seemed abnormal. Did they have whole-body lifts?

Before going to sleep these nights she often sat up in bed reading *People* and

*Vanity Fair*, searching out articles on Older Women, Elizabeth Taylor, Jane Fonda, Shirley MacLaine. Studying their photos made for a depressing night—though she knew all about makeup and high cameras, low lights, soft focus to cover up years. If it were true as Jim Pollock said, that ninety-eight percent of the atoms in your body weren't there a year ago, why did you age at all? Was it similar to what happened to the great old buildings in Athens and Paris—roughening, darkening, crumbling from air pollution? Was some chemical in the air responsible? Or in the food? Or in the relationships?

What would thoroughly healthy aging be like? Did we even know?

Max still lived in the mausoleum on Odana Street, contributing generously to her support. He could have the house, she often thought, if he'd help her buy a smaller one on the edge of the city. Living with Zoe was not ideal; but the question was, what did she really want to do? After six months of separation Clara still wasn't sure. In retrospect, and in low moments, life with Max didn't seem all that bad.

"Mother," Barbara said on her Sunday night call, "is it just the stuffed animals? Because it could be a lot worse, you know, it could be human heads." Such were the artifacts Barbara's mate brought back from his anthropological jaunts.

"It's not just the animals, dear."

"What then?"

"Oh, I was bored, Barbie."

"Bored? Ma, there must be another reason! I mean, *why* were you bored? What was it you wanted that you weren't getting with Dad? Travel? Good sex? What was it?"

How can I know if I don't know? Clara wondered.

Though Jim Pollock could remember the Depression, he looked a youthful forty-five; his shining face smiled out at the world beneath fleecy hair Clara longed to run her fingers through. He was a sharp dresser, tending to shirts of pink, orange and lavender, flowered ties, checked sports jackets. Once in a while he overdid it and looked a little like a racehorse tout, his gold tooth flashing in the sunlight.

"What's your secret, Jim?" Clara asked daringly one afternoon. "How do you look so young?"

"Never take things seriously," he told her, "that's the thing."

"Never?"

"Don't get caught in your own melodrama, my dear."

Another day she tried a different tack. "I'm so tired this week! I'm just getting old; look at me, Jim, I feel like a physical wreck!"

"Ah," he said, "you don't like that bodysuit you're zipped up in, do you?"

"Not a bit."

"I bet you *never* liked it."

Transported back to adolescence Clara felt a forgotten lust for a larger bra size, thinner calves, a clear complexion. Yes, and ten years later when Barbara came she'd longed for a flat stomach again, no stretch marks, twenty pounds gone. It was true, she'd never really liked her body, there were too many things wrong with that particular bodysuit.

"Never, never," Jim nodded. "About the only thing that's different now is you think it's age."

"*Society* thinks it's age, Jim! How can I *not*!"

"What? They've got a mind control switch in your head?"

"Oh Jim, you're unreal!"

"Now you're getting it," he agreed.

What's the youngest you can die of old age?" she asked her doctor during her annual physical before her birthday.

"Don't be morbid, Clara." He was brisk, professional, barely forty. "The less you think about such things the better."

The day before Clara's fifty-ninth birthday a huge bouquet of white roses arrived from Max with an invitation to lunch next day. Clara thought about it. She'd run into Max one day in Victor's and they'd had mochas together; it had been innocuous enough. Rather nice, in fact. She decided to accept.

Entering The Ovens of Brittany on University she caught a glimpse of Max up the steps by the window and was shocked by how ancient he looked—it wasn't just that he was nearly bald, it was the way he *sat*, it was everything about him.

Now he saw her and waved.

"Lunch, Clara," he explained, seating her, "because I was afraid you wouldn't go to dinner with me." There was a flat wrapped package on the table beside his place. (Was he, could he possibly be, courting her? Part of Clara's heart lifted unexpectedly at the thought.)

Whether he was or not, the lunch went well; they spoke of Barbara, of Zoe, of Clara's job. Max said he'd taken up calligraphy, which she was sure he'd pursue as he did everything else, with thoroughness and determination. Max was a careful man, a cautious man, with a strange and beguiling romantic streak when he was younger. He'd never had a sense of humor though, nor had Barbara. Was *that* Jim's secret, Clara wondered? A fraud perhaps, yet somehow appealing.

Max handed her the package and Clara unwrapped it quickly—a framed, beautifully scripted familiar poem on exquisite vellum, looking quite professional:

> *Grow old along with me*
> *The best is yet to be,*

*The last of life, for which the first was made...*
Robert Browning to his wife Elizabeth. Tears filled Clara's eyes.

"I worked on it all month," Max said.

"It's beautiful, Max." She found she could not say more.

"A toast," he smiled, pouring out the last of the champagne, "to years to come."

"Whatever they may bring," she said, finding her voice, looking at him over the rim of her glass.

"Ma, he really does love you," Barbara said. Her UPS package had arrived that afternoon containing a brilliant scarf from Tanzania wrapped around a book entitled *Deconstructing Psychic Phenomena.* "He talks about you all the time. Why don't you try couples counseling? I think he's game."

Clara smelled conspiracy here, Barbara had always been a Daddy's girl.

"Not yet, dear, not till I know how I feel." Over the wire she heard her daughter sigh.

"Don't let Barbie pressure you," Zoe approved a few minutes later, "or Max either. You're absolutely right, Clara, you're still much too vulnerable. Wait a while before making any decisions."

Clara knew it would be all too easy to slip back into old patterns, much less grueling. Now and then she thought of herself as a huge collection of patterns something like a patchwork quilt, forming, dissolving, mellowing. And it seemed to her too many lives around her re-echoed old themes across the years—themes which gave a certain continuity and structure and yet at the same time held people back from other possibilities. A person had to have lived a long time, she thought, before such patterns became visible. It was one of the perks of growing old.

Late at night Clara lay in bed thinking; she listened to sporadic traffic on the street, a deep-voiced dog barking, a siren on the other side of town. In geology there was something called *deep time*, billions of years, impossible to comprehend. If you imagined the age of the earth being similar to the old English yard—a measurement based on the distance from the king's nose to the tip of his outstretched hand—then a single stroke from a nail file erased human history. Clara felt she existed in a sort of deep time herself now, with whole eras rolling past in a flash—wars and police actions, presidencies, pregnancies, marriages, divorces. Fashions and returning fashions, loves and animosities, sadnesses, joys. Deaths and births.

The body remembers, she thought in the dark; every part of us remembers everything that's ever happened...Ah, we know so much, if only we could believe it.

Stephanie was coming back to Jim's office on Monday. Outside the window of the reception room a hardy daffodil blew in the cold March sunlight as it slanted through the trees; in a week or so the streets of Madison would be full of bare legs and sleeveless shirts, a university town full of human daffodils.

It was Friday and Clara began putting her desk in order. She could see Jim through the open door leaning back in his chair, the phone at his ear, his grey hair shining in the sunlight. He looked like a spry old fox, lively and unpredictable, a wild thing resistant to custom.

Next week the temporary agency was sending her to Hovde and Bradshaw, a legal firm off State Street; she wondered if she'd survive the culture shock. Jim's ideas *were* truly outlandish, but his clients seemed to benefit from seeing him. Clara couldn't believe he was part of what Barbie called The Swami Mafia. He'd been good to her. And occasionally she wondered if the metaphysical interests the world scorns might be just as natural in later years as sexual leanings were in adolescence.

Feeling a bit down today, a bit agitated, Clara blamed it on her lack of sleep. This morning her mirror reflected a face somewhere between sixty and a thousand—they just weren't making mirrors like they used to.

"Clara, my dear," Jim suddenly appeared at her elbow. "You're leaving today? I can't believe it."

"Yes I am," she said sadly.

"I'm really going to miss you; you've been absolutely terrific!" He squeezed her shoulder and sat down on the edge of her desk looking at her speculatively. "I've been watching you a long time, Clara. You may not realize it but you've been traveling around in a Volkswagen bus all your life when you've got the motor of a Ferrari. Why don't you get out on the road and see what you can really do?"

"Why, I'd bust a gasket," she said. "Jim, I'm not what I used to be—even a Volkswagen bus."

"Nobody's what they used to be, bless your heart. What about taking the Ferrari out for dinner tomorrow night?"

He fixed her with those pale blue eyes as she hesitated.

"You think I'm full of baloney, don't you?" he laughed. "But it's *marvelous* baloney, Clara! Let me tell you something, my dear—don't identify with the baloney! Or with Jim Pollock either. It's the *energy* that's important. Can you feel it?" He threw back his head and laughed, gold tooth flashing. "Don't you know, my dear, when you really connect with someone on the energy level it's like being together in a cosmic jacuzzi! Do you feel it?"

Clara had a sensation of hurtling through space, spiralling along infinite possibilities of a lifetime.

"How about tomorrow night?" he leaned toward her. "What d'you say, my dear?"

Clara took a deep breath, and replied.

# Estrus

## Elizabeth Cunningham

"*estrus.*"

I am crouching over *The American Heritage Dictionary*, having sneaked downstairs after breakfast to what I call the stacks—three shelves of my own personal library in a corner of what other people in Suburbia refer to as the family room, or worse, the entertainment center. The books give some dignity, some tone, to a room otherwise dominated by technology: a VCR, a computer, and a nautilus machine.

"n. Also oestrus," I read. "A regularly recurrent period of ovulation and sexual excitement in female mammals other than humans."

But why "other than humans"? Without those three words the definition is an accurate description of what I experience for two or three days every month, of what, in fact, I am going through now.

"Because," I can hear my husband Richard explaining when last month I advanced my theory of cyclical sexual interest in human female mammals (namely me), "what differentiates the human female from females of other species is the human female's continuous receptivity."

"Ah, yes," I replied. "That's the Universal Male Fantasy, isn't it?"

"Come again?" he said, no pun, I am sure, intended.

"Richard," I sighed," why do you suppose it is that more women than men suffer from migraines?"

"What's that got to do with it?"

Despite his degree from M.I.T. and his job on the Route 128 Boston Brain Belt, Poor Richard, as I sometimes think of him, can be quite dense.

" 'Not tonight, dear, I've got a headache'?"

"Oh!" He finally caught on. "But that's just a sitcom cliche. *You've* never pleaded a headache," he said with more than a touch of masculine pride as he reached for me. And that ended that discussion.

But then, I have never needed such hackneyed defenses as headaches. My cycle has determined the pattern of our marital relations for years—at least since Sybil, our youngest, now eleven, went off to nursery school. (Sybil, six and nine years younger than her siblings, was a brilliant afterthought, as her father puts it.) It's when childbearing is finally over, with its wake of night feedings, early risings, and the physical demands of keeping a death-defying toddler alive, that the subtle rhythms become obvious again. At least they are obvious to me. Richard, as noted, is oblivious, though quite responsive, to the ebb and flow of my desire. He is the one who is continuously receptive, available on demand— the dear.

"You're an animal, Cyn," he protested happily this morning when I made a purposeful move in his direction a full twenty minutes before the alarm, having woken from a night of dreams that kept me on the brink of orgasm. "A bitch in heat," he elaborated fondly, if without much originality.

I am an English major and—well, why not say it?—a poet, and I tend to be fussy about metaphors, but at that moment I was in no position (pun intended) to object. Moreover it seems *The American Heritage* concurs with Richard.

"Also called 'heat,' " I continue to read, relinquishing my crouch and sitting down fully on the floor. Reading the dictionary is an addictive activity for me, just like eating potato chips or M&Ms. I can't stop with just one word. I suspect it's not definition but derivation that's the real hook, the deadly additive, the sugar, the salt.

"[New Latin, from Latin *oestrus* gadfly, frenzy, from Greek *oistros*. See *eis-* 1 in Appendix.*]"

Of course I look up the root: "In words denoting passion...4. Suffixed o-grade form *ois-tro*, madness, in Greek oistros gadfly, goad, anything causing madness: ESTRUS (ESTRONE)."

I wonder, as I flip back to the definition, how many words that mean crazy can be traced somehow to female sexuality. Hysterical (from hustera, womb); insane, unclean (we all know who and what that means; why else are products to staunch menstrual flow called sanitary?).

"Estuary," I read on. "1. The part of the wide lower course of a river where its current is met and influenced by the tides." Nicely put, I think. "2. An arm of the sea that extends inland to meet the mouth of a river." I find this image strangely erotic. "[Latin *aestuarium*, estuary, tidal channel, from aestus, heat, swell, surge, tide..."

Heat, swell, surge, tide. What marvelous words. I look up from the page, willing estrus and estuary to share a common root. That's the sort of discovery that could make my day.

"...See *aidh-* in Appendix*]"

Disappointed but obedient, I look up the entry. "To burn," I read; then I find repeated, "*aestus*, heat, swell, surge, tide: ESTUARY."

"Mom!" It's Sybil calling me from the top of the basement stairs. "Mom!"

"I'll be right there. Are you all ready to go?"

I drive her to school on my way to work, our quality time.

"Of course I'm ready. What are you doing down there?"

Lately Sybil always seems suspicious of me, a classic case of projection, surely—or a studied tactic. I'm not sure which.

"Nothing," I give the classic reply. I'm hardly going to admit that I've been voraciously—not to mention salaciously—reading the dictionary.

"Well, hurry up. I don't want to be late."

"Neither do I."

I take the steps two at a time despite my heels. I always feel springy in the fall, optimistic, adventurous. Maybe it's the rhythm of the school year established in childhood, that sense of starting fresh that's reinforced by my birthday's falling at the beginning of October. Though I admit that since I saw forty almost six years ago, I've been somewhat ambivalent about my birthday as a sign of renewal.

This fall I have a new job, a full-time one after years of part-time: substitute teaching here, a stint as a florist's assistant there, a spot or two of waitressing, and once even a season as a delivery person of singing telegrams. I've taken these odd jobs to support my poetry habit, but now with my older daughter Kate a Junior in college, and my son Peter threatening to enter as a freshman next year, a second full-time income is no longer optional.

So just before Labor Day I began work as a receptionist in a proctologist's office—a position which embarrasses to varying degrees the various members of my family. Peter reverts to a prurient five-year-old with jokes about assholes. Sybil merely shudders at the mention of proctology and wrinkles her nose as if someone had made a particularly noisome fart in her vicinity. Kate, who is premed, can handle the anatomical implications of the job but finds it appalling that her mother would be willing to be something as lowly as a receptionist. "Less than a secretary!" as she puts it. Richard tends to agree with Kate that if I'm going to work full-time I should find a position with more status, at least, attached. Although he restrains himself (just barely) from making crude and worn-out jokes, he feels a sort of horrified fascination with the nature of my bosses' work. With the brain available, or the nervous system, even the heart, why choose the lowly rectum? Finding it an object of such derision, I am beginning to feel a sort of perverse tenderness for that part of the body. Also, it occurs to me, its poetic possibilities must be largely unexplored...

The redeeming feature of my job, as far as Richard is concerned, is that I have at long last become computer literate, more or less. Not that I get a chance at our P.C. with Sybil and Peter both wanting to do their homework on it as well as play and design games in their spare time, that is, if their father isn't hooked up. I exercise my new word processing skills at the office. Between answering the phone, receiving payments and writing the odd irate letter, usually to insurance companies, I type drafts of poems and prepare submissions to magazines and contests.

My bosses are pretty easy-going. Looking at assholes all day, then listening to stupid, repetitive jokes at parties must keep proctologists grounded, in touch with the earthy and the absurd. The two nurses, with whom I work more closely, don't mind what could be considered slacking on my part. The last receptionist apparently had a tendency "to get above herself" and "play nurse." She was fired for giving detailed—and erroneous—medical advice over the phone.

"You're not going to the office looking like THAT!" Sybil states with all her juvenile authority as I emerge from the basement. She plants herself firmly between me and the front door.

"Like what?" My mind runs to the obvious: slip showing? Run in my pantyhose? Make-up smeared?

"Like Madonna having menopause."

Despite my Catholic girlhood I somehow know she means Madonna as in MTV and not the Ever Blessed Virgin.

"And just what do you know about menopause, Miss?" I keep my tone light as I check my purse for the keys, but I feel as if I've just been slapped.

"I know it has to do with hormones," she says seriously. "And older women (like her mother, it goes without saying) start going crazy and dying their hair and wearing red a lot, because their periods have stopped."

"Oh, I see." I sling my bag over my shoulder and head resolutely for the door. Sybil is referring to what I have to admit is a rather snug, red (let's call it crimson) sweater, which I am wearing over a narrow black skirt. A wide belt with a flashy gold buckle makes my waist look narrower than it is (I hope) and (theoretically) my hips and bust voluptuous rather than merely ample. I have crimson high-heeled shoes to match the sweater and, I confess, the lipstick.

Sybil may have a point.

On the other hand, I have finally, in my forties, after a lifetime of eschewing bright colors, red in particular, as cheap and whorish, discovered that they suit my strong coloring.

"Sybil, you know I don't dye my hair. You can see the gray in it." Ten hairs at last count; I am determined to age with dignity, if not with grace. "As for menopause, I haven't even thought about it." Well, that's a slight exaggeration. "I still have my period every month."

Unlike Sybil, who hasn't had her first period yet, although many of her classmates have. She is built like her father: hollow bird bones and no flesh to spare. She won't reach that critical one hundred and ten pounds for a couple of years. I pause at the door to look at her still regarding me severely through owl-shaped glasses, her long virgin braids tossed over her shoulders. Sybil is something of an anomaly in our slick suburb where people are wont to bemoan the ever earlier onset of puberty. She is the leader of a resistance movement against hormonal and cultural folly, shunning what we used to call "boy craziness" and designer fashion. More remarkable, she is not considered a nerd or a dweeb or whatever is the current term. She is popular with boys and girls, a sort of sixth grade Joan of Arc. I adore her.

"Come on," I say, unable to resist giving her a hug, which she, I am pleased to note, is unable to resist returning. "Let's go."

As Sybil and I step out of the house my son's ride arrives: Johnny Masserelli pulling up to the curb in an all but antique Buick convertible, a real heap.

"Run and tell Peter Johnny's here," I say to Sybil.

"He's probably still blow-drying his hair." Her contempt for her brother is total. "I don't know why he bothers. It'll just get messed up again on the way to school." But she goes back into the house, and I can hear her bellowing "Peter!" at the foot of the stairs.

Johnny, meanwhile, gives me an understated nod of recognition, which includes a tossing of hair out of his eyes, and I find that I am walking (well, swaying, in these heels) down the walk to greet him instead of turning towards my own car in the driveway. Other mothers have warned me that Johnny is a bad influence and that I should discourage a close association between him and my son. Not that any of us has ever found an effective form of "discouragement." I did tail Johnny once to satisfy myself of his driving ability, and when I discovered him speeding, I engaged in a mild chase scene and actually succeeded in forcing him off the road. That impressed him. There's been a bond of sorts between us since then.

"So how's Senior year so far?" I ask.

Johnny looks up at me from under that shock of black hair that's already in his eyes again.

"Well, you know..." He shrugs; his shoulders are far more articulate than the rest of him.

I notice that he's wearing a T-shirt, black of course, though the temperature is only in the fifties. All the boys, it seems to me, as soon as they're large enough or swift enough to resist their mothers, wear T-shirts in all weathers. I am momentarily torn between annoyance at this compulsive puerile flouting of maternal wisdom and a quite non-maternal interest in the way his biceps strain at the absurdly thin material.

"I hear you got a new job, Mrs. O." (Short for Osika.) Johnny can't help smirking but at least he refrains from making obvious jokes.

"Well, you know..." It is my turn to make an eloquent motion with my shoulders, which, I am afraid, draws attention not to my biceps but to my rather prominent scarlet (excuse me, crimson) breasts. "It keeps me off the streets."

Is it possible that I am being suggestive? It is.

I ask a few more banal questions about school to re-establish the generation gap, all the while wondering why we leave boys like Johnny to wreak havoc in their back seats with ignorant young girls of their own age. With those hormones running riot, young boys so obviously need to be taken in hand by a mature woman, initiated and instructed, first-hand, about birth control and prevention of STDs, not to mention other subtler arts...

"It is time," I picture myself addressing the Parents and Teachers Organization, "to get serious about sex education."

Fortunately my fantasies are interrupted by Peter hurtling by and vaulting into the passenger seat. Then, from the driveway comes Sybil's martyred "Mom!" recalling me to my primary function.

At the office, where I arrive half an hour before anyone else, I make myself at home in what I think of as my "pen," the area being secure and enclosed. Like the prisoners in old movies, I communicate through a glass window, except that my window is open during business hours to permit crucial transactions, such as payment for services rendered. Like a playpen, my pen contains various toys to keep me amused.

I putter about efficiently, checking the thermostat, playing back the messages on the answering machine and jotting them down for their recipients. Then I check the appointment book and pull the charts for the day. Most important, I activate the coffee machine and set out the artificial additives, which are clearly marked as hazardous to health. The plants, which are real, though they don't look it, must be watered. Finally, I pour myself a cup of coffee, sit down at my desk and retrieve a folder of poems from the back of the accounts overdue file. By the time the aptly named Nurse Jane Powers walks through the door, I have the computer humming, and I am contemplating an expanse of pristine screen.

"At our morning meditations, are we?"

Jane Powers is the sort of good-natured, maternal bully one sometimes encounters in the nursing profession. She never accords anyone but doctors an individual identity. The rest of us, patients and underlings, are enveloped in the folds of her ample being. She has a more difficult time with her colleague, Nurse Stephanie Anderson, who, with all the rigidity of youth, rejects Nurse Powers as a mother by proxy and moreover has the effrontery to be coldly gorgeous and professionally ambitious. Stephanie will soon be a Nurse Practitioner, which is to say a quasi-doctor. The only good thing about Stephanie's imminent apotheosis from Jane's point of view is that she will then leave the office of Doctors Woods, Jordan, and Winchester. Those are my bosses whom my husband rather unkindly (and again without much originality) refers to as the three stooges.

"Yes," I say agreeably, typing the first line of a poem called "Bottomless." As an unsung poet I am accustomed to scorn and condescension. "I'm trying to complete a cycle of poems. For a chapbook contest," I add, hoping that to Jane this phrase will sound esoteric and impressive.

She merely snorts and locks her enormous black pocketbook that almost looks like a doctor's bag in a cabinet drawer. I return to the screen and rather absently type another line. I am thinking of cycles: poetic cycles, bicycles, hormonal cycles. Perhaps I should write a cycle of twenty-eight poems evoking the rhythms and mood of menstruation and ovulation. Or a life cycle of poems from menarche to menopause. I glance at Nurse Powers who is both rounded and severe. The word stalwart comes to mind, and bulwark. Sixty if a day, she must have experienced the mysteries of menopause. I find myself wondering if, as a nurse, she remarked about her hormonal cycles. Did she experience estrus as a goad to madness? Did she become a gadfly, a danger to the male doctors who dominated her professional life?

Before I can contemplate the subtle phrasing of these questions, the phone rings, and I must focus on making an appointment for someone who is determined to give me a detailed account of his suffering with hemorrhoids. I have learned that it does little good to try to halt the flow of description by explaining that I'm just the receptionist. As I listen, more or less sympathetically, waiting for the moment when I can bring the conversation back to the appointment, Stephanie Anderson stalks in, greeting her colleague with a curt nod and hurling her purse, like a hand grenade, onto the top of a cabinet. She never bothers to lock it in a drawer.

"My, my, we don't seem to be in a very good mood today, do we?" With my free ear I hear Jane muttering loudly.

"We are having PMS today, so we would be well advised not to mess with us!" Stephanie, who is usually more restrained, snaps at Jane.

"PMS! PMS! You girls are always whining about PMS. It's just a fad." Jane dismisses it with a wave of her hand. "It's a fashionable excuse for lack of good old-fashioned self discipline, that's what it is. What's more it's self-defeating. You girls want to be just like men and do everything men do, be soldiers, astronauts, presidents, brain surgeons. Don't you know that one of the oldest arguments against letting a woman have any responsibility is that they go crazy when they have their periods and they might set off the H-bomb!"

"Mmm hmm," I murmur to the man on the phone, who has reached in his anal saga the most recent bowel movement of two days ago.

"You girls ought to have the sense to just keep quiet about it. Play it down," she concludes.

"Well, that's easy for you to say, Jane," sniffs Stephanie.

"Why? Because I've had the change of life?"

I find it fascinating, as I listen to Jane and Stephanie instead of the man's description of the consistency of his stools, that Jane, a nurse, says "change of life" instead of menopause.

"All right, I have. But I want you to know," Jane continues, "that I had the curse every month for forty years—except when I was pregnant, of course—and I never missed a day of work and never made a fuss."

I wonder, I almost say aloud to my phone partner, why it is that only the menstrual part of the cycle receives any societal attention. Whose purposes does PMS serve? Obviously, the pharmaceutical companies'. And Jane has a point. Our hormonal cycle—read instability—has been used against us. Perhaps I'd better keep my theory of estrus in human females quiet. Why make a case that women go crazy not once but twice a month? A full blown manic-depressive cycle.

"Yes," I finally break into a soliloquy longer and more lugubrious than all of Hamlet's strung together. "Yes, I understand how you feel. Yes, we do have an opening today. Three o' clock. I'm afraid that's the earliest I have. With Dr. Jordan. Jordan. Yes. Yes, he's the one with the thinning red hair." I wink at Bob Jordan who has just stuck his balding pate through my window.

"I heard that, Cyn, and you're fired." He winks back.

Still on the phone, I roll my eyes and hand him his messages.

"Cyn," he hisses. "If that's Mr. Peck, just tell him: Never strain at stool, and hang up."

"Yes, Mr. Peck. I'll see you at three o' clock. And meanwhile, remember: Never strain at stool." I set down the receiver with relief.

Jane and Stephanie lapse into silence, a sort of enforced female solidarity, as the other two doctors also arrive and pick up their messages. It occurs to me how depressingly traditional and patriarchal my workplace is: three male doctors and their handmaidens, of whom I am, without doubt, the lowliest.

In addition to Bob Jordan there is Justin Winchester. I privately think of him as a TV doctor. He has the air of mystery and the glamorous good looks; moreover, he is single. "I'm surprised he didn't become an OB-GYN," Jane confided one day. "He's the type. Although there would have been hell to pay," she added. I personally find him too flawlessly handsome for flirtation and fantasy, except, perhaps, of the most detached and impersonal kind. He takes his good looks so seriously—not in the sense of being conceited but as if he had a grave moral responsibility to act with restraint in order to protect women from the full force of his charm. He and Stephanie behave with such extreme correctness and propriety in each other's presence they become positively Victorian.

Completing this medical trio is Dan Woods, the senior doctor, and, in some ways, Nurse Powers's counterpart. He cultivates a wise, benevolent, doctor-knows-best mystique. I would not be surprised if one day he reached through my receptionist's window and patted me on the head, mistaking me, perhaps, for one of his seven grown children whose photographs vie with his medical diplomas for wall space in his office.

Of the three, Bob Jordan is the most accessible, with his humorous approach and his tendency to flirt. Perhaps he feels that the revelation of his freckled scalp relieves him of the moral responsibility that goes with a full head of hair.

The patients begin to arrive, pausing anxiously at my window to confirm their appointments and to reassure themselves that someone knows of their existence in the waiting room. I try to provide a comforting presence. Because my ambitions are purely literary, I have never been corrupted by the petty powers of my office as guard dog to the doctors. My boldest maneuver has been to subscribe on the behalf of Woods, Jordan & Winchester to magazines other than *Sports Illustrated*. I have even taken out subscriptions to several literary journals. I take a personal interest in watching what patients choose to peruse.

I now have my playpen mostly to myself except for the periodic hustle and bustle of Nurses Jane and Stephanie as they come in and out with patient charts. I often wonder which nurse it would be worse to have in attendance at a rectal examination: the gorgeous and frosty Ms. Anderson or the officious Mrs. Powers instructing: Let's take off our pants now. 'At-a-boy. Ups-a-daisy, honey buns.

The morning progresses routinely. Between phone calls and payments, I manage to type a couple of short poems, but I am conscious of a phenomenon I have come to associate with estrus: a subliminal awareness of my own sexual organs. I say subliminal, because I am perfectly focused on whatever task is at hand. It is not a matter of thinking but rather of images that persistently surface and float at the edge of consciousness. But the images are not just visual; they are embodied. How to say it? I feel myself opening, blossoming, all those pink, vaginal folds—so many petals. And I know that I am slippery with secretions (secret secretions) and giving off a scent that we've been taught not to admit we can detect. The image of a flower opening and enticing with its fragrance is apt. Although I will not, a few days from now, literally strew faded blooms as I pass, I will experience a closing, a folding back into itself of my sex. And I will wonder why I ever wanted to go to bed with anything other than a book.

Another more cultivated image that recurs is of my ripened egg, round and shining like a full moon, as it sails the dark channel of my fallopian tube to the red sea of my womb where it wanes and dissolves. Channel...I knew there was a connection between those words. The fallopian tube is an estuary! I have the unmistakable feeling—similar to when you know, yes, I'm going to come—of a poem beginning.

Then the door of my playpen opens. It is Doctor-knows-best-Woods ushering in an elderly gentleman—that's the phrase that comes to mind.

"Our girl here will explain the coverage," he says to his patient. "Cyn, help Mr. Mills with the Medicare forms."

I feel my face turning red (crimson does not seem the appropriate word in this context) as I wonder what I did that was so bad I wound up in this feminist hell. Maybe it's punishment for taking the job in the first place—for the sake of my "art." Who am I kidding?

"Please sit down, Mr. Mills."

Dr. Woods withdraws before I can say anything to him. Well, I tell myself, it would be unprofessional to confront my boss in front of a patient, but I promise myself that I will—later.

"Thank you, Ms..."—or it may be the old all-purpose predecessor Miz— "I'm sorry I didn't quite catch your name."

I find myself looking straight into Mr. Mills's eyes. They are hazel, almost green, and look quite striking with his white hair. I replace the word elderly with the word courtly. Mr. Mills is a courtly gentleman. I am completely smitten.

"Osika," I say, deciding to let him choose the title.

"Well, Ms. Osika..."

This could be love, I think.

"I am certainly glad this chair has a cushion."

We look at each other for a moment. Another old fashioned word comes to mind. Merriment. Then we both burst out laughing.

"I guess cushions are crucial in a proctologist's office," I muse. "After I had my second child, I know I couldn't stand to sit down for six months."

"Stand to sit down. Now there's an interesting turn of phrase!"

Someone attentive to language! Perhaps I could elope with this man on my lunch hour?

"About these dratted forms, Ms. Osika..."

Dratted! How long since I've heard that word. He put the forms on my desk and I swiveled closer to him.

"Let's have a look." Oh God, I think. I'm starting to talk like Nurse Jane! "Although I must warn you, Mr. Mills, I'm new at this job, and I might not be able to understand them either, but I've had enough experience to know that insurance forms are satanic devices. Filling them out is dress rehearsal for hell."

"My sentiments exactly, Ms. Osika. But surely Satan cannot stand against two such intrepid souls as you and I."

"Oh surely not."

So we set to work and spend a very pleasant and stimulating half hour together making a game of filling out the forms almost as if we were lost together in an eighteenth century maze—where, as I understand it, many an erotic adventure occurred. We part with what I can only describe as "expressions of mutual esteem."

By one o'clock the waiting room is empty, the patients scheduled for twelve having been seen at last. Lunch hour is officially from one to two. Appointments begin again at two-fifteen, but the doctors aren't usually back until two-thirty.

Technically, we "girls" are allowed to lock up and leave, though frequently one or more of us eats in, using the time to update records, file charts, or, in my case, settle down to some serious revision, or even—if the muse is rampant—composition. The "boys" always leave. They lunch collegially in smart places about town where they are recognized by embarrassed or titillated patients. I consider ambushing Dan Woods on his way out but decide that it is not wise to come between a physician and his lunch. I will wait until he is better fed. Or perhaps I will spend my lunch hour writing amusing but instructive verse.

> There once was a medical churl
> Who called his receptionist "girl"

The lines appear on my screen, but then Jane walks in, and I press delete.

"Eating in today, are we?"

"Well, I am," I say, not entirely certain in this context who "we" includes.

"I'm having lunch with my daughter." Jane uses "I" as a sort of royal prerogative. "We've just found out we're preggers."

"Congratulations. Her first?" I ask, deducing that the "we" means the daughter.

Jane snorts, as she unlocks the drawer and retrieves her bag. "Her third! We're not celebrating, I'm afraid. We're campaigning to get Grandma to quit her nice comfy job to run a private daycare center. Ha! Fat chance."

"Well, good luck."

"Are we gone?" Stephanie appears a few moments later.

"She's having lunch with her daughter." I resist the temptation to join in making fun of Jane. My unwritten job description, I sense, is to act as a buffer between the nurses.

"Good. Excuse me," says Stephanie opening a drawer of my desk where we keep a sample of more or less over-the-counter drugs. She pops a couple of Midol. "I'm going to succumb to modern-day moral and physical weakness and take a nap in Room 2. Don't tell."

"My lips are sealed. But aren't you going to eat?"

"When I wake up. Check on me by ten of, would you?"

"Sure."

I get up and file the charts, then settle happily into my solitude, kicking off my crimson shoes and unwrapping my peanut butter and jelly sandwich. This almost daily dose of peanut butter is carcinogenic, Bob Jordan assures me. His health lectures are part of a campaign to get me to have lunch with him on a regular basis.

"At least use the microwave," he once said, as if to prove his concern for my health was genuine. "That's what it's there for!"

"Microwaved peanut butter and jelly?" I quipped. "Even my son hasn't tried that."

Bob threw up his hands, conceding defeat once more.

Estuary, I think to myself, trying to coax the poem back, as I eat my sandwich. When I'm done, I wipe my fingers and rummage in a drawer for scrap paper. I generally don't compose on the machine—not serious verse, anyway. Heat, swell, surge, tide, I write experimentally. Each of those words seems almost a poem in itself. Maybe I should just send them out singly to that journal of one-word poems that keeps calling for manuscripts in *Poets & Writers*. Moon, I say invitingly to my creative unconscious. The great shining O of ovulation, orgasm. O...

"I hear you got a new job, Mrs. O."

My mind plays back Johnny's voice, and I am suddenly blushing scarlet (yes, scarlet is apt) as I remember that little shimmy I did with my shoulders. Then, too, there was my wink at Bob Jordan, who hardly needs encouragement, and my cozy huddle over the insurance forms with the courtly Mr. Mills. I have been sending out signals all day, an unmistakable scent of heat that male mammals inevitably detect.

The trouble is, I consider, that human beings, particularly the males, have persuaded themselves that there is no such thing as estrus in the human female. Thus these inadvertent signals are subject to gross misinterpretation. What havoc it must wreak, this unacknowledged monthly madness! Men assume that a woman's heightened interest has to do with their own irresistible charms when it's really nothing but a temporary surfeit of hormones. Women, ignorant of estrus, may mistakenly suppose they are discontented with their mates. Estrus unrecognized is doubtless the origin of many a messy and unnecessary affair. Despite the fact that today I might lust for a roll in the back seat with Johnny or an elegant interlude with Mr. Mills at a nice hotel or a good scratch of the itch in Room Two with Bob Jordan, I have no desire for anything so personal or open-ended as an affair.

I am on to something, I sense, but I'm not sure it's a poem.

"What I want—" I pause with my pen poised. It is not a poem that is coming but a full-blown X-rated fantasy. Well, why not? I ponder briefly a career as a pornographer. The pay would be better than what I get for answering phones and filing. But then, I would probably only be able to put my heart (so to speak) into porn at estrus. The rest of the month it would probably seem too silly, too adolescent. Hormonally that's what estrus is, a resurgence (surge!) of adolescence. "What I want—" I read the words again, then I begin to write.

On the banks of the Estuary stood the Temple of Estrus, round like the ancient beehives and full of luxuriant cells surrounding a central courtyard where there was a pool in the shape of a yoni fed by hot springs. Here each suppliant male had to bathe before being blindfolded and led by the High Priestess to one of the cells where a woman waited to administer the sacrament.

These women, maidens and matrons of the City, would come to the Temple of Estrus freely, remaining for a night or a week as they chose, to consecrate their sacred lust, their only vow being to receive all suppliants indiscriminately and anonymously. (There is no AIDS in this fantasy.) Unmarried women who offered themselves received no censure and wives could not be reproached by their husbands. Children born of these rites were considered to have been divinely conceived, but each woman could choose whether or not she wished to open her womb. (This is getting a little technical for a fantasy but since it's mine, I insist on access to contraception. Maybe I'll start a new genre of pornography: feminist utopian.)

Each cell was furnished with warm scented oils, incense, a sumptuous couch with plenty of pillows to encourage experimentation with positions, and a variety of condoms—some exotic, all functional—from which the woman made a selection, it being understood that the man must submit to her will in this matter.

And it came to pass that a certain provincial matron by the name of Diana (that's me, of course, Cynthia and Diana both being names of the moon goddess), having been harassed and preoccupied for many years by the performance of her household duties, resolved at last to make a pilgrimage to the famed Temple of Estrus.....

"You were supposed to wake me up!"
I am startled by Stephanie's bursting back into my pen. As I look at her wolfing a bag of corn chips, I am reminded of my own pre-menstrual preferences: solitude, a bowl of salted popcorn, and a book. I decide that in this utopia I am creating there will also be plush menstrual (and pre-menstrual) huts, complete with saunas and hot tubs as well as shelves full of trashy paperbacks. The trouble with the old menstrual taboos is that they became riddled with misogyny. What I want is a feminist revival and revision of some ancient customs. So: three days a month at the Temple of Estrus and five a month at Club Menses. With pay. Of course.
"Some of us don't have to go out to lunch to be out to lunch," Stephanie grumbled.
Poor Stephanie. She could definitely use some time in the whirlpool.
"Sorry Stephanie. You're right. I'm completely out to lunch. It's an occupational hazard. And speaking of occupational hazards, you better watch yourself. You're starting to talk like her."
"Never."
"You just referred to me as us."

"I didn't!"

"Well, did we have a nice lunch break?" Nurse Jane is back.

The phone starts to ring; the waiting room begins to accumulate patients. By the time Dan Woods returns twenty minutes late, all I can do is hand him his messages. Confrontation deferred again. The hemorrhoidal Mr. Peck, on the other hand, arrives twenty minutes early and hovers by my window, hoping, no doubt, to resume our conversation. But after I confirm his appointment, I heartlessly return to composing pornography (taking care to shield the paper with my left arm).

All afternoon, between phone calls and payments, I follow the adventures of that bold matron Diana. Having left her demanding and ungrateful family behind, she arrives at the Temple. As a first time Celebrant she must go through admissions procedures with the High Priestess, who explains the house rules and instructs Diana in various erotic techniques. (Really, I see no reason to keep this fantasy strictly heterosexual.) The High Priestess also details how to handle any nasty or truculent suppliants. At the first hint of violence, a woman has but to pull a bell rope and the eunuchs (who got that way for a reason) will come and take the offender away to a dungeon where he can expect to consume bread and water in the company of rats until the severity of his penalty is decided. Under those circumstances, there is usually no trouble.

Diana's first suppliant is a luscious not-quite-virgin boy of eighteen, seeking refinement of his technique. That takes all of one night. Next Diana receives a charming older man who desires to be restored to full potency. No problem for our Diana. So passes another night. Then the High Priestess brings her a robust man of about her years, un joli laid (somehow his plainness, his ordinariness is exciting) who, like Diana, enjoys the spice of variety...

"TGIF!" exclaims Stephanie, who is suddenly standing by my desk shouldering her purse.

"You said it, sister!" for once Jane and Stephanie are in full accord.

"Are all the patients gone?" I ask, somewhat dazed.

"It's five thirty, Cyn," says Stephanie. "Where've you been?"

Where indeed?

"Are the boys still here?" I inquire.

"The *boys!*" Nurse Jane is disapproving; this, after calling grown men sugar face and dearie pie all day.

"I've got to talk to Dr. Woods."

"You better grab him fast," advises Stephanie, as she and Jane leave together.

I leave the safety of my pen and head down the hall where I knock more timidly than I'd like on Dan Woods's open door. He is just closing up his big black bag.

"May I speak with you for a moment, Dr. Woods?"

"Why sure, hon, what's on your mind?"

"It's just that, well, I'd appreciate it if you didn't refer to me as 'girl' when you're speaking to patients. I am forty-six years old, well, next week I will be..." (Including that detail makes me feel more like I'm going on six.)

"I didn't know you were one of those women's libbers, Cyn."

"Well"—don't deny it, I order myself— "I think it would sound more professional if you referred to me as Mrs. Osika."

"If that's the way you want it, hon, I'll try to remember," he sighs. "Hard to teach an old dog new tricks."

You old dog you, I think.

Back in my pen, I put the computer to bed, then finish filing charts. I am often the last one to leave. Supposing myself to be alone, I am startled almost to the point of being frightened when Bob Jordan opens the door.

"At last!" he says. "I thought we'd never be alone."

There is enough comic exaggeration in his tone that I am not unduly alarmed—or impressed. I briskly continue filing. Then Bob comes up behind me and stands too close. I can smell his aftershave, which I suspect has been freshly applied. The inch or so of air between us heats up several degrees.

Heat, swell, surge, tide.

"I thought it was adorable the way you told my venerable colleague not to call you girl."

Adorable?

"You were eavesdropping."

"Not on purpose. I can't help it if all the doors were open."

I slam the file cabinet shut, side step Bob, and carefully squat rather than bend over as I retrieve my bag from under my desk. God help him if he says: You're so cute when you're mad. I won't be responsible for my actions. I'll plead temporary insanity.

"Have a drink with me, Cyn."

"I never drink and drive."

"Keep me company then."

"I'm afraid I really can't."

"Why are you so nervous all of a sudden? Come on, Cyn. Don't be so uptight. We're both mature adults. Happily married. We're not going to do anything we both don't want to do. Relax. It's harmless. I'm harmless. Swear to God!" He holds up one hand as if taking a boy scout oath.

I look at him, thinking: You may be harmless, but I'm not. I'm dangerous. I'm a natural force, surging with estrogen. I am an opening rose, a full moon, a rising tide. What is more, I happen to think you're a jerk. I wouldn't have anything to do with you unless I was bound by a sacred vow to receive all suppliants and my old pal the High Priestess led you to me blindfolded.

I briefly contemplate asking Bob if he has ever considered estrus as a phenomenon affecting human female mammals, but reject the idea. He would probably consider it a come-on and call me a bitch in heat.

"Sorry, Bob," I say. "I'm busy. I've got to see a man about an estuary. Do me a favor and lock up? Don't forget to turn down the thermostat," I add, just a tad suggestively.

With that I'm gone, driving east into a full autumn moon to pick out a site for the Temple on the banks of the Charles.

# Dead Heat
## Clarinda Harriss Raymond

Oh lord, kill the beast in me. But not yet.

—St. Augustine

I want her back, the beast,
the bloody bitch.
Tonight, tonguing you an easy goodbye
I missed
the way she used to whine
on the porch
and strain at the leash
sniffing
your retreating crotch.

# Contributors

**Gaye Todd Adegbalola** is one of the three blues women in Saffire. She bought her first guitar while attending Boston University and went on to teach high school, was named Virginia Teacher of the Year in 1982. She has a grown son who is a "young, young man." Saffire's recordings include *The Uppity Blues Women* and *Hot Flash.*

**Karen Alkalay-Gut** lectures in English and American poetry at Tel-Aviv University. She has published six books of poetry. Her most recent books, *Ignorant Armies* and *Love and War* are concerned with politics.

**Mary Allison** lives in the Blue Ridge Mountains where she is a nurse, caterer and builder. She writes to challenge her mind and to save her soul. She regularly attends Wild Acres Writers Retreat in North Carolina. Her work appears in *Sexual Harassment: Women Speak Out.*

**Brenda Bankhead** is a Black writer born and raised in Los Angeles. She is presently working on a collection of short stories about poor Black women and children and their survival in this place called America. She is employed by the University of Southern California.

**Elisabeth Boone** graduated from the Iowa Writers' Workshop in 1968. Two decades later she settled down to write. She has been published in *Spectacles, Thema* and *Paragraph.*

**Victoria Branch** is a Los Angeles based free-lance writer/editor specializing in corporate communications. Her short fiction has appeared in *Playgirl* and *eNvee.*

**Clare Braux** is 65 and has been writing for 12 years. She is an American citizen as well as a Canadian and has published over a dozen stories in Canadian and U.S. literary magazines. Her novel, *Medusa & Her Sisters* will be published in 1993.

**Claire Braz-Valentine** is a widely published playwright; her plays about Susan B. Anthony and Frida Kahlo are produced in theatres across the country. She is currently working on a play about Amelia Earhart and a poetry collection which exposes her continued erotic fascination with Godzilla.

Maria Bruno is assistant professor of women's studies and writing at Michigan State University. She has published fiction in *Ms., Earth's Daughters, Midway Review* and in *Women's Friendships,* an anthology.

Thea Caplan lives in Toronto where she has worked as a consultant in addictions and as director of a hostel for assaulted women and children. Her collection of short stories, *What Passes For Love,* is seeking a publisher.

Naomi Feigelson Chase has published in *Ploughshares, Lear's* and *The New York Times* and in the anthologies, *A Wider Giving* and *Lovers.* She is the author of *The Underground Revolution, A Child Is Being Beaten* and two books of poetry.

Erica Lann Clark is 55, with two grown sons and three grandchildren. She works as a storyteller, a writer, a teacher and an acupressure massage therapist. Long after the wrinkles and flab, she plans to exercise her wildness and power. Her work has appeared in *Sexual Harassment: Women Speak Out* and *Women of the 14th Moon.*

Portia Cornell has had work published in numerous women's magazines and anthologies. The "Eleanor Roosevelt Erotic Letter Writing Club" was originally performed in Ashford, CT. in 1990. She works with an improvisational theatre group called Crone Players.

Elizabeth Cunningham lives in New York near the Hudson River, which is an estuary. She does not, however, work in a proctologist's office. Her novel, *The Return of the Goddess, A Divine Comedy,* was published by Station Hill Press in 1992.

Rosemary Daniell is the author of *The Hurricane Season.* Her previous books include *Sleeping With Soldiers, Fatal Flowers: On Sin, Sex and Suicide in the Deep South,* and three collections of poetry. She is the originator of "Zona Rosa," writing workshops in Savannah, Georgia.

Corinne Davis, under a different name, is married with three adopted children and has worked with abused children and dysfunctional families for 25 years. She has a degree in journalism and was a newspaper editor for several years.

Regina deCormier-Shekerjian is the author of *Growing Toward Peace,* which has been translated into 15 languages, and *Hoofbeats On The Door.* She has published in *The Nation, American Poetry Review, The American*

*Voice* and *Looking For Home* (Milkweed Editions).

**Deborah DeNicola** is the winner of the 1992 *Embers* Chapbook Poetry Competition for her manuscript *Psyche Revisited*. Her poetry has appeared in *Antioch Review, Fiction International* and *The Cimarron Review*. She is a Visiting Lecturer at The Massachusetts College of Art.

**Gail Donovan** lives in Maine where she has recently completed a novel about twins, *We Are Running North And South*. Her work has been published in *Clerestory* and she was a finalist in the University of Illinois Short Fiction Series in 1989.

**Ayofemi Folayan** is a Black poet, playwright, journalist and activist living in Los Angeles. She teaches creative writing at the Gay and Lesbian Community Services Center and the Exceptional Children's Foundation. Her work has appeared in *Sojourner, Vanguard, off our backs, Indivisible* and *Riding Desire*.

**Martha Gies** teaches creative writing at Marylhurst College and Portland State University. She has published in *Zyzzyva, Crazyquilt,* and *Seattle Weekly*. Her story, "O'Keefe Sober" was a PEN Syndicated Fiction winner and was broadcast nationally on NPR in 1991.

**Constance Hester** began writing at 50 and is currently part of a writing group of ten San Francisco Bay Area poets. She has had several poems published and has a book in progress.

**June Hudson** won a 1991 Jessamyn West Writing Award and has had poetry published in numerous literary journals. She lives with her husband in Sonoma, CA, in a retro deco diner style home.

**Lynn Kanter** lives in Washington, DC. Her novel, *On Lill Street,* was published in 1992. She is a founding member of Virago Video, a women's television production company. She has written fiction, nonfiction, scripts and innumerable grant proposals for worthy causes.

**Chris Karras** has published work in *Women of the 14th Moon: Writings on Menopause* and *Sexual Harassment: Women Speak Out*. She lives rurally in Ontario, Canada with her husband of 38 years.

**Claudia Kenyon** is a freelance English teacher now training in Aikido and other forms of conflict resolution. She lives in Santa Cruz, CA.

**Phyllis Koestenbaum** teaches at West Valley College and is an Affiliated Scholar at Stanford University's Institute for Research on Women and Gender. She is a widely published poet and has received grants from the NEA and Money for Women/Barbara Deming Memorial Fund.

**Candida Lawrence** has published stories and non-fiction in the anthologies *If I Had A Hammer* and *Women of the 14th Moon,* and in *Sonora Review, Passages North* and *Ohio Journal.* She lives with her dog in Santa Cruz, CA.

**Janice Levy** is the first place winner of the 1992 Fiction Contest sponsored by *Painted Hills Review.* Her work appears in the anthologies *Lovers* and *Patchwork of Dreams* and in *The Sun, Kalliope,* and *Brooklyn Free Press.* She lives in Merrick, NY with her husband and two children.

**Ginny MacKenzie** teaches at the School of Visual Arts in New York City and is the editor and co-translator of two anthologies of contemporary Chinese and American poetry. Her poetry and criticism appear in *Ploughshares, The Iowa Review* and *Women of the 14th Moon.* Her fiction appears in *New Letters* and *Caesura.*

**Nancy Mairs** is the author of *Ordinary Time,* a collection of essays on being a Catholic feminist, *Remembering the Bone House: An Erotics of Place and Space, Carnal Acts, Plaintext: Deciphering A Woman's Life* and *In All the Rooms of the Yellow House.* Her short fiction appears in *Lovers.*

**Irene Marcuse** lives in NYC where she recently completed her M.S.W. She is currently looking for work which combines writing and social work. Her work has been published in *Touching Fire: Erotic Writings By Women, Nimrod,* and *Moonjuice.*

**Barbara McDonald** teaches junior high school in the San Francisco Bay area, where she was born. She is the mother of three adult children. Her work has been published in *North American Review.*

**Susan B. McIver** is a former Presbyterian, closeted lesbian, and academic. She lives on Salt Spring Island, British Columbia, with her partner, Anne, and writes humorous stories.

**Maude Meehan** is the author of *Chipping Bone,* a collection of ten years of poetry, and the newly published *Before the Snow.* She is widely published and teaches extension courses in poetry at University of California, Santa Cruz, as well as women's writing workshops.

**Deena Metzger** is a poet, novelist, playwright and psychotherapist. Her books include *Writing for Your Life, A Sabbath Among the Ruins, Looking for The Faces of God, What Dinah Thought, Tree* and *The Woman Who Slept with Men to Take the War Out of Them.* She lives rurally in Southern California.

**Susan Moon** won a 1991 Pushcart Prize for her story "Bodies" which appears in the anthology *Lovers.* She teaches at St. Mary's College and is the editor of *Turning Wheel,* a magazine about Buddhism and social activism. She is the author of *The Life and Letters of Tofu Roshi.*

**Constance Mortenson** lives in Powell River, British Columbia, and writes for *Women's Weekly* in London. She is a contributor to *Women of the 14th Moon: Writings on Menopause* and has published in many small magazines. She has written three novels and is working on a trilogy about a Logging Clan.

**Tema Nason** is the author of *Ethel: The Fictional Autobiography of Ethel Rosenberg* and *A Stranger Here Myself,* a collection of short stories. She is a research associate in the Sociology Department at Brandeis University and the mother of five children.

**Linda Norlander** has published short humor and stories in *The Minneapolis Tribune, The American Journal of Nursing* and the New Rivers Press anthology, *The House on Via Gombito.* "Postage Stamps" is part of *The Alice Stories,* a work-in-progress.

**Carol Potter** received the *New Letters* Poetry Award in 1990. Her first collection of poems, *Before We Were Born,* was published by Alice James Books. Her poetry appears in *The Women's Review of Books, Out/Look,* and *Lovers.*

**Clarinda Harriss Raymond** teaches writing at Towson State University in Maryland and edits/directs the New Poets Series, Inc./Chestnut Hills Press. Her work has appeared in *Touching Fire: Erotic Writings by Women* and *Sexual Harassment: Women Speak Out.*

**Trudy Riley** is 60 and lives in Los Angeles, where she started writing seven years ago. Her work has been published in *Women of the 14th Moon, Common Lives/Lesbian Lives* and *Indivisible.* She is presently working on a novel.

**Carly Rivers** is a writer and performer with Mothertongue Feminist Theatre Collective, a lesbian, mother, and grandmother, happily living in Berkeley with her life partner, Toni, and Rutherford "The Cat."

**A.D. Ross** has worked as a typesetter, statistician, therapist, scientific editor, librarian, high school teacher, and political activist. She now writes full time in California.

**Elizabeth Searle** is the author of *My Body to You,* a collection of short stories that won the 1992 Iowa Short Fiction Award. Her fiction has appeared in *The Kenyon Review, Redbook, Boulevard,* and in the anthology *Lovers.* She teaches fiction writing at Emerson College.

**Eva Shaderowfsky** is a writer, artist and photographer living in Rockland County, New York. Her stories have appeared in *Touching Fire: Erotic Writings By Women, Sexual Harassment: Women Speak Out* and *Lovers.*

**Tilly Washburn Shaw** is originally from New England. She teaches literature at the University of California, Santa Cruz. She has published on modern poetry and has been writing poetry for many years.

**Enid Shomer** has published stories and poems in *The New Yorker, Poetry, The Paris Review* and *Lovers. Stalking the Florida Panther* is her first collection of poetry. Her new books are *This Close to the Earth: Poems* and *Imaginary Men,* which won the 1992 Iowa Short Fiction Award.

**Deborah Shouse** is spending her mid-life, so far, in Kansas. Her work has appeared in *Good Housekeeping, The Sun,* and *New Letters* ; her story, "Diner," was selected by the PEN Syndicated Fiction Project.

**Laurel Speer** is a poet, essayist and book reviewer. She edits the journal *Remark* and regularly contributes to *Small Press Review.* Her poetry has been published in numerous literary magazines and anthologies.

**Madelon Sprengnether** is a professor of English at the University of Minnesota, where she teaches both critical and creative writing. She is the author of *Rivers, Stories, Houses, Dreams* and *The Normal Heart* (New Rivers Press) and is currently at work on *The Body of Mourning,* a creative prose manuscript.

**Judith W. Steinbergh** is a poet and teacher living in Boston who performs, leads poetry workshops and creates tapes for children with Troubadour. She has published three books of poetry for adults, *Marshmallow Worlds* for children and co-authored *Beyond Words: Writing Poems with Children.*

**Jennifer Stone** hosts a weekly radio show on KPFA/ Pacifica Public Radio in Berkeley. Her collection of essays on literature and politics, *Stone's Throw* was published in 1989. Her novel, *Telegraph Avenue Then: Loose Leaves from a Little Black Book,* was published in 1992.

**Amber Coverdale Sumrall** has published poetry most recently in *IKON: The Nineties.* Her fiction appears in *Eating Our Hearts Out: Women And Food, My Father's Daughter* and *Catholic Girls.* She is going through a second adolescence in mid-life.

**Christina Sunley** has recently completed an MA in English/Creative Writing at San Francisco State University. Her work has appeared in *Backbone, Conditions, Common Lives/Lesbian Lives* and *Word of Mouth.*

**Dena Taylor** is the author of *Red Flower: Rethinking Menstruation,* and co-editor of *Sexual Harassment:Women Speak Out* and *Women of the 14th Moon: Writings on Menopause.* She lives on the Northern California coast, is a part-time disc-jockey and makes her living from books. She is enjoying the feisty fifties with her friends, family and work.

**Abigail Thomas** is fifty, happily married (at long last) with four adult children and two grandchildren. Two of her children's books will be published by Henry Holt in 1993. Her first collection of stories will also be published in 1993, by Algonquin Books.

**Barbara Unger** is the author of *Dying for Uncle Ray and Other Stories.* Her work appears in *American Fiction: The Best Unpublished Short Stories, If I Had a Hammer* and *Sexual Harassment: Women Speak Out.*

**Rima de Vallbona** was born in Costa Rica and presently resides in Houston, Texas, where she teaches at the University of St. Thomas. She is the mother of four children. Her most recent book, *Los infiernos de la mujer y algo mas* (short stories) was published in 1992.

**Gloria Vando** has published in *The Kenyon Review, Seattle Review* and *New Letters,* among others. Her first book of poems, *Promesas: Geography of the Impossible* will be published by Arte Publico Press in 1993. She has won several awards and grants and currently publishes *Helicon Nine* Editions.

**Lisa Vice** is a former unwed teenage mother, high school drop-out, welfare recipient, silversmith's apprentice, nurse's aid, farmer, birth control counselor, batik artist and cleaning woman. She now teaches writing. Her story, "The House of Blue Lights," won a 1992 PEN Syndicated Fiction Award. *Reckless Driver* is her current, award-winning novel.

**Gail Weber** grew up in Toronto where she is now the Coordinator of Programs for Midlife and Older Women/Menopause Education at the Regional Women's Health Centre. She has recently completed a study of older women in six ethnic minority communities which will be published soon.

**Verna Wilder** is a technical writer at Apple Computer. She has a Master's degree in English from San Jose State University and teaches English Composition occasionally at West Valley College. "Stepping Out" is her first published story.

**Hannah Wilson** is the fiction editor of *Northwest Review.* Her story, "Early Delivery," appears in the Norton anthology, *A Wedding Cake in the Middle of the Road.* She lives in Oregon.

**Lea Wood** lives with her daughter in Vermont on twelve acres of pasture and pine forest. She is a feminist and environmental activist. Her work appears in *Women of the 14th Moon: Writings on Menopause.*

The Crossing Press publishes many books
of interest to women. To receive a catalog,
please call toll free **800/777-1048**
and ask for our general catalog.